Beside Still Waters

Beside Still Waters

Devotional Thoughts for Each Day of the Year

by
Hughes W. Day, M.D.

*He maketh me to lie down in
green pastures: he leadeth me
beside the still waters.*
—PSALM 23:2

Beacon Hill Press of Kansas City
Kansas City, Missouri

Permission to quote from the following copyrighted versions of the Bible is acknowledged with appreciation:

The Holy Bible, The New International Version (NIV), copyright © 1978 by the New York International Bible Society.

The *Revised Standard Version of the Bible* (RSV), copyrighted 1946, 1952, © 1971, 1973.

The Living Bible (TLB) © 1971 by Tyndale House Publishers, Wheaton, Ill.

The *Good News Bible, Today's English Version* (TEV) © American Bible Society, 1966, 1971, 1976.

The Bible: A New Translation (Moffatt), copyright 1954 by James A. R. Moffatt. By permission of Harper and Row, Publishers, Inc.

The *New Testament in the Language of the People* (Williams), Copyright 1937 by Bruce Humphries, Inc. Assigned 1949 to Moody Bible Institute, Chicago.

The *Weymouth New Testament in Modern Speech* (Weymouth), Copyright 1929 by Harper and Brothers, New York.

Dedication

To Lorene
for her love and faith

Preface and Acknowledgments

The preparation of a daily devotional book is a tedious but rewarding task. This one has been prepared with the hope that it will be a blessing in the lives of God's people during these difficult and perilous times.

Many publishers have graciously consented for us to quote from their copyrighted material. These are: The Nazarene Publishing House, The Radio Bible Class, Fleming H. Revell Co., Zondervan Publishing House, *Herald of Holiness*, *Decision Magazine*, Beacon Hill Press of Kansas City, Word Books, Moody Press, The Abingdon Press, American Bible Society, The New York International Bible Society, and Tyndale House Publishers.

Pastors, teachers, and friends have kindly allowed us to use portions of their writings. This list includes Robert G. Lee, Henry G. Bosch, J. W. Macauly, Richard DeHaan, W. T. Purkiser, Paul R. Van Gorder, Vance Havner, George Coulter, David A. Hubbard, C. Fred Dickason, Fletcher Spruce, Ruby Franklin, Hal Bonner, Billy Graham, Kenneth Grider, Edward Lawlor, William Fisher, Arthur Fallon, U. S. Grant, E. Russell Lynn, Robert H. Thompson, Kenneth Dodge, Leslie VanInwegen, Robert Belton, and A. F. Harper.

We have used several quotations from books by Norman B. Harrison, and extensive material from Richard Ellsworth Day and Charles Haddon Spurgeon. All of their books are worthy of deep devotional study and are now in the public domain.

Annie Johnson Flint's poetry has, through the years, brought encouragement and comfort to many people. We are grateful, therefore, to Miss S. Hodgson of Evangelical Publishers, Toronto, for the privilege of quoting extensively from this famous Christian poet. Poetry of Ira Stanphil, Mosie Lister, and Margaret Clarkson has been printed through the kindness of Singspiration, Lillenas, and Union Gospel Press. The poem by Edgar Guest is used by permission of the Henry Regnery Company. In addition we are indebted to the late Kathryn B. Peck for her beautiful poems and to Miss Theo Oxenham of Sussex, England, for the right to quote her father's poetry—the works of John Oxenham.

We acknowledge our indebtedness to poets and authors that we have not been able to trace. We have thus not been able to secure permission for a small portion of the compilation and we ask indulgence and forgiveness of these writers. If the poet is unknown, this has been so indicated. Any information as to the true author would be deeply appreciated and will be corrected in future editions. Literature and poems from the author's pen are unsigned.

I also wish to acknowledge the counsel and help given to me by my friend, M. A. Lunn, general manager of the Nazarene Publishing House. He furnished to me needed counsel, correction, and helpful criticism.

A new year is breaking as these final lines are written. It is the author's prayer that this book, in some small way, may be used to "strengthen with might by his Spirit" the hearts of all of God's people, and "that Christ may dwell in your hearts by faith; that ye being rooted and grounded in love, may be able to comprehend with all saints what is the breadth, and length, and depth, and height; and to know the love of Christ, which passeth knowledge, that you might be filled with all the fullness of God" (Eph. 3:17-19).

—HUGHES W. DAY

Mission, Kansas
January 3, 1979

8

Foreword

Less than three years ago I was lying in the intensive care unit after coronary bypass surgery. Through those first pain-punctuated hours of fitful consciousness and narcotic haze, I was vaguely conscious of:

the tubes protruding from various areas of my anatomy;

the wire electrodes which connected me to the various clicking, flashing, humming, and chiming monitors;

the limp plastic bags of blood and fluids perfusing my body with life-sustaining nourishment;

the wall clock recording the interminable hours by hands that dragged their unwilling way across the face;

the measured cadence of my rib cage as it rose and fell to the will of the pulmonary life-support machine;

But most of all, I remember the little nurse who sat beside my bed. Each time I opened my eyes, Tammy was intently watching the dials, the bleeps, my face; and I would doze again serenely confident that Tammy would see that the gadgets continued to function uninterruptedly.

Later I remembered that my friend, Dr. Hughes Day, had designed the first coronary care unit; and I thanked God for the creative ingenuity and professional skill of this cardiologist extraordinaire. It was not the first time (or the last) that I have thanked God for Hughes Day and his spiritual sensitivity.

In the pages of this devotional omnibus Dr. Day takes us into a spiritual intensive care unit. With his carefully selected daily devotional sketches he portrays God's "intensive care" of His children. In these pages one sees:

a) the monitors which measure our spiritual vital signs: "The fruit of the Spirit . . . is joy" (Gal. 5:22), February 3.

b) the soul nourishment to perfuse us: "No good thing will he withhold from them that walk uprightly" (Ps. 84:11), March 16.

c) eternity's clock to encourage and sober us: "We know that if our earthly house of this tabernacle were dissolved, we have a building of God, an house not made with hands, eternal in the heavens" (2 Cor. 5:1), October 7.

d) the life support systems to supplement our own weak efforts: ". . . an hiding place from the wind, and a covert

9

from the tempest; as rivers of water in a dry place, as the shadow of a great rock in a weary land" (Isa. 32:2), October 21.

e) and the ever watchful eye of our God, on us continually even as we go down through the valley of the shadow of death: "He brought me up also out of an horrible pit, out of the miry clay" (Ps. 40:2), January 9.

—HOWARD H. HAMLIN, M.D., F.A.C.S.

January 1

*Now, behold, I go bound in the spirit unto
Jerusalem, not knowing the things that shall
befall me there* (Acts 20:22)

Brave soldier of the Cross! Paul had faithfully followed all
of his Commander's marching orders and now he felt compelled
to go to Jerusalem. He could not see the dangers that awaited him
nor the long night journey under Roman guard to the governor in
Caesarea. There, in chains, he would make his defense before
King Agrippa as the Spirit directed.

But Paul belonged to the risen and victorious Christ, so he
was not afraid. Let the tempestous winds of Euroclydon blow and
the ship be wrecked at sea. Faithful he would remain and un-
shaken would be his trust. In due time he would yet walk the
Appian Way to Rome with his King's message!

The Savior who loved and kept Paul is our Lord too, and He
is able to safely and surely lead us through the coming days. As
we enter an unknown year with an unseen way, not "knowing
the things that may befall," Let us take courage and not fear. He
will be our Guide—and He is all we need!

I know not what awaits me;
  God kindly veils mine eyes,
And o'er each step of my onward way
  He makes new scenes to rise;
And every joy He sends me comes
  As a sweet and glad surprise.

One step I see before me;
  'Tis all I need to see.
The light of heaven more brightly shines,
  When earth's illusions flee;
And sweetly through the silence comes
  His loving, "Follow me."

Oh, blissful lack of wisdom:
  'Tis blessed not to know;
He holds me with His own right hand,
  And will not let me go;
And lulls my troubled soul to rest
  In Him who loves me so.

11

So on I go—not knowing,
I would not if I might;
I'd rather walk in the dark with Christ
Than go alone in the light;
I'd rather walk by faith with Him
Than go alone by sight.

—MARY G. BRAINARD

January 2

Thus saith the Lord, Because the Syrians have said, The Lord is God of the hills, and he is not God of the valleys, therefore will I deliver all this great multitude into thine hand, and ye shall know that I am the Lord (1 Kings 20:28).

The Syrians had an erroneous opinion of the God of Jacob. Though their armies had been defeated by Israel from the Golan Heights, they were determined to go to war again. The Word says that they had a saying among themselves that "the Lord is God of the hills but not God of the valleys," and therefore they thought they could annihilate Israel if they fought on the plains. The great slaughter that occurred showed to all that He was the Almighty God—both of the hills and of the valleys.

How wonderful to read and know that Jesus Christ is the same "yesterday, and to day, and for ever." He is there in the mountaintop experiences. But most of life is lived in the valleys and He is there also. He is the God of the hills and the Lord of the valleys!

Refreshing indeed are mountaintop experiences. But like the Mount of Transfiguration, it is in the valley below that the sick and the sorrowing are gathering for the Master's touch, and it is there we need to be. Let us claim His promises and go to them. Our wonderful Lord of the hills and valleys will be with us everywhere, and He will manifest His love through us and in us as we serve Him—even in the far valleys of the earth.

January 3

Thy shoes shall be iron and brass; and as
thy days, so shall thy strength be (Deut. 33:25).

Have you felt at times that you could go no farther? Remember you belong to a Lord who has promised to lead you all the days of your life, and He also has promised to provide shoes for your weary feet. The shoes He gives never need repairs and will last you the long journey through. When the day is weary, the trials hard, the road extremely steep, He will be your strength for the day's travel. "As thy days, so shall thy strength be." This is His sure promise.

Day by day, and with each passing moment,
  Strength I find to meet my trials here.
Trusting in my Father's wise bestowment,
  I've no cause for worry or for fear.
He whose heart is kind beyond all measure
  Gives unto each day what He deems best.
Lovingly its part of pain and pleasure,
  Mingling toil with peace and rest.

Every day the Lord himself is near me,
  With a special mercy for each hour.
All my cares He fain would bear and cheer me,
  He whose name is Counselor and Power.
The protection of His child and treasure
  Is a charge that on himself He laid.
"As thy days, thy strength shall be in measure,"
  This the pledge to me He made.

Help me, then, in every tribulation,
  So to trust Thy promises, O Lord,
That I lose not faith's sweet consolation,
  Offered me within Thy Holy Word.
Help me, Lord, when toil and trouble meeting,
  E'er to take, as from a Father's hand,
One by one, the days, the moments fleeting,
  Till I reach the promised land.

—Carolina V. Sandell-Berg

Say it over to thyself, O Christian, when the going seems hard. Remember thy God proposes to equip thy feet for work and for war: "Thy shoes shall be iron and brass"! Notice how fittingly the rest of the sentence follows: ". . . and as thy days, so shall thy strength be." The help which comes from God is based on our needs, not our notions; is adjusted to facts, not our fears; and is given according to our days, not our decades.

—RICHARD ELLSWORTH DAY

January 4

After they were come to Mysia, they assayed to go into Bithynia: but the Spirit suffered them not (Acts 16:7).

No angels with flaming swords barred the road to Bithynia. No clarion voice from heaven prohibited the journey. No! Rather, the Lord stopped the apostle in another way.

Beside Paul's bed of sickness, faithful Luke the physician ministered. Slowly the fever left him and the weary limbs which had walked the byways of Galatia with the gospel received strength once more. And when the Book of Acts was written, no word of wondering at the ways of His grace is mentioned. Rather, "the Spirit suffered us not."

Take courage, O believer! He guides thy steps aright. From beds of illness, from unexplained hindrances, from depths of tragedy, "the Spirit suffered us not." In His good time, the door to Troas will open!

> *If, on a quiet sea,*
> *Toward heaven we calmly sail,*
> *With grateful hearts, O God, to Thee,*
> *We'll own the favoring gale.*

> *But should the surges rise,*
> *And rest delay to come,*
> *Blest be the tempest, kind the storm,*
> *Which drives us nearer Home.*

14

Soon shall our doubts and fears
 All yield to Thy control;
Thy tender mercies shall illume
 The midnight of the soul.

Teach us, in every state,
 To make Thy will our own;
And when the joys of sense depart,
 To live by faith alone.

—Augustus M. Toplady

January 5

The trial of your faith, . . . much more precious than of gold that perisheth (1 Pet. 1:7).

Faith untried may be true faith, but it is sure to be little faith, and it is likely to remain dwarfish so long as it is without trials. Faith never prospers so well as when all things are against her. Tempests are her trainers, and lightnings are her illuminators. When a calm reigns on the sea, spread the sails as you will, the ship moves not to its harbor, for on a slumbering ocean the keel sleeps too. But let the winds rush howling forth, and let the waters lift up themselves, then, though the vessel may rock, and her deck may be washed with waves, and her mast may creak under the pressure of the full and swelling gale, it is then that she makes headway towards her desired haven. No faith is so precious as that which lives and triumphs in adversity.

Tried faith brings experience. You could not have believed your own weakness had you not been compelled to pass through the rivers; and you would never have known God's strength had you not been supported amid the floodwaters. Faith increases in solidity, assurance, and intensity, the more it is exercised with tribulation. Faith is precious, and its trial is precious too.

—Charles Haddon Spurgeon

January 6

This is the day which the Lord hath made;
we will rejoice and be glad in it (Ps. 118:24).

C. Neil Strait writes concerning an eight-year-old boy named Jeffrey. He finished grace at the breakfast table one morning with these words: "We thank Thee for this beautiful day."

His mother, looking out the window, viewed the dark clouds of an approaching storm. Then she asked her son, "Why did you say that? This day is anything but beautiful."

"Mother," replied the boy, "we should never judge a day by its weather."

Many years ago as a young lad, I climbed the steps of our old church on a cold Sunday morning. Snow was falling. One of the elders stood at the door and shook my hand, as I made some comment against the winter day. He replied in the words of our text, "This is God's day. Let us be happy in it."

Yes, days should not be judged by their weather.

What should they be judged by? C. Neil Strait suggests: "Days should be judged by their opportunities. Days should be judged by smiles, more than by storms. By service rendered, more than by a snowfall. By responses to life, more than by rain falling. By love flourishing, rather than by lightning flashing and by concerns expressed rather than by clouds hanging low.

"Days should be judged by things accomplished, and not by tasks unfinished. By joyous moments, rather than by monotonous routines. Days should be judged by memories, not by mistakes. Each day thus dawns with new appeal and expectation. Each day comes with gladness to the one who has learned that days are not judged by the weather."

"Teach us to number our days, that we may apply our hearts unto wisdom" (Ps. 90:12).

January 7

I thank my God upon every remembrance
of you, always in every prayer of mine for you
all making request with joy (Phil. 1:3-4).

What a lovely testimony Paul records about the saints at Philippi! This church was dear to his heart, because the believers there did not fail either Paul or their Lord. Can this be said of us?

William Barclay wrote, "The Christian life is the only effective advertisement for Christianity. Just how well do we measure up? Christianity claims that it gives rest and joy and peace and power. Is there in our lives a calm serenity, a radiant happiness, a power to cope with life that the non-Christian does not possess? Or are we just as worried and anxious—just as gloomy and grumbling?"

The Christians at Philippi were glorious advertisements for their Lord. They not only professed Christ, they radiated Christ! And Paul thankfully remembered them, even from a prison cell in Rome! What shall *we* be remembered for?

I want you to know you are never forgotten,
That the old, old days hid in memory sweet
Are still a part of my life that I cherish,
Without them so much would be incomplete.
And you are mixed up with so much I remember,
Your name so often I utter in prayer;
Never forgotten, on earth or in heaven,
Always the child of God's tenderest care.

I want you to know you are never forgotten,
That my thoughts and my prayers are folding you round,
Rest in His promises, go where He sends you,
Do what He bids you, faithful be found.
Look up and trust Him, a new day is dawning,
Stretch out your hand and take His today;
Bought by Him, loved by Him, never forgotten,
Hid in His heart forever and aye.

—AUTHOR UNKNOWN

"When Timotheus came from you unto us, and brought us good tidings of your faith and [love], and that ye have good remembrance of us always, desiring greatly to see us, as we also to see you: therefore, brethren, we were comforted over you in all our affliction and distress by your faith" (1 Thess. 3:6-7).

January 8

Without faith it is impossible to please him; for he that cometh to God must believe that he is, and that he is a rewarder of them that diligently seek him (Heb. 11:6).

"In the evening I went very unwillingly to a society in Aldersgate Street where one was reading Luther's preface to the Epistle to the Romans. About a quarter before nine, while he was describing the change which God works in the heart through faith in Christ, I felt my heart strangely warmed. I felt I did trust in Christ, Christ alone, for salvation; and an assurance was given me that He had taken away my sins, even mine, and saved me from the law of sin and death" (JOHN WESLEY, *Journal*).

Thus John Wesley described and affirmed his conversion: the "change which God works in the heart through faith in Christ." No one could say it better than this great missionary preacher.

When America's evangelist Billy Graham was asked by a college student, "Tell me plainly, what do I do to find God?" Dr. Graham gave this answer. "First, you must acknowledge that God is, that He exists. Second, you must accept the fact that He loves you in spite of all your sins, and that He gave His Son to die on the Cross for your sins. Third, you must be willing to repent of your sins, confess your transgression of His laws, and be willing to give up your sin. Fourth, you must receive by faith Jesus Christ as your very own Lord and Savior."

This is conversion!

January 9

They rose up the same hour, and returned to Jerusalem, and found the eleven gathered together, and them that were with them, saying, The Lord is risen indeed (Luke 24:33-34).

In the art museum in Bern, Switzerland, hangs Robert Zund's great painting, "The Way to Emmaus." It shows two bewildered men walking along the road with a Stranger. These two disciples were defeated, disappointed, and discouraged. They walked to Emmaus with but one desire, to leave Jerusalem with its sad memories.

On the way to Emmaus, the risen Christ joined the two and walked with them, but they didn't know Him. They did know that very early in the morning, some women had found the stone in front of the sepulchre rolled away and "had found not the body of the Lord Jesus." These two Emmaus disciples had seen Him die. They no longer had any hope. Their faith was a past faith.

But Luke wrote, "It came to pass, as he sat at meat with them, he took bread, and blessed it, and brake it, and gave it to them. And their eyes were opened, and they knew him." Oh, glorious recognition!

Although night had fallen, these two disciples, perhaps with lanterns to light their way, hastened back to the city they left but a few hours before. They had seen the risen Lord! He was alive! With great joy they spread the good news. And so the return from Emmaus is another great proof of His resurrection. "The Lord is risen indeed."

> They did not know Christ as they walked along,
>   Although their hearts contained an inner glow;
> And when they reached their home and broke the bread,
>   I wonder what it was that made them know.
>
> It might have been the way He looked or spoke
>   That caused their hearts at last to understand—
> Or maybe as He reached to take the bread
>   They saw the nail print marked upon His hand.

—FLORENCE FRENCH

January 10

The Lord is my shepherd; I shall not want
(Ps. 23:1).

If sheep could talk, and a wise and a foolish sheep were speaking together, I fancy the foolish one would talk after this fashion: "I know where the crystal brook babbles, and I shall never want for drink. I know where the great oak spreads its leafy branches, and I shall not want for shade. I know where the green pastures of tender grass grow, and I shall never want for food. I know where the door of the fold stands wide open, and I shall never want for refuge."

Then I hear the wise sheep answering: "O foolish sheep! I have a better reason than yours for not wanting. I have the best Shepherd in the world, therefore, I shall not want. If the brook dries up He will find another for me. If the tree is cut down by the woodsman's ax, He will lead me to the shadow of a great rock. If the pastures dry up under the summer's sun, He knows how to find others. And when the wolf comes, He will lay down His life, if need be, for His sheep. O foolish sheep! I shall never want; not because I trust in things that may change, or men that prove false, but in the Shepherd who does not change, nor does He ever fail."

Men and women argue after this same fashion. They say, "I am keen of brain and skillful of hand, therefore I shall not want. The balance in my bank account is a comfortable one, therefore I shall not want. I have influential friends at court, therefore I shall not want. I am strong in body and able to make a good living, therefore I shall not want."

But the bank may fail, the skillful hands lose their cunning, friends may prove false, health may end, and wealth may disappear. When these are gone, where will we be? Then it is that we need this supreme truth—it is not the favorableness of our circumstances, but the fact of the Lord's Shepherdship which is the perpetual pledge that we shall not want!

—JAMES H. McCONKEY

January 11

They were all filled with the Holy Ghost
(Acts 2:4).

The Book of Acts is filled with excitement. It announces the ushering in of a new era. Pentecost marked the dawn of a new age—the age of the Holy Spirit. There were many supernatural incidents and accompaniments that day. But the greatest miracle was that "they were all filled with the Spirit:"

It was the filling of the Spirit which met the central need of those who tarried in the Upper Room. When "they were all filled" their preaching was then with power and their witnessing was dynamic. Self-centered attitudes and personal ambitions were purged from their hearts.

It was because of the infilling of the Holy Spirit that those early Christians were conscious of a spiritual adequacy which enabled them to meet every situation of life with poise and strength. The Spirit's fullness within gives victory over every pressure exerted by the world without.

The miracle of Pentecost needs to be repeated today. Believers filled with the Holy Spirit will be freed from the inner conflict of the carnal mind and set free to do His holy will with joy and power. Let it be "noised abroad" that the Holy Spirit is waiting to "fill" the hearts of Christ's followers and to make their lives fruitful in service.

—GEORGE COULTER

"I desire . . . that he would grant you, according to the riches of his glory, to be strengthened with might by his Spirit in the inner man" (Eph. 3:13, 16).

When a group of clergymen met one morning to discuss extending an invitation to Dwight L. Moody to hold a city-wide evangelistic campaign, one of their number seemed unimpressed with the evangelist. He arose and asked, "Does Mr. Moody have a monopoly on the Holy Spirit?"

The moderator of the meeting was quiet for a moment and then he answered, "No, but the Holy Spirit does have a monopoly on Mr. Moody."

"Be filled with the Spirit."

January 12

I will lead on softly, according as the cattle that goeth before me and the children be able to endure (Gen. 33:14).

> Lead softly on, dear Lord,
>   Lead softly on—
> My Guide and Shepherd be!
> Knowing Thy love for me,
> Safely I'll trust in Thee—
>   Lead softly on!

> Lead softly on, dear Lord,
>   Lead softly on—
> Past all my doubts and fear,
> Sorrows and falling tears.
> God of my youthful years,
>   Lead softly on!

Lead softly on, dear Lord,
    Lead softly on—
'Til by Thy side I stand,
    All dangers gone.
Until the night is past,
Until my anchor's fast,
And I am Home at last—
    Lead softly on!

What a beautiful picture of Jacob's thoughtfulness for the cattle and the children! He would not allow them to be overdriven even for one day. He knew exactly how far they could go and he made that his only consideration in arranging the marches. Jacob had gone the same wilderness journey years before, so he knew of its roughness and length. Thus he said, "I will lead on softly."

We too have not passed this way heretofore, but the Lord Jesus has. It is all untrodden and unknown ground to us but not to Him. The steep bits that take away our breath, the stony bits that bruise our feet, the hot, shadeless stretches that exhaust us, the rushing rivers we have to pass through—Jesus has gone through it all before us. Many waters went over Him, and yet His love was not quenched. He knows our frame. Think of that when you are tempted to question the gentleness of His leading. He is remembering all the time; and not one step will He make you take beyond what your feet can endure. The step that comes next is known to Him. He will strengthen you for it or He will call a sudden halt in the journey and you will not have to take it. "I will lead on softly."

—Frances R. Havergal

January 13

**The elder unto the well-beloved Gaius,
whom I love in the truth** (3 John 1).

John wrote his Third Epistle to Gaius. Gaius appears to be entirely outside the dignataries of the Early Church. He was probably just a humble follower of the Lord Jesus, unknown and unsung. Yet he stood firm in his loving Christian witness and was noted for his bountiful hospitality toward the working friends of Jesus.

The last written message, therefore, from the apostolic

fathers is this short letter to a humble and poor man, yet one who was rich in faith and love and service. Wealth, education, refinement, and prominence are always the marks which the world applauds. But God is always looking for a faithful and honest man—even though he be humble, poor, and unknown.

> Does the place you're called to labor
> Seem too small and little known?
> It is great if God is in it,
> And He'll not forget His own.
> Little is much when God is in it;
> Labor not for wealth or fame.
> There's a crown, and you can win it
> If you'll go in Jesus name.
>
> —Mrs. F. W. Suffield

Let it never be forgotten that glamour is not greatness; applause is not fame; prominence is not eminence. The man of the hour is not apt to be the man of the ages. A stone may sparkle, but this does not make it a diamond; a man may have money, but this does not make him a success. It is what the unimportant do that really counts and determines the course of history. The greatest forces in the universe are never spectacular. Summer showers are more effective than hurricanes, but they get no publicity. The world would soon die but for the fidelity, loyalty, and consecration of those whose names are unhonored and unsung.

—John R. Sizoo

January 14

I am persuaded, that neither death, nor life, nor angels, nor principalities, nor powers, nor things present, nor things to come, nor height, nor depth, nor any other creature, shall be able to separate us from the love of God, which is in Christ Jesus our Lord (Rom. 8: 38-39).

The word *persuaded* was a favorite expression in St. Paul's vocabulary. He used it many times in his writings. To Timothy he wrote that he was "greatly desiring to see thee, being mindful of thy tears, that I may be filled with joy; when I call to remembrance the unfeigned faith that is in thee, which dwelt first in thy grandmother Lois, and thy mother Eunice; and I am persuaded that in thee also."

The word *persuaded* spoke of Paul's sure faith and the Rock upon which he stood. "I am not ashamed: for I know whom I have believed, and am persuaded that he is able to keep that which I have committed unto him against that day" (2 Tim. 1:12).

Dr. Donald Grey Barnhouse, after preaching a soul-stirring message on the sufficiency of Christ, closed the sermon with the words of our text. He then went to the vestibule of the sanctuary to greet the congregation. A young boy of 12 extended his hand to the great preacher and looking up at him said, "Dr. Barnhouse, we're in great shape, aren't we?"

"I am persuaded." O believer, rejoice evermore! "We know that in everything God works for good with those who love Him."

Yea I am with thee when there falls no shadow
Across the golden glory of the day,
And I am with thee when the storm clouds gather,
Dimming the brightness of the onward way;
In days of loss and loneliness and sorrow,
Of care and weariness and fretting pain,
In days of weakness and of deep depression,
Of futile effort when thy life seems vain;
When youth has fled and Death has put far from thee
Lover and friend who made the journey sweet,
When age has come with slowly failing powers,
And the dark valley waits thy faltering feet;
When courage fails thee for the unknown future;
And the heart sinks beneath its weight of fears;
Still I am with thee—Strength and Rest and Comfort,
Thy Counsellor through all earth's changing years,
Whatever goes, whatever stays,
Lo, I am with thee all the days.

—Annie Johnson Flint

January 15

Be not drunk with wine, wherein is excess,
but be filled with the Spirit (Eph. 5:18).

To be filled with the Holy Spirit is not merely a privilege, it is not merely a possibility, it is a command. Therefore it logically follows that not to be filled with the Spirit is a sin.

It is first of all a sin against God, because only as we are filled with the Spirit can we honor and glorify Him or be "to the praise of His glory." Should not the work praise its Master? But how can it unless it portrays the Master's Spirit? His indwelling and in-filling alone becomes the enabling for a life pleasing to Him.

And it is a sin against self, for if we are not filled with the Spirit we are living the miserably unhappy life of Romans seven; constantly defeated, constantly under bondage of sin and fear, while we should be walking and talking with the King. Our lives lack the upward look and the forward movement; the courage that smiles in the face of seeming defeat; the faith that lights a lamp of hope in the darkest hour; the gladness that sings its sweetest melodies in the night of pain; the unconscious radiance that makes of the humblest task a sacred rite in the temple of God.

A privilege? Oh, yes it is! A possibility? Praise His name, yes! A command? O my God, how I have sinned! Forgive me! Cleanse me! Fill Me!

—Anna J. Lindgren
from *In His Presence*, Moody Press, © 1934, 1962

O the Spirit-filled life: is it thine, is it thine?
Is thy soul wholly filled with the Spirit divine?
O thou child of the King, has He fallen on thee?
Does He reign in thy soul, so that all men may see
The dear Saviour's blest image reflected in thee?

Has He swept through thy soul like the waves of the sea?
Does the Spirit of God daily rest upon thee?
Does He sweeten thy life, does He keep thee from care?
Does He guide thee and bless thee in answer to prayer?
Is it joy to be led of the Lord anywhere?

Is He near thee each hour, does He stand at thy side?
Does He gird thee with strength, has He come to abide?
Does He give thee to know that all things may be done
Through the grace and the power of the Crucified one?
Does He witness to thee of the glorified Son?

Has He purged thee of dross with the fire from above?
Is He first in thy thoughts, has He all of thy love?
Is His service thy choice, and is sacrifice sweet?
Is the doing His will both thy drink and thy meat?
Dost thou run at His bidding with glad eager feet?

Has He freed thee from self and from all of thy greed?
Dost thou hasten to succor thy brother in need?
As a soldier of Christ dost thou hardness endure?
Is thy hope in the Lord everlasting and sure?
Hast thou patience and meekness, art tender and pure?

O the Spirit-filled life may be thine, may be thine,
In thy soul evermore the Shekinah may shine;
It is thine to live with the tempests all stilled,
It is thine with the blessed Holy Ghost to be filled;
It is thine, even thine, for thy Lord has so willed.

—AUTHOR UNKNOWN

January 16

All with one voice about the space of two hours cried out, Great is Diana of the Ephesians (Acts 19:34).

The Psalmist declared, "It is time for thee, Lord, to work (Ps. 119:126). However, God often does His best work by apparently doing nothing.

At Ephesus a strong witness for Christ was established through Paul's ministry. God did extraordinary miracles through Paul and, as a result, the Word of the Lord grew and prevailed mightily.

But Satan also found himself a man to work through—a certain Demetrius, a silversmith, who manufactured silver images of "the great goddess Diana." Under his influence, the whole city was agitated against the Christians.

An angry mob grabbed Gaius and Aristarchus, companions of Paul, and rushed into the amphitheater. Chaos and confusion followed. Some shouted one thing and some another. The gathering was in tumult and most of them didn't know why they had come together. And so the mob as with one voice broke into a shouting that lasted for two hours:

"Great is Diana of the Ephesians."

Over and over they cried it!

And what did God do to interfere and to save His two servants? Not one thing! Not one solitary thing! He accomplished His purposes by just watching and waiting . . . by biding His time and letting them wear themselves out.

Our God is practical! He deals with wilful people, and with the realities of physical exhaustion, headaches, and sore throats! He waited until their voices were almost silent from hoarseness.

26

Admittedly, the town clerk who finally was able to "dismiss the gathering" was an influential leader, but he could not have been heard at the beginning of the riot. No! But after two hours of shouting the mob would be in such a worn-out condition that they would be not only able to hear his voice, but also ready to be sent home!

So in God's good time, the Christians were free. And the Word of the Lord was not made "void." Let us never forget that our Lord is always in control. And frequently He is doing some of His most effective work when He appears to be doing "nothing."

He is just biding His time!

—Virginia Corfield

"Be still and know that I am God" (Psalm 46:10).

January 17

Jesus sat over against the treasury, and beheld how the people cast money into the treasury (Mark 12:41).

The widow who cast her two mites into the treasury of the Temple was giving because she loved God. Man looks at what is in the hand of the giver; God looks at the heart of the giver. The world calculates how much is given; God is interested in how much is left after the gift!

The Holy Spirit used only nine words to reveal how much the widow gave. "She threw in two mites, which make a farthing." The Lord is interested in our motives. Do we give cheerfully? There is great joy in being a faithful and loving steward. There is also a great blessing!

Over the entrance to an old cathedral in France, these words stand out clearly, "He who bringeth no gift to the altar, beareth no blessing away."

> *One by one He took them from me,*
> *All the things I valued most;*
> *Until I was empty-handed,*
> *Every glittering toy was lost.*

And I walked earth's highways, grieving
  In my rage and poverty,
Till I heard His voice inviting,
  "Lift your empty hands to me."

So I held my hands toward heaven
  And He filled them with a store
Of His own transcendent riches
  Until they could hold no more.

And at last I comprehended,
  With my stupid mind and dull,
That God could not pour His riches
  Into hands already full!

—MARTHA SNELL NICHOLSON

A rich man once said to his pastor, "Why do people criticize me for being miserly, when many of them know that I have made provision in my will to leave all of my wealth to charity?"

"Let me tell you a story," the minister replied. "A pig was lamenting his lack of popularity. He complained to the cow that people were always talking about the cow's gentleness and kind eyes. He admitted that the cow gave milk and cream, but maintained that pigs also gave—bacon, ham and even pickled feet. He demanded to know the reason for such a lack of appreciation.

"The cow thought a while and said, 'Maybe it's because I give while I'm still living.'"

"Give, and it shall be given unto you; good measure, pressed down, and shaken together, and running over" (Luke 6:38).

January 18

The third day there was a marriage in Cana
of Galilee; and the mother of Jesus was there.
And both Jesus was called, and his disciples to
the marriage (John 2:1-2)

Jesus was invited to a wedding. Wise indeed is the couple who invites Christ, not only to their marriage, but also to their courtship!

It was here at this Cana wedding celebration that they ran out of wine. Mary came to Jesus and said very simply, "They have no wine." To the servants she said, "Whatsoever he saith unto you, do it."

There were six stone waterpots nearby. Jesus said to the servants "Fill the waterpots with water." And they filled them up to the brim. Then the servants bore some of the miraculous draught to the ruler of the feast. How impressed he was! He called to the bridegroom, "Thou hast kept the good wine until now."

This miracle reveals Christ as the giver of joy. But there is more than just ordinary joy symbolized here. It is the best joy—full, overflowing, and in abundant supply. The waterpots each held several firkins and a firkin equalled nine gallons. Thus over 100 gallons of the very best wine was made available.

This generous miracle speaks of abundance. It teaches us that all good things are in reserve and are available to those who love the Lord. Like the miracle of the loaves and fishes, Christ produces more than we can eat or drink or need or use!

And at the last, we have more of Him than we did at the beginning. Fear not life's feasts or famines, He is the Christ of the abundant life. He keeps you and also keeps all good things for you—even to the last of the feast.

> When from life's feast the glory has departed
>   And weariness creeps on,
> When on thy lips the bread has turned to ashes
>   And all the wine is gone.
>
> Then fill the jars once more, though but with water,
>   And fill them to the brim;
> And to the waiting guests about thy table
>   Pour out the best—for Him.
>
> His power only waits for thy small effort,
>   To add His mighty touch,
> Transmuting thy poor gift to His rich vintage,
>   Making thy little much.
>
> So shalt thou know again the joy of service
>   That thou hadst thought was past,
> And find the Master of the Feast has given
>   The best wine at the last.
>
> —ANNIE JOHNSON FLINT

"Thou hast put gladness in my heart, more than in the time that their corn and their wine increased" (Ps. 4:7).

January 19

*I will ask the Father, and he will give you
another Helper, the Spirit of truth, to stay with
you for ever* (John 14:16, TEV).

The Holy Spirit is not the companion of the hours of mourning alone, although He is that; He is the strength of the soul in every time when life is difficult, when problems are insoluble, when the way is dark, when we are near the breaking point of life.

The Holy Spirit is the Person who enables us to cope with life. Of course, that is exactly what "Comforter" meant in the 17th century; for the word "comforter" has in it the Latin adjective *fortis* which means brave; and a comforter was one who put courage into a man.

I am not forgetting how precious the word "Comforter" is, and I am not forgetting how great a function of the Holy Spirit comfort is, in the modern sense of the word. But to limit the function of the Holy Spirit to that takes much of the strength and iron and virility and gallantry out of the doctrine of the Holy Spirit.

It is very difficult to get an English translation for *parakletos*; it may well be that Moffatt was right when he translated it simply but cogently and beautifully as "the Helper."

No translation is sacred and immutable and unchangeable; and the translation of *parakletos* by the word "Comforter" is very apt to make the Holy Spirit the refuge of age rather than the inspiration of youth, the consoler of the sad rather than the spur and stimulus to chivalrous and gallant living. The Holy Spirit is both, and the word "Helper" includes both.

—William Barclay

from *Daily Celebration*, Word Books, © 1971

More holiness give me, more strivings within;
More patience in suffering, more sorrow for sin;
More faith in my Saviour, more sense of His care;
More joy in His service, more purpose in prayer.
More purity give me, more strength to o'ercome;
More freedom from earth-stains, more longings for home;
More fit for the kingdom, more used I would be;
More blessed and holy—more, Saviour, like thee.

—Philip P. Bliss

January 20

*Having therefore these promises, dearly
beloved, let us cleanse ourselves* (2 Cor. 7:1).

The promises Paul referred to in this verse are found in the
preceeding verses: "Come out from among them, and be ye separate," (6:17) was his plea. Obedience brought the sure promises
of God: "I will receive you" (6:17); "I will be a Father unto you"
(6:18); "You shall be my sons and daughters" (6:18). These
promises were spoken first to Israel, but Paul writes that these are
also our promises from the Father.

We need to be clean! God wants a holy church as the bride of
His Son. The apostle John wrote of the Father's love and said,
"Behold, what manner of love the Father hath bestowed upon us,
that we should be called the sons of God. . . . Now are we the sons
of God, and it doth not yet appear what we shall be: but we know
that, when he shall appear, we shall be like him; for we shall see
him as he is. And every man that hath this hope in him purifieth
himself, even as he is pure" (1 John 3:1-3).

This is the blessed hope of the Church—the coming of the
Bridegroom (Jesus) for His Bride (the Church). She must be
chaste. She must be clean!

Dr. William Pettingill once told the story of a young mother
who expected her husband home on the late afternoon train. She
bathed and dressed their two small girls and drove to the village
station to meet him. But he was not aboard. Hiding her disappointment, she returned to their home. A telegram was delivered,
later, stating that he had been delayed but would arrive the following day. The second day the procedure was repeated but the
father failed to appear. Later that evening, he called to tell his
family that his arrival on the morrow was certain. All business
had been completed and he was eager to see them. So once again
they bathed and dressed for his arrival.

As they were leaving again for the depot, a nosy neighbor
called to her and said, "When that man finally arrives, I'd sure
give him a piece of my mind, if I were you." To this the young
wife replied, "I don't mind the inconvenience, for we will be so
glad to have him home. But one thing is certain, the fact that my
husband is coming has kept us clean for three days!"

Paul was saying this. John was saying this. Let us be clean,
"blameless and harmless, the sons of God, without rebuke, in the
midst of a crooked and perverse nation, among whom ye shine as
lights in the world" (Phil. 2:15).

January 21

A man shall be as an hiding place from the
wind, and a covert from the tempest; as rivers
of water in a dry place, as the shadow of a great
rock in a weary land (Isa. 32:2).

We live in a weary land. The noon day heat oppresses. Life's
fierce fevers come. But our Christ is a sure hiding place from all of
life's trials. When we are tired and worn, we may rest in His
shadow. He is our Rock. And for all of life's thirsts, Jesus is also
sufficient. If our lives are parched and dry, we need but drink of
Him and find "rivers of living water." Like the woman at the well,
we can leave our earthen waterpots behind, for all who drink of
Him need never thirst again!

But not only for the trials of life and the thirsts of life is
Jesus sufficient, He is also sufficient for the tempests of life.
When great sorrow and tragedy come, when temptations almost
overwhelm the soul, in Him we have a secure hiding place and a
safe covert.

O fearful heart, hush thy needless poundings. Let the storms
rage. He who stilled the restless waves of Galilee bids thee to
hide safely in Him. Christ is sufficient!

I could not do without Thee;
I cannot stand alone,
I have no strength or goodness,
No wisdom of my own;
But Thou, beloved Saviour,
Art all in all to me;
And weakness will be power,
If leaning hard on Thee.

I could not do without Thee;
For, oh, the way is long!
And I am often weary,
And sigh replaces song.
How could I do without Thee?
I do not know the way.
Thou knowest and Thou leadest
And wilt not let me stray.

I could not do without Thee,
O Saviour of the lost!

Whose precious blood redeemed me
At such tremendous cost.
Thy righteousness, Thy pardon,
Thy precious blood must be
My only hope and comfort,
My glory and my plea!

I could not do without Thee!
For years are fleeting fast
And soon, in solemn loneliness,
The river must be passed.
But Thou wilt never leave me
And though the waves roll high,
I know Thou wilt be near me
And whisper, "It is I."

—FRANCES R. HAVERGAL

January 22

In this was manifested the love of God toward us, ... that God sent his only begotten Son into the world, that we might live through him. Herein is love, not that we loved God, but that he loved us, and sent his Son to be the propitiation for our sins (1 John 4:9-10).

Upon the wall of one of the offices in our hospital, a secretary had placed some signs. One reads, "Yesterday was the last day to receive complaints." Another states, "Wear something new today —smile." An attractive sign says this: "Spread the rumor—God loves you."

This is no rumor, this is a fact. The arms of the Cross reveal the outstretched arms of God's love, for God sent His Son into the world that through Him the world might be saved!

Henry Moorehouse was called "the boy preacher" of England. He came to Chicago and reluctantly Mr. Moody let him preach. For six nights he preached on the text, "For God so loved the world, that he gave his only begotten Son, that whosoever believeth in him should not perish, but have everlasting life" (John 3:16).

Mr. Moody later wrote, "The seventh night came, and Henry

Moorehouse went into the pulpit. Every eye was upon him. He said, 'Beloved friends, I have been hunting all day for a new text, but I cannot find anything so good as the old one; so we will go back to the third chapter of John and the sixteenth verse,' and he preached the seventh sermon from those wonderful words, 'God so loved the world.' At the end of the sermon, Henry Moorehouse said, 'My friends, for a whole week I have been trying to tell you how much God loves you, but I cannot do it with this poor stammering tongue. If I could borrow Jacob's ladder and climb up to heaven and ask Gabriel, who stands in the presence of the Almighty, to tell me how much love the Father has for the world, all he could say would be: "God so loved the world, that He gave His only begotten Son, that whosoever believeth in Him should not perish, but have everlasting life."'"

> The love of God is greater far
> Than tongue or pen can ever tell;
> It goes beyond the highest star,
> And reaches to the lowest hell.
> The guilty pair, bowed down with care,
> God gave His Son to win;
> His erring child He reconciled,
> And pardoned from his sin.
>
> Could we with ink the ocean fill,
> And were the skies of parchment made;
> Were every stalk on earth a quill,
> And every man a scribe by trade;
> To write the love of God above
> Would drain the ocean dry;
> Nor could the scroll contain the whole,
> Though stretched from sky to sky.

—F. M. LEHMAN
from "The Love of God," © 1945,
Nazarene Publishing House

January 23

Always labouring fervently for you in prayers, that ye may stand perfect and complete in all the will of God (Col. 4:12).

Sometimes we feel that the will of God for our lives is hard to discover. But I can tell you from Scripture one of the most important features of His plan for you, if you are a Christian. It is the same as what He plans for me—He wants to make us like Christ.

This is His purpose which He conceived for you and me before the world began. "Whom he did foreknow, he also did predestinate [that is, decided the destiny ahead] to be conformed to the image of his Son" (Rom. 8:29).

Here is the intended direction of our whole lives. Do you want to know the will of God for you? It has something to do with you becoming like Christ. It is not just where you will go and what you will do, but what you will become.

This is so important to God that He arranges every event in our lives to work toward that result. "All things work together for good to them that love God, to them who are the called according to his purpose" (Rom. 8:28). They work together for good; but the good toward which they work is not our comfort. Most of us have discovered that. Nor is it our peace of mind. The good toward which they work is our transformation—that we shall be like Christ! God is not satisfied with us the way we are.

What is Christlikeness? Jesus characterized His own life in two ways. First, "I do always those things that please him" (John 8:29). The Psalmist described Him by writing, "I delight to do thy will, O my God: yea, thy law is within my heart" (Ps. 40: 8). To be like Him is to obey the Father.

Secondly, Christ said, "A new commandment I give unto you, That ye love one another; as I have loved you, that ye also love one another" (John 13:34). The quality of Jesus' love is to be ours. He offers it to us, that we may love one another.

Christlikeness . . . this is God's will for us. Are you growing more like the Master?

—Robert H. Thompson

January 24

A man prepared a great feast and sent out many invitations (Luke 14:16, TLB).

In this parable, the supper represents the feast of salvation and God has issued the invitations to it. It is called in the King James Version "a great supper" because the whole world is invited. This is a feast that all may enjoy and find complete satis-

35

faction from the hungers of life. Kings and potentates, doctors and lawyers, bricklayers and painters, rich and poor, bond and free—they shall come from the east and the west and the north and the south to this great dinner which cost so much, yet is free to all who come. To attend this feast, special dress is required: a robe of righteousness imputed by God through faith to all those who believe in His Son.

In this parable are excuses and turned-down invitations. One man claims a business deal prevents his attendance—he had purchased some property. One has acquired oxen and he must go and prove them. One has just married and the wife keeps him away. How typical of the day in which we live: money, pleasure, sex all come before the kingdom of God.

"Go out quickly into the streets," the Host of the feast said, "and bring in here the poor and the maimed, and the lame, and the blind. Tell them to come, for all things are ready."

So God called them, and so He calls today. Come just as you are! Come now! Come and bring *someone* with you—don't bother bringing *something* with you, for it is "by grace are ye saved through faith; and that not of yourselves: it is the gift of God: not of works, lest any man should boast" (Eph. 2:8-9).

"The servant said, Lord, it is done as thou hast commanded, and yet there is room. And the Lord said unto the servant, Go out into the highways and hedges, and compel them to come in, that my house may be filled. For I say unto you, That none of those men which were bidden shall taste of my supper" (Luke 14:22-24).

> There's room at the Cross for you;
> There's room at the Cross for you.
>   Tho' millions have come,
>   There's still room for one.
> Yes, there's room at the Cross for you.

—IRA STANPHILL
"Room at the Cross for You" © 1946 Singspiration, Inc.

January 25

When he asks, he must believe and not doubt, because he who doubts is like a wave of the sea, blown and tossed by the wind (Jas. 1:6, NIV).

Richard DeHaan records the story of a small church that became disturbed over a night club which had opened on the village's main street. Members met to pray for its removal from their community. Some even asked the Lord to burn it down. A few weeks after the prayer groups started, a storm struck the community, lightning hit the tavern, and it was destroyed by fire. The owner, knowing of the prayer groups, sued the church for damages with the owner's attorney filing briefs in court that the church's prayers had caused the loss of the drinking establishment. The congregation hired another lawyer to defend them and to fight the charges. After due deliberation the judge ruled: "It is the opinion of this court that the tavern keeper obviously believes in the power of prayer while the church members do not."

Do we pray expecting God to answer?

"Therefore I tell you, whatever you ask for in prayer, believe that you will receive it, and it will be yours" (Mark 11:24, NIV).

"Many a fellow is praying for rain with his tub wrong side up" (Sam Jones).

"Ask and it will be given to you; seek and you will find. . . . For everyone who asks receives; he who seeks finds, and to him who knocks the door will be opened" (Matt. 7:7-8, NIV).

"Keep praying, but be thankful that God's answers are wiser than some of your petitions" (William Culbertson).

January 26

They brought to him a man sick of the palsy, lying on a bed (Matt. 9:2).

Here was a man with a desperate need. Cerebral palsy had finally confined him to bed. He could not walk. His situation was hopeless. But where there is a great need, the Master comes to heal and to save.

According to the Gospel account, four faithful friends were needed to carry the man to Jesus. A crowd pressed around the house where Jesus was speaking. It was impossible to get inside. But hope always removes obstacles. The faithful bearers lifted the sick man to the roof of the small house, removed some of the tiles, and lowered the man to Christ.

There are still many "palsied" in the world today, and Jesus is still the good and true Physician. We need men who will bring them to the Savior. Obstacles may have to be removed. The task may be difficult, yet the divine call still goes out: "Wanted—litter bearers for the Lord Jesus." Will you be one?

> *The bearers are unsteady. Racked and worn*
> *With long disease, and clumsily upborne,*
> *What is my anguish with their stumbling feet*
> *And all the push and clamor of the street?*
> *But any way, however rough it be,*
> *O Good Physician, if I get to Thee!*
>
> *The crowd is great about Thee. How they press*
> *Each in his own absorbing wretchedness,*
> *Unheeding me, the sick man borne of four,*
> *Halting despondent at the crowded door.*
> *But any way, however thronged it be,*
> *O Good Physician, if I get to Thee!*
>
> *Upon the roof a glaring light is spread,*
> *Blistering underneath and overhead,*
> *They tear the tiles; the smarting dust is thick—*
> *O men, ye four, be mercifully quick!*
> *But any way, however hard it be,*
> *O Good Physician, if I get to Thee!*
>
> —Amos R. Wells

"When Jesus saw their faith, he said unto the sick of the palsy, Son, thy sins be forgiven thee. . . . I say unto thee, Arise, and take up thy bed, and go thy way into thine house. And immediately he arose, took up the bed, and went forth before them all; insomuch that they were all amazed, and glorified God, saying, We never saw it on this fashion" (Mark 2:5, 11-12).

January 27

*These that have turned the world upside
down are come hither also* (Acts 17:6).

The world turned upside down! What a marvelous testimony to the power of the gospel, the grace of God, and the zeal of Paul and Silas, is expressed in these words by the unbelievers in Thessalonica. The message of the Cross had proven to be the power of God. Sorcerers were losing their power, ancient cults were threatened, and Diana of the Ephesians was losing influence. The world was really being turned "rightside up." Paul and Silas were not only faithful to the message of the Cross, but also faithful to the Great Commission of the Christ of the Cross. If the gospel is to be preached to the world, the gospel must go to the world. The world can only be turned upside down if the "go ye" finds fulfilment with the words, "These . . . are come here also."

"It has always been my ambition to preach the gospel where Christ was not known . . . But now there is no more place for me to work in these regions, and since I have been longing for many years to see you, I plan to do so when I go to Spain" (Rom. 15:20, 25, NIV).

"The early Christians did not say in dismay, 'Look at what the world has come to,' but in delight, 'Look who has come into the world!'" (E. Stanley Jones).

"If God could turn some of us inside out, He might send us to turn the world upside down" (Leonard Havenhill).

Have you seen any worlds turned upside down lately?

January 28

· *Do thy diligence to come shortly unto me:
for Demas hath forsaken me, having loved this
present world* (2 Tim. 4:9-10).

Paul realized that his earthly journey was nearing an end. "I have fought a good fight, I have finished my course . . . I am now ready to be offered, and the time of my departure is at hand"

(2 Tim. 4:7, 6). These were the apostle's parting words to Timothy.

The prison was cold and damp. Paul asked Timothy to bring his cloak and books and his beloved parchments (scriptures).

And then he mentions Demas. Demas, as well as Mark and Luke, had been with Paul during his first imprisonment in Rome. (Philem. 24). However, as Paul's life and ministry came to a close, Demas left him. Whatever the reasons, he had pulled his own hands back from the plow. He did not complete the task the Lord had given him. Paul simply said, "Demas left me for this present, evil world." Our love for Christ needs to be strong!

> My soul, be on thy guard;
> Ten thousand foes arise;
> The hosts of sin are pressing hard
> To draw thee from the skies.
> Ne'er think the victory won,
> Nor lay thine armor down;
> The work of faith will not be done
> Till thou obtain the crown.
>
> —GEORGE HEATH

Demas started out in dead earnest, maybe with plenty of fire, but the pull of the old life and the charm of the world were too much for him. The spirit of the times got to Demas. Christians, free from the grosser sins and unaffiliated with the fun and frolic of low living, may, nevertheless, still be worldlings. The Christian's citizenship is in heaven and whatever does not savor of that is of the world. Any interest that is ahead of the will of God, be it business or pleasure or ambition, is of Demas (Vance Havner in *Rest Awhile*).

> Tell me the old, old story of unseen things above,
> Of Jesus and His glory, of Jesus and His love.
> Tell me the story simply, as to a little child;
> For I am weak and weary, and helpless and defiled.
>
> Tell me the story slowly, that I may take it in—
> That wonderful redemption, God's remedy for sin.
> Tell me the story often, for I forget so soon,
> The "early dew" of morning has passed away at noon.
>
> Tell me the same old story when you have cause to fear
> That this world's empty glory is costing me too dear.
> Yes, and when that world's glory is dawning on my soul,
> Tell me the old, old story: Christ Jesus makes thee whole.
>
> —KATE HANKEY

January 29

*He brought me up also out of an horrible
pit, out of the miry clay* (Ps. 40:2).

The Holy Spirit is the Lord of the harvest. He woos and calls
and reveals the Lord Jesus to sinful men. Some come to Christ
early in life and some reject Him forever. Some are won by His
love. Others are reached only after they have lived in the "far
country" and from the deepest pit. Some seek Him only after
great tragedy.

Kenneth Dodge writes of a farmer who had three sons, Jim,
John, and Sam. No one in the family ever attended church or had
any interest in the things of God. Then one day Sam was bitten
by a rattlesnake and the doctor was called.

He did all he could to help Sam but the situation was very
grave so they sent for the pastor of the local church. He came and
prayed as follows:

"O wise and righteous Father, we thank Thee that in Thy
wisdom Thou didst send this rattlesnake to bite Sam. He has
never been inside the church and it is doubtful that he has, in all
this time, ever prayed or acknowledged Thee. Now we trust that
this experience will be a valuable lesson to him and that it will
lead him to genuine repentance and faith in our Lord Jesus Christ.

"And now, O Father, wilt Thou send another rattlesnake to
bite Jim and another one to strike John and a really big one to bite
the old man, their father. For years we have done everything we
know to beg them to turn to Thee but all in vain. Where our efforts failed, the rattlesnake has succeeded. We thus conclude that
the only thing that will do this family any real good is rattlesnakes; so Lord, send us bigger and better rattlesnakes until they
turn to Thee. Amen."

—KENNETH DODGE

Isaiah made the promise plain but with a warning. Men do
well to heed his word. "Seek ye the Lord while he may be found,
call ye upon him while he is near: Let the wicked forsake his way,
and the unrighteous man his thoughts: and let him return unto
the Lord, and he will have mercy upon him; and to our God, for
he will abundantly pardon" (Isa. 55:6-7).

January 30

*Now is not Boaz of our kindred, with
whose maidens thou wast? Behold, he win-
noweth barley tonight in the threshing floor*
(Ruth 3:2).

One of nature's grandest views can be seen in western Kansas
at sunset with the pink rays of the dying sun moving across the
fields of waving grain. It is a sky that the master artist Corot
would love to have painted. And in certain seasons across those
fields of grain move the great threshing combines garnering wheat
for the hungry of the world.

In the days of Boaz threshing was done by hand. Sheaves of
grain were brought to the barn and then flailed until the precious
chaffless nuggets of grain were left on the threshing floor.

Thus God's people are separated from the chaff. He wants
pure wheat. Samuel Rutherford wrote, "Be content; you are the
wheat growing in the Lord's field; and, if wheat, you must go
under our Lord's threshing instruments. He will make you good
bread in His house."

May our prayer be, "Flail me, dear Lord, 'till all the chaff
is gone and I am found pure and wholesome for my Master's use."

> *When the wheat is carried home*
> *And the threshing time has come,*
> *Close the door.*
> *When the flail is lifted high,*
> *Like the chaff I would not fly;*
> *At His feet, oh, let me lie*
> *On the floor!*
> *All the cares that o'er me steal,*
> *All the sorrows that I feel*
> *Like a dart.*
> *When my enemies prevail,*
> *When my strength begins to fail—*
> *'Tis the beating of the flail*
> *On my heart!*
> *It becomes me to be still,*
> *Though I cannot all His will*
> *Understand.*
> *I would be the purest wheat*
> *Lying humbly at His feet,*
> *Kissing oft the rod that beats*
> *In His hand!*

By and by I shall be stored
In the garner of my Lord
Like a prize;
Thanking Him for every blow
That in sorrow laid me low,
But in beating made me grow
For the skies!

—Author Unknown

January 31

**Let no man despise thy youth; but be thou
an example of the believers, in word, in conversation, in charity, in spirit, in faith, in purity**
(1 Tim. 4:12).

The closing chapters of Paul's first letter to young Timothy
can be called "advice to a young man." In them Paul urges his son
in the faith to set a good example in word, in speech, in conduct,
in love, and in purity. He urges Timothy to meditate upon the
Word and to adhere to its counsel. The apostle wanted his young
friend to be a good witness both in speech and in conduct.

Paul added additional and important counsel near the end of
his letter. "Flee, O man of God" (6:11), he wrote. What was Timothy to flee? He was urged to flee ungodliness, unholy living,
sexual impurity. Timothy was also warned to guard against "the
love of money." The apostle further advised him to flee from
temptation. "Run as though your very life and soul depended on
it," Paul was saying.

Paul also said, "Follow" (6:11). What was Timothy to follow? He was told to follow after righteousness, godliness, faith,
love, and other fruits of the Spirit-filled life. Timothy was to be
like Barnabas, "a good man, full of faith and of the Holy Spirit."

Finally Paul said, "Fight the good fight of faith" (6:12). The
battle rages, but do not give up. "Lay hold on eternal life. Make
a good profession before many witnesses."

Flee! Follow! Fight! O man of God, there is a place for all
of these. Flee from temptation, to Christ. Follow with a whole
heart the will and righteousness of God. Fight with His full armor
upon you. Victory is assured in the fullness of the Holy Spirit.

43

February 1

Make thee two trumpets of silver; of a whole piece shalt thou make them . . . And it came to pass on the twentieth day of the second month, in the second year, that the cloud was taken up from off the tabernacle of the testimony. And the children of Israel took their journeys out of the wilderness of Sinai (Num. 10:2, 11-12).

This had been a time of waiting for Israel. Tarrying at Sinai, they had received the law and the ordinances. The tribe of Levi had been appointed to serve in the tabernacle, and Aaron and his descendents had been anointed for the holy priesthood.

All was in order. At last the silver trumpets blew and the cloud hanging over the tabernacle lifted. The trumpets' note and the ascending cloud were signs that the children of Israel were about to embark on the next stage of their God-directed journey. The cloud, designed to lead them, was also a limiting factor. Because of it, they were unable to see the path ahead with clear vision. The future for them, as now for us, was hidden by the wise foreknowledge of God. Thus the lifting cloud was not only a time for rejoicing, but also provided a time for trusting! God knows our frame. He knows our weariness. He does not allow us to be tried beyond our endurance. The length of the day's journey lies in His tender care.

So when the trumpets blow again for you and the cloud lifts, these are His marching orders. Move forward then with confidence and trust.

> *I have traveled long in the weary way*
> *Over mountain and sea and plain,*
> *Through the burning heat of the summer's day*
> *And the winters of wind and rain;*
> *I have journeyed on through the dark and light,*
> *By the dimness of dusk and dawn,*
> *For I rise and go, be it noon or night,*
> *When the pillar of God moves on.*
>
> *I may know no home on my pilgrim way,*
> *But a tent and a camp instead;*
> *I may murmur not if He bids me stay*
> *When my spirit would forge ahead;*

For my home is far in the Promised Land
  Where my Risen Lord has gone,
And I trace the touch of His wounded hand
  As the pillar of God moves on.

Oh, it matters not if I go or stay,
  For I know He has planned aright,
And His snowy cloud is my guide by day,
  And His column of fire by night.
So I follow on in His winding ways,
  Be it darkness or day or dawn,
And my heart o'erflows with its pilgrim praise
  As the pillar of God moves on.

I will fear no ill on my homeward way,
  For my Master is by my side,
And He points my pathway by night and day—
  And I know I can trust my Guide.
So I'll follow on where His hand may lead
  While a pilgrim on earth I roam,
For I know my Saviour is all I need
  Till the pillar of God moves Home.

—E. Margaret Clarkson

If by chance there is a museum in heaven, thy servant doth much desire to see and handle the two silver trumpets. Quite plainly the Word affirms that any movement in the camp which began *without* their silvery peal was merely the ugly action of an unsubdued will. To move *forward* without the trumpets was *rebellion*. To remain quiet, if the trumpets said "Go," was *rebellion*. To move *before* they sounded was to *move* into the dark; and to refuse to move after they spoke was to *remain* in the dark.

—Richard Ellsworth Day

February 2

When he had gone a little farther thence, he saw James the son of Zebedee, and John his brother, who also were in the boat mending their nets. And straightway he called them: and they left their father Zebedee in the ship with the hired servants, and went after him (Mark 1:19-20).

Zebedee must have loved his two sons very dearly. He had undoubtedly held their little hands as they had learned to walk and into his outstretched arms they had fled for comfort and from childish dangers. Zebedee had taught them well, not only how to be brave men, but he had also taught them the promises of God. Perhaps often at night in their home they had prayed for the coming of the promised Messiah.

Then Jesus came and called James and John. They responded to Him. They "left their nets" and their father to follow and serve the Lord. Tears must have fallen on Zebedee's weathered face. They were tears of separation and also tears of joy. He would miss them, and yet how proud of his sons he must have been!

We rejoice in the "Jameses and Johns" of our day who have left all for Christ. He demands the best of our youth, but let us not forget to pray for the "Zebedees" who have given their children to Him. There is joy in experiencing a son's or daughter's answering the Spirit's call, but there are tears too. So pray often for the "Jameses and Johns" and also for the "Zebedees."

It must have been a blow to Zebedee
When James and John, on hearing, "Follow me!"
Seemed to forget the plans already made
That they should carry on the fishing trade
When Zebedee grew old and felt he must
Surrender it to someone he could trust.

Ah, how they knew the fishing business! He
Had seen them come through storms on Galilee
That would have tested older fishermen.
They understood the seasons and knew when
To set a trap of nets, knew how to haul,
And where to sail. Yes, he had taught them all.

He knew of fishing, but had taught them, too,
The law, the prophets, and what one must do

To live beyond reproach with God and men
While waiting for the day of promise when
The Lord should sent to earth a chosen One—
His Servant, His Emmanuel, His Son.

But, as they worked, a strong young Teacher came
And spoke to them as One who has a claim
Upon all men—One not to be denied.
"Come, I will make you fish for men," He cried.
"You, John and James!" What could they do but go?
Should he go too? He, Zebedee? But no.

Someone must stay behind to man the boat.
But they must go; he must not let them note
How disappointment struggled with his pride
In them, and tears were hard to hide.
"Boys, when you fish for men, remember me
And try to catch a few for Zebedee."

—MARY S. THOMAS

February 3

The fruit of the Spirit . . . is joy (Gal. 5:22).

"In the Lord Jesus Christ every believer has a treasure which cannot be described solely in terms of material wealth and possession. God is our Father and we are members of His wealthy family. All gold and silver are His and through Him, they are ours. His Son is ours. His Salvation is ours. Sanctification is ours. Glorification is ours. All the promises of the Book are ours" (M. R. DeHaan)

With such great possessions and a wonderful family, we should radiate love, joy, and peace to the saddened world around us. Jesus has given us His wonderful peace. It was Jesus who said: "Peace I leave with you, my peace I give unto you" (John 14:27). Our hearts should not be troubled or afraid and our countenance should radiate His joy. Our Lord said, "Ye shall be my witnesses." We are not just to *bear* a witness, we are to *be* a witness. God cannot use a gloomy messenger. The Spirit-filled life is not a life filled with defeat, discouragement, or depression.

Dr. W. E. Sangster, well known interpreter of John Wesley,

was pastor for many years of the Westminster Central Hall in London. He once spoke concerning a friend of his, a Dr. Farmer who was the great organist at Harrow. The musician had attended a service and had become disturbed over a loud Salvation Army drum that was being beaten ferociously. Finally he could stand it no longer so he quietly asked the drummer not to beat so hard.

The beaming bandsman replied to Dr. Farmer, "Lor' bless you, sir, but since I've been converted I'm so 'appy I could bust the blooming drum."

The fruit of the Spirit is joy. Let us keep the "drums beating loudly."

February 4

Be still, and know that I am God (Ps. 46: 10).

It is not easy to be still in this rough and restless world. Yet God says, "Be still." He also says, "In returning and rest shall ye be saved; in quietness and in confidence shall be your strength" (Isa. 30:15). Listen to Him!

"Be still, and thou shalt know I can put all enemies to shame. He that sitteth in the heavens shall laugh; the Lord shall hold them in derision!

"Be still, and thou shalt know that I can uphold My own truth in a day of error. Is not My Word precious to Me and My Book of truth, is it not above all books in Mine eyes?

"Be still, and thou shalt know that I can say to the nations, 'Peace be still.' The waves rise, but I am mightier than all. The tumults do not touch My throne. Take no alarm. I am still God.

"Be still, and thou shalt see the glorious issue of all the confusions. The world is My world, and thou shalt see it to be such; the earth shall yet see My Kingdom."

—HORATIUS BONAR

"Ye shall not need to fight in this battle: set yourselves, stand ye still, and see the salvation of the Lord" (2 Chron, 20:17).

> *I know not how God works His purpose out,*
> *But this I know, He'll bring His plans about.*
>
> *I know not how He makes my spirit whole,*
> *But this I know, He satisfies my soul.*

I know not how His grace will conquer sin,
But this I know, His victory He will win.

I know not how His nature He'll impart,
But this I know, He'll fill the longing heart.

I know not how my strength He will renew,
But this I know, His promises are true.

I know not how His Word He will fulfill,
But this I know—He's promised, and He will.

—E. Margaret Clarkson

February 5

I pray for them (John 17:9).

John records four gifts given to the Lord Jesus by His Father: "The work which thou gavest me . . . the words which thou gavest me . . . the glory which thou gavest me . . . the men which thou gavest me" (John 17:4, 8, 22, 6).

In His priestly prayer, Jesus reminded the Father of His gift of men: "That [I] should give eternal life to as many as thou hast given [me]. . . . I have manifested thy name unto the men which thou gavest me . . . I pray for them . . . which thou hast given me . . . keep thou through thine own name those whom thou hast given me . . . While I was with them in the world, I kept them in thy name: those that thou gavest me I have kept . . . Father, I will that they also, whom thou hast given me, be with me where I am" (John 17:2, 6, 9, 11, 12, 24).

How amazing His grace that sinners so vile could yet be a gift from God to His Son and a gift worth thanking the Father for. These were His men and Jesus loved them and His prayer requests for them were: "Father, keep [them] . . . sanctify them . . . that they might have my joy . . . I pray not that thou shouldest take them out of the world, but that thou shouldest keep them from the evil. . . . I will that they also . . . be with me where I am; that they may behold my glory" (John 17:11, 17, 13, 15, 24).

Peter, James, Andrew, John, and the others—the Master prayed earnestly for them. But He did not stop there. Listen! "Neither pray I for these alone, but for them also which shall believe on me through their word" (John 17:20). Jesus prayed for us, and the Father will honor His Son's requests.

49

What was His last request? "That the love with which thou
hast loved me may be in them, and I in them" (John 17:26). We
are the possessors of the Father's wonderful love!

February 6

*Brethren, when I came to you, [I] came
not with excellency of speech or of wisdom,
declaring unto you the testimony of God. For
I determined not to know any thing among
you, Save Jesus Christ, and him crucified* (1
Cor. 2:1-2).

Paul thus declares himself to be a preacher of the Cross! No
vain or idle babblings fell from his lips. He gave no book reviews
or sermons on philosophy! His message was the Cross: Christ
cruficied for our sins, Christ buried, and Christ risen again. The
preaching of the Cross! This is the message of God that can save
a dying world!

One day upon the green-clad slope
Of Calvary's mountain fair,
There fell a shadow, grim and cold,
That told a cross was there.
Upon its outstretched arms it bore
The form of One divine;
Though sinless, yet condemned to die,
Your Advocate and mine.

Around its base in silent grief
Stood those who loved Him best;
The vital meaning of that Cross
Burned deep within each breast.
They through the years, to all the world,
Proclaimed its power to save,
Its message of redeeming love
And life beyond the grave.

They preached that Cross with fervent zeal,
They told its fearful cost,
But somewhere down the path of time
Its deepest sense was lost.

No longer stained with precious blood,
But gilded now with gold;
No longer warm with life and love,
But formal, vain, and cold.

It dangles now from golden chain,
Or gleams from lifted spire,
Too seldom shines from hearts aflame
With love's eternal fire.
Yet mid the chaos of the world,
Its strife and selfish greed,
That sacrificial cross of Christ
Remains its greatest need.

—Clarence H. Alquist

Without Christ crucified in her pulpit, a church is little better than a dead carcass, a well without water, a barren fig tree, a sleeping watchman, a silent trumpet, a dumb witness, an ambassador without terms of peace, a messenger without tidings, a lighthouse without fire, a stumbling block to weak believers, a comfort to infidels, a hotbed for formalism, a joy to the devil, and an offense to God.

—J. C. Ryle

February 7

God shall wipe away all tears from their eyes; and there shall be no more death, neither sorrow, nor crying, neither shall there be any more pain; for the former things are passed away (Rev. 21:4).

Perhaps today with aching heart, you stand where the road bends, gazing with straining eyes down the path where last you saw someone who through the years had walked near your side.

When the way was pleasant you laughed together, and lingered beside the clear streams to gather flowers of happiness. When there were storms of grief, you clung to each other for comfort. When the dark clouds of war and hate broke above your heads, you looked into each other's eyes, and there found courage and faith to go on. When there were threatenings of discouragement, misunderstanding, and doubt, you threw your shoulders back and smiled away your fears—for you were together.

But today you walk alone.

For, answering a call which your ear did not hear, your loved one hastened on ahead, following the final bend in the road. Take heart, dear one. Faith whispers, "The way is not long. Soon you, too, will follow the bend in the road, and beyond its turning you will discover the most glorious morning that ever dawned! And in its eternal light you will see clearly all that now seems dim and confusing."

The Savior is strong and true, and He has promised never to leave or forsake us. Trust Him, and hold fast to His hand. He will take you through.

—K. B. P.

Near the end of a journey long and steep,
    As you toiled 'neath a cumbering load,
Have your eyes, so lately prone to weep,
Beheld with joy through the shadows deep
    The final bend in the road?

Oh, the road of life winds in and out,
    Over time's vast plains outspread,
And to him who travels with fear and doubt,
And to him of faith, with courage stout,
    There is always a turn ahead.

And the man of faith undaunted goes,
    And the craven lags behind;
While the trail of life, with its joys and woes
Leads on, and bends—and neither knows
    At the turn what he shall find.

And fear cries out, "See, the pathway bends,
    How I dread the way unknown!
Lo, the hill before me steep ascends,
And I know not where the journey ends,
    And I fear to walk alone!"

But faith exults, "See the bend in the road?
    Ah, my journey soon shall end,
And there waits for me a blest abode,
With a smooth, bright path, and a lightened load,
    And the welcome of a Friend!"

—Kathryn Blackburn Peck

February 8

*The fruit of the Spirit is love, joy, peace,
longsuffering, gentleness, goodness, faith,
meekness, temperance; against such there is
no law* (Gal. 5:22-23).

Beloved Christians! Christ Jesus longs for you in order to
make you, amid those who surround you, a very fountain of love.
The love of heaven would fain take possession of you, in order
that, in and through you, it may work its blessed work on earth.
Yield to its rule. Offer yourself unreservedly to its indwelling.
Honor it by the confident assurance that it can teach you to love
as Jesus loved. As conformity to the Lord Jesus must be the chief
mark of your Christian walk, so love must be the chief mark of
that conformity. Be not disheartened if you do not attain it at
once. Only keep fast hold of the command, "Love, even as I have
loved you." It takes time to grow into it. Say to Him, "Lord Jesus,
in Thy strength be pleased to reveal Thy love to me. Shed abroad
Thy love in my heart through Thy Holy Spirit."

Child of God! It was according to the Scriptures "that Jesus
Christ lived and died." O give thyself up with an individual heart
to learn in the Scriptures what God says to thee. Let the Word be
thy daily food and meditation. Go to God's Word each day with
the joyful and confident expectation that through the blessed
Holy Spirit who dwells in thee, the Word will indeed accomplish
its divine purpose in thee—that thou shalt be like Christ.

Beloved followers of Jesus! Called to manifest His likeness
to the world, learn that as forgiveness of your sins was one of the
first things Jesus did for you, forgiveness of others is one of the
first things you can do for Him. And remember that to the new
heart there is a joy even sweeter than that of being forgiven; even
the joy of forgiving others. The joy of being forgiven is only that
of a sinner and of earth; the joy of forgiving is Christ's own joy,
the joy of heaven.

You would be like Christ? Here is the path. Gaze on the glory
of God in Him. Look to Him, the living, loving Christ. Look to
Him in adoration. Look to Him in faith. Look to Him with strong
desire. And as you behold Him, above all, let the look of love not
be wanting. Tell Him that to please Him, the beloved One, is your
highest, your only joy.

—Andrew Murray
in *Like Christ*

Oh, to be like Thee! Blessed Redeemer,
This is my constant longing and prayer.
Gladly I'll forfeit all of earth's treasures,
Jesus, Thy perfect likeness to wear.

Oh, to be like Thee! While I am pleading,
Pour out Thy Spirit, fill with Thy love;
Make me a temple meet for Thy dwelling,
Fit me for life and heaven above.

—T. O. CHISHOLM

February 9

**Looking unto Jesus the author and finisher
of our faith** (Heb. 12:2).

There are three "looks" in the Christian life: the backward look, the onward look, and the upward look.

The backward look is dangerous. We are admonished to not look back. "This one thing I do," said Paul, "forgetting those things which are behind . . . I press toward the mark" (Phil. 3: 13-14). We cannot change the tide of the years, and life's golden opportunities seldom come again. But sin can be forgiven by His grace and all is not lost. Practice, therefore, the "onward look." Greater joy and usefulness lie ahead if you submit "to do His will and to seek His good pleasure." Press on "toward the mark of your high calling in Christ." Live with the "onward look."

And then look up! The upward look must be your total commitment. Look not at surroundings or circumstances but look up unto Jesus. He is the Author and the Finisher of your faith. Human friends may fail but Jesus, never. Live with the upward look of devotion, faith, and trust.

I don't look back; God knows the fruitless efforts,
The wasted hours, the sinning, the regrets;
I leave them all with Him who blots the record,
And mercifully forgives, and then forgets.

I don't look round me; then would fears assail me,
So wild the tumult of earth's restless seas;
So dark the world, so filled with woe and evil,
So vain the hope of comfort or of ease.

54

I don't look in; for then am I most wretched;
  Myself has naught on which to stay my trust;
Nothing I see save failures and shortcomings,
  And weak endeavors crumbling into dust.

But I look up—into the face of Jesus,
  For there my heart can rest, my fears are stilled;
And there is joy, and love, and light for darkness,
  And perfect peace, and every hope fulfilled.

—ANNIE JOHNSON FLINT

February 10

If he hath wronged thee, or oweth thee aught, put that on mine account; I Paul have written it with my own hand, I will repay it: albeit I do not say to thee how thou owest unto me even thine own self besides (Philem. 18-19).

In the city of Colossae, in Phrygia, lived a wealthy Christian by the name of Philemon. He was the head of a large household and, like many in that day, he had a number of slaves and bondmen. Christianity did not immediately overturn this evil custom, but eventually it was driven out by the message of the Cross.

This man Philemon evidently was converted to Christ through the ministry of the apostle Paul. Years went by, and one of Philemon's slaves, Onesimus, robbed his master and fled to Rome. Onesimus did not take God into account, but God's eye was nevertheless upon him in his journeyings. In the imperial city this Phrygian slave was brought into contact with the very man through whom his master had found Christ. Possibly Onesimus was arrested because of some further mischief, and in that way came into contact with Paul in prison. But through the same gospel that had blessed Philemon, Onesimus, the runaway slave, was also saved, and another star added to the Redeemer's crown.

One evidence that people are really born of God is their effort to make restitution for wrong done in the past. They want a good conscience both before God and before men. And so Onesimus tells Paul of his stealing and of his desire to go back to his master and make amends. Paul could have just written a tender letter to Philemon asking him to forgive. But he did not do this. I believe he wanted to give a picture of the great gospel of vicarious sacrifice. And so Philemon reads of Paul's hand, "put the debt on my account. I will repay it when I come."

This is a picture of the gospel, of what the Savior has done for every repentant soul. I see Him as He brings the needy, penitent wrongdoer into the presence of God, and says, "My Father, he has wronged Thee, he owes Thee much, but let him go free. It has all been charged to my account. I have paid it."

Paul writes to Philemon, "If thou count me therefore a partner, receive him as myself" (v. 17). What a glorious description of substitution and heavenly welcome. We are accepted in the Beloved. Christ has settled our debt, and provided for our future!

—Harry Ironside

Scholars believe that in Ephesus, about A.D. 90, the letters of St. Paul were first collected and issued in the form of a book. Some years after that, Ignatius, Bishop of Antioch, was writing letters to the Churches of Asia, as he was being taken to Rome to be flung to the beasts in the arena. Amongst the letters is one to Ephesus which pays rare tribute to the Bishop of Ephesus and to his beautiful nature and to the usefulness of his life—just like his name. And the name of the Bishop of Ephesus was Onesimus.

—William Barclay

February 11

Then said Ahimaaz the son of Zadok, Let me now run, and bear the king tidings, how the Lord hath avenged him of his enemies. And Joab said unto him, Thou shalt not bear tidings this day, but thou shalt bear tidings another day; but this day thou shalt bear no tidings, because the king's son is dead. Then said Joab to Cushi, Go, tell the king what thou hast seen. And Cushi bowed himself unto Joab, and ran. Then said Ahimaaz, the son of Zadok, yet again to Joab, But howsoever let me, I pray thee, also run after Cushi. And Joab said, Wherefore wilt thou run, my son, seeing thou hast no tidings ready? But howsoever, said he, let me run. And he said unto him, Run (2 Sam. 18:19-23).

Poor, silly Ahimaaz. There he goes with legs moving, feet flying, arms flailing, nostrils dilating. He runs so well that he outdistances Cushi, but he arrives with no message to give the king. Ahimaaz was the first "minister without portfolio," a "well without water," a watchman on the tower who had no time to proclaim.

But do not laugh too loudly. Many people, like Ahimaaz, have mounted a "pulpit" without a message from God to deliver. "Thou hast no tidings ready." Will this be God's appraisal of your ministry? Are you too attempting to do His work without "carrying His Word"? "I give you this charge," said St. Paul to young Timothy, "Preach the Word; be prepared in season and out of season; correct, rebuke and encourage—with great patience and careful instruction" (2 Tim. 4:1-2, NIV).

Young Timothys, do not be overly concerned with the manner of delivery, but only with the message. Run with the good tidings of the gospel. A dying world is waiting to hear it!

> Sweetly echo the gospel call,
>   Wonderful words of Life!
> Offer pardon and peace to all,
>   Wonderful words of Life!
> Jesus, only Saviour,
> Sanctify forever,
> Beautiful words, wonderful words,
> Wonderful words of Life!
>
> —Philip P. Bliss

Now there is one curious fact over which thy servant has for a thousand times been lost in wonder, love, and praise, namely, The telling of the story of the cross requires no preliminary or introductory action upon the souls of men!

Never mind how ignorant or vile, debased or brutal, pagan or polished, men may be. To effectively tell them about the atonement, waste no time in vapid introductions. Start right off with the story of the cross! Behold, that glorious message immediately attracts attention, arresting human interest, and unmistakably enlists the power of the Holy Spirit in causing men to hear it.

—Richard Ellsworth Day

February 12

Love never faileth (1 Cor. 13:8).

Paul had been writing about the Holy Spirit, and for Paul, love is the supreme gift of the Spirit. It is love which marks the church as the Body of Christ, and the first fruit of the Spirit in the believer is love (Eph. 5:22). Note the exquisite courtesy of Paul in the use he makes of the first person singular. "If I had the gift of prophecy and knew all about what is going to happen in the future, knew everything about *everything*, but didn't love others, what good would it do? Even if I had the gift of faith so that I could speak to a mountain and make it move, I would still be worth nothing at all without love. If I gave everything I have to poor people, and if I were burned alive for preaching the gospel but didn't love others, it would be of no value whatever" (1 Cor. 13:2-3, TLB).

Paul writes of love's priority over the power of language. Without love, "I am become as sounding brass, or a tinkling cymbal." Paul gives us love's priority over the power of learning. "Though I have the gift of prophecy, and understand all mysteries, and all knowledge; . . . I am nothing." Paul shows us love's priority over the power of liberality. "If I gave everything I have to poor people, and if I was burned alive for preaching the gospel but didn't love others, it would be of no value whatever."

May the Holy Spirit guide us and remind us that without love's priority over language . . . we *say* nothing; without love's priority over learning . . . we *know* nothing; without love's priority over liberality . . . we *give* nothing.

May He teach us the way of love!

—E. Russell Lynn

February 13

Father, the hour is come; glorify thy Son,
that thy Son also may glorify thee (John 17:1).

John 17 is truly the Lord's Prayer. These sacred words are holy ground. It has been called the chapter of glory. Eight times the Lord Jesus uses some form of the word "glory" in this prayer.

"Father . . . glorify thy Son, that thy Son also may glorify thee . . . I have glorified thee on the earth: I have finished the work which thou gavest me to do. . . . All mine are thine, and thine are mine; and I am glorified in them. . . . The glory which thou gavest me I have given them . . . Father, I will that they also, whom thou hast given me, be with me where I am; that they may behold my glory . . . And now, O Father, glorify thou me with thine own self with the glory which I had with thee before the world was."

The Father glorified His Son. The Son glorified His Father by finishing the work He began. But He is also glorified in us. All heaven honors Him. Jesus is the fairest of ten thousand, the One altogether lovely, and yet His ransomed ones add glory unto His glory.

Paul wrote to Titus saying, "Adorn the doctrine of God, our Saviour in all things" (Titus 2:10). The word means to add beauty or to glorify. Elisha Hoffman sang, "Let me tell the old, old story / Of His love so full and free; / For I feel like giving Him the glory / For His wondrous love to me." How do we do this? Paul gives us the answer. "For the grace of God that bringeth salvation hath appeared to all men, teaching us that, denying ungodliness and worldly lusts, we should live soberly, righteously, and godly, in this present world; looking for the blessed hope, and the glorious appearing of the great God and our Saviour Jesus Christ; who gave himself for us, that he might redeem us from all iniquity, and purify unto himself a peculiar people, zealous of good works" (Titus 2:11-14). As His people, we adorn and glorify Him in good works. When we live like this, we are "giving Him the glory."

February 14

So shall my word be that goeth forth out of my mouth: it shall not return unto me void, but it shall accomplish that which I please, and it shall prosper in the thing whereto I sent it (Isa. 55:11).

Voltaire, the noted 18th-century infidel, bragged that in 100 years from the day he published his thesis, the Bible would be outmoded and forgotten—a book to be found only in a museum. But God knew otherwise. When the century had passed, Voltaire's house, where he wrote his treatise against God's Word, was owned by the Geneva Bible Society, and it was sending out Bibles to a needy world.

This Holy Book I'd rather own
Than all the golden gems
That e'er in monarch's coffers shone,
Or all their diadems!

Nay, were the sea one chrysolite,
The earth a golden ball,
And diamonds all the stars of night,
This Book is worth them all.

For here a blessed balm appears
To heal the deepest woe,
And he that seeks this Book in tears,
His tears shall cease to flow.

Author Unknown

"Do you know a Book that you are willing to put under your head for a pillow when you are dying? Then that is the Book you should want to study while living" (Joseph Cook).

We search the world for truth. We cull
The good, the true, the beautiful,
From graven stone and written scroll,
And all old flower-fields of the soul;
And, weary seekers of the best,
We come back laden from our quest,
To find that all the sages said
Is in the Book our mothers read.

—John Greenleaf Whittier

"For ever, O Lord, thy word is settled in heaven" (Ps. 119: 89).

February 15

In the beginning was the Word, and the Word was with God, and the Word was God. The same was in the beginning with God. . . . And the Word was made flesh, and dwelt among us, (and we beheld his glory, the glory as of the only begotten of the Father,) full of grace and truth (John 1:1-2, 14).

"Jesus Christ is the Very God, begotten, not made, being of one substance with the Father, and by whom all things were made.

He became flesh for us men, being conceived by the Holy Spirit and born of the Virgin Mary. He lived a miraculous life and suffered death on the cross in atonement for the sins of the whole world. He arose from the dead in a bodily form, and is now at the right hand of God ever living to make intercession for His believing people. He is coming again, even as He was seen to go, when He will set up His kingdom on the earth. We feed on Him by faith, and we are alive in Him forever more" (James M. Gray).

The purpose of John's Gospel was plainly stated. "These are written, that ye might believe that Jesus is the Christ, the Son of God; and that believing ye might have life through his name" (John 20:31).

Jesus is! He is called by Isaiah the Wonderful Counsellor, the Everlasting Father, the Mighty God, the Prince of Peace. He is the Lamb of God, the Good Shepherd, the Bread of Life, the Bright and Morning Star. John's Gospel opens by declaring that Jesus is the Word. Revelation closes by declaring that Jesus is the Alpha and the Omega, the First and the Last, the Faithful and True, and "he was clothed with a vesture dipped in blood; and his name is called The Word of God" (Rev. 19:13).

He is all of this and yet it will do us no good unless Jesus is—our Savior! our Master! our Lord!

Jesus is:
>Heaven's bread for earth's hunger,
>Heaven's clothing for earth's nakedness,
>Heaven's riches for earth's poverty,
>Heaven's light for earth's darkness,
>Heaven's grace for earth's guilt,
>Heaven's gladness for earth's grief,
>Heaven's gain for earth's loss,
>Heaven's love for earth's hate,
>Heaven's peace for earth's strife,
>Heaven's hope for earth's despair,
>Heaven's comfort for earth's sorrows,
>Heaven's salvation for earth's damnation,
>Heaven's life for earth's death.
>This is what Jesus is!

—ROBERT G. LEE

February 16

*Thomas, one of the twelve, called Didy-
mus, was not with them when Jesus came*
(John 20:24).

This is one of the saddest verses in John's Gospel. Thomas
was one of the 12 apostles. He had walked with Jesus on His
earthly journey. He had sat at His feet and heard His words, and
he had witnessed the miracles the Lord had performed. But this
man Thomas was away from the apostolic group after the Resurrection miracle.

Why was Thomas absent? I think it was due to indifference.
Thomas had simply lost his hope. He had seen Jesus die and he
thought that the end had come. When the joyous disciples found
him and exclaimed, "We have seen the Lord," he retorted that
unless he could see the wounds in Christ's hands, and thrust his
hand into His side, he would not believe.

Thomas thus missed the fellowship of the other disciples and
of course he missed seeing Jesus. He was not with them, and what
a loss that was! He truly loved his Master and he would have
been present in the Upper Room if he had understood the promise and hope of the Resurrection.

Because Thomas was absent, he missed Christ's gift of peace.
When His peace flowed into their hearts, their fears disappeared.
Thomas missed this and he likewise missed being recommissioned
by the living Lord. What a costly absence! Had he known, had he
suspected that Christ was going to come into the Upper Room, he
surely would have been there. Someone once wrote, "God does
not label His richest experience, nor does He underline in red the
day He intends to make great." We must not forsake the assembling together or we may miss the Lord's presence.

But Thomas came back. Now they are all together again and
Jesus came and stood in their midst. He said to Thomas, "Reach
hither thy finger, and behold my hands; and reach hither thy
hand, and thrust it into my side: and be not faithless, but believing." Thomas cried out, "My Lord and my God."

The Lord met Thomas when he came back to the place where
he belonged. This is the history of God's dealing with His straying
children. Lost communion and fellowship can be found again if
we will but go back to where we belong. There and there alone
faith meets the risen Savior and cries, "My Lord and my God."

—ROBERT H. BELTON

February 17

I will remember the years of the right hand of the most High (Ps. 77:10).

> I remember the years of His hand's deep shadow—
> The sun was darkened, the stars were veiled,
> The glory of life was a fading flower,
> And mirth was over and music failed;
> But in that shade I was safely hidden,
> From wind and tempest I knew release,
> And for the old, new songs were given,
> My heart learned patience, my soul found peace.

"I will uphold thee with the right hand of my righteousness" (Isa. 41:10).

> I remember the years of His hand's upholding—
> Its help how mighty, its clasp how strong;
> Almost I slipped when my feet were sliding,
> Almost I fell when the way was long;
> But never once did His strength forsake me,
> And when I leaned on His wondrous might,
> On wings I mounted, I ran unwearied,
> I walked unfainting, by day or night.

"Thou shalt remember all the way which the Lord thy God led thee" (Deut. 8:2).

> I remember the years of His hand's sure leading—
> How safe His guidance, His way how wise;
> Often my thoughts and my heart would wander,
> My feet would follow my straying eyes;
> But never once did His patience fail me,
> And through it all did His love restrain,
> And when I followed where He would lead me,
> How all the way and the end grew plain.

"He will hear him from his holy heaven with the saving strength of his right hand" (Ps. 20:6).

> I remember the years of His hand's safe keeping—
> When danger threatened or sin beset,
> When, the rudder fallen from nerveless fingers,
> My life-bark drifted where wild seas met;

But through it all did His power keep me,
    And now I know, when my foes assail,
Strong to deliver, He waits to succor,
    And prays for me lest my faith should fail.

"Behold, I have graven thee upon the palms of my hands" (Isa. 49:16).

Oh, I know that my name on Thy palms is graven,
    I remember the years of Thy hand, Most High!
How it has sheltered and held and guided
    'Neath clouded heaven or open sky;
I lean on Thine arm and Thy hand upholds me,
    Its power protects and its strength defends;
Still it shall hide me and keep and lead me
    Till Home is reached and the journey ends.

—ANNIE JOHNSON FLINT

February 18

When they had prayed, the place was shaken where they were assembled together; and they were all filled with the Holy Ghost, and they spake the word of God with boldness (Acts 4:31).

Every man is a marked man. Some are marked for death and some carry the marks of life. The Early Church was no exception, and in Acts, chapter 4, we read of these marked men. They were marked because they belonged to Christ and were filled with the Spirit.

Spirit-filled men are marked by potent praying (v. 31). Something happened when they prayed—"the place was shaken." And not only the place but the people also. Do our prayers get results today?

Spirit-filled men are marked by frequent fillings of the Holy Spirit (v. 31). This was the same crowd who were filled on the Day of Pentecost—now they were filled again. And it happened again and again. This does not downgrade Pentecost; it upgrades the saints of God!

Spirit-filled men are marked by a holy boldness (v. 31). They do not tremble easily under human threats. They tell forth the good tidings with joyful abandon. They leave the results to God.

Spirit-filled men are marked by an organic unity (v. 32). This group had a heavenly togetherness that no organizational merger could produce. It was a heart-and-soul unity which made them truly one.

Spirit-filled men are marked by intuitive stewardship (v. 32). These disciples likely had not heard much preaching about the matter, but God gave them an awareness because they were listening. Sharing and giving were natural for them.

Spirit-filled men are marked with an effective witness (v. 33). "With great power gave the apostles witness"—it was more of a passion than a method. It was not powerful because it was correct; it was correct because it was powerful.

Spirit-filled men are marked by "great grace" (v. 33). They enjoyed the unmerited favor of God—peace, pardon, holiness, blessing, assurance, approval, and acceptance—in abundant measure! Small wonder, then, that they were happy—and powerful! They were marked men!

—FLETCHER SPRUCE

A rushing wind the Spirit came!
Purge us from all that would defame,
    O Cleansing One.

Our sins lost in Thy holiness,
Let worthy lives our faith confess,
    O Sinless Son.

The gift of tongues the Spirit brought!
May our dull tongues by Thee be taught,
    Master of Love.

May words and deeds tell every land
The word we preach at Love's command,
    Father above.

The Spirit came in tongues of fire!
Now our cold hearts with flame inspire,
    Spirit Divine.

Give us a holy zeal for Thee
To labor for eternity
    Our will all Thine.

—CATHERINE BERNARD BROWN

February 19

Christ sent me not to baptize, but to preach the gospel: not with wisdom of words, lest the cross of Christ should be made of none effect. For the preaching of the cross is to them that perish foolishness; but unto us which are saved it is the power of God (1 Cor. 1:17-18).

The old cross is a symbol of death. It stands for the abrupt violent end of a human being. The man in Roman times who took up his cross and started down the road had already said good-by to his friends. He was not coming back. He was not going to have his life redirected; he was going out to have it ended.

The race of Adam is under a death sentence. There is no commutation and no escape. God cannot approve of any of the fruits of sin, however innocent they may appear or how beautiful to the eyes of men. God salvages the individual by liquidating him, and then raising him again to new life.

God offers life, but not an improved old life. The life He offers is life out of death. It stands always on the far side of the Cross. Whoever would possess it must pass under the rod. He must repudiate himself and concur in God's just sentence against him.

What does this mean to the individual, the condemend man who would find life in Christ Jesus? Simply this. He must repent and believe. He must forsake his sins and then go on to forsake himself. Let him cover nothing, excuse nothing. Let him bow his head before the stroke of God's stern displeasure. Having done this, let him gaze with simple trust upon the risen Savior, and from Him will come life and rebirth and cleansing and power. The cross that ended the earthly life of Jesus now puts an end to the sinner, and the power that raised Christ from the dead now raises him to a new life in Christ.

—A. W. TOZER

"What shall we say then? Shall we continue in sin, that grace may abound? God forbid. How shall we, that are dead to sin, live any longer therein? . . . Therefore we are buried with him by baptism into death: that like as Christ was raised up from the dead by the glory of the Father, even so we also should walk in newness of life" (Rom. 6:1-2, 4).

February 20

*Speaking the truth in love ... grow up into
him in all things* (Eph. 4:15).

The Christian's speech does not have to be taken with "a grain of salt."

> "Let your speech be always with grace, seasoned with salt, that ye may know how ye ought to answer every man" (Col. 4:6).

The Christian's speech should not be wild or careless.

> "Sound speech, that cannot be condemned; that he that is of the contrary part may be ashamed, having no evil thing to say of you" (Titus 2:8).

The Christian's speech should not be of doubtful context.

> "Let it not be once named among you, as becometh saints; neither filthiness, nor foolish talking" (Eph. 5: 3-4).

The Christian's speech should be characterized by honesty.

> "Putting away lying, speak every man truth with his neighbour" (Eph. 4:25).

The Christian's speech must contain conscious restraint.

> "Let no corrupt communication proceed out of your mouth, but that which is good to the use of edifying, that it may minister grace unto the hearers" (Eph. 4:29).
> "If any man among you seem to be religious, and bridleth not his tongue, but deceiveth his own heart, this man's religion is vain" (Jas. 1:26).

> *Oh that my tongue might so possess*
> *The accent of His tenderness*
> *That every word I breathe should bless!*
>
> *For those who mourn, a word of cheer;*
> *A word of hope for those who fear;*
> *And love to all men, far and near.*
>
> *Oh, that it might be said of me,*
> *"Surely thy speech betrayeth thee*
> *As friend of Christ of Galilee."*
>
> —THOMAS R. ROBINSON

February 21

Their rock is not as our Rock (Deut. 32: 31).

A party of tourists travelling in the mountains of Colorado were listening to their guide describe the grandeur and beauty of the Rockies and the geological age of some nearby rocks. William Jennings Bryan was in the group and, although impressed by the wondrous handiwork of the Creator, he confessed to the guide, "I'm not so much interested in the ages of the rocks as I am in the Rock of Ages."

By divine inspiration Isaiah wrote, "Thus saith the Lord God, Behold I lay in Zion for a foundation a stone, a tried stone, a precious cornerstone, a sure foundation" (Isa. 28:16). We are told in the letters of both Paul and Peter that Christ is this Stone (1 Cor. 10:4; 1 Pet. 2:6-8). Moses, speaking of the rocks of the world said, "Their rock is not as our Rock." Our Rock is "a tried stone." Our Lord is called a Tried Stone because He never fails or disappoints. Down through the centuries, those who have committed their all to Him have been completely satisfied. Moreover, He is also "a precious stone." There is no stone on earth of greater value—He is the Pearl of Great Price (Matt. 13:45).

Jesus is also called "a cornerstone and a sure foundation" (1 Pet. 2:7). Such stones are needed to build a great edifice that will withstand the ravages of time. A foundation stone gives a sure footing. With Christ as our true foundation we cannot fail or fall. He stands as our Rock of safety and security. His salvation endures within our heart.

The "Rock of Ages" is a sure stone. Hiding in the "cleft of the rock" we have a safe refuge from all storms and a safe place from the temptations that can overwhelm the soul. Joining with Moses we sing triumphantly, "Their rock is not like our Rock."

> O safe to the Rock that is higher than I,
> My soul in its conflicts and sorrows would fly;
> So sinful, so weary, Thine, Thine would I be;
> Thou blest "Rock of Ages," I'm hiding in Thee.

> —William O. Cushing

February 22

Jesus answered and said unto him, Verily, verily, I say unto thee, Except a man be born again, he cannot see the kingdom of God (John 3:3).

Jesus Christ is unquestionably not only the world's greatest teacher, but He is the only teacher who teaches with divine authority. There are many teachers, but He is The Teacher. Men of His day said that Jesus did not speak as the scribes and Pharisees, but as One having authority.

When Mary called Him "Rabboni" she used a word that means the supreme authoritative teacher, a teacher of teachers—one over all. This One, who is Lord of All, said, "Except a man be born again, he cannot see the kingdom of God. . . . Ye must be born again."

All of our respectability, our church membership, our profession of goodness will not give us an inheritance among those who are sanctified. "Ye must be born again." We must have a new birth in righteousness. We must have our hearts changed by the Holy Spirit. We must be "born from above."

With all the force of Deity and with the command of authority, Jesus said, "Ye must." There is no possibility of evasion. There is nothing vague or indefinite. The command is absolute and final. We are either "born again" or we lose eternal life.

Spiritual birth is a blessed reality to all who trust the Lord Jesus Christ. The primary step to receiving the new birth is found in 1 John 5:1: "Whosoever believeth that Jesus is the Christ is born of God." We must believe in Christ with all our heart and accept Him as our personal Savior. He is the Christ, the appointed One of God who shed His precious blood for us. Paul made it very plain when he wrote, "If thou shalt confess with thy mouth the Lord Jesus, and shalt believe in thine heart that God hath raised him from the dead, thou shalt be saved. For with the heart man believeth unto righteousness; and with the mouth confession is made unto salvation" (Rom. 10:9-10).

This is being born again. This is the new birth!

—COLVIN G. BUTLER

February 23

Be careful [anxious] for nothing; but in
every thing by prayer and supplication with
thanksgiving let your requests be made known
unto God (Phil. 4:6).

Paul is found presenting an interesting combination as he outlines the secret peace of God. As we pray, we must praise. Asking, we must adore. Requesting further favors, we must remember past provisions. Our supplications must be accompanied with a song. Too often we approach the throne of grace as beggars. Ours is the spirit of the Prodigal—"give me, give me." We are so taken up with immediate cares that we do nothing but request. Eager to receive from God, we forget what He expects from us. Greedy, we take all we can, but fail to satisfy God's bountiful heart as it yearns for the gratitude of those He blesses.

God's bounty in giving should produce thanksgiving. Paul never sent belated thanks. Gifts were immediately recognized and acknowledged in his letters. Since there is no darker sin than ingratitude, may we always be found praising and thanking God for all blessings and prayers answered.

—HERBERT LOCKYER
in *All the Promises of the Bible*

"No prayer is lost. Praying breath was never spent in vain. There is no such thing as prayer unanswered or unnoticed by God, and some things we count refusals or denials are simply delays" (Horatius Bonar).

> For all Thy blessings given
> There are many to thank Thee, Lord
> But for the gifts withholden
> I fain would add my word.
> For the good things I desired
> That barred me from the best;
> The peace at the price of honor,
> The sloth of a shameful rest;
> The poisonous sweets I longed for
> To my hungering heart denied;
> The staff that broke and failed me,
> When I walked in the way of pride;
> The tinsel joys withheld that
> So content might still be mine;

The help refused that might have
Made me loose my hand from Thine;
The light withdrawn that I might
Not see the dangers of my way;
For what Thou hast not given,
I thank Thee, Lord, today.

—ANNIE JOHNSON FLINT

February 24

I will therefore that men pray every where, lifting up holy hands, without wrath and doubting (1 Tim. 2:8).

Our world is a sick world—disillusioned, war-scarred, head-dizzy, body-weary, sin-smitten—a world in despair. Human philosophy is bankrupt. Nations, weary and wicked, walk on the edge of abysses. Men and women everywhere are bewildered and distracted by the problems and difficulties of life. Some leaders "loose wild tongues that hold not God in awe."

There are so many problems that cannot be solved, so many dangers that cannot be averted, so many burdens that cannot be borne by human strength, ingenuity, and genius. What we need is what God can do! What God can do will be done for us when God's people pray. It is the conviction of all who have proved the faithfulness of God that nothing lies beyond the reach of prayer except that which lies outside the will of God. Intercessory prayer is our mightiest weapon and the supreme call for all Christians today.

Let there be prayer then at sunup, at noonday, at sundown, at midnight—all through the day. Pray for our children, our youth, our aged, our pastors, our homes. Let us pray for our churches that they may fill their God-appointed missions. Let us pray for our missionaries at home and in foreign lands. Let us pray for ourselves, that we may not lose the word *concern* out of our Christian vocabulary. Pray for nations in distress, for our own nation, for those who have never known the redeeming love of Jesus Christ, for moral forces everywhere, and for all hearts that they may hold no malice; for our tongues and pens, that we be not hurtfully critical.

Let prayer be our portion. Let prayer be our pastime. Let

prayer be our passion. Let prayer be our practice. Let us be found at the throne of grace, not only with holy boldness, but with serene confidence—knowing that God is faithful to perform that which He has abundantly promised, and that God is able to do exceedingly abundantly above all that we ask or think, according to the power that in us worketh.

—Robert G. Lee

"Praying always with all prayer and supplication in the Spirit, and watching thereunto with all perseverance and supplication for all saints; and for me, that utterance may be given unto me, that I may open my mouth boldly to make known the mystery of the gospel, for which I am an ambassador in bonds" (Eph. 6:18-20).

Lord, I have shut the door;
Speak now the word
Which in the din and throng
Could not be heard.
Hushed now my inner heart.
Whisper Thy will,
While I have come apart,
While all is still.

Lord, I have shut the door,
Here do I bow;
Speak, for my soul, attent,
Turns to Thee now.
Rebuke Thou what is vain,
Counsel my soul;
Thy holy will reveal,
My will control.

In this blest quietness
Clamorings cease;
Here in Thy presence dwells
Infinite peace;
Yonder the strife and cry,
Yonder, the sin:
Lord, I have shut the door,
Thou art within.

—William M. Runyan

February 25

Seeing then, that we have a great high priest, that is passed into the heavens, Jesus the Son of God, let us hold fast our profession (Heb. 4:14).

This man, after he had offered one sacrifice for sins for ever, sat down on the right hand of God; from henceforth expecting till his enemies be made his footstool (Heb. 10: 12-13).

When our Lord Jesus on the cross cried, "It is finished!" He proclaimed that He had finished the redeeming work which God the Father had sent Him to do. Then the Father raised Him from the dead as a convincing and lasting "Amen" that confirms a perfect salvation accomplished.

The Resurrection and Ascension gave Christ glory and the place of highest honor at the right hand of God. There He sat down, resting from His finished work; and He now saves perfectly and freely those who trust Him.

We can also rejoice in His unfinished work! He is still actively carrying on vital ministries which promote His present program, ministries without which we could not carry on our Christian life and service. Among His several offices are two that relate to His program for us as individuals and as His church.

Christ is appointed, by God's oath, as a high priest forever. He replaced all other priests and stands a perfect high priest, offering a perfect salvation. He is the living mediator of the New Covenant which grants forgiveness of sins through His shed blood.

He is also our Intercessor. He knows our weaknesses and trials because He has suffered also in life and death. He prays for us much as He did for Peter—that he be kept from Satan and that his faith not fail. He is our Preserver in trials and the provider of grace. We can come boldly to the throne of grace in His name to find help in time of need.

His ministry today also includes that of Head of the Church. Christ planted the Church by His death on the cross and the coming of the Holy Spirit. Today He directs her activities and builds the Church in quantity and quality. He uses those who submit to His will to do His work and the Church under Him will be victorious. What a wonderful Savior!

—C. Fred Dickason

"For we have not an high priest which cannot be touched with the feeling of our infirmities, but was in all points tempted like as we are, yet without sin. Let us therefore come boldly unto the throne of grace, that we may obtain mercy, and find grace to help in time of need" (Heb. 4:15-16).

February 26

God shall wipe away all tears from their eyes; and there shall be no more death (Rev. 21:4).

So I lay down upon the cross, and I rest upon it even unto this day. And the Angel of Suffering watches upon my left hand, while upon my right is one who comes always with him—the Angel of His Presence. And of late there has been another, the Angel of Peace. And the three abide always with me. And a loving Father bends over me. The way has brought me almost to His feet. There is but a narrow valley that divides us, the Valley of the Shadow, and the angel who shall lead through it is the Angel of Death.

I wait his coming with a tranquil heart, for beneath the mask that frights the timid human hearts which dread his summons I shall see a face I know—the face of the Son of God, who has walked beside me in the furnace of affliction, so that I passed through without even the smell of fire on my garments.

And when I go down into the deep waters, it is His arm I shall lean upon, and the voice that welcomes me upon the other side will be His.

And from the bank of the river the path leads upward to the city which hath foundations, whose builder and maker is God, and they that enter in shall go no more out forever.

*Blessed are they who love Him and they who keep His
    Word;
They shall enter into the city and dwell in the house of the
    Lord;
And oh, the joy of knowing, as the Lord's redeemed can
    know,
While often sad and lonely, through this earthly life they go,
There shall be no more sickness; there shall be no more
    pain;*

There shall be no more parting, loved from the loved again;
There shall be no more weeping, kneeling beside earth's
*   biers;*
There shall be no more dying, through the eternal years!

—ANNIE JOHNSON FLINT

February 27

I know whom I have believed (2 Tim. 1:12).

Ira Stanphill has given the church some great singing music. It is difficult to choose "the brightest and best." Perhaps such a selection depends upon the hour's trial or the particular day's journey. But one I have always loved reads thus:

> *I don't know about tomorrow,*
> *   I just live from day to day.*
> *I don't borrow from its sunshine,*
> *   For its skies may turn to gray.*
> *I don't worry o'er the future,*
> *   For I know what Jesus said,*
> *And today I'll walk beside Him,*
> *   For He knows what is ahead.*
>
> *I don't know about tomorrow,*
> *   It may bring me poverty;*
> *But the One who feeds the sparrow,*
> *   Is the One who stands by me.*
> *And the path that be my portion,*
> *   May be through the flame or flood,*
> *But His presence goes before me,*
> *   And I'm covered with His blood.*

There is much that we do not understand. Even books of church doctrines and disciplines leave us bewildered sometimes. But the plain words of the Lord Jesus are easily understood. They need no ecclesiastical explanations.

"The Son of man is come to seek and to save that which was lost" (Luke 19:10).

"For God so loved the world, that he gave his only begotten Son, that whosoever believeth in him should not perish, but have everlasting life" (John 3:16).

"Verily, verily, I say unto you, He that heareth my word, and believeth on him that sent me, hath everlasting life, and shall not come into condemnation; but is passed from death unto life" (John 5:24).

"My sheep hear my voice, and I know them, and they follow me: and I give unto them eternal life; and they shall never perish, neither shall any man pluck them out of my hand. My Father, which gave them to me, is greater than all; and no man is able to pluck them out of my Father's hand. I and my Father are one" (John 10:27-30).

These are precious promises and His Word is true. Believe Him!

> Many things about tomorrow
> I don't seem to understand;
> But I know who holds tomorrow,
> And I know who holds my hand.
>
> —IRA STANPHILL
> © 1950, Singspiration, Inc.

February 28

I commend unto you Pheobe our sister, which is a servant of the church which is at Cenchreae: that ye receive her in the Lord, as becometh saints, and that ye assist her in whatever business she hath need of you: for she hath been a succourer of many, and of myself also (Rom. 16:1-2).

At the close of his great doctrinal epistle, the Book of Romans, the apostle Paul reveals his heart of love and interest in the individual believers. He mentions them one by one, including Phoebe.

Four things are written about her in these first two verses, namely; a Sister, a Servant, a Saint, and a Succourer of many. Here is a miniature judgment seat.

"Our sister" would remind us of the eternal bond that unites believers together. Earthly ties will end with time, but the heaven-born family union will last for all eternity. "A servant of the church." Could that be truthfully said of you and me? In one of

John's chapters, we see the Lord Jesus himself taking the lowly place of service, and He did this as an example for us. Phoebe was a "servant of many." A noble occupation!

"A saint"—Phoebe knew something of the practical truth of being separated from this godless and worldly scene, and separated unto God.

Then lastly, we are told Phoebe was a "succourer of many." This included Paul also. It means a helper and protector. It is the only place in the Word where this expression occurs. What a commendation! Do we ever sit down and quietly think of someone to whom we might be of some help? Is there someone who might need our care? Oh, how different the church and the world would be today if there were many Phoebes to succor! Trials and distress are everywhere. How many might be won to the Lord if we would but care! Let us shun this spirit of sham and indifference so manifest today, and be of service to God. Let us be like Phoebe!

—JOHN SCROGGIE

March 1

He lets me rest in the meadow grass and leads me beside the quiet streams (Ps. 23:2, TLB).

How comforting to know that the Great Shepherd leads us. It may be "beside still waters." Here the sheep can drink and rest. But all is not always peaceful. At times the rains pour down, the waters are at flood, and there is grave danger. Still, the Shepherd advises His followers not to be fearful. He is leading and He says: "I will bear; even I will carry, and will deliver you" (Isa. 46:4). Be not afraid. He is the Shepherd of the still waters but He is also the Shepherd of the swift and deep waters. Safely, He will guide you through.

> *In pastures green, not always—*
> *Sometimes He who knoweth best*
> *In kindness leadeth me in weary ways,*
> *Where heavy shadows be, out of the*
> *Sunshine, warm, and soft, and bright,*
> *Out of the sunshine into the darkest night.*
> *I oft would faint with sorrow and affright—*

Only for this—I know He holds my hand.
Whether it be in green or desert land
I trust, although I may not understand.

And by still waters? No not always so.
Ofttimes the heavy tempests round me blow;
And o'er my soul the waves and billows go.
But when the storms beat loudest, and I cry
Aloud for help, the Master standeth by,
And whispers to my soul, "Lo, it is I."
Above the tempest wild I hear Him say:
"Beyond this darkness lies the perfect day;
In every path of thine I lead the way."

So, whether on the hilltop high and fair
I dwell, or in the sunless valleys where
The shadows lie—what matters? He is there.
And more than this: where'er the pathway lead
He gives to me no helpless, broken reed,
But His own hand, sufficient for my need.
So where He leads me I can safely go;
And in the blest hereafter I shall know
Why in His wisdom He hath led me so.

—BARRY

"When thou passest through the waters, I will be with thee; and through the rivers, they shall not overflow thee" (Isa. 43:2).

March 2

Now Peter and John went up together into the temple at the hour of prayer ... And a certain man lame from his mother's womb was carried, whom they laid daily at the gate of the temple which is called Beautiful, to ask alms of them that entered into the temple (Acts 3:1-2).

This is the story of a man lying lame at the gate of the Temple. Whether it be a man with a withered hand, as Mark wrote of, or a man with withered feet, Christ is the Great Physician and He is able to heal and restore.

78

The lame man had faithful friends and they brought him daily to a good place to ask alms, for God's people are to be giving people, "zealous of good works."

But the true purpose of the Church is not to give just silver and gold, but to say to the halt and the lame, "In the name of Jesus Christ rise up and walk."

C. William Fisher once said, "After many, many years of receiving coins of silver and gold, this man was still a cripple, his fundamental need still unmet. On this day, he was still asking for a handout but God gave him a cure!

"What a picture of our world. After all the panaceas of the politicians and the philosophers, humanity still lies lame and is still asking for a handout when it so desperately needs healing.

"Let a man go to a psychiatrist, but he can become only an adjusted sinner.

"Let a man go to a physician but he can become only a healthy sinner.

"Let a man achieve wealth and fame, but he can become only an affluent sinner.

"Let a man join a church but he can become only a religious sinner.

"But if a man in sincere repentance and faith comes to the foot of the Cross and receives God's Son as his Savior, he becomes a new creature in Christ, forgiven, and reconciled, and with a new life. The healing of lame men is the true ministry of the Church of Jesus Christ."

At the Beautiful Gate lay a man lame from his birth. This man symbolizes a crippled world at the door of the church. The Book of Acts, where this story is recorded, is not the Acts of the Apostles, but the Acts of the Lord Jesus. He is still ministering to the *lameness* at the gate.

In the story in Acts He worked through Peter and John. The lame man looked on them "expecting to receive something." He was not disappointed, for with the *look* came the *lift*. Peter took him by the right hand and lifted him up. With the *lift* came *life!* "And immediately his feet and ancle bones received strength."

The Church must thus be in the "uplift business." If Peter and John had merely lifted the lame man to drop him again, he would have been more crippled than ever. He must have *life* also. "In the name of Jesus Christ of Nazareth rise up and walk." This is *life!*

But there was a *leap* here also. "And he, leaping up, stood and walked, and entered with them into the temple, walking, and leaping, and praising God." Sometimes I have stood in a very dignified morning service while the congregation sang rather thoughtlessly:

Hear Him, ye deaf; His praise, ye dumb,
Your loosened tongues employ;
Ye blind, behold your Saviour come;
And leap, ye lame, for joy.

I have wondered what would happen if someone took the admonition seriously and actually leaped. I'm sure there would have been an exodus of scandalized saints. But we need the "leap" today in our churches, and if we have lost it, it is because we have lost the "lift" and the "life" also.

All Jerusalem was shaken by this wonderful miracle. This sort of thing will always shake "Jerusalem." The hearts of men are not moved by conventions and programs and teas, but by cripples who have looked and been lifted and who leap because they have found life.

—VANCE HAVNER

March 3

Take heed that ye do not your alms before
men, to be seen of them: otherwise ye have
no reward of your Father, which is in heaven
(Matt. 6:1).

The Father loves a cheerful giver. Paul urges each believer to purpose in his heart to give generously, not grudgingly (2 Cor. 9:7). Be not like one described by Versteeg:

Once there was a Christian,
He had a pious look;
His consecration was complete
Except his pocket book.
He'd put a nickle in the plate
And then, with might and main
He'd sing, "When we asunder part
It gives us inward pain."

Not only are we urged to be *cheerful* givers, we are also admonished to be *secret* givers. The Master preached this in His Sermon on the Mount and warned His followers not to "sound a trumpet" over charities. Do you give to see your name in print or to have the preeminence? If you do, Christ said, "You have your reward." He looks not only at what you have in your hand but what you have in your heart!

Three times the Savior warned of this in Matthew's Gospel: there is no reward in giving alms before men; there is no reward for praying to be seen of men; and there is no reward for fasting before men to impress them with one's piety.

Men seem bent on accumulating vast treasures of one kind or another. But on earth moth and rust corrupt and thieves abound everywhere. Wise indeed is he who seeks Christ's rewards. He has promised them in bountiful measure to those who are faithful in the stewardship of their time, their talents, and their treasures.

"No man can outgive God."

March 4

There shall not any man be able to stand before thee all the days of thy life: as I was with Moses, so I will be with thee: I will not fail thee, nor forsake thee (Josh. 1:5).

The men of Ai were "but few," and yet the people who had conquered mighty Jericho "fled before the men of Ai." It was not the strength of their enemy, nor had God failed them. The cause of their defeat lay somewhere else. The Lord himself declared it: "Israel hath sinned, and they have also transgressed my covenant which I commanded them: for they have even taken of the accursed thing, and have also stolen, and dissembled also, and they have put it even among their own stuff. Therefore the children of Israel could not stand before their enemies" (Josh. 7:11-12). It was a hidden evil that conquered them. Buried in the earth, in an obscure tent in that vast army, was hidden something against which God had a controversy. "There is an accursed thing in the midst of thee, O Israel."

The lesson here is simply this, that anything cherished in the heart which is contrary to the will of God, let it seem ever so insignificant, or be ever so deeply hidden, will cause us to flee before our enemies. Any conscious root of bitterness cherished toward another, any self-seeking, any harsh judgments, any slackness in obeying the voice of the Lord, any doubtful habits or surroundings—these things or any one of them, consciously indulged, will effectually cripple and paralyze our spiritual life.

We may seem to ourselves and to others to have reached an almost impregnable position of victory, and yet we may find ourselves suffering bitter defeats. We may wonder, and question, and despair, and pray. Nothing will do any good until the wrong thing is dug up from its hiding place, brought out to the light, and laid before God.

—HANNAH WHITALL SMITH
in *The Christian's Secret of a Happy Life*

March 5

He called his ten servants, and delivered them ten pounds, and said unto them, Occupy till I come (Luke 19:13).

There are many truths in the parable of the 10 pounds, but one is very evident: *all our talents must be used for the Master.* He has given to each of us a sacred trust, and praise or condemnation depends upon our use of those abilities.

A critic suggested one day to Dwight L. Moody that he should realize his limitations and not speak in public.

"You make too many mistakes in grammar," his critic complained.

Mr. Moody faced him and said, "I know that. I know I lack a great many things, including an education, but I am doing the best I can with what I've got for the Lord."

He paused and then asked, "Look here, man. You've got lots of grammar. What are you doing with it for the Master?"

> *A sacred trust my Lord to me has given;*
> *The pounds are His; to use them is my task.*
> *Whether 'neath skies all bright or tempest-riven*
> *His service leads, it is not mine to ask;*
> *He tells me not how long the time shall be*
> *Till He shall deem it best to call me home;*
> *I only hear Him saying unto me,*
> *"Occupy thou until I come."*
>
> *He does not say that I may choose my toil*
> *And only do the things that please me best;*
> *Nor does He tell me when I've served awhile*
> *That I may lay His armor by and rest;*

But He asks for calm endurance to the end,
  Alike through joy or pain, through light or gloom;
And promises to be my Guide, and Friend;
  So I must occupy until He comes.

How dare I, then, enwrap the precious pounds
  In folds of uselessness, and lay aside!
On every side rich fields of toil abound
  Where they may be increased and glorified.
I may not understand why He to me
  Gives but perchance one talent, while to some
He gives the five or ten; yet faithfully
  Must I still occupy until He come.

Why should it matter whether one or ten,
  Since all are His, and but a trust retained
To use for Him until He comes again
  To see how much my toil for Him has gained?
But it does matter whether I, at last,
  Among the faithless meet a saddened gloom,
Or hear Him say to me, "Well done! Thou hast
  Been faithful unto Me. Behold—I come!"

—M. C. HAYWARD

March 6

When he had called the people unto him with his disciples also, he said unto them, Whosoever will come after me, let him deny himself, and take up his cross, and follow me (Mark 8:34).

What did our Lord really mean when He said, "Take up [your] cross, and follow me"? One thing is certain, crossbearing is intimately associated with denial and death of self. The world and its religions preach that one should know himself, or enrich himself, or enjoy himself. Only the Savior says, "Bury yourself, shoulder your cross, and follow Me."

The cross carries the stigma of death! Thus if we are to really follow Christ, we must die. The self-life must be buried—for "to die is gain, to live is Christ." The true Christian crossbearer must

83

have been to a funeral—his own! He must die to self-will and self-desire. Death must bring him to the place where he can say "that in all things He might have the preeminence."

This means that lamenting over life's problems and life's burdens—the drunken husband, the tragic divorce, the sorrows, the illnesses, the desertions—is not truly "bearing one's cross."

Paul made this concept plain in his Roman letter: "Therefore we are buried with him by baptism into death: that like as Christ was raised up from the dead by the glory of the Father, even so we also should walk in newness of life" (Rom. 6:4).

> Who answers Christ's insistent call
> Must give himself, his life, his all,
>   Without one backward look.
> Who sets his hand unto the plow,
> And glances back with anxious brow,
>   His calling hath mistook.
> Christ claims him, wholly, for His own;
> He must be Christ's and Christ's alone.
>
> —JOHN OXENHAM

"What things were gain to me, those I counted loss for Christ. Yea doubtless, and I count all things but loss for the excellency of the knowledge of Christ Jesus my Lord: for whom I have suffered the loss of all things" (Phil. 3:7-8).

March 7

**Being brought on their way by the church,
they passed through Phoenicia and Samaria,
declaring the conversion of the Gentiles: and
they caused great joy unto all the brethren**
(Acts 15:3).

William Barclay, Scotland's great theologian, said this of conversion: "The first step is for a man to be convinced of the wonder of Jesus Christ, and to know that Jesus Christ can do for him what he can never hope to do for himself. The second step in conversion is the conviction that this experience brings both the privilege and the responsibility of becoming a member of the fellowship of people who have had the same experience.

"The third step in conversion is the awareness that we are

not converted only for our own sake, that we are not converted to gain entry only into a society of believers, but that there is laid on the Christian man the obligation to take upon his shoulders and into his heart the sin and the suffering and the sorrow of the world.

"A conversion is incomplete if it does not leave Jesus Christ in the central place in a man's life. A conversion is incomplete if it does not leave a man integrated into the Church. A conversion is incomplete if it does not leave a man with an intense social consciousness, if it does not fill him with a sense of overwhelming responsibility for the world—a love for his fellowman.

"The Church must never be in any sense a little huddle of pious people shutting the doors against the world, lost in prayer and praise, connoisseurs of preaching and liturgy, busy mutually congratulating themselves on the excellence of their Christian experience. Commitment to Christ brings caring love for men. A man is not saved by his good works, but he is saved for good works!" (from *Daily Celebration*, © 1971, Word Books).

March 8

The king spake and said to Daniel, O Daniel, servant of the living God, is thy God, whom thou servest continually, able to deliver thee from the lions? (Dan. 6:20).

King Darius, in this haunting question, confirms that Daniel was a faithful servant of the Lord who continually served the living God. This king did not believe in the "God is dead" theory.

Daniel had been cast into a den of angry beasts by cunning, evil men. Darius had sought to save him, but the law of the Medes and the Persians could not be revoked once it had been signed. Still, Daniel's enemies failed to take into consideration the power of the Living God. The man of God was preserved by One who could stop the mouths of hungry lions. His God, and our God, is the One who "delivereth and rescueth and worketh."

"Is He able, O Daniel?" And the answer rings back across the centuries, "Our God is able to deliver thee." If Daniel, however, had not been cast into the pit and spent the night in dire danger, he would not have seen God's mighty deliverance with his own eyes. Deliverance is associated with dangers.

Sometimes the deliverance we pray for does not come. There are times when the lions' roar is not stopped. What then? God is still able to deliver, but He may have other plans. We must always leave the outcome of the cry for deliverance to His perfect will. Above the noise and the tumult, above the pounding of our heart, we must pray, "Lord, whatever be the outcome, let it add to Your glory. I know You can deliver; but, whatever come, continue Your work through me that men may know that You are the Living Redeemer!"

"I will deliver thee in that day, saith the Lord: and thou shalt not be given into the hand of the man of whom thou art afraid" (Jer. 39:17).

March 9

His mother said unto him, Son, why hast thou thus dealt with us? behold, thy father and I have sought thee sorrowing. And he said unto them, How is it that ye sought me? Wist ye not that I must be about my Father's business? (Luke 2:48-49).

"I must be about my Father's business." The servant is not greater than his Lord. He asks for our time, our talents, our days. We are to work for Him until the night falls "when no man can work." The Christian has a vocation: God's business must be our business!

Dwight L. Moody, on his way home from a meeting one night, saw a man leaning against a lamppost. Placing his hands on his shoulders, he asked:

"Are you a Christian?"

"Mind your own business," the man roared back at him.

"I'm sorry if I have offended you," Mr. Moody replied, "but this *is* my business."

Three months later, on a bitter cold morning, the man knocked on Mr. Moody's door and said, "I want to become a Christian. I haven't had any peace since that night you spoke to me. I have been haunted and troubled. Will you pray for me?"

Early that morning, Mr. Moody led the man to an acceptance of Christ as his own personal Savior.

Are you busy about His business?

I said, "Let me walk in the fields."
  He said, "No, walk in the town."
I said, "There are no flowers there."
  He said, "No flowers, but a crown."

I said, "But the skies are black;
  There is nothing but noise and din."
And He wept as He sent me back—
  "There is more," He said, "there is sin."

I said, "But the air is thick,
  And fogs are veiling the sun."
He answered, "Yet souls are sick,
  And souls in the dark undone!"

I said, "I shall miss the light,
  And friends will miss me, they say."
He answered, "Choose tonight,
  If I am to miss you or they."

I pleaded for time to be given.
  He said, "Is it hard to decide?
It will not seem too hard in heaven
  To have followed the steps of your Guide."

—GEORGE MacDONALD

March 10

Blessed be God, even the Father of our Lord Jesus Christ, the Father of mercies, and the God of all comfort; who comforteth us in all our tribulation, that we may be able to comfort them which are in any trouble, by the comfort wherewith we ourselves are comforted of God (2 Cor. 1:3-4).

Many a rapturous minstrel
  Among the sons of light,
Will say of his sweetest music,
  "I learned it in the night."
And many a rolling anthem
  That fills the Father's throne,
Sobbed out its first rehearsal
  In the shade of a darkened room.

—AUTHOR UNKNOWN

I've come through the darkest days of my years shipwrecked on God and stranded on omnipotence. I've learned the difference between God the Rewarder and God the Reward. Sometimes our dear ones are taken and sorrow comes and help fails—all to drive us to the Lord himself.

I've learned in a new way that God is a very present help in trouble. I've learned that "weeping may endure for the night, but joy cometh in the morning." God doesn't want us to sit up with our dead. They are gone but they are in His care. Think of that word "gone." One of these days—sin will be gone. Sorrows, gone. Pain, gone. Death, gone. Darkness, gone. Then we'll have again those we've loved and lost awhile, because Christians never meet for the last time.

—Vance Havner

> If I should die and leave you here awhile
>   Be not like others, sore undone, who keep
>   Long vigil by the silent dust and weep.
> For my sake turn again to life and smile,
>   Nerving thy heart and trembling hand to do
>   That which will comfort other souls than thine:
>   Complete these dear unfinished tasks of mine
> And I perchance may therein comfort you.

—Mary Lee Hall

March 11

For ever, O Lord, thy word is settled in heaven (Ps. 119:89).

What rejoicing is ours today that we have God's Book—the Bible—the strangest, the mightiest, the loveliest, the best of books, to guide us in our gloom, to prompt us in our perplexities, to help us in our hazards, to direct us in our doubts, to be a "lamp unto our feet and a light unto our path." Wondrous Book! Book above and beyond all books as a river is beyond a rill in reach, as the sun is above and beyond a roadside bush in majesty, as the wings of an eagle are beyond the sparrow's wings in strength. Book that has withstood storms of fire! Book against which tyranny has issued its edicts! Book against which infidelity has thrown its sharpest shafts and strongest spears of scorn and ridicule! Book against which snipers from behind some pulpits have "whacked" like butchers and do attack now like savages on a midnight raid!

But withal, all its enemies have not torn one hole in its holy vesture nor stolen one flower from its wondrous garden nor diluted one drop of honey from its abundant hive nor broken one string on its thousand-stringed harp nor drowned one sweet word in infidel ink nor made dim one ray of its perpetual light nor stayed its triumphant progress by so much as one step nor shortened its life by so much as one grief hour! It is still the pilgrim's Staff, the pilot's Compass, the soldier's Sword! And more besides!

—Robert G. Lee

> Last eve I passed beside a blacksmith's door,
>   And heard the anvil ring the vesper chime;
> Then, looking in, I saw upon the floor
>   Old hammers, worn with beating years of time.
>
> "How many anvils have you had," said I,
>   "To wear and batter all these hammers so?"
> "Just one," said he, and then, with twinkling eye,
>   "The anvil wears the hammers out, you know."
>
> And so, thought I, the anvil of God's Word,
>   For ages skeptic blows have beat upon;
> Yet, though the noise of falling blows was heard,
>   The anvil is unharmed—the hammers gone.

—Author Unknown

March 12

They drank wine, and praised the gods of gold, and of silver, of brass, of iron, of wood, and of stone. In the same hour came forth fingers of a man's hand, and wrote over against the candlestick upon the plaster of the wall of the king's palace: and the king saw the part of the hand that wrote (Dan. 5:4-5).

It was Belshazzar's last night on earth and he spent it drinking, carousing, and praising the gods of gold and silver. As drunkenness increased, his values lowered and he ended up praising even gods made of wood and stone. He was enjoying what the world calls "a good time."

But in the same hour judgment fell. "MENE, MENE, TEKEL, UPHARSIN," wrote the moving fingers. "Thou art weighed in the balances, and art found wanting. . . . God hath numbered thy kingdom, and finished it" (Dan. 5:25-27). God wrote this message of judgment on the wall of the great palace dining room near the candlesticks so that all could see it clearly.

This account of Belshazzar's vision teaches that all nations are subject to God's timetable. There is a judgment day, for both men and nations. Sometimes the end is closer than most believe possible. On this very night, Belshazzar was slain and the glorious empire of Babylon passed away forever into the hands of the Medes and Persians.

How tragic it is to forget God! The "hand that is not shortened so it cannot redeem" is also the hand that pronounces judgment when salvation is rejected. There is an hour when men go beyond the mercy of the Cross! If Belshazzar had turned in repentance to the God whom his father knew, he would have been spared. The Lord is long-suffering, "not willing that any should perish." But today is the day of salvation—not tomorrow!

"Seek ye the Lord while he may be found, call ye upon him while he is near; let the wicked forsake his way, and the unrighteous man his thoughts; and let him return unto the Lord, and he will have mercy upon him; and to our God, for he will abundantly pardon" (Isa. 55:6-7).

> Wide is the gate that leads to death,
> Smooth is the slope where your feet may stray,
> Broad is the road for the sinner's feet,
> The easy path of the downward way,
> But close beside you at every turn
> Love and pardon and welcome wait,
> Close beside you the Saviour walks,
> Down, clear down to the last dark gate.
>
> Down, clear down to the gates of death;
> Deep are the billows that meet you there,
> Swift are the waves your feet must pass,
> Chill are the waters your soul must dare;
> Down, clear down to the gates of hell,
> And Christ is calling you, every day,
> Christ is pleading at every step,
> Christ is loving you all the way.
>
> And when sometimes on the downward way
> Your heart grows sick with a sudden fear,

If you breathe His name it will be enough,
  For the ear of the Lord is quick to hear;
If you reach your hand through the lonely dark,
  His hand will clasp it, for He is nigh,
His heart is waiting to heed your call,
  His voice will answer your lightest cry.

But some sad hour will be the last,
  Some one moment will be too late,
At the last dark gate He must turn away
  And love and pardon no longer wait.
Turn, oh, turn from the downward path,
  From the way of death where your feet are set,
Turn to the Lord while the Lord is near,
  To the Christ who lingers and loves you yet.

—ANNIE JOHNSON FLINT

March 13

We have not an high priest which cannot be touched with the feeling of our infirmities; but was in all points tempted like as we are, yet without sin (Heb. 4:15).

At the close of a service in Germantown, a stranger accosted the late Dr. D. M. Stearn and said to him, "I don't like your preaching. I do not care for the cross. I think instead of preaching the death of Christ on the cross it would be far better to preach Jesus as the Teacher and the Example."

"Would you then be willing to follow Him?" Dr. Stearn asked.

"Yes, I would," the young man replied.

"Then," said Dr. Stearn, "Let us take the first step. 'He who did no sin.' Can you take this step?"

The young man looked confused. "No," he finally said, "I do sin and I acknowledge it."

"Well then," said the minister, "Your first need of Christ is not as an Example, but as a Savior."

The next verse in Hebrews reads, "Let us therefore come boldly unto the throne of grace, that we may obtain mercy, and find grace to help in time of need" (Heb. 4:16).

G. Campbell Morgan once said, "I am never tired of pointing out that the Greek phrase translated 'in time of need,' is a colloquialism of which 'in the nick of time' is the exact equivalent." Yes, we may find grace and mercy when we need it most because Christ is the Savior, not just a Teacher. Wherever we are, when flaming temptations come, we have a Redeemer who was tempted as we are, "yet without sin." He is One who is able, "in the nick of time," to keep us and sustain us by His grace and mercy!

March 14

Finally, brethren, pray for us, that the word of the Lord may have free course, and be glorified, even as it is with you: and that we may be delivered from unreasonable and wicked men; for all men have not faith (2 Thess. 3:1-2).

"Pray for us." Over and over again Paul makes this request in his letters to the young churches. He knew that effectual work for Christ could only be done with prayer. He coveted the prayers of all the saints. He asked them to pray, not for his personal wealth or fame, but that the Word of God might be proclaimed in mighty power. This prayer request was fully granted by our Lord.

Paul's second request, that he be "delivered from unreasonable and wicked men," was only partially granted. On three occasions he was beaten with rods and five times his back bore 40 stripes. Outside the city of Lystra he was stoned by an angry mob. He suffered shipwreck, and as he penned this particular prayer request the angry seas at Malta threatened to engulf him once again. Ahead of him lay a Roman prison and a martyr's death.

"Brethren, pray for me." Paul asked for prayer that he might faithfully run the race set before him and complete his task with joy. But above all he sought the prayers of believers that he might be a faithful preacher of God's Word. There is no greater calling.

> *I do not ask that crowds may throng the temple,*
> *That standing room be priced;*
> *I only ask that as I voice the message*
> *They may see Christ!*

I do not ask for churchly pomp or pageant,
  Or music such as wealth alone can buy;
I only ask that as I voice the message
  He may be nigh!

I do not ask that men may sound my praises
  Or headlines spread my name abroad;
I only pray that as I voice the message
  Hearts may find God!

—RALPH SPAULDING CUSHMAN

March 15

**Then we turned, and took our journey
into the wilderness** (Deut. 2:1).

"Then we turned." These words are the sad epitaph of Israel.
Because of unbelief and hardness of heart, not a soul who left
Egypt, save Caleb and Joshua and their families, lived to enter
"the land flowing with milk and honey." For 40 years their children wandered in a wilderness while their bodies fell by the wayside. Only the "little ones" whom they said would be "a prey to
the Hittites and Amorites" crossed over the Jordan. With their
frequent sinning and unbelief, and their cries of repentance, God
forgave Israel again and again. But now, in the scripture narrative,
they had passed beyond the reach of His promise. They were not
given a second chance.

Let no false pride arise in our hearts. Unbelief can also keep
us from the fulfillment of His promises and His choicest desires
for our lives. Whittier wrote, "Of all sad words of tongue or pen;
the saddest are these: It might have been!" May this not be our
regretful song! Choosing the permissive will of God instead of His
expressed will, is choosing second best. This falls far short of the
blessed life found only in a surrendered will.

They came to the land of Canaan,
  But they never entered in;
They came to the land of promise,
  But they perished in their sin.
And so we are ever coming
  To the place where the two ways part;
One leads to the land of promise
  And one to a hardened heart.

—AUTHOR UNKNOWN

March 16

*No good thing will he withhold from them
that walk uprightly* (Ps. 84:11).

Someone has written: "I asked for strength that I might
achieve; He made me weak that I might obey. I asked for health
that I might do great things; I was given grace that I might do
better things. I asked for riches that I might be happy; I was given
poverty that I might be wise. I asked for power that I might have
the praise of men; I was given weakness that I might feel the need
of God. I asked for all things that I might enjoy life; I was given
life that I might enjoy all things. I received nothing that I asked
for and yet received more than I had hoped for."

"My God shall supply all your need according to his riches
in glory by Christ Jesus" (Phil. 4:19).

The promise is secure—He "shall supply." His storehouse of
help is unlimited for it is filled with "riches in Christ Jesus."
God's larder is full! There is no shortage. No thieves can reduce
its inventory, for it is "according to his riches in glory." Take
heart, therefore, O child of God. Be not afraid. Divine supplies
are assured to meet your "need" as your Heavenly Father designs.
They will come at the appointed time!

> *God hath not promised*
> *Skies always blue,*
> *Flower-strewn pathways*
> *All our lives through;*
> *God hath not promised*
> *Sun without rain,*
> *Joy without sorrow,*
> *Peace without pain.*
>
> *But God hath promised*
> *Strength for the day,*
> *Rest for the labor,*
> *Light for the way,*
> *Grace for the trials,*
> *Help from above,*
> *Unfailing sympathy,*
> *Undying love.*

—ANNIE JOHNSON FLINT

March 17

Unto the angel of the church of the Laodiceans write; These things saith the Amen, the faithful and true witness, the beginning of the creation of God; I know thy works, that thou art neither cold nor hot (Rev. 3:14-15).

There is a well-known physical ailment commonly called "hardening of the arteries." Its medical name is arteriosclerosis. This disease is usually associated with advancing years, and high fat metabolism plays an early part.

There is also a spiritual ailment called "hardening of the ardor-ies." It means a decreased sensitivity, a reduced fervency, a dying down of love's flame, a cooling of the heart's devotion, and a subtle and progressive change from compassion to callousness, and from tenderness of spirit to "hardness of heart."

This is a serious malady! Laodicea suffered from it. They had "left their first love!" Their ardor had cooled—they had grown cold in their love for Christ. Associated with it came spiritual blindness.

This spiritual ailment of "hardening of the ardor-ies" not only affects individuals and churches but entire denominations. Declining membership, decreasing finances, and diminished involvement with gospel outreach are all signs of the disease. How easy it is to use quack remedies! Gimickry, bingo, and entertainments are substituted for prayer, the Word of God, and the ministry of the Holy Spirit. Form and ritual cannot replace holy fire!

But this is eventually a fatal disease. Its only cure for both an individual or a church is repentance and a return to His Word. Hardening of the arteries cannot be cured, but "hardening of the ardor-ies" can be!

—C. William Fisher

Spirit of God, descend upon my heart.
  Wean it from earth, through all its pulses move;
Stoop to my weakness, mighty as Thou art,
  And make me love Thee as I ought to love.

Hast Thou not bid us love Thee, God and King?
  All, all Thine own, soul, heart and strength and mind;
I see Thy cross—there teach my heart to cling;
  Oh, let me seek Thee, and Oh, let me find.

Teach me to feel that Thou art always nigh;
Teach me the struggles of the soul to bear,
To check the rising doubt, the rebel sigh;
Teach me the patience of unanswered prayer.

Teach me to love Thee as Thine angels love,
One holy passion filling all my frame;
The filling of the heaven descended Dove,
My heart the altar, and Thy love the flame.

I ask no dream, no prophet ecstasies,
No sudden rending of the veil of clay,
No angel visitant, no opening skies,
Just take the dimness of my soul away!

—GEORGE CROLY

March 18

Yea, in the shadow of thy wings will I make
my refuge (Ps. 57:1).
As birds flying, so will the Lord of hosts
defend Jerusalem (Isa. 31:5).

What a comforting promise this is! It is indeed heartening to know that as the birds flutter over their nests with quivering and palpitating wings, so the Lord protects us. No matter what perils may shadow us, even though it be the last shadow of death, all is well if we enjoy the shadow of God's guardian wings. He shelters, protects, and preserves His Blood-washed ones. In the shadow of His wings, we have power and peace, and heaven itself.

"He shall cover thee with his feathers," the Psalmist declares (Ps. 91:4). We have here another aspect of the promised covering of the divine wings, which we can accept without hesitation and find sure. Past centuries justify our reliance on such a promise. A great company no man can number have proved how faithful God has been to the promised covering of His soft feathers. Did our Lord have this precious verse in mind when He used the simile of the hen protecting her brood, allowing them to nestle under her wings? Because His promise must stand, let us shelter in Him and experience the overflowing peace that comes through the knowledge that He is guarding us.

—HERBERT LOCKYER
in *All the Promises of the Bible*

March 19

Jesus called a little child unto him, and set him in the midst of them, and said, Verily I say unto you, Except ye be converted, and become as little children, you shall not enter into the kingdom of heaven (Matt. 18:2-3).

Helen is growing up.

When she left her mountain home and came to live with us for a year, she wasn't what she is now. She is so appropriately called "civilized," so much more mature than when she came.

Now her prayers have taken on the even-spoken "Our Kind Heavenly Father" instead of her confiding "Dear Jesus."

The pointedness of "Bless Aunt Marge in the housework and help Albert to hear better" has given way to "Bless our friends and loved ones all over the world."

Helen used to pray—before she grew up—"Thank You for all the cardinals and the chickadees and the little lame grosbeak that came to Uncle Dan's feeder—and thank You for the warm house and my shiny new shoes." Now she says, "Thank You for everything."

Must she have learned "Except you become adults"? Or should we learn "Except you . . . become as little children"?

—CAROL ANN MARLOW

Tell me the old, old story of unseen things above,
Of Jesus and His glory, of Jesus and His love.
Tell me the story simply, as to a little child;
For I am weak and weary, and helpless and defiled.

—KATHERINE HANKEY

"Jesus called them unto him, and said, Suffer little children to come unto me, and forbid them not: for of such is the kingdom of God" (Luke 18:16).

March 20

At that feast the governor was wont to re-
lease unto the people a prisoner, whom they
would. And they had then a notable prisoner,
called Barabbas. Therefore when they were
gathered together, Pilate said unto them,
Whom will ye that I release unto you? Barab-
bas, or Jesus which is called Christ? . . . But the
chief priests and elders persuaded the multi-
tude that they should ask Barabbas, and de-
stroy Jesus. . . . They said, Barabbas (Matt. 27:
15-17, 20-21).

As Barabbas emerged from the prison into the free, glorious
sunshine, the crowd was already surging out toward the Place of
the Skull. And then, if not before, the desire must have arisen to
know who had been condemned to die in his place. One can easily
imagine how Barabbas followed the throng, striving eagerly to see
the Man who was to die for him. Perhaps it was not until the
sound of the hammer driving the nails had ceased, and the cross—
Barabbas's cross—had been upreared, bearing its awful burden,
that Barabbas saw the Sufferer and looked up into the face of
Jesus—the One who died in his place.

Now Barabbas was not a theologian, but he could easily
understand the doctrine of the Atonement.

First, he knew that he was a guilty wretch, under the righteous condemnation of the law. And in both these respects
Barabbas was a representative of all men.

Second, Barabbas knew that the Sufferer before him had
done no wrong; and

Third, he knew that Jesus was, for him, a true Substitute. He
was verily and actually dying in his place. This One was innocent
and holy and He was bearing the very penalty which the law had
justly decreed to him—Barabbas. He could never question Christ's
death as vicarious and substitutional.

Fourth, he knew that he had done nothing whatever to merit
the marvelous interposition of that death. It reached him as an
act of pure grace!

Finally, Barabbas knew that Christ's death for him was perfectly efficacious. There was, therefore, nothing for him to add
to it. Just because Christ was dying, he was living. The only question before Pilate was whether Christ should die or Barabbas, and
when it was decided that Christ should die, Barabbas was set free.

My brethren, may I commend to you Barabbas's message of the Atonement. It is the only word to preach on, to live on, and to die on. No other plan of salvation will do.

—C. I. SCOFIELD

"He was wounded for our transgressions, he was bruised for our iniquities: the chastisement of our peace was upon him: and with his stripes we are healed" (Isa. 53:5).

March 21

He was sad at that saying, and went away grieved: for he had great possessions (Mark 10:22).

Of all the dramatic happenings recorded in the Gospels, one of the most tragic is that of the rich young ruler who sorrowfully refused to pay the price of Kingdom entrance. He had all the admirable qualities inherent in formal religion—wealth, position, education, and excellent moral character. Outwardly at least, he was a man of high standards and exemplary living.

There were so many things in his favor: He was reverent, for he knelt and addressed Jesus as "Good Master." He was eager, for he came running. He was discerning, for he saw his need. He was sincere, for when he found the requirements too rigid he went away sorrowful. He was courageous, for he came out from his family and friends, risking criticism and ridicule.

Externally he passed inspection. He had wronged no man, *But*—what a world of tragedy in that three-letter word. According to the Master's analysis, the core, the root, the impelling motive of the young man's life was defective. He wasn't willing to lose his life in order to find it again in Christ. He rebelled at the thought of dying to wealth, position, and honor that he might find the satisfaction these things failed to give. Sorrowfully he went back to his property and his life of luxury and creature comfort. The demands of discipleship were too drastic.

The greatest hazard in life is the peril of the lesser good. The supreme test is not, "Can you withstand the evil?" but "Can you rise superior to the lower values, the second best?" Each day sets before us the choice. The constant challenge is to respond to the call of the High Road. The first step in that direction is taken when you resist the lure of the lowland!

—M. A. LUNN

I'm going by the upper road, for that
still holds the sun,
I'm climbing through night's pastures where
the starry rivers run!
If you should think to seek me in my
old dark abode,
You'll find this writing on the door,
"He's on the Upper Road."

—Author Unknown

March 22

Then shall be brought to pass the saying
that is written, Death is swallowed up in victory
(1 Cor. 15:54).

I dropped in on an old friend of boyhood days. She was one of God's rare saints—rich in experience—ripe for the coming glory. She had gone so far in life's pilgrimage that her mind was clouded and her memory affected.

As I rose to leave, she arose also and said, "I want to go home." Then her daughter said, "But Mother, you are home." She looked at me with a tender smile and replied with a profound touch of pathos, "I want to go home before it gets dark."

I opened the door and started on my way. The twilight sky was still aglow with the vanishing beauty of the sunset. Beyond it lay the glory of the Father's house. The words that I had heard bore down upon me. What an unspeakable blessing for God's redeemed to reach Home before it gets dark. Home before the darkness of a broken body and failing health; of dimmed senses and clouded faculties; of physical sufferings and infirmities; of vanished faces and voices and fellowships. What an unspeakable blessing for God's redeemed to reach Home "before it gets dark."

—James H. McConkey

"Eye hath not seen, nor ear heard, neither have entered into the heart of man, the things which God hath prepared for them that love him" (1 Cor. 2:9).

When death touches a young girl in her bloom of maidenhood; when it reaches out to a youth in the freshness of his stirring; when it comes to a man in his prime of creative and productive living; or when its cold breath touches the beautiful child

100

leaving that awful void in loving hearts and arms—how difficult —how hard to understand! In the midst of it all, remember that the Father's home is the cure for the troubled heart—that our loved ones in Christ are safely there before dark!

> When for a little walk we went
> On errand or on pleasure bent,
> As we drew near the vine-clad gate,
> My always present walking mate
> Would slip his chubby hand from mine,
> And toddling on past shrub and vine,
> Would turn and say with baby wit:
> "I beat you home—a little bit."
>
> God was so good to him and me
> As to permit our lives to be
> Like those of two frank, boyhood chums
> Together solving life's hard sums.
> I, as elder, sometimes knew
> Where, in his path, lay bog and slough.
> So I might point it out in time
> And save him from the fall and grime.
>
> Today some friends came by and spoke to me,
> And then awoke a slumbering memory,
> I dreamt he was a babe again,
> That on before my feet had sped
> To reach our door a step ahead.
> Through trembling lips I whispered it,
> "He beat me home—a little bit."
>
> —AUTHOR UNKNOWN

"The Harbor almost reached after a splendid voyage, with such companions all the way, and my boy awaiting me" (Sir William Osler).

March 23

Then was Jesus led up of the Spirit into the wilderness to be tempted of the devil (Matt. 4:1).

Temptation is common to men but God has provided a way of escape. The record of Christ's victory is an encouragement to beleaguered saints and an example to all who would live victoriously.

The areas of attack against the believer are threefold: *Preservation* (changing stone to bread)—the lust of the flesh; *Presumption* (Christ casting himself from the Temple)—the pride of life; and *Power* (giving homage to Satan)—the lust of the eyes. The devil invariably strikes at our weakest points. But the Lord Jesus set the pattern for victory. The method He used is guaranteed. It never fails.

First, His prolonged communion in the wilderness with the Father strengthened His spirit (although His body hungered) against the onslaught of evil. If we would be strong we must keep our fellowship with the Father unbroken.

Second, the Savior wielded the Word of God ("It is written") as His Sword against the devil's thrusts. This is still the saint's offensive weapon. Know your Bible. Keep your Sword untarnished and available for instant action. And use it!

Third, Christ triumphed because He refused to permit the devil's subtle suggestions to cross even the threshold of His heart. He recognized and spurned Satan's wiles before they made the slightest inroad into His thinking. He refused to toy with any diabolical ideas. We too must stedfastly resist the initial appeal of sinful desires. It is no sin to be tempted. But to cater to temptation is dangerous. The foul bats of unworthy thoughts must not be allowed to roost in the chimneys of our hearts.

—J. C. MACAULAY

"There hath no temptation taken you but such is common to man: but God is faithful, who will not suffer you to be tempted above that ye are able; but will with the temptation also make a way of escape, that ye may be able to bear it" (1 Cor. 10:13).

March 24

As much as in me is, I am ready (Rom. 1: 15).

St. Paul used the expression "I am" in a most unique way in the opening verses of his glorious Epistle to the Romans.

In verse 14 he said, "I am debtor." To whom? Why to the Greeks and to the barbarians. As someone has expressed it: "He was not in debt because of what *they had done for him* but he was in debt because of what *he could do for them.*"

Then in verse 15 he says, "I am ready." Ready to go or ready to stay but always ready to do God's will. How these three little words testify to the great apostle's loyalty and ownership by his Savior.

But more, he writes, "I am not ashamed" (v. 16). Paul, the Roman citizen; Paul, the Greek scholar; Paul, who sat at the feet of Gamaliel was not ashamed of Jesus nor of the blessed gospel which was and which is the power of God unto salvation.

Are you also ready in all things to do His complete will?

> *Ready to suffer grief or pain,*
> *Ready to stand the test;*
> *Ready to stay at home and send*
> *Others, if He sees best.*
>
> *Ready to go, ready to bear,*
> *Ready to watch and pray;*
> *Ready to stand aside and give,*
> *Till He shall clear the way.*
>
> *Ready to go, ready to stay,*
> *Ready my place to fill;*
> *Ready for service, lowly or great,*
> *Ready to do His will.*
>
> —S. E. L.

Listen to Paul again. "God forbid that I should glory, save in the cross of our Lord Jesus Christ, by whom the world is crucified unto me, and I unto the world" (Gal. 6:14).

"Not ashamed," cries the great apostle; and those who know His name must also respond, "I am not ashamed. Christ is my all in all."

> *Jesus, and shall it ever be,*
> *A mortal man ashamed of Thee?*
> *Ashamed of Thee, whom angels praise,*
> *Whose glories shine through endless days?*
>
> *Ashamed of Jesus! yes, I may,*
> *When I've no guilt to wash away;*
> *No tear to wipe, no good to crave,*
> *No fears to quell, no soul to save.*
>
> *Till then, nor is my boasting vain,*
> *Till then I boast a Savior slain;*
> *And O, may this my glory be,*
> *That Christ is not ashamed of me!*
>
> —Joseph Grigg

March 25

We came unto the land whither thou
sentest us, and surely it floweth with milk and
honey; and this is the fruit of it. Nevertheless
the people be strong that dwell in the land,
and the cities are walled, and very great: and
moreover we saw the children of Anak there
(Num. 13:27-28).

Kadesh-barnea! O fateful stopping place on Israel's journey! Faith proclaimed, "We are well able to possess the land," but unbelief cried "We are not." The giants of Anak were more impressive than God's sure word of deliverance and the promise of a land "flowing with milk and honey." Forty days of spying led to 40 years of wandering. Disbelief ended in death.

Do not pitch the tent of your life at Kadesh-barnea! Trust God's Word. Believe His promise. Move forward, "for the Lord thy God bringeth thee into a good land, a land of brooks of water, of fountains and depths that spring out of valleys and hills; a land of wheat, and barley, and vines, and fig trees, and pomegranates; a land of olive oil, and honey; a land wherein thou shalt eat bread without scarceness" (Deut. 8:7-9).

> *Oh, there are heavenly heights to reach*
> *In many a fearful place,*
> *While the poor, timid heir of God*
> *Lies blindly on his face;*
> *Lies languishing for light divine*
> *That he shall never see*
> *'Til he goes forward at Thy sign,*
> *And trusts himself to Thee.*

> —C. A. Fox

March 26

He said unto Jesus, Lord, remember me
when thou comest into thy kingdom (Luke
23:42).

"Remember me," the penitent thief asks. Not a throne, not a seat of glory among the angels, not a place at the right or left hand of Jesus; but just a thought, a crumb for a dog, a drop of your love. The voice that quivers with pain has in it a tone of hope. Jesus has forgiven those villains below—perhaps He will forgive a wretch like me. As he looks at the Savior, light breaks into his dark soul. And the Spirit touches him to make him alive. Burdened with wrong, he flees to the Savior to hide there.

Jesus answered him immediately. He had disappointed King Herod by His silence and surprised Pilate by not answering him. But He's eager to speak to this thief. Here we see His purpose. He ate and drank with sinners and publicans. He came for them too! He was counted among criminals to be their friend. He loved and wanted them also. For them, for us—He died to take away every sin and to make us clean and holy through His blood. He came to bring us to God. He will go after a sinner to the end and snatch him as a brand from the fire. Here on the cross, Jesus is dying for the sins of the whole world. But He takes time out to turn to the thief and open the door for him. "Today thou shalt be with me in Paradise. Come in. It isn't too late."

Heaven is a gift! This thief had nothing good about him, either before or after his conversion, which could have counted with God. It has been said that he couldn't walk the right way because his feet were nailed to a cross. He couldn't do any good with his hands, not even fold them in prayer, because they too were fastened. He couldn't live a better life because he was dying. He had no baptism or Lord's Supper. He could offer no church membership nor gifts to charity. If anyone had reason to despair, he did. All he could do was to call on Christ for salvation. But that is all it takes, for it is written, "Whosoever shall call upon the name of the Lord shall be saved" (Rom. 10:12).

Jesus did not forget him. He remembered him and took him to Paradise. And who is this Jesus that can give heaven away in such a lordly fashion to this wretch? It is the Christ—the Son of the Living God who can give away heaven. And He wants, also, to give it to you!

"To day shalt thou be with me in paradise."

—E. RUSSELL LYNN

See, Father, I have brought with me
  This trophy rare;
We both were hanging on a tree—
  I heard his prayer;
And since for sinners there I bled,
For him the crimson stream was shed.

I heard that cry—"Remember me!"
  My soul it stung.
So piteous his agony,
  As there we hung.
My word I pledged within a trice—
"Today . . . with Me in Paradise!"

The first fruits of My dying there
  To Thee I yield;
O Father, what the harvest rare
  From that world field!
This malefactor, first to come,
Leads all the ransomed sinners Home!

—WILLIAM MARION RUNYAN

March 27

**The land, whither ye go to possess it, is a
land of hills and valleys, and drinketh water of
the rain of heaven; a land which the Lord thy
God careth for** (Deut. 11:11-12).

Troubled heart traveling the lonely pathway of sorrow today, remember this truth: the scene will change!

As surely as the path led down into the valley, it must climb again to the heights. For there could be no valley if there were no hills. The hills are what make the valley a valley!

The sun glimmers through the shadows even along the valley road, and if you listen you may find a song. Though tuned to a minor key, you will find it very beautiful, and when you emerge to the heights again, you will keep it in your heart.

And you will find that you have grown, during your sojourn in the valley, and henceforth you will have sympathy and love to share with all who walk a lonely way.

—K. B. P.

I do not know why sorrows bow the heart,
  Or why temptations sweep in like a flood;
I do not know why those who love must part—
  But this I do believe: Our God is good!

I do not know why still He waits to send
  The answer to some prayer His child has prayed;
But while above the earth His heavens bend,
  I shall pray on, and trust, nor be afraid!

I cannot always see the pathway clear,
  And, looking back, can see no laurels won.
But what we shall be doth not yet appear;
  So I shall walk by faith till life is done!

No need have I to know the plan complete;
  No need have I today to see the goal.
It is enough to know who guides my feet—
  In Him I confidently rest my soul!

—KATHRYN BLACKBURN PECK

March 28

**If the dead rise not, then is not Christ
raised; and if Christ be not raised, your faith is
vain; ye are yet in your sins** (1 Cor. 15:16-17).

"If Christ be not risen," then where is the proof of His deity?
What is there to back up all those claims he made for himself?
What is there to fortify the story that He was the virgin-born Son
of God? If the spear and the spikes ended it all, then how did Jesus
differ from other good men who died as martyrs?

"If Christ be not risen," then I have been cheated. If there is
no living Savior, then my faith has failed me and it is vain.

"If Christ be not risen," then He is still dead, and churches
are monuments to man's stupidity.

"If Christ be not risen," all Christian creeds and books are
false and meaningless. All songs and sermons in His name are
hollow and ineffective.

"If Christ be not risen," then all who sleep in the silent city
of the dead will never wake again. If He did not rise from the
grave, no one will.

"If Christ be not risen," the greatest tragedy of all is that you and I are still sinners. Our hope in a risen Christ, a dead one.

"But now is Christ risen from the dead." The Son of God lives! He conquered death! He is alive today! He will live forever! Therefore my faith is secure. My sins are gone; my hope is steadfast; my resurrection is certain; my title to eternal life is a blessed reality! Thank God for Easter—the dawn without a dusk!

—FLETCHER SPRUCE

On the third day the friends of Christ coming at daybreak to the tomb found the grave empty and the stone rolled away. In varying ways they realized the new wonder, but even they hardly realized that the world had died in the night. What they were looking at was the first day of a new creation, with a new heaven and a new earth; and in a semblance of the gardener, God walked again in the garden, in the cool not of the evening but of the dawn.

—G. K. CHESTERTON

Jerusalem's streets had never seen
   Anxiety at such a race
As that which whirled through morning mist
   At reckless pace.

In fear, in hope, in unbelief—
   Scarce knowing whom or what they faced;
Competitors from Galilee
   Set out in haste.

An eagerness born out of love
   Was impetus enough for them
To Speed—impatient for the truth
   Toward Joseph's tomb.

They ran, The younger finished first,
   But stopped short of the victor's view.
The older persevered to find
   The news was true.

—D. BRUCE LOCKERBIE

March 29

I saw a new heaven and a new earth (Rev. 21:1)

Long will be eternity but not longer than the joys of eternity. Long will be the eternal years, but not longer than the companionship we shall enjoy with the redeemed, in fellowship with those who are "arrayed in white . . . and have washed their robes and made them white in the blood of the Lamb." And there in the land of eternal day, where no grave digger plies his spade and where no roll of hearse wheel is ever heard, where no tears bedim the eyes and no fears beset the heart, "they shall hunger no more, neither thirst any more . . . For the Lamb which is in the midst of the throne shall feed them, and shall lead them unto the living fountains of waters: and God shall wipe all tears from their eyes."

There will not be many earthly sunsets until there will be an eternal heavenly sunrise. Only a little while until the shadows will flee away. Only a little while until we lay our burdens down at the end of the journey. Only a little while until all of God's redeemed of all the ages will be gathered in that glorious resurrection morning. Soon we shall see Jesus and, with Him, the faces of redeemed loved ones. We have in Christ a resurrection that can never be thwarted, a destiny that can never be changed, a hope that can never be disappointed, and a glory that can never be denied.

—Robert G. Lee

March 30

I will declare what he hath done for my soul (Ps. 66:16).

Think of what He has done for your soul! He it was who saw you lost and helpless and in His love and mercy provided a way of deliverance. It was your sinful condition that brought the Savior above to die on Calvary. By His blood He secured a priceless redemption for your soul. . . . He meets your every need. To adapt what a gifted writer has said of Philip, one of the least of the disciples, "I may not be able to reason and debate. I may have little skill in logic and apologetic. My words may be destitute of the orator's passion and poetry and color. But at least I can say, 'Come, for you shall see; come, and you shall find for yourselves how good He is.'"

in *All the Promises of the Bible*

I have found no satisfaction in the fleeting joys of earth;
I have hewed me broken cisterns that have mocked me by
*   their dearth;*
All the springs my soul had tested failed to meet my deepest
*   need;*
Christ alone has met my longing, He has satisfied indeed.

I have tried the world for pleasure, but it could not satisfy;
Tho' it promised much, it failed me, all its wells and springs
*   were dry*
Everything I tried was empty, and I thought that life was
*   vain;*
But He came and tuned my heartstrings, and I learned to
*   sing again.*

I was tempted not to trust Him, for so many things had
*   failed;*
But so patiently He waited, and His tenderness prevailed;
So I swung my heart's door open, and His promises I tried;
Christ is not a disappointment, He has fully satisfied.

Christ is not a disappointment, every longing in my breast
Finds in Him complete fulfillment, He has brought me into
*   rest.*
I have tested Him and proved Him more that all I dreamed
*   He'd be;*
Christ is not a disappointment, He is all in all to me.

—C. W. WAGGONER

March 31

*Not many days after the younger son gath-
ered all together, and took his journey into a
a far country, and there wasted his substance
with riotous living* (Luke 15:13).

In this chapter Jesus introduces us to the Prodigal Son, a
young man who asked for and received his inheritance, without
any restraints being placed upon him. He left home of his own
free will. He chose the right to sow and to reap. The boy was a
rich prodigal, and just as much a prodigal in the father's house as
in the far country. Where our hearts are really determines where
we are!

The Word tells us that "he gathered all together and took his
journey into a far country." We do well to keep our eyes on the
end of the road.

In the far country he first encountered the pleasures of sin.
But Moody once said, "Shame, contempt, and distress are wedded
to sin, and can never be divorced." Paul wrote, "The wages of sin
is death" (Rom. 6:23). Too often God is blamed for the want and
distress of the far country when it is simply the devil collecting
the wages due him.

Fortunately the story doesn't end there: this boy came to his
senses with a wonderful decision to turn from his sinning and
head back toward his home. There the father waited to greet him
with outstretched arms of love.

Fletcher Spruce wrote concerning the prodigal son: "He
came to himself. He admitted that sin had made him morally in-
sane and spiritually enslaved. Sin had made him a pauper inside,
and he said so. Sin had lowered him to the animal level, and he
was not hiding it. To repent is to admit enslavement to sin.

"'I have sinned,' he said. He acknowledged that he personal-
ly was guilty. He did not blame his father, his brother, society,
nor his companions. He did not try to hide his sins nor shift the
responsibility. This is repenting.

"'I . . . am no more worthy.' He was aware of the moral havoc
of sin. Once arrogant and haughty he had said, 'Give me.' But
none of that now. No bragging about his past fling. Now he was
not too good to kneel, to cry, to pray. Until a sinner comes to this
place, he has not repented.

"'Make me as one of thy hired servants.' Repentance includes a willingness to bear the punishment for sins committed.
He knew he deserved no favors—and he asked none.

"'He arose, and came to his father.' Repentance means complete rejection of the practices and fetters of sin. His father did not have to pull him out of the muck—he left the pigpens on his own volition. Nor did he beg the family to put a fence around it to keep him from returning. He was through with the mess. True repentance means a break with the old life, now and forever."

"Him that cometh to me I will in no wise cast out" (John 6: 37).

April 1

The fool hath said in his heart, There is no God (Ps. 14:1).

On this "April Fools' Day," God reminds us that those who deny His reality are atheistic fools. They look at a golden sunrise and are unable to see Him. They cannot trace His creative hand in the beauties of nature, nor do they see His majesty in the towering mountains.

God writes in His Word of other fools. Those who despise His wisdom and truth are called ignorant fools (Prov. 1:7). Those who build great barns to store their earthly riches and rejoice in them, He labels as industrious fools (Luke 12:20). Those who laugh at sin and choose evil, He describes as shameless fools (Prov. 14:9). The entrance of His Word alone brings light and truth, and men who are wise in their own conceits are named as self-confident fools (Rom. 1:22). There is also the self-righteous fool who knows "there is a way which seemeth right unto a man but the end thereof are the ways of death" (Prov. 16:25).

There is another fool spoken of in the Bible. This man is a fool "for Christ's sake," and like the apostle Paul, he willingly bears the reproaches of Christ. He desires the Lord's approval and His riches above all that the world can offer. We do well to ask our hearts, "What kind of a fool am I?" (See 1 Cor. 4:10.)

What will it profit, when life here is o'er
Though great worldly wisdom I gain,
If seeking knowledge—I utterly fail
The wisdom of God to obtain?

112

What will it profit, when life here is o'er
Though gathering riches and fame,
If, gaining the world—I lose my own soul
And in heaven unknown is my name?

What will it profit, when life here is o'er
Though earth's fleeting love has been mine,
If seeking its gifts—I fail to secure
The riches of God's love divine?

—GRACE E. TROY

"What shall it profit a man, if he shall gain the whole world, and lose his own soul? Or what shall a man give in exchange for his soul?" (Mark 8:36-37).

April 2

If ye then be risen with Christ, seek those things which are above, where Christ sitteth on the right hand of God. Set your affections on things above, not on things on the earth. For ye are dead, and your life is hid with Christ in God (Col. 3:1-3).

When it comes to living the Christian life, many lose sight of this principle. Having been saved by faith, many think that they are to live by works and efforts; instead of continuing to receive they are now to begin to do! The life hid with Christ in God is to be entered by faith. "As we have received Christ Jesus the Lord, so we are to walk in him." We received Him by faith and by faith alone; therefore we are to walk in Him by faith and by faith alone. And the faith by which we enter into this hidden life is just the same as the faith by which we were translated out of the kingdom of darkness into the kingdom of God's dear Son, only it lays hold of a different thing.

Then we believed that Jesus was our Savior from the guilt of sin, and according to our faith it was unto us; now we must believe that He is our Savior from the power of sin. We took Him as a Savior in the future from the penalties of our sins; now we must take Him as Savior and Lord in the present from the bondage of sins. Then He was our Redeemer; now He is to be our Life—the

Lord of our life. He lifted us out of the pit; now He wants to seat us in heavenly places with himself.

—Hannah Whitall Smith
in *The Christian's Secret of a Happy Life*

April 3

I know that my redeemer liveth, and that he shall stand at the latter day upon the earth (Job 19:25).

It is a cold, dreary Lord's day as I write these lines. A snowstorm lies just to the west of my city, and only a few brave trees and some startled tulips testify that spring arrived a few weeks ago. But it is also Easter Sunday—the day of Christ's resurrection. As I sat in the old pew, I thought of other Easters and of familiar faces "which I have loved long since and lost awhile."

I thought of an old Sunday school teacher who lived and prayed that his class of young boys might be led to Jesus; of a faithful pastor and dear friend who preached his last sermon on "the Cradle, the Cross, and the Crown," and then quietly slipped into His presence as he prayed in the pulpit; of two faithful "Priscillas" who earnestly taught "young Timothy" to be grounded and rooted in the Word; of a godly mother whose joy was found in service to others; of a great gospel singer, who sang before presidents and kings, and then gave up his famous career to "sing and make melody" only for the Lord; of friends from youthful days in the old church who already have joined "the Church Eternal."

The day of resurrection! "Now is Christ risen from the dead, and become the firstfruits of them that slept" (1 Cor. 15:20). How wonderful not to be counted with those "who have no hope." How glorious to know that "we shall not all sleep, but we shall all be changed, in a moment, in the twinkling of an eye, at the last trump; for the trumpet shall sound, and the dead shall be raised incorruptible, and we shall be changed" (1 Cor. 15:52).

Blow on, O cold north wind. The lilac will yet bloom and the iris will wave in the late spring wind. "Death is swallowed up in victory."

Christ is risen!

The Lord is risen indeed!

> I know that my Redeemer liveth,
>   And on the earth again shall stand;
> I know eternal life He giveth,
>   That grace and power are in His hand.
>
> I know His promise never faileth;
>   The word He speaks, it cannot die.
> Though cruel death my flesh assaileth,
>   Yet I shall see Him by and by.
>
> I know my mansion He prepareth,
>   That where He is there I may be.
> Oh, wondrous thought, for me He careth,
>   And He at last will come for me!
>
> I know, I know that Jesus liveth,
>   And on the earth again shall stand;
> I know, I know that life He giveth,
>   That grace and power are in His hand.
>
> —JESSIE BROWN POUNDS

"'Where, O death, is your victory? Where, O death is your sting?' The sting of death is sin, and the power of sin is the law. But thanks be to God! He gives us the victory through our Lord Jesus Christ. Therefore, my dear brothers, stand firm. Let nothing move you. Always give yourselves fully to the work of the Lord, because you know that your labor in the Lord is not in vain" (1 Cor. 15:55-58, NIV).

April 4

When he had by himself purged our sins, [he] sat down on the right hand of the Majesty on high (Heb. 1:3).

"*Di eautou*"—by himself! Never have we found two words more suggestive of evangelical truth, and, therefore, more worthy of being guarded against omission. There is a purposeful ambiguity in these two words which makes it necessary for us to regard three shades of meaning.

"By himself" indicates the lonely, the unique, the exclusive character of Christ's redemptive work for us. There was no one to help Him. No one could help Him. In all the universe there was no other who could represent both God and man. Therefore, like the solitary high priests on the great Day of Atonement, He went alone to Pilate's hall, to dark Gethsemane, to the kingdom of death. See thy lonely Savior!

"By himself" implies, also, the competency of our Lord to redeem us. He needed no help. Through Him the worlds were made. Note how this passage labors to express His power. He is the effulgence *(apaugasma)* of God; He is the carbon copy, *(charakter)*, exact reproduction, of God's substance. See thy mighty Savior!

And, "by himself" designates the means whereby He redeemed us. He was himself the Price of our healing. He brought not the blood of bulls or calves, but His own blood. And so effective is this precious redemption that it is "once for all." See thy suffering Savior!

—RICHARD ELLSWORTH DAY

April 5

He was wounded for our transgressions, he was bruised for our iniquities: the chastisement of our peace was upon him; and with his stripes we are healed (Isa. 53:5).

The Man of Sorrows became the Man of Suffering, for our Lord died a vicious death. There was shame and indignity and brutality at the Cross. Jesus suffered! He was wounded!

Our Lord bore five bleeding wounds. Among them was the *contused* wound or heavy bruise. This is described in John 19:3: "They smote him with their hands." They took their fists and rods and hit Him in the face until "his visage was so marred more than any man" (Isa. 52:14). And again, "I gave my back to the smiters, and my cheeks to them that plucked off the hair; I hid not my face from shame and spitting" (Isa. 50:6).

They also scourged Him: "Pilate, willing to content the people, released Barabbas unto them, and delivered Jesus, when he had scourged him, to be crucified" (Mark 15:15). This was the *lacerated* wound. It means to be torn. The soldiers had taken leather cords tipped with metal and had viciously beaten Jesus' back. Thus they fulfilled what the Psalmist had said, "The plowers plowed upon my back: they made long their furrows" (Ps. 129:3). With evil hands they whipped and tore the Son of God until His precious blood dripped "like rain from a low eave" to the marble floor of Pilate's judgment hall.

There was also the *penetrating* wound—piercing deeply. Cruel thorns were pressed into His brow—a brow that now wears a crown of glory. On His head they laid a tearing crown of thorns. "They clothed him with purple, and platted a crown of thorns, and put it about his head" (Mark 15:17).

Then came the Cross, and with it came the nails. His hands and His feet bore the *perforated* wound. The Cross and nails were His, but by those nail prints He blotted out "the handwriting of ordinances that was against us, which was contrary to us, and took it out of the way, nailing it to his cross" (Col. 2:14).

The final wound He bore that day was the deep thrust of the spear—the *incised* wound. John tells us in his Gospel that "one of the soldiers with a spear pierced his side, and forthwith came there out blood and water" (John 19:34). The precious blood poured forth, and a fountain for sin's cleansing was opened. How glorious to know that Jesus became the Man of Suffering by whose "stripes we are healed." Wonderful grace! Wonderful redemption! Wonderful Savior!

> My sins laid open to the rod
>   The back which from the law was free;
> And the Eternal Son of God
>   Received the stripes once due to me.
>
> No beam was in His eye, nor mote,
>   Nor laid to Him was any blame;
> And yet His cheeks for me were smote—
>   The cheeks that never blushed for shame.
>
> I pierced those sacred hands and feet
>   That never touched or walked in sin;
> I broke the heart that only beat
>   The souls of sinful men to win.
>
> That sponge of vinegar and gall
>   Was placed by me upon His tongue;
> And when derision mocked His call,
>   I stood that mocking crowd among.
>
> And yet His blood was shed for me,
>   To be of sin the double cure;
> And balm there flows from Calvary's tree
>   That heals my guilt and makes me pure.
>
> —JAMES M. GRAY

April 6

Who hath saved us, and called us with an holy calling (2 Tim. 1:9).

Now here is a touchstone by which we may try our calling. It is "an holy calling, not according to our works, but according to His own purpose and grace." This calling forbids all trust in our own doings, and conducts us to Christ alone for salvation; but it afterwards purges us from dead works to serve the living and true God. As He that hath called you is holy, so must you be holy. If you are living in Sin, you are not called, but if you are truly Christ's, you can say, "Nothing pains me so much as sin; I desire to be rid of it; Lord, help me to be holy." Is this the panting of thine heart?

Paul in Philippians spoke of "the high calling of God in Christ Jesus." Is then your calling a high calling? Has it ennobled your heart, and set it upon heavenly things? Has it elevated your hopes, your tastes, your desires? Has it upraised the constant tenor of your life, so that you spend it with God and for God? Another test is found in Heb. 3:1—"partakers of the heavenly calling." Heavenly calling means a call from heaven. If man alone call thee, thou art uncalled, Is thy calling from God? Is it a call to heaven as well as from heaven? Unless thou art a stranger here, and heaven thy home, thou hast not been called with a heavenly calling; for those who have been so called, declare that they look for a city which hath foundations, whose builder and maker is God, and they themselves are strangers and pilgrims upon the earth. Is thy calling holy, high, and heavenly? This is the calling wherewith God doth call His people.

—CHARLES HADDON SPURGEON

April 7

Be careful [anxious] for nothing; but in every thing by prayer and supplication with thanksgiving let your requests be made known unto God (Phil. 4:6).

Paul remembers the words of David; "Commit thy way unto the Lord, trust also in him" (Ps. 37:5). Cease your worrying!

It is said of Bishop Quayle that for years he worried over his church, his clergy, his work, and all the things he had to do. William Barclay writes of him, "He used to sit up half the night worrying about all kinds of things. Then one night as he sat worrying he tells us that he heard God's voice as clearly as if it had been someone sitting in the same room, and God was saying, 'Quayle, you go to bed. I'll sit up for the rest of the night!' And thereafter there was in Quayle a wonderful serenity, for he had learned to cast his burden upon the Lord."

"Casting all your care upon him; for he careth for you" (1 Pet. 5:7). Do we believe this? Lord, hush our pounding pulses! Quiet our fearful hearts! Fill us with faith that we may cast our burdens and our fears upon You—and leave them there!

If the world from you withholds of its silver and its gold,
And you have to get along with meager fare,
Just remember, in His Word, how He feeds the little bird;
Take your burden to the Lord and leave it there.

If your body suffers pain and your health you can't regain,
And your soul is almost sinking in despair,
Jesus knows the pain you feel, He can save and He can heal;
Take your burden to the Lord and leave it there.

When your enemies assail and your heart begins to fail,
Don't forget that God in heaven answers prayer;
He will make a way for you and will lead you safely
through;
Take your burden to the Lord and leave it there.

When your youthful days are gone and old age is stealing
on,
And your body bends beneath the weight of care;
He will never leave you then, He'll go with you to the end;
Take your burden to the Lord and leave it there.

—G. Albert Tindley

"Commit thy way unto the Lord; trust also in him; and he shall bring it to pass" (Ps. 37:5).

April 8

Naaman said, Shall there not then, I pray thee, be given to thy servant two mules' burden of earth? for thy servant will henceforth offer neither burnt offering nor sacrifice unto other gods, but unto the Lord. In this thing the Lord pardon thy servant, that when my master goeth into the house of Rimmon to worship there, . . . the Lord pardon thy servant in this thing (2 Kings 5:17-18).

Poor Naaman! He had lost his leprosy in Samaria and had found the "sweet knowledge of the Lord." But now he was willing to go only so far in spiritual living.

Matthew Henry wrote that Naaman committed the mistakes of both "overdoing and underdoing." He wanted to take back with him some bags of earth from the land of Israel so that when he bent his knees they would rest on holy ground. However, the Lord wants more than bended knees—He wants "bended hearts" that are fully consecrated to Him. Vance Havner once said, "We can become so busy hauling holy dirt that we forget God."

Naaman was willing to pay only part of the price for God's blessing. He felt it was important that he not offend the idolatrous king of Assyria who still believed in the pagan god Rimmon. So Naaman wanted to bend his knees to both Jehovah and Rimmon. He typifies the believer who is saved for full service and born of the Spirit but who has not been filled with the Spirit and sanctified wholly or completely committed to God. This was Naaman's underdoing.

But let us not criticize Naaman too harshly. He has lots of company. Many a Christian offers his Lord "bended knees," but not a "heart meet only for the Master's use." It is the latter that the Savior wants. Are we too busy "hauling holy dirt" and failing to live holy and surrendered lives? "Holy dirt" plus "the house of Rimmon" are not compatible with victorious living!

"Lovest thou me more than these?" (John 21:15).

April 9

As God's chosen people, holy and dearly loved, clothe yourselves with compassion, kindness, humility, gentleness and patience (Col. 3:12, NIV).

My friend, Pastor U. S. Grant, wrote in one of his pastoral letters, "The apostle Paul gives a marvelous prescription for living in his letter to the Philippians. Among other things he says, 'Let your moderation be know unto all men, the Lord is at hand' (Phil. 4:5).

"The word 'moderation' can be defined as 'restraint, avoidance of extremes, or temperance.' These are all good words. The Amplified Version translates this as 'Let all men know and perceive your unselfishness, your consideration, your forebearing spirit.' Take a good long look at these words. They all reveal attributes that should be in the fiber of a genuine Christian.

"An expository dictionary gives these thoughts: 'The word moderation implies gentleness, sweet reasonableness, and equitable and fair patience.' It is a word that really describes one who is not insisting on the letter of the law. Such a Christian shows long-suffering to others, that quality of self-restraint which should be manifest in the face of provocation.

"In my own personal version this is its meaning: 'In light of the glorious anticipation of the Lord's soon return, it is time for all Christians to begin to act like Christians.'"

The Spirit-filled life is a life in which the fruits of the Holy Spirit are manifest. We speak often of love, joy, and peace. But let us not forget that long-suffering, temperance, and moderation are also a part of that life. Can it be said of us that we are living such a life—a life of "sweet reasonableness," unselfish and considerate of all? These are the marks of the life truly lived in the Spirit.

April 10

> *Such were some of you: but ye are washed, but ye are sanctified, but ye are justified in the name of the Lord Jesus, and by the Spirit of our God* (1 Cor. 6:11).

Genuine holiness is not the inability to sin, but the ability not to sin. It is not freedom from temptation, but power to overcome temptation. It is not exemption from conflict, but victory through conflict. It is not freedom from liability and falling, but gracious ability to prevent falling. It is not the end of progress, but deliverance from standing still. What real Christian would not desire the beauty and blessedness of such a life?

—G. Campbell Morgan

Hannah Whitall Smith in *The Christian's Secret of a Happy Life:*

Man's part is to trust and God's part is to work. We are to be delivered from the power of sin, and are to be made perfect in every good work to do the will of the Lord. We are to be transformed by the renewing of our minds, that we may prove what is that perfect will of God. A real work is to be wrought in us and upon us. Besetting sins are to be conquered; evil habits are to be overcome; and wrong dispositions are to be rooted out. A positive transformation is to take place. We have most of us tried to do it for ourselves at first, and have grievously failed; then we discover, from the Scriptures and from our own experience, that it is something we are unable to do, but that the Lord Jesus Christ has come on purpose to do it, and that He will do it for all who put themselves wholly into His hands and trust Him without reserve.

Say to Him: "Lord Jesus, I am going to trust Thee to keep me. I have tried keeping myself and have failed. I give myself to Thee. I keep back no reserves. I present myself to Thee as a piece of clay, to be fashioned into anything Thy love and Thy wisdom shall choose. And now I am Thine; take possession of my foolish heart. Begin to work in me to will and to do of Thy good pleasure. I trust Thee utterly, and I trust Thee now."

> *Jesus, Thy boundless love to me*
> *No thought can reach, no tongue declare;*
> *O knit my thankful heart to Thee,*
> *And reign without a rival there!*
> *Thine wholly, Thine alone, I'd live,*
> *Myself to Thee entirely give.*

O grant that nothing in my soul
　　May dwell, but Thy pure love alone;
O may Thy love possess me whole,
　　My joy, my treasure, and my crown!
All coldness from my heart remove;
May every act, work, thought, be love.

O Love, how gracious is Thy way!
　　All fear before Thy presence flies;
Care, anguish, sorrow, melt away,
　　Where'er Thy healing beams arise.
O Jesus, nothing may I see,
Nothing desire, or seek, but Thee.

—PAUL GERHARDT

April 11

**If any man be in Christ, he is a new crea-
ture: old things are passed away; behold, all
things are become new** (2 Cor. 5:17).

Before my conversion, I worked toward the Cross, but since
then I have worked from the Cross; then I worked to be saved,
now I work because I am saved. I remember the morning on which
I came out of my room after I had first trusted Christ. I thought
the old sun shone a good deal brighter than it ever had before—I
thought that it was just smiling upon me; and as I walked out
upon Boston Commons and heard the birds singing in the trees, I
thought they were all singing a song to me. Do you know, I fell
in love with the birds. I had never cared for them before. It seemed
to me that I was in love with all creation. I had not a bitter feeling
against any man, and I was ready to take all men to my heart. If a
man has not the love of God shed abroad in his heart, he has never
been regenerated. If you hear someone finding fault with everybody, you may doubt whether he has a genuine conversion; it
may be counterfeit. It has not the right ring, because the impulse
of a converted soul is to love and not to be complaining and finding fault.

—DWIGHT L. MOODY

Heaven above is softer blue,
Earth around is sweeter green!
Something lives in every hue
Christless eyes have never seen;
Birds with gladder songs o'erflow,
Flowers with deeper beauties shine,
Since I know, as now I know,
I am His and He is mine.

—WADE ROBINSON

April 12

When Jesus therefore had received the vinegar, he said, It is finished: and he bowed his head, and gave up the ghost (John 19:30).

It is now over 40 years since I heard a Plymouth Brethren minister preach from this verse in a revival meeting held in an old Presbyterian church. How graciously the Holy Spirit opened the eyes of that seeking teenage boy sitting in the back pew. That night I saw that not my goodness or works—nor my own righteousness—could ever pay the debt of sins.

The great sacrifice had been paid. The Savior's blood had been shed. God's mercy and salvation was free in His Son. That night as I received Jesus Christ as my personal Savior, trusting Him to save my soul, my deaf ears were opened, and my blind eyes were made to see His finished work.

The years have passed swiftly and the steps go a little slower. But lo, these 40 years, He has never failed me yet. I revisit the place of "my anniversary" each year. The old church has long been gone and a parking facility now stands on the sacred ground. But thanks be to God, the message of the Cross still is the same and He stands today, seeking and willing to save. The Savior is still "able to save to the uttermost" because He ever lives to make intercession for His own.

You ask me how I gave my heart to Christ?
O yes, I know!
There came a yearning in my soul for Him,
So long ago.

I found earth's fairest flowers would fade and die;
I wept for something that would satisfy;
And, in my grief, somehow, I seemed to dare
To lift my broken heart to Him in prayer.
O yes, I know!
    And I can tell you how;
    I know, I know He is my Saviour now.

You ask me when I gave my heart to Christ?
    Yes, I can tell!
The day, and just the hour, indeed,
    I now remember well.
It was when I was struggling all alone,
The light of His forgiving Spirit shone
Into my heart, all clouded o'er with sin,
That I unlocked the door and let Him in.
O yes, I know!
    And I can tell you when;
    I know, I know He is so dear since then.

You ask me where I gave my heart to Christ?
    Yes, I can say!
That sacred place can never fade from sight,
    As yesterday.
Perhaps, He thought it better I should not
Forget the place, that I should love the spot;
And until I behold Him face-to-face,
'Twill be to me, on earth, the dearest place.
O yes, I know!
    And I can tell you where;
    I know, I know He came and saved me there.

—W. H. O. and CHARLES H. GABRIEL

April 13

He answered, Fear not; for they that be
with us are more than they that be with them
(2 Kings 6:16).

The prophet Elisha was in a very difficult situation. It appears that he was vastly outnumbered. During the night the enemy came in with all their army on horses, ready for battle. When the day dawned, Elisha's servant surveyed the host that compassed the city, ready for battle—and he cried out in despair. But God's man replied, "They that be with us are more than they that be with them." Then Elisha prayed for the Lord to help his servant see the unseen. And it was so! The entire mountain was full of friendly warriors on horses—ready to rescue God's man with chariots of fire!

God's people have always had eyes for invisibles! Abraham believed God's promises and saw the Promised Land long before anyone else saw it. Joseph kept true to his convictions and saw his destiny as God's leader long before he sat on the throne. Of Moses it was said, "He endured as seeing him who is invisible" (Heb. 11:27).

Lift up your heads, O Christians! This is no time to tread a slow step with downcast eyes! These dismal circumstances about us are not the full story! God is very much alive—and active in our behalf. Victory is assured the faithful!

—FLETCHER SPRUCE

April 14

In the end of the sabbath, as it began to dawn toward the first day of the week, came Mary Magdalene and the other Mary to see the sepulchre (Matt. 28:1).

Luke wrote, "Very early in the morning." Mark proclaimed, "When the sabbath was past." And John said, "When it was yet dark . . . the first day of the week." The Resurrection message starts "at the dawning." It was the end of the old—the beginning of the new. The dispensation of law had closed. The veil in the Temple was torn apart, the tomb was empty, and the darkness was ending. God's dispensation of grace was beginning. Hope had come! Dawn came to a sinful world when Jesus Christ arose!

Mary Magdalene was the first to come. She came bringing spices and ointments to anoint His body. She came expecting to find Him in the grave. The greatest verse in the Gospel accounts of the Resurrection is found in Luke: "They found not the body of the Lord Jesus" (Luke 24:3). Every effort had been made by the high priests and Pilate to see that Jesus' body would be untouched. What consternation must have gripped their souls when the fact of the empty tomb was made known to them!

Here is one of the great proofs of Jesus' resurrection. In spite of their worries over His pronouncements, in spite of the tomb being sealed, in spite of Rome's finest guarding His grave, they could not find the body of the Lord Jesus. The grave was empty! Thank God for the message, "He is not here. . . . Come, see the place where the Lord lay" (Matt. 28:6).

Because they found *not* His body, our preaching is *not* vain; our faith is *not* vain; our witness is *not* false; our dead are *not* perished; our sins are *not* charged to us; our hope is *not* transient; and our joy is *not* empty! (1 Corinthians 15).

April 15

Then shall appear the sign of the Son of man in heaven . . . and they shall see the Son of man coming in the clouds of heaven with power and great glory (Matt. 24:30).

I like to ponder that word of Scripture:
  "Then shall the sign of the Son appear";
To meditate on the many symbols
  By which He speaks to His people here.

I like to wonder which sign is chosen
  His glorious coming at last to bring;
Will it be the sword of our Victor-Captain?
  The shining crown of the conquering King?

Will it be the Star in the darkness gleaming
  That led men's feet to His manger bed?
Or the rising Sun with its wings of healing
  Breaking bright through the clouds of dread?

Will it be the Dove in the heavens flying
  That heralds the Prince of Peace once more?
Or the Smiting Stone that shall grind to powder,
  And scatter the dust of the men of war?

Is it any of these? I muse and ponder
  And closer, closer the page I scan;
These are the words the scribe has written:
  It shall be "the sign of the Son of Man."

And what was the sign by His own rejected—
 The sign of failure and death and loss?
The sign still spurned by a world that scorns Him?
 The sign of the Cross—the Cross—the Cross!

Is this the sign that shall show in heaven,
 Rising in wrath where it rose in love?
Looming high in the skies of judgment,
 A world of terror and doom above?

The sign of shame and the sign of glory,
 Tenderest pity and love sublime,
Of a Lamb once slain, of a dying Savior,
 "Towering o'er the wrecks of time."

We do not know, but I muse and wonder;
 He has not told us, we may but guess;
But I like to think that the Cross is chosen,
 The sign of His love and righteousness.

—ANNIE JOHNSON FLINT

April 16

Every man according as he purposeth in his heart, so let him give (2 Cor. 9:7).

Blessed is the man who gives cheerfully and liberally from his heart and thus honors God. Some ask, "Why should I give— did I not earn it all myself?" God says no! You are just a steward of your possessions, not an owner.

"But why should I give? I will never get it back," some souls echo. But the Lord of glory says that you will, and His Word cannot be broken. "Give, and it shall be given unto you; good measure, pressed down, and shaken together, and running over" (Luke 6:38). Christ gave so much—dare you give so little?

A Christian young man entered the contracting business and made a vow to tithe his income. With industry and honesty his profits increased until he was giving hundreds of dollars a week to the Lord's work.

But he could see places where this money could be put to good financial use. New equipment could be bought and new investments made that would produce even greater revenue. So he met with his pastor and explained his vow and his problem. He asked, "Do you suppose the Lord would mind if I now reduced my gifts one-half. After all, this would still be a lot of money."

The minister was quiet for a few moments and then said, "I have never had such a problem presented to me before, but I believe I have the correct answer for you. Let's both of us get down on our knees, now, and ask God to shrink your business and then you won't owe Him so much."

> May we Thy bounties thus
>   As stewards true receive,
> And gladly, as Thou blessest us,
>   To Thee our first-fruits give.
>
> To comfort and to bless,
>   To find a balm for woe,
> To tend the lone and fatherless,
>   Is angels' work below.
>
> The captive to release,
>   To God the lost to bring,
> To teach the way of life and peace,
>   It is a Christ-like thing.
>
> —WILLIAM W. HOWE

"Ye know the grace of our Lord Jesus Christ, that, though he was rich, yet for your sakes he became poor, that ye through his poverty might be rich" (2 Cor. 8:9).

April 17

They spake against God; they said, Can God furnish a table in the wilderness? (Ps. 78:19).

Can God? Oh, fatal question! It shut Israel out of the Land of Promise, and it will do as much for us. Israel had seen the wonderful works of God, cleaving the sea, lighting the night, and giving water from rocks. Yet they questioned God's ability to give bread, and to spread a table in the wilderness. Surely it was a slur on His gracious providence to suppose that He had begun what He could not complete, and had done so much but could not do all.

But we are in danger of making the same mistake. Though behind us lay the gift of the Cross, the miracles of Resurrection and Ascension, the care exercised by God over our early years, the goodness and mercy of our after lives, we are disposed to say, "Can God?" Can God find me a position or provide food for my children? Can God keep me from yielding to that besetting sin? We look at the difficulties, the many who have succumbed, the surges that are rolling high, the poor demon-possessed child, and we say, "*If* Thou canst do anything, help us!"

Nay, nay, there is no *if* with God; there is no limit to His almightiness but thy unbelief. The words are wrongly placed. Never say again, "Can God?" but "God can." Never *if* thou canst; but *if* I can believe. Never, *if* Thou canst Thou wilt; but *if* Thou wilt Thou canst; and Thou wilt, since Thou hast made and redeemed me. And Thou canst not forsake the work of Thine own hands.

—F. B. Meyer

April 18

Whatever ye do, do all to the glory of God (1 Cor. 10:31).

There goes my church in work shoes! He works at the assembly line and lives the life of a saint where it's not the easiest thing to do. And he is a witness too.

There goes my church in a nurse's uniform. She endures hours of listening to problems and some criticism with a radiance that's hard to replace. Her kind words and Christlike spirit have often wedged open a way for her to tell of Jesus.

There goes my church in a business suit. Every customer receives some sort of prod towards God. And my church also goes in cowboy boots—under a ten-gallon hat. He's for real. And his cattle don't keep him from Christ. He has family prayers and pays his tithe and speaks when others are silent.

There goes my church with an armload of books. She not only teaches for money—she teaches for love—and her pupils have caught her praying. She reaches them for Christ.

And I could go on. There goes my church—all across the city and country. I am proud of them and to be a member and pastor of such a fine church. I hope they are proud of me.

—Fletcher Spruce

God bless the Church on the Avenue
  That hears the city's cry;
The Church that sows the Word of the Lord,
  Where the masses of men go by.
The Church that makes, midst the city's roar,
  A place for an altar of prayer;
With a heart for the rich, and a heart for the poor,
  And rejoices their burdens to bear.

The Church that's true to the call of Christ
  Who wept o'er a city's need;
And sent His disciples to labor for Him,
  Where the forces of evil breed.
The Church that gives, and the Church that lives,
  As seen by the Master's eye—
God bless the Church on the Avenue
  That answers the city's cry.

—RALPH WALKER

April 19

Who for the joy that was set before him endured the cross, despising the shame, and is set down at the right hand of the throne of God (Heb. 12:2).

The believer is the possessor of joy—the same kind of joy which the Lord Jesus had. "These things have I spoken unto you, that my joy might remain in you, and that your joy might be full" (John 15:11). It is possible for the saints of God to wear radiant faces and not be found with sullen and somber countenance.

The writer of the book of Hebrews said that because of joy, Christ was able to endure the Cross. What was this deep and wonderful joy? Dr. Bruce Dunn suggests that it was the joy of a completed task. Finishing an important work always brings satisfaction and joy. Of our Lord it is written, "Lo, I come (in the volume of the book it is written of me) to do thy will, O God" (Heb. 10:7). And one can hear the Father say, "This is my beloved Son, in whom I am well pleased" (Matt. 3:17). Christ had joy unspeakable and full of glory, for He had completed the work which His Father had given Him to do!

Then, too, there was the joy of His redeemed people. The

work was finished but He would not be going back to heaven empty-handed. The redeemed thief would accompany Him, followed by a host of others who discovered saving grace. The Lord Jesus had been given a great gift by His Father. "All mine are thine, and thine are mine; and I am glorified in them. . . . Father, I will that they also whom thou hast given me, be with me where I am; that they may behold my glory" (John 17:10, 24).

There was also the joy of His returning home. How this must have warmed the heart of the Son of God. "Lift up your heads, O ye gates; even lift them up, ye everlasting doors; and the King of glory shall come in" (Ps. 24:9). If the angels in heaven rejoice over one sinner who repents, how mightily rang the chords of the angelic hosts when He who left the "ivory palaces for a cross of woe" returned triumphant over sin and death and the grave! The joy of His homecoming! "Thou art worthy, O Lord, to receive glory, and honour and power" (Rev. 4:11).

And finally, there was the joy of His coming coronation. All things have been delivered to Him by His Father. "Wherefore God also hath highly exalted him, and given him a name which is above every name, that at the name of Jesus every knee should bow, of things in heaven, and things in earth, and things under the earth; and that every tongue should confess that Jesus Christ is Lord, to the glory of God the Father" (Phil. 2:9-11). The Coronation Day, when He shall reign as King of kings and Lord of lords, is coming!

When Paul admonishes us to "rejoice evermore," he is simply saying: "Be joyous evermore with His joy." Christ has bequeathed it to us. Receive it—claim it—and shine with His joy in a dark world!

April 20

*I thank God that I baptized none of you,
but Crispus and Gaius* (1 Cor. 1:14).

When my dear friend L. D. Boatman died, I found this story by an unknown author among his pulpit messages. A church was in need of a new minister so one of the elders prepared the following letter of application:

"Gentlemen: I understand that you are seeking a new minister and I would like to apply for the position. I have many qualifications. I have been blessed to preach with power and am both an evangelist and teacher. I also am a writer and some say that I am a good organizer. I have been a leader in most places where I have been.

"Some people hold certain things against me, however. I am more than 50 years of age. I have never preached in one place more than three years at a time. I have had to leave town because of my ministry and some disturbances have been associated with me. Three or four times I have been in jail, but only because I preached the gospel of redeeming love.

"My health is not too good and my vision is failing. My churches have been small and I have urged my fellow Christians to be filled with the Spirit and to live a holy life. I would expect to preach the message of the Cross in every sermon.

"I should tell you that I am not too good in keeping records and I have been known to forget whom I have baptized. However, if you can use me, I shall do my best to watch over you in love and to be faithful. I am accustomed to working to help in my support."

The elder read this at the pastoral seeking committee and asked if they were interested. All members replied that the man would never do for their church. The applicant's name was Paul.

"Christ sent me not to baptize, but to preach the gospel; not with wisdom of words, lest the cross of Christ should be made of none effect" (1 Cor. 1:17).

April 21

They . . . first gave themselves to the Lord
(2 Cor. 8:5).

Before these Macedonian Christians began any work for Christ, before they undertook the support of foreign missions, before they even began to preach or to sing they first gave themselves to the Lord. So many saints fail to do this. The reason that hearts are so cold, lives so barren of His grace, service to the Lord so fruitless, is because people have given Him everything but themselves!

These believers in Macedonia knew that dedication must be first and complete. If we long for peace and for increased faith, then all must be laid on the altar of commitment.

The Christian life is a failure apart from dedication. Love

must be the compelling motive in giving. Like the ancient slaves in Israel, who, rather than leave their master, had the mark of the "love slave" placed in their ears, so we too must bear the mark of belonging to Jesus. However, never forget that the giving of a gift is made only once. Some are so busy repeatedly coming to the altar "dedicating" that they have forgotten to make the gift, once and for all.

"They gave themselves." This dedication is not money, nor talent, nor singing, nor even service—it is a dedication of the whole heart and will. If you will give yourself, then He will have all of you. The Son of God deserves and wants your all—or none at all! He wants you!

April 22

*I have given unto them the words which thou gavest me; and they have received them.
. . . I have given them thy word* (John 17:8, 14).

How can we know if the words Jesus spoke were divinely authentic? What is the test? I believe it to be the Resurrection from the dead.

In the beginning of John's memoirs, he made a remarkable observation. In chapter two, when Christ drove out the money changers from the Temple, they challenged Him. "What sign showest thou unto us, seeing that thou doest these things?"

He answered, "Destroy this temple, and in three days I will raise it up" (John 2:18-19). They thought He spoke of the ancient temple, but John said He spoke of "the temple of his body" (John 2:21). "When he was risen from the dead, his disciples remembered that he had said this unto them, and they believed the scripture and the word which Jesus had said" (John 2:22).

If Christ had not risen from the dead, His words would not have been remembered. They would have proved to be the words of a mere man. He knew they were His Father's words, but His disciples needed proof. That proof was the Resurrection!

Jesus lifted up His voice one day in the Temple and cried, "If any man thirst, let him come unto me and drink. He that believeth on me, as the scripture hath said, out of his . . . [heart] shall flow rivers of living water" (John 7:37-38).

John said He spoke of the Holy Spirit which they should

receive after Jesus was glorified. Had Christ not risen from the dead and ascended to His Father, there would be no flowing for us of that living water. But thank God He was glorified and the rivers do flow!

The resurrection of Jesus from among the dead is a vital and wondrous truth. It is God's witness that Jesus is His Son and our High Priest. Paul writes that Jesus was "declared to be the Son of God with power . . . by the resurrection from the dead" (Rom. 1:4). He is God's Son; He is risen from the dead; He has been glorified; and you can depend on His words. They are God's words!

—Pastor U. S. Grant

April 23

They that were in the ship came and worshipped him, saying, Of a truth thou art the Son of God (Matt. 14:33).

There is something about a storm that is indeed frightening. In this storm the disciples were at sea and they were badly frightened. The winds were strong, the waves were high, and the boat tossed dangerously. Yet a miracle was occurring: Jesus appeared on the sea and walked toward them. He said, "Be of good cheer: it is I; be not afraid." These words should have produced calm and assurance in each heart. But bold Peter cried out, "Lord, if it be thou, bid me come unto thee on the water."

How we love the spectacular rather than simple faith. Should not His word be enough? Could not faith believe "It is I?"

All the disciples save Peter stayed in the boat. Staying in the boat can imply more faith in believing Christ than asking for the miracle of movement.

Arthur Fallon once wrote, "It took more faith to stay in the boat than to walk on the sea. There is a great miracle in just staying in the boat. For years I had been waiting for God to perform the 'spectacular' when living miracles were all around me. The fine laymen who were true to their Lord and kept on believing whether sick or well or poor or prosperous. They never doubted nor needed a spectacular happening. Before my very eyes they lived as faithful saints 'staying in the boat.' My daily prayer now is, 'Lord Jesus, help me to stay in the boat and let me accept Thy promises and keep my trust in Thee, not because of miracles but because Thou art the Christ.'"

This is the miracle above all miracles—simply believing what He has said. Let us stay in the boat!

Fierce was the wild billow,
Dark was the night,
Oars labored heavily,
Foam glimmered white;
Trembled the mariners,
Peril was nigh;
Then said the God of God,
"Peace! It is I."

Ridge of the mountain-wave,
Lower thy crest!
Wail of Euroclydon,
Be thou at rest!
Sorrow can never be,
Darkness must fly,
Where saith the Light of Light,
"Peace! It is I."

Jesus, Deliverer,
Come Thou to me;
Soothe Thou my voyaging
Over life's sea;
Thou, when the storm of death
Roars, sweeping by,
Whisper, O Truth of Truth,
"Peace! It is I."

—ANATOLIUS (8TH CENTURY)
tr. JOHN NEALE, 1818-1866

April 24

Simon Peter saith unto them, I go a fishing. They say unto him, We also go with thee. They went forth, and entered into a ship immediately; and that night they caught nothing (John 21:3).

Christians who drift away from the Lord soon find that their lives are empty and fruitless. Peter had denied the Savior three times. Forsaking his high calling as one of Jesus' disciples, he went back to his old occupation. As often happens, he dragged others down with him; for Thomas, Nathanael, and the sons of Zebedee followed his bad example. Contrary to their Lord's command, they had fished for fish instead of men, hence "they caught nothing."

What an embarassing situation! Seasoned fishermen working all night, and not a minnow to show for their efforts! With hopes of an immediate kingdom having been shattered, Peter suggested that they revert to their old life and occupation. Their empty nets served as an object lesson to teach them that they should not turn back after they had decided to follow Christ.

August Van Ryn wrote: "Why were the disciples unsuccessful that night? Did they lack ability or experience? No, they knew their job. Leadership? No, Peter had that quality. Had they put forth insufficient effort? No, they had toiled all night. But they lacked Christ. He had said, 'Without me ye can do nothing.' That is the lesson to be learned from this distressing incident."

—HENRY G. BOSCH
From *Our Daily Bread*, © 1974, Radio Bible Class.
Used by special permission.

April 25

We love him, because he first loved us. If a man say, I love God, and hateth his brother, he is a liar; for he that loveth not his brother whom he hath seen, how can he love God whom he hath not seen? And this commandment have we from him, That he who loveth God love his brother also (1 John 4:19-21).

"John was helped by loving hands to mount the rostrum, and to seat himself in a chair beside the pulpit. Fourscore and almost 10 years had put their ruinous marks upon his aged body. It seemed hardly possible that this old man was once the wholesome youth who leaned on Jesus' bosom. And this was to be his last sermon. Everyone realized it would be very short. So everyone sensed that John would say that which summed up the holy meditation and prayers of nearly 70 years. His sensitive right hand was lifted tremblingly, a mere shadow of the vigor he had possessed when his world was young. Now he's speaking; listen closely, for thou shalt hear the wisdom of God! And in this last sermon, he uttered but one sentence, 'Little children, love one another!'"

So runs the form of an ancient tradition as to John's last words. From that church service the Christians departed, their memories repeating a thousand times John's final public utterance, "Little children, love one another." And into that ancient world the infant Church flung itself, "moved empires off their hinges," with one instrument. The instrument of love!

"Behold, how they love one another."

—RICHARD ELLSWORTH DAY

April 26

Behold, the Lord stood upon a wall made by a plumbline, with a plumbline in his hand (Amos 7:7).

The plumb line was a cord composed of many fine strands ending with a cone-shaped brass weight at the bottom with the apex pointing down. It indicated quite accurately the bowing of walls and leaning of buildings. Amos said that the Lord was using His plumb line. Our God is quite concerned about "out of plumb" lives! We often pass over them and excuse sin on the basis of weakness of the flesh, but the plumb line of God does not. God has a standard and He accepts no excuses.

Amos said that men had built the wall and used their own plumb line. Undoubtedly the makers of the wall were quite satisfied with their work. Then the Lord measured and found it wanting. The wall did not come up to His standard.

Are you measuring your righteousness by your own plumb line? Beware of error. "All have sinned and come short of [His] glory" (Rom. 3:23). Men need more than a Teacher and an Example. They need a Savior!

> *In peace let me resign my breath*
> *And Thy salvation see.*
> *My sins deserved eternal death,*
> *But Jesus died for me.*

—DR. VALBY

April 27

I will lead them in paths that they have not known. I will make darkness light before them, and crooked things straight. These things will I do unto them, and not forsake them (Isa. 42:16).

"Being saved is not the end of the journey, but it is the end of our wandering" (William S. Stoddard).

He was better to me than all my hopes;
He was better than all my fears;
He made a bridge of my broken works,
And a rainbow of my tears.
The billows that guarded my sea-girt path,
But carried my Lord on their crest;
When I dwell on the days of my wilderness march
I can lean on His love for the rest.

He emptied my hands of my treasured store,
And His covenant love revealed,
There was not a wound in my aching heart,
But the balm of His breath hath healed.
Oh, tender and true was the chastening sore,
In wisdom, that taught and tried,
Till the soul that He sought was trusting in Him,
And nothing on earth beside.

He guided by paths that I could not see,
By ways that I have not known;
The crooked was straight, and the rough was plain
As I followed the Lord alone,
I praise Him still for the pleasant palms,
And the water-springs by the way,
For the glowing pillar of flame by night,
And the sheltering cloud by day.

Never a watch on the dreariest halt,
But some promise of love endears;
I read from the past, that my future shall be
Far better than all my fears.
Like the golden pot, of the wilderness bread,
Laid up with the blossoming rod,
All safe in the ark, with the law of the Lord,
Is the covenant care of my God.

—AUTHOR UNKNOWN

"For the Christian there is a silver lining in every cloud; a blue patch in the darkest sky; a turn in the longest lane; a mountain view which will compensate for the steepest ascent. Wait on the Lord. Wait on Him and keep His way" (F. B. Meyer).

April 28

His elder son was in the field; and as he came and drew nigh to the house, he heard music and dancing (Luke 15:25).

The prodigal son's brother was the prodigal who stayed at home. L. Wayne Sears said, "In the parable of the prodigal son, the younger wasted his substance with riotous living; the elder with selfish living." E. Russell Lynn wrote, "It was fortunate for the returning prodigal that he met his father first. Had he come upon his brother first, he might have turned and taken the road again."

The elder brother was guilty of the horrible sin of self-pity. It was manifested by anger and the nursing of a grievance. This can destroy all peace and joy in the heart. We may be full of orthodoxy, but we must never forget that the fruit of the Holy Spirit is love, joy, peace!

Pastor Larsen in a sermon said, "The elder brother had virtue, but it was outraged; he had vision, but it was restricted; he had values, but they were distorted."

The father gave the prodigal son a calf to celebrate his return. The elder brother asked for a goat to entertain his friends. With self-pity he was satisfied with small portions. All that the father had was his but he did not understand that he was living with his father—not serving a hard taskmaster.

The father had given the prodigal the family robe and the ring of sonship on his finger. He had given him shoes for his weary feet. Still the elder brother refuse to love him and spoke only of his past. "He who has devoured thy substance with harlots." This was probably true, but only he revealed it. He said, "Thy son." He had no love for him and couldn't bring himself to call him "brother."

The elder brother was self-centered. When the prodigal came home he used the word "I" only once. "I have sinned," he said. But listen to the elder brother. "Lo, these many years do *I* serve thee, neither transgressed *I* at any time thy commandment; and yet thou never gavest *me* a kid, that *I* might make merry with *my* friends" (Luke 15:29). Five times he used the pronouns *I, me, my*. The sin of self-centeredness.

Two brothers! Both guilty of self: self-gratification for the one, total selfishness for the other. Both needed repentance and both needed love. The father in Jesus' parable welcomed both of them to himself and both back into his home. Thus does God deal with us. Love and forgiveness are offered equally to prodigal sons and to prodigal brothers.

April 29

Grieve not the Holy Spirit of God, where-by ye are sealed unto the day of redemption (Eph. 4:30).

All that the believer has must come from Christ, but it comes solely through the channel of the Spirit of grace. Moreover, as all blessings thus flow to you through the Holy Spirit, so also no good thing can come out of you in holy thought, devout worship, or gracious act, apart from the sanctifying operation of the same Spirit. Even if the good seed be sown in you, yet it lies dormant except He worketh in you to will and to do of His own good pleasure.

Do you desire to speak for Jesus—how can you unless the Holy Spirit touches your tongue? Do you desire to pray? Alas! What dull work it is unless the Spirit maketh intercession for you! Do you desire to subdue sin? Would you be holy? Would you be like the Master? Do you desire to rise to superlative heights of spirituality? Are you wanting to be made like the angels of God, full of zeal and ardor for the Master's cause? You cannot without the Spirit—"without me ye can do nothing."

O branch of the vine, thou canst have no fruit without the sap! O child of God, thou hast no life within thee apart from the life which God gives thee through His Spirit! Then let us not grieve Him or provoke Him to anger by our sin. Let us not quench Him in one of His faintest motions in our soul; let us foster every suggestion and be ready to obey every prompting. If the Holy Spirit be indeed so mighty, let us attempt nothing without Him. Let us begin no project, and carry on no enterprise, and conclude no transaction, without imploring His blessing. May this be our prayer, "Open Thou my heart and my whole being to Thine incoming."

—CHARLES HADDON SPURGEON

April 30

I know the plans I have for you, says the Lord. They are plans for good and not for evil, to give you a future and a hope (Jer. 29:11, TLB).

How marvelous to know that God has a plan for each believer. This is His word of promise. He cares for His own.

His plan gives us a bright future. We do not rely on sorcerers or horoscopes, for our day is not determined by the stars. Our times are in His hands, the hands of Him who is "the bright and morning star." We cannot drift beyond His love and care.

When the path is unknown or the way is dark, rely on Him who has promised, "I know the plan I have for you." If sorrows or sufferings come, or storms arise, lift your head and sing, "He has a plan for me to give me hope." Trust with a joyful heart, for He will give you light in His time. Walk close to Him and wait to see His will made plain. He has "a plan for you for good."

> I know not where tomorrow's road
> May turn my pilgrim way,
> I may not taste its joy or care,
> Nor see beyond today;
> But this I know—my Father plans
> The path I cannot see;
> He knows each turn, each hill and dale,
> And He will walk with me.
>
> I know not if my way be bright,
> Or dark with storm and rain;
> I know not what it holds for me
> Of pleasure, or of pain:
> But this I know—my Savior's love
> Prepares my path each day,
> And held within His mighty hand
> I need not fear the way.
>
> I know not what the future holds,
> Nor what life's evening brings,
> But with the glad salute of faith
> I hail its opening wings;

For this I know—in God the Lord
Shall all my needs be met;
I'll trust tomorrow to His love
Who has not failed me yet.

—E. Margaret Clarkson

During World War II the King of England quoted these words to his people. They come from the pen of an unknown English author: "I said to a man who stood at the gate of the year, 'Give me a light that I may tread safely into the unknown.' And he replied, 'Go out into the darkness and put your hand into the hand of God. That shall be to you better than a light, and safer than a known way.'"

May 1

If I then, your Lord and Master, have washed your feet; ye also ought to wash one another's feet (John 13:14).

All was ready for the Last Supper, to the very water to wash the feet of the guests, according to custom. But there was no servant to do the work. Each one of the Twelve waits for the other: none thinks of humbling himself to do the work. All at once Jesus rises, lays aside His garments, girds himself with a towel, and begins to wash their feet. O wondrous spectacle on which angels gazed with adoring wonder! Christ chooses the servant's place for His own and He takes the soiled feet in His own holy hands and washes them.

In thus taking the form of a servant, Jesus proclaims the law of rank in the Church of Christ. The higher one wishes to stand in grace, the more it must be his joy to be servant to all. "Whoever will be chief among you, let him be your servant." "He that is greatest among you shall be your servant." The higher I rise in the consciousness of being like Christ, God's beloved Son, the deeper shall I stoop to serve all around me.

John writes, "Having loved His own which were in the world, he loved them to the end." Love never speaks of sacrifice. It was love that made Jesus a servant. It is love alone that will take the servant's place and work such blessedness to us that we shall persevere in it at all cost. We may perhaps, have to wash the feet

143

of some Judas who rewards us with ingratitude and betrayal. We shall probably meet many a Peter, who first, with "never my feet" refuses, and then is dissatisfied when we do not comply with his impatient "not only the feet, but also the head and the hands." Only love, a heavenly unquenchable love, gives the patience, the courage, and the wisdom for this great work the Lord has set before us in His holy example: "Wash ye one another's feet."

My Lord, I give myself to Thee. Thou everlasting Love, dwell in me, and my life shall be like Thine, and the language of my life to others as Thine, "I am in the midst of you as he that serveth."

—ANDREW MURRAY

May 2

The Lord Jesus, the same night in which he was betrayed, took bread; and when he had given thanks, he brake it, and said, Take, eat; this is my body, which is broken for you: this do in remembrance of me. After the same manner also he took the cup, when he had supped, saying, This cup is the new testament in my blood: this do, as often as ye drink it, in remembrance of me. For as often as ye eat this bread, and drink this cup, ye do shew the Lord's death till he come (1 Cor. 11:23-26).

The Savior instituted this Communion service so that we would have a constant, lasting, and visible reminder of His death. The broken bread was ever to remind us of His body, torn, broken, and bruised for us. The wine was to be ever a constant memorial of His blood shed at Calvary. He knew that the things which are seen would crowd out the things that are not seen. This communion, therefore, is a constant reminder of the Cross!

Our Lord also knew that there would be grievous divisions among His followers, and thus He gave the loaf as an emblem of the unity He so much desired among His people. The loaf is one loaf, representing the whole of the body of Christ, no matter by what name God's people are called. When we partake of that loaf by breaking and eating it, we confess that we are all His! We drink the cup as a testimony to our faith in the value of His atoning blood that cleanses us from all sin and that paid the complete penalty for all our guilt.

—WALTER L. WILSON

"Till He come!" oh, let the words
Linger on the trembling chords;
Let the little time between
In their golden light be seen:
Let us think how heaven and home
Lie beyond that "Till He come."

When the weary ones we love
Enter on their rest above,
Seems the earth so poor and vast,
All our life-joy overcast?
Hush, be every murmur dumb;
It is only "Till He come."

See, the feast of love is spread,
Drink the wine, and break the bread:
Sweet memorials—till the Lord
Calls us around His heavenly board;
Some from earth, from glory some,
Severed only "Till He come."

—EDWARD H. BICKERSTETH

May 3

The Spirit said unto Philip, Go near, and join thyself to this chariot (Acts 8:29).

Just before William Carey, the great missionary, left for India, his sister said to him, "Finding a lost soul in India is like looking for a needle in a haystack." Carey replied to her, "Yes, Sister, but the Holy Spirit knows where that needle is."

All of God's great soul winners have been Spirit-led men. Philip was such a man. He received a *call* and a *commission* from the Spirit of God, and he responded to the order "Go and tell." God's Spirit-filled men are to "go into all the world," but it could mean carrying the gospel to our next door neighbor as well as on "the road to Gaza."

Philip was sent and led to a man who was trying to find God. This is a part of the Holy Spirit's ministry in this day of grace, for the Savior said, "He shall testify of me."

But Philip not only had a *call* and a *commission*, he also had a *conviction*. He believed that the Ethiopian treasurer was lost without Christ. Do we really believe this? Do we really want to bring Christ to the needy of the world?

Philip also had *confidence*—yes, a *great confidence*. He believed that this rich politician could be transformed and redeemed by Jesus Christ. He "ran" to meet him. He was eager to climb up into the seeker's chariot and to present Christ to the Ethiopian. Philip proclaimed the Christ of Isaiah 53—the Man of Sorrows and the Man of Suffering. He showed him Jesus, who "was wounded for our transgressions, . . . [and] bruised for our iniquities"; but best of all, "with his stripes we are healed."

Gladly was Christ received. So we see also a *conversion*. The Ethiopian believed, and not only was his soul saved but transformation of his heart and life began. Luke wrote that the "man saw Philip no more; and he went on his way rejoicing." It is ever thus when Christ comes into the life. He brings not only salvation but a song on the lips and gladness in the heart!

May 4

Behold, there came a leper and worshipped him, saying, Lord, if thou wilt, thou canst make me clean. And Jesus put forth his hand, and touched him, saying, I will; be thou clean. And immediately his leprosy was cleansed (Matt. 8:2-3).

Although multitudes followed the Lord Jesus, as recorded in this scripture passage, only one came to worship him. He was a hopeless leper but he came believing. He believed that the Christ could heal and receive him. He said, "Lord, if thou wilt, thou canst make me clean." There was no doubt concerning Christ's ability. There need be no doubt concerning Christ's willingness!

Jesus touched him. No one else in all Israel would have done this—but Jesus did. In that touch the Master received him. Christ's promise is secure even to the vilest man—"Him that cometh to me I will in no wise cast out" (John 6:37).

Jesus touched him with his leprosy and said "be thou clean." Someone has said that "Christ is a far greater Saviour than any man ever dared to be a sinner." He can make the vilest pure! Have you by faith cried out to Him, "Lord, make me clean"? From leprosy to holiness when Jesus is passing by!

"Hearing the multitude pass by, he asked what it meant. And they told him, that Jesus . . . passeth by. And he cried, saying, Jesus . . . have mercy on me" (Luke 18:36-38).

> This is the season of hope and grace,
>   Jesus is passing by;
> This, for salvation the time and place,
>   Jesus is passing by.
>
> This is the moment to seek the Lord,
>   While He is passing by;
> This is the time to believe His Word,
>   While He is passing by.
>
> Trust in the Lord in this hour of need,
>   While He is passing by;
> And you will find Him a Friend indeed,
>   Jesus is passing by.
>
> —E. A. HOFFMAN

May 5

I call to remembrance my song in the night (Ps. 77:6).

It is said that the world's best supply of perfume comes from roses on the Balkan Mountains. The flowers from which the lovely fragrance is distilled must be gathered in the darkest part of the night. The laborers pick only in the very early hours of the morning. Tests have shown that during this gloomy interval the blossoms give their most precious scent. Much of the sweet aroma disappears in the light of day.

The children of the Heavenly King also find the sweetest communion and the most pleasant spiritual experiences in the dark shadows of adversity. To sing in the day with its sunshine and glad fellowship is not difficult, but to make melody in the lonely hours of anguish, sickness, and sorrow requires a song of grace which can be put into the soul only by the Chief Musician. Such a hymn of praise cannot be sung "by note," for the light is often too dim to read the score. No, the music of the Spirit must be rendered "by heart." As we think of the past blessings of God's consolations and His overruling love, we echo with joy the words of the Psalmist, "I call to remembrance my song in the night!" In the bright light of happy days and joyous prospects, we often hum little tunes not worth repeating; but in the murky hours of temptation and trial, the melody the Lord provides becomes a thrilling oratorio of blessing.

—Henry G. Bosch

From *Our Daily Bread*, © Radio Bible Class.
Used by special permission.

May 6

Wilt thou not revive us again: that thy people may rejoice in thee? (Ps. 85:6).

O Lord, revive thy work in the midst of the years (Hab. 3:2).

Saviour, visit Thy plantation,
    Grant us, Lord, a gracious rain!
All will come to desolation,
    Unless Thou return again.
Keep no longer at a distance,
    Shine upon us from on high,
Lest, for want of Thine assistance,
    Every plant should droop and die.

Surely once Thy garden flourished!
    Every part looked gay and green;
Then Thy Word our spirits nourished;
    Happy seasons we have seen!
But a drought has since succeeded,
    And a sad decline we see;
Lord, Thy help is greatly needed,
    Help can only come from Thee!

Where are those we counted leaders,
    Filled with zeal and love and truth—
Old professors, tall as cedars,
    Bright examples of our youth?

Some, in whom we once delighted,
    We shall meet no more below;
Some, alas! we fear are blighted,
    Scarce a single leaf they show.

Younger plants—the sight how pleasant!—
    Covered thick with blossoms stood;
But they cause us grief at present,
    Frosts have nipped them in the bud!
Dearest Saviour, hasten hither;
    Thou canst make them bloom again;
Oh, permit them not to wither,
    Let not all our hopes be vain!

Let our mutual love be fervent,
    Make us prevalent in prayers;
Let each one esteemed Thy servant
    Shun the world's bewitching snares.
Break the tempter's fatal power,
    Turn the stony hearts to flesh;
And begin, from this good hour,
    To revive Thy work afresh.

—JOHN NEWTON

May 7

Put affection into your love for the brotherhood; be forward to honour one another; never let your zeal flag; maintain the spiritual glow; serve the Lord (Rom. 12:10-11, Moffatt).

"Maintain the spiritual glow." These four words convey the solution to the problem of meeting the humanly impossible standards of living set forth in Romans 12, the "most demanding chapter in all of Paul's disturbing letters." The implication is that religious activities, church attendance, and program participation are not enough. Victorious Christian living centers in a state of the soul—an inner spiritual condition.

The word "glow" connotes fire; not a roaring flame but an energy that radiates light and heat; something that makes itself known to the possessor and the onlooker.

The suggestion is that the glow may be lost. It may be lost by disobedience or by neglect. But there are more subtle enemies. The disillusionments and frustrations of life, the wearying routines that have been called "the 'dailyness' of living," lead to questioning, cynicism, and bitterness.

But the spiritual glow can be maintained. God's imperatives are never impossible. The glow, however, is not self-sustaining. The inner devotional life must be fed and nourished. The result is apparent in countenance, attitude, and action, and is much more convincing to the skeptic than verbal testimony or logical argument.

This radiance reflecting His Presence is sustained only as we zealously guard it by constant communion with our Lord, by prayer and meditation, and by reading and growing in the Word. And the glow is retained by sharing. As it reflects into the lives of others it is intensified within ourselves.

There's a lot of darkness and despair in this old world. Illuminate it by the glow of God's presence shining out of your life each day!

—M. A. Lunn

May 8

Behold, there was a man named Zacchaeus, which was the chief among the publicans, and he was rich (Luke 19:2).

Our Lord found Nicodemus on a housetop; the woman of Samaria by a well; the man of Gadara in a cemetery; Matthew at a tax booth; the penitent thief on a cross, and Zacchaeus in a sycamore tree. The Master came to seek, to find, and to save the lost.

Zacchaeus "sought to see Jesus who He was; and could not for the [crowd]." The "crowd" has kept many a man from accepting Jesus, but not Zacchaeus! He climbed into a tree to see Jesus, and just a glimpse of Him began a change that affected his whole life. Jesus can change us, too. If we have not changed, but may be only religious, we have not met the Master!

"Zacchaeus stood, and said unto the Lord; Behold, Lord, the half of my goods I give to the poor; and if I have taken any thing from any man by false accusation, I restore him fourfold. And

Jesus said unto him, This day is salvation come to this house"
(Luke 19:8-9a).

Two brothers were in the coal business; one of them joined
the church. In a few weeks he began to talk to his brother concerning his salvation. After several attempts at conversation, the
brother finally said, "Look here John, it's all right for you to get
'religion,' but if I get it, who's going to weigh the coal?"

When Zacchaeus found His great salvation, both his life and
his works were changed. It is still that way. In Christ we become
"a new creation"—old things pass away and all things are new.

> I sought the Lord, and afterward I knew
>   He moved my soul to seek Him, seeking me;
> It was not I that found, O Savior true,
>   No, I was found of Thee.
>
> Thou didst reach forth Thy hand and mine enfold;
>   I walked and sank not on the storm-vexed sea—
> 'Twas not so much that I on Thee took hold,
>   As Thou, dear Lord, on me.
>
> I find, I walk, I love, but oh, the whole
>   Of love is but my answer, Lord, to Thee;
> For Thou wert long beforehand with my soul,
>   Always Thou lovedst me.
>
> —AUTHOR UNKNOWN

May 9

Finally, brethren (Phil. 4:8).

Paul thus comes to the end of the letter to his beloved church
at Philippi. How poignant his parting words! "Be careful for
nothing; but in every thing by prayer and . . . thanksgiving, let
your requests be made known unto God. . . . And the peace of
God which passeth all understanding, shall keep your hearts and
minds through Christ Jesus" (Phil. 4:6-7). And the promises to
them are also for us today!

"Finally, brethren." Paul thus lets his gracious and Spirit-
filled counsel give advice that can keep us from a psychiatrist's
couch! "Whatsoever things are true, whatsoever things are
honest, whatsoever things are just, whatsoever things are pure,

whatsoever things are lovely, whatsoever things are of good report; if there be any virtue, and if there be any praise, think on these things (Phil. 4:8). Fill your heart and mind, not on the sordid world, not on financial worries, not on earthly desires, not on envious greed, but on things worthy of praise.

What marvelous words for this dark and dangerous day in which we live! We have the peace of God, but best of all we have the God of peace guarding our hearts and minds. No wonder Paul can victoriously sing, "I can do all things through Christ." We too can sing this song if Christ is ours!

> O blessed Lord, whose hand has led me on
>   By paths no vulture's eye hath seen;
> I thank Thee for each upward step, though rough,
>   Though bare of brooks and pastures green;
> For Thou wast there, my All in All.
>
> Yes, Lord, I thank Thee too for tears that cleansed,
>   That purged mine eyes from dimming dross,
> When I had wept till I could weep no more,
>   And heaven seemed to me my cross
> Thou, Thou wast then my All in All.
>
> And if the vale of deathly gloom I tread,
>   With tears for drink, and grief for bread;
> I'll know that Thou hast planned it so for me,
>   That I have nothing now to dread,
> For Thou art still my All in All.
>
> And though the road ahead may still look steep,
>   And rough the path that leads me home,
> The perfect day for me has dawned, and soon
>   Where every tear is dried I'll come
> To be with Thee, My All in All.
>
> —CARL ARMERDING

The testimony of God's adequate man is in! The record stands for these Philippians who knew Paul so well. He has borne witness. Follow the little word "all." There was the "all" of circumstances to be borne, but Paul is adequate. God has given him poise. There is the "all" of needs to be met, but Paul is adequate—and God has given him plenty. He is enough—and more. The greatest of human hands has written the warmest of his letters. The love-task is finished. The day is done. The chain is still there upon the apostolic wrist. The soldier is still on guard. But never mind! Paul's spirit is free. His mind is clear. His heart is glowing. And in the morning, Epaphroditus will stride away to Philippi with his last letter!

—PAUL S. REES

May 10

I call to remembrance the unfeigned faith
that is in thee, which dwelt first in thy grand-
mother Lois, and thy mother Eunice (2 Tim.
1:5).

Paul called Timothy his dearly beloved son in the faith, but Timothy also had a godly mother who prayed for him and showed him the ways of righteousness. How marvelous to have a godly mother. Many a son who has wandered into the "far country" has returned back again because of his mother's prayers.

Thackeray wrote, "Mother is the name for God on the lips and in the hearts of little children." Henry Ward Beecher said, "The mother's heart is the child's schoolroom." And an old Spanish proverb reads, "An ounce of mother is worth a pound of the clergy."

> *I have worshipped in churches and chapels;*
> *I've prayed in the busy street;*
> *I have sought my God and have found Him*
> *Where the waves of His ocean beat;*
> *I have knelt in the silent forest*
> *In the shade of some ancient tree;*
> *But the dearest of all my altars*
> *Was raised at my mother's knee.*
>
> *I have listened to God in His temple;*
> *I've caught His voice in the crowd;*
> *I have heard Him speak when the breakers*
> *Were booming long and loud;*
> *Where the winds play soft in the treetops*
> *My Father has talked to me;*
> *But I never have heard Him clearer*
> *Than I did at my mother's knee.*
>
> *The things in my life that are worthy*
> *Were born in my mother's breast,*
> *And breathed into mine by the magic*
> *Of the love her life expressed.*
> *The years that have brought me to manhood*
> *Have taken her far from me;*
> *But memory keeps me from straying*
> *Too far from my mother's knee.*

God, make me the man of her vision
And purge me of selfishness!
God, keep me true to her standards;
And help me to live to bless!
God, hallow the holy impress
Of the days that used to be,
And keep me a pilgrim forever
To the shrine at my mother's knee!

—JOHN H. STYLES, JR.

"The babe who feeds upon his mother's bosom is always on her heart" (Henry Ward Beecher).

As Thou didst walk the roads of Galilee,
So, loving Saviour, walk with him for me.
For since the years have passed and he has grown,
I cannot follow, so now he walks alone.

Be Thou my feet that I have had to stay,
For Thou canst comrade him along the way;
Be Thou my voice when sinful things allure,
Plead with him to choose things that endure.

Be Thou my hand that once held his in mine,
Be all things else that mothers must resign.
When he was little, I could walk and guide,
But now I pray that Thou be at his side.

And as Thy loving mother folded Thee,
So, precious Saviour, hold my son for me.

—AUTHOR UNKNOWN

May 11

To me to live is Christ, and to die is gain. . . . For I am in a strait betwixt two, having a desire to depart, and to be with Christ; which is far better (Phil. 1:21-23).

And should I be afraid of Death?
The pall of darkness and abating breath?
More surely would I fear to stand
Upon the shores of my fair native land.

Or tremble at His voice, deep, tender, mild,
Who loved me when I was a little child.
I take thy hand, O Death, within my own,
Thou canst but lead me to my Father's throne!

—Catherine Baird

Gaze not through moistened eyes at flowered coffin and lifelessness that herein lies. At peace? At rest? *No!* . . . a thousand no's. . . . For a spirit, long captive of mortality, has in victory at long last shaken earthly bounds of pain and sorrow and heartache. And now in immortal robes walks in heavenly places worshipping the Christ who conquered death. Eternal rest? Eternal peace? *No!* Eternal life! Eternal glory! For the sepulchre before you is empty; Only the mortal wrappings of a spirit remain. Gaze not with saddened heart, and let your tears be tears of joy. He is *free!*

—Gordon L. Hanna

"Earth recedes; Heaven opens before me. It is beautiful. It is like a trance. If this is death, it is sweet. There is no valley here. God is calling me, and I must go" (Dwight L. Moody's dying words).

His love is sufficient—yea boundless and free;
As high as the mountains, as deep as the sea.
Ah, there I will rest till the darkness is o'er,
And wake in His likeness to dwell evermore.

—Avis Burgeson

May 12

Sirs, be of good cheer; for I believe God, that it shall be even as it was told me (Acts 27: 25).

"I believe God." A noble declaration! The storm was still fearful; the ship was floundering, but Paul's trust was in the word of the living God.

Dr. Vance Havner once wrote, "Throw your doubts to the winds, stand on your feelings, laugh at your circumstances, though you sometimes feel like a fool doing it. The devil will scare you out of it if he can, but although, as with Paul, the storm may rage and all hope seem out of the question, let the world know that you have had word from higher quarters, and shout in the teeth of the gale, 'I believe God.' There may be hardships ahead. We may be cast 'upon a certain island.' The ship may be wrecked. But fear not. We shall not be wrecked."

"Be strong and of good courage; be not afraid, neither be thou dismayed: for the Lord thy God is with thee withersoever thou goest" (Josh. 1:9).

The writer to the Hebrews quotes from Deut. 31:6 and says "I will never leave thee, nor forsake thee" (Heb. 13:5). A certain professor sought to add joy to the heart of a humble saint by telling her that this could be literally translated, "I'll never, no never, no never, forsake thee." The dear old lady replied to him, "Well, the Lord may have to say it three times for you to understand it, but once is enough for me."

> Though the storm-clouds dark may low'r and threaten,
>   And no friendly light I see;
> Behind the clouds the sun is shining
>   And will soon break through on me.
>
> The storms of life may beat around me,
>   And the breakers dash and foam;
> But my Pilot's at the wheel beside me,
>   I shall safely reach my home.
>
> His eye is true, though lightning's flashing,
>   And a faithful watch He'll keep;
> His ear's not deaf from thunders crashing,
>   And He'll slumber not nor sleep.
>
> So I'll sail my barque o'er life's broad ocean,
>   And will trust my Pilot true;
> 'Mid quiet sea or wild commotion
>   He will keep the port in view.
>
> When I reach that calm and glorious haven,
>   With life's stormy voyage o'er;
> I'll sing around His throne in heaven,
>   And will praise Him evermore.
>
> —Flora B. Tupper

"Paul stood forth . . . and said . . . be of good cheer . . . fear not . . . I believe God . . . and it came to pass that they escaped all safe to the land" (Acts 27).

May 13

Let us consider one another to provoke unto love and to good works: not forsaking the assembling of ourselves together, as the manner of some is, but exhorting one another: and so much the more, as ye see the day approaching (Heb. 10:24-25).

When asked if a prominent community leader was a member of his church, a minister replied, "No, John doesn't belong to my church although his name is on the roll." "What is the difference" inquired the friend, "in having one's name on the roll and belonging?" "Well, it's like this," the pastor explained, "John's time does not belong to the church, nor his affections, nor his energies, nor his thoughts. And the ministries of the church do not really belong to John."

It makes a great deal of difference if one loves God's house and God's people. This is not to say that we should not have friends in the world, for there are some very find people out there. We should seek their friendship and attempt to influence them for Christ. But we must realize the necessity of fellowship with other believers in His church.

David loved God's house so much that when he was compelled to be away from it by unavoidable circumstances, he begrudged the sparrow that nested in its eaves. He said, "My soul longeth . . . for the courts of the Lord . . . the sparrow hath found a house . . . the swallow a nest where she may lay her young, even thine altars . . . blessed are they that dwell in thy house" (Ps. 84: 2-4). Treasure the joy of worshipping in His house. Do not leave your first love. Really belong and make Him the desire of your heart.

—Pastor U. S. Grant

"Christ loved the church and gave himself up for her to make her holy, cleansing her by the washing with water through the word, and to present her to himself as a radiant church, without stain or wrinkle or any other blemish, but holy and blameless" (Eph. 5:25-27, NIV).

May 14

Enoch walked with God: and he was not;
for God took him (Gen. 5:24).

He walked with God! This speaks of companionship for the journey and divine direction for the steps. Through the valleys and across the hills—in pleasant places in bright sunshine, and o'er perilous paths facing dark and gathering storms—Enoch walked with God. "I will fear no evil." "For all things work together for good to them that love God, and are the called according to his purpose" (Rom. 8:28). Why should my soul be fearful since I have full assurance that "neither death, nor life, nor angels, nor principalities, nor the present, nor the future, nor evil forces above or beneath, nor anything else in all creation, will be able to separate us from the love of God as shown in Christ Jesus our Lord" (Rom. 8:38-39, Williams).

He "walked with God!" Could grander words be written?
　Not much of what he thought or said is told;
Not where or what he wrought is even mentioned;
　He "walked with God"—brief words of fadeless gold!

How many souls were succoured on his journey—
　Helped by his words, or prayers, we may not know;
Still, this we read,—words of excelling grandeur—
　He "walked with God," while yet he walked below.

And, after years, long years, of such blest walking,
　One day he walked, then was not, God said "Come!
Come from the scene of weary, sin-stained sadness!
　Come to fuller fellowship of Home!"

Such be the tribute of thy pilgrim journey
　When life's last mile thy feet have bravely trod—
When thou hast gone to all that there awaits thee,
　This simple epitaph—He walked with God!

—J. Danson Smith

May 15

As he entered into a certain village, there met him ten men that were lepers, which stood afar off: and they lifted up their voices, and said, Jesus, Master, have mercy on us. And when he saw them, he said unto them, Go shew yourselves unto the priests. And it came to pass, that, as they went, they were cleansed. And one of them, when he saw that he was healed, turned back, and with a loud voice glorified God, and fell down on his face at his feet, giving him thanks: and he was a Samaritan. And Jesus answering said, Were there not ten cleansed? but where are the nine? (Luke 17:12-17).

These 10 lepers, outcasts from their families and friends, had a great need. Thus they cried to Jesus for mercy—their only plea being their suffering against His sufficiency; their need against His grace; their hopelessness against His great mercy.

Many great acts of faith are recorded in Luke's Gospel. There is the miraculous draught of fishes by Simon Peter; the healing of the palsied man let down through the roof; the raising of Jarius's daughter; the redemption of the penitent thief—but this is perhaps the greatest act of faith in Luke's account.

Under the law, the leper was unclean and an outcast. If he were healed, then he could show himself to the priest who would then command him to be cleansed and restored within the city. These lepers, acting on Jesus' word, turned *with* their leprosy toward the city, and *as they went* they were healed! They had faith in His word!

Joyfully nine go on. But one sees his skin become like that of a little child, so he turns back to fall at the Master's feet in worship and praise and thanksgiving. Tenderly the Lord responded by saying, "Arise go thy way: thy faith hath made thee whole. . . . But where are the nine?"

The world needs witnesses! Today, many are neglecting Him. Today, many are rejecting Him. Will you be a witness?

I meant to go back, but well you may guess
I was filled with amazement I cannot express.

To think that after those horrible years,
That passion of loathing and passion of fears,
My sores unendurable, eaten, defiled,
My flesh was as smooth as the flesh of a child!
I was drunken with joy, I was crazy with glee,
I scarcely could walk and I scarcely could see
For the dazzle of sunshine where all had been black;
But I meant to go back, oh, I meant to go back!

I had thought to return, when my people came out.
There were tears of rejoicing, and laughter, and shout;
They embraced me—for years I had not known a kiss;
Ah, the pressure of lips is an exquisite bliss!
They crowded around me, they filled the whole place,
They looked at my feet and my hands and my face;
My children were there, my glorious wife,
And all the forgotten allurements of life.
My cup was so full I seemed nothing to lack;
But I meant to go back, oh, I meant to go back!

I had started—yes, Luke, I had started to find
The Healer so mighty, so tender and kind;
But work pressed upon me: my business, you know,
For all of those years I was forced to let go;
I had tools to collect, I had orders to get,
I found my poor family all burdened with debt,
My time was all taken with labor and care,
The days went more swiftly than I was aware
With the practical problems I had to attack;
But I meant to go back, oh, I meant to go back!

I never supposed He would wait my return,
Just one of the ten, and would linger, and yearn
As you tell me He did; why, Luke, had I thought,
There is no one on earth I would sooner have sought.
I'd have shown Him my body, all perfect and strong;
I'd have thanked Him and praised Him before the great throng;
I'd have followed Him gladly forever and aye
Had I thought that He minded my staying away.
He so great—I so little and paltry! Alack—
Had I only gone back! Had I only gone back!

—Amos R. Wells

160

May 16

It came to pass in the third year, that Jehoshaphat the king of Judah came down to the king of Israel. And the king of Israel said ... Wilt thou go with me to battle to Ramoth-gilead? And Jehoshaphat said to the king of Israel, Inquire, I pray thee, at the word of the Lord today (1 Kings 22:2-5).

King Jehoshaphat made a covenant with Ahab to go to war and then he became concerned. His fears were valid. He knew of Israel's idolatry and infidelity to Jehovah, and the wickedness of her rulers. He knew that the prophets of Baal were the real advisers to the throne. And so he belatedly asked, "Is there any word from the Lord today?" The answer was not long in coming. The lone prophet of God foretold death and disaster at the end of the day's battle.

Jehoshaphat was a little late in asking for God's guidance. Are we like him? Do we ask for the Lord's blessings upon decisions that we have already made? Like Jehoshaphat, are our associations wrong? Paul warned the Christians at Corinth that business associations and marriages should be within the family of God: "Be ye not unequally yoked together with unbelievers: for what fellowship hath righteousness with unrighteousness? and what communion hath light with darkness" (2 Cor. 6:14).

Many of our tears would never fall if we walked in His will and sought His ways. Spending time in prayer seeking God's guidance avoids the restless nights of insomnia. We need to wait upon the Lord. He has a word for us today!

"It may seem an easy thing to wait on the Lord, but it is one of the postures a Christian soldier learns not without years of teaching. Marching is much easier than waiting. There are hours of perplexity and you must learn to simply wait. Wait in prayer. Wait in faith. Wait in patience. Say, 'Lord, not my will, but Thine. I know not what to do; I am brought to extremities, but I will wait until Thou shall cleave the flood, or drive back my foes. I will wait, if Thou keep me many a day, for my heart is fixed upon Thee alone. My spirit waiteth for Thee in the full conviction that Thou wilt yet be my joy and my salvation, my refuge and my strong tower'" (Charles Haddon Spurgeon).

"Wait on the Lord: be of good courage, and he shall strengthen thine heart" (Ps. 27:14).

161

May 17

Precious in the sight of the Lord is the death of his saints (Ps. 116:15).

This is one of the sweetest verses in all of David's psalms. He writes of the death of a child of God and calls it "precious" in God's sight. How can death be called "precious"?

Perhaps it is because God's saints leave a sin-cursed and sorrow-filled earth for the joyous courts of heaven. No more shall they live in the scenes of tears and sadness for "joy comes in the morning," and all tears shall "he wipe away from their eyes."

This verse also reminds us that the believer has been bought with an expensive payment by God the Father—the blood of His own dear Son. When something is bought, one desires to take it home. Paul emphasizes this in Eph. 1:14 when he wrote that the Holy Spirit has been given to us as "the earnest of our inheritance until the redemption of the purchased possession." He is the Father's guarantee that we have been bought and that He will complete the transaction of what He has paid for!

The death of a saint also means that the one who has walked with Him by faith may now see Him face-to-face. The believer's death is therefore an answer to Jesus' prayer, "Father, I will that they also, whom thou hast given me, be with me where I am; that they may behold my glory, which thou hast given me: for thou lovedst me before the foundation of the world" (John 17:24).

And then, when the Christian dies, his death is declared "precious" because the Lord has proven once again that He is able to save, and to satisfy and to sustain on the pilgrim journey of life all those who trust in Him. We are wonderfully secure!

I'm nearing the end of my journey;
The lengthening shadows creep
Silently over the meadows,
And across the path at my feet;
But I look away to the hilltops,
Aglow in the setting sun,
And think of the hills of glory
And the day that is never done.

The gentle breeze grows cooler
As eve draws on apace;
It lifts the thin and faded hair
Away from my heated face;

It cools my brow, and soothes me,
  With its fragrant, balmy breath;
And my soul in song mounts upward
  On wings of living faith.

I have a loved One's promise,
  That somewhere on the way
He will meet me as I journey,
  But He came not through the day;
And now that the hush of evening
  Is falling on vale and hill,
I am longing for His greeting,
  And trusting, watching still.

Thus I wait my dear Lord's coming;
  I list for the sound of His feet
Amid the lengthening shadows,
  So peaceful, cool, and sweet;
And I know He will not tarry,
  For morning and noon are past,
But here in the quiet evening
  I'll hail my Lord at last.

—ANNA M. HICKS

May 18

Thou hast not lied unto men, but unto God (Acts 5:4).

Ananias left tragic footprints upon the sands of time. He desired the preeminence in the Early Church. He gave to gain the praise of men. Many have followed in his train.

The great sin of Ananias was not in holding back part of his gift, but in lying! By his act he said, "Here is my all," but his gift was not completely on the altar. God does not take lying lightly!

Let us beware of what we say and sing!

We sing, "Onward Christian Soldiers" and never enter His army.

We sing, "Sweet Hour of Prayer" and then seldom pray.

We sing, "O for a Thousand Tongues to Sing" and keep silent with the one we have.

163

We sing, "Blest Be the Tie That Binds" but express little loyalty to Christ or His Church.

We sing, "I Love to Tell the Story" and never mention the gospel to our neighbors.

We sing, "Cast Thy Burden upon the Lord" and then "an ulcer is the badge of our faith."

The Ananias Club has many members. You can become a charter guest by singing, "I'll Go Where You Want Me to Go, Dear Lord" and then stay at home! Beware of lying to God!

May 19

Lead me, O Lord, in thy righteousness . . .
make thy way straight before my face (Ps. 5:8).

David prayed to know the will of God. He asked to be led by the Lord and that his way might be straight. His will is delightful and if the Christian will live in His expressed will he will walk in His way. This leads to a transformed life in Christ—a life lived in the Spirit.

Dr. F. B. Meyer once wrote of an experience he had in the home of Dr. Wilberforce. An elderly minister attending this meeting arose and spoke not on giving things up but appropriating the very life and nature of our Lord. He stated that he had had great difficulty with his temper. One day he was trying to interest some children who were anxious to break away and play outside. He was aggravated but he saw the Lord Jesus there standing among the children. He said, "Lord Jesus, Thy patience, please," and the Savior dropped a large lump of patience into his heart, so that he could have borne with twice as many boisterous boys and girls. "And so the Lord is always with me when the tempter comes. If it is a temptation to impurity, I cry, 'Thy purity, Lord.' If it is a temptation to pride, I say 'Dear Lord, give me Thy humility,' and to whatever sin I am tempted, I turn to Christ and receive the opposite grace from that to which the evil one is tempting me."

"Make Thy way straight before my face." If we ask Him, He will! The victorious life is the life lived in Christ.

—F. B. Meyer

May 20

His name shall be called Wonderful (Isa. 9:6).

In the realms of astronomy, He is the Sun of Righteousness and the Bright and morning Star.

In the realm of geology, He is the Rock of Ages.

In the realm of botany, He is the Rose of Sharon and the Lily of the Valley.

In the realm of zoology, He is the Lion of Judah and the Lamb of God.

In the realm of medicine, He is the Great Physician.

In the realm of government, He is the King of Kings and the Lord of Lords.

He is the Everlasting Father, the Prince of Peace, the Mighty God.
At His birth, the angel announced, "Thou shalt call his name JESUS: for he shall save his people from their sins." That name, Jesus, is still the hope of earth and the joy of heaven. Jesus the Savior! What a wonderful, wonderful name.

"Jesus Christ, the same yesterday, and today, and for ever."

> Today on the road I met Him;
> The very same Jesus who trod
> The old, old lanes and highways—
> Jesus, the Son of God!
>
> I was troubled and heartsick and weary
> With a load too heavy to bear;
> I cried aloud in my weakness,
> And suddenly He was there.
>
> His gentle hand on my shoulder
> Was lifting the burden from me;
> And He dried my tears, and I knew Him
> It was Jesus of Galilee.
>
> No different at all from the Master
> On the Jericho road that day;
> No different at all from the Saviour
> Along the Calvary way.

And I am so glad that I met Him!
I knelt and I called out His name,
And I am so grateful I found Him
Unchanged and forever the same!

May 21

**Unto him that loved us, and washed us
from our sins in his own blood** (Rev. 1:5).

*When the heavenly hosts shall gather and the heavenly courts
    shall ring,*
*With the rapture of the ransomed, and the New Song they shall
    sing,*
Though they come from every nation, every kindred, every race,
*None can ever learn that music till he knows God's pardoning
    grace.*
All those vast eternities to come will never be too long
To tell the endless story and to sing the endless song;
"Unto Him who loved us and who loosed us from our sin"—
We shall finish it in heaven, but 'tis here the words begin.
"Unto Him who loved us"—we shall sing it o'er and o'er,
"Unto Him who loved us"—we shall love it more and more;
"Unto Him who loved us"—song of songs most sweet and dear;
But, if we would know it yonder, we must learn the music here.

*Here, where there was none to save us, none to help us, none to
    care;*
Here, where Jesus came to seek us, lost in darkness and despair;
*Here, where on that cross of anguish He redeemed us from our
    sins;*
Here, where first we know the Saviour, it is here the song begins.
Here, amid the toils and trials of this fleeting earthly life;
Here, amid the din and turmoil of this troubled earthly strife;
Here, in suffering and sorrow; here, in weariness and wrong;
We shall finish it in heaven, but 'tis here we start the song.
"Unto Him who loves us"—we must sing it every day;
"Unto Him who loves us"—who is Light and Guide and Way;
"Unto Him who loves us"—and who holds us very dear;
If we'd know it over yonder, we must learn the music here.

There will be no silent voices in that ever-blessed throng;
There will be no faltering accents in that hallelujah song;
Like the sound of many waters shall the mighty paean be
When the Lord's redeemed shall praise Him for the grace that set
   them free.
But 'tis here the theme is written; it is here we tune our tongue;
It is here the first glad notes of joy with stammering lips are
   sung.
It is here the first faint echoes of that chorus reach our ear;
We shall finish it in heaven, but our hearts begin it here.
"Unto Him who loved us"—to the Lamb for sinners slain;
"Unto Him who loved us"—evermore the joyful strain;
"Unto Him who loved us"—full and strong and sweet and clear;
But, if we would know it yonder, we must learn to sing it here.

—ANNIE JOHNSON FLINT

"They sung a new song, saying, Thou art worthy to take the book, and to open the seals thereof: for thou wast slain, and hast redeemed us to God by thy blood out of every kindred, and tongue, and people, and nation" (Rev. 5:9).

May 22

He that saith he abideth in him ought himself also so to walk, even as he walked (1 John 2:6).

Abiding in Christ and walking like Christ: These are the two blessings of the new life which are here set before us in their essential unity. The fruit of a life in Christ is a life like Christ.

To the first of these expressions, abiding in Christ, we are no strangers. The wondrous parable of the Vine and the branches, with the accompanying command, "Abide in me, and I in you," has often been to us a source of rich instruction and comfort. And though we feel as if we had but very imperfectly learned the lesson of abiding in Him, yet we have tasted something of the joy that comes when the soul can say: *Lord, Thou knowest all things. Thou knowest that I do abide in Thee.* And He knows, too, how often the fervent prayer still arises: *Blessed Lord, do grant me the complete unbroken abiding.*

The second expression, walking like Christ, is not less significant than the first. It is the promise of the wonderful power which the abiding in Him will exert. The two are inseparably connected. The abiding in Him always precedes the walking like Him. When the Saviour said, "If ye keep my commandments, ye shall abide in my love," He meant just this: the surrender in walk like Me is the path to the full abiding in Me. Many will discover that just here is the secret of his failure in abiding in Christ; he did not seek it with the view of walking like Christ! He that seeks to abide in Christ, must walk as He walked, and he that seeks to walk like Christ must abide in Him.

With some there is the earnest desire and effort to follow Christ's example, without any sense of the impossibility of doing so, except by deep, real abiding in Him. They fail because they seek to obey the high command to live *like* Christ, without the only power that can do so—the living *in* Christ. To walk like Christ one must abide in Him; he that abides in Him has the power to walk like Him. Therefore, abide in Him! Abiding in Him is to consent with our whole soul to His being our life, to reckon upon Him to inspire us in all that goes to make up life, and then to give up everything most absolutely for Him to rule and work in us.

—Andrew Murray
in *Like Christ*

May 23

Unto the praise of his glory (Eph. 1:14).

Paul divides the first chapter of Ephesians, after his introductory remarks, into three parts: (1) the Work of the Father; (2) the Work of the Son, and (3) the Work of the Holy Spirit. Then he adds the words "to the praise of his glory."

Here is the Work of the Father. He has blessed us with all spiritual blessings in heavenly places. God's people are not poor people. We are rich in Christ. He has chosen us in His Son before the very foundations of the world. He has predestinated us unto the adoption of children by Jesus Christ to himself, and He has made us accepted in His Beloved.

Paul further adds, "He has abounded toward us in all wisdom and prudence." The greek word translated *abounded* means to "draw some bigger circles." God drew a big circle and took us in. And finally, the Father's work was to make known to us the mystery of His will.

What is that mystery? Paul writes that the mystery (something which has been hidden prior) is "that in the dispensation of the fullness of times he might gather together in one all things in Christ, both which are in heaven and which are on earth, even in him" (Eph. 1:10).

The Father loves to glorify and honor His Son! "What think ye of Christ?" (Matt. 22:42) is the doctrine that separates false cults from the Father's work. "Wherefore God also hath highly exalted him, and given him a name which is above every name: that at the name of Jesus every knee should bow, of things in heaven, and things in earth, and things under the earth; and that every tongue should confess that Jesus Christ is Lord, to the glory of God the Father" (Phil. 2:9-11).

This is the mighty Work of the Father. No wonder that Paul adds the words, "To the praise of the glory of his grace."

May 24

Blessed be God, even the Father of our Lord Jesus Christ, the Father of mercies, and the God of all comfort; who comforteth us in all our tribulation, that we may be able to comfort them which are in any trouble, by the comfort wherewith we ourselves are comforted of God (2 Cor. 1:3-4).

We are to be comforters. But to be such we must first pass through tribulations and trials and partake of His care and comfort. If we have walked through the valley, we shall then be able to show the "God of all comfort" to others who are sorrowing. When trials and tribulations abound and when sorrows and sickness enter the sphere of our lives, let us rejoice and learn of Him that we may be able to say to others, "We are troubled . . . yet not distressed; we are perplexed, but not in despair; [we are] persecuted, but not forsaken; [and we are] cast down, but not destroyed" (2 Cor. 4:8).

> *I shall know by the gleam and glitter*
> *Of the golden chain you wear,*
> *By your heart's calm strength in loving,*
> *Of the fire you have had to bear.*

Beat on, true heart, forever;
Shine bright, strong golden chain;
And bless the cleansing fire
And the furnace of living pain!

—ADELAIDE PROCTOR

"George Mueller once said, 'The only way to learn strong faith is to endure trial.' Learn faith by standing firm amid severe testings. The time to trust is when all else fails. If you are passing through great afflictions, let go. He will teach you in these hours the mightiest hold upon His throne you can ever know. If you are afraid, just look up and say, 'What time I am afraid I will trust in thee.' You will yet thank God for the school of sorrow which was to you the school of faith" (A. B. Simpson).

For I learn as the years roll onward
And leave the past behind,
That much I have counted sorrow
But proves that our God is kind;
That many a flower I longed for
Had a hidden thorn of pain,
And many a rugged bypath
Led to fields of golden grain.

The clouds but cover the sunshine,
They cannot banish the sun,
And the earth looks out the brighter,
When the wearisome rain is done.
We must stand in the deepest shadow
To see the clearest light,
And often from wrong's own darkness
Comes the very strength of right.

The sweetest rest is at evening
After the wearisome day,
When the heavy burden of labor
Is borne from our hearts away.
And those who have never known sorrow
Cannot find the infinite peace
That falls on the troubled spirit,
When it finds a sweet release.

We must live through the dreary winter
To value the bright, warm spring;
The woods must be cold and silent
Before the robins sing;

The flowers must be buried in darkness
Before they can bud and bloom,
And the purest and warmest sunshine
Comes after the storm and gloom.

So the heart from the hardest trial
Gains the purest joy of all,
And the lips that have tasted sadness
The sweetest songs that fall.
Then as joy comes after sorrow,
And love's the reward of pain,
So after earth is heaven,
And out of loss is gain.

—AUTHOR UNKNOWN

May 25

**He that dwelleth in the secret place of the
most High shall abide under the shadow of the
Almighty (Ps. 91:1).**

The 90th psalm closes with the words, "Let the beauty of the
Lord our God be upon us." The opening verse of the 91st psalm
gives the secret of how God imparts that beauty into the life of
each believer. The verse speaks of a permanent abode. "He that
dwelleth." His beauty is imparted to the surrendered heart only
when it abides in Him. It does not come by merely visiting in the
secret place occasionally.

The Psalmist's words also speak of a place of private association—"the secret place." It is the *secret* place because so few of
God's people dwell there. This is sad, for many lives are barren of
the Spirit's fruit because they lack a personal affiliation with Him.
He longs for complete surrender!

Not only does this verse tell of a permanent abode and a
private association, but it infers a personal affiliation—"In the
secret place of the most High." What a lofty union—abiding in
Him! And those who "abide under the shadow of the Almighty"
are given a promised assurance! If we dwell and abide in Him, He
will deliver us from the snares of life and from the awful pesti-
lence. "He shall cover thee with his feathers, and under his wings
shalt thou trust." Those who thus abide shall not be afraid or

171

terrified, no evil shall befall them, and His love is eternally set upon them.

Are you living and abiding in His secret place?

In the secret of His presence how my soul delights to hide!
Oh, how precious are the lessons which I learn at Jesus' side!
Earthly cares can never vex me, neither trials lay me low;
For when Satan comes to tempt me, to the secret place I go.

When my soul is faint and thirsty, 'neath the shadow of His
wing
There is cool and pleasant shelter, and a fresh and crystal spring;
And my Saviour rests beside me, as we hold communion sweet:
If I tried, I could not utter what He says when thus we meet.

Only this I know: I tell Him all my doubts, my griefs and fears;
Oh, how patiently He listens! and my drooping soul He cheers:
Do you think He ne'er reproves me? What a false friend He
would be,
If He never, never told me of the sins which He must see.

Would you like to know the sweetness of the secret of the Lord?
Go and hide beneath His shadow: this shall then be your reward;
And whene'er you leave the silence of that happy meeting place,
You must mind and bear the image of the Master in your face.

—ELLEN LAKSHMI GOREH

May 26

God, who at sundry times and in divers manners spake in time past unto the fathers by the prophets, hath in these last days spoken unto us by his Son (Heb. 1:1-2).

The writer of the Letter to the Hebrews declares that down through the ages God spoke to men by His prophets. But men would not listen! David asked this question in the second psalm, "Why do the [nations] rage, and the people imagine a vain thing? The kings of the earth set themselves, and the rulers take counsel together, against the Lord, and against his anointed, saying, Let us break their bands asunder, and cast away their cords from us."

In this day, God still speaks to men, but He speaks through

His Son. This is what He has to say (Hebrews 1:2-4): His Son has been "appointed heir of all things." By His Son He "made the worlds." His Son, Jesus, is "the brightness of his glory and the express image of his person." By His Son, God "purged away our sins," and then, His Son, "sat down on the right hand of the Majesty on high." This One, is "better than the angels," and He has "a more excellent name than they." Thus God speaks today concerning His only begotten Son. Are we listening?

"Wherefore God also hath highly exalted him, and given him a name which is above every name: that at the name of Jesus every knee should bow, of things in heaven, and things in earth, and things under the earth, and that every tongue should confess that Jesus Christ is Lord, to the glory of God the Father" (Phil. 2:9-11).

May 27

Quench not the Spirit (1 Thess. 5:19).

The Holy Spirit is portrayed in scripture as a gentle dove, as a mighty rushing wind, and as tongues of fire. As the flame of fire, He enlightens our minds, warms our hearts, and consumes our dross. He is the Purifier as well as the Comforter.

We are told not to grieve or quench the Spirit. Don't bank or let the fire go out. Let it burn! Vance Havner once had a friend who quoted this verse as "Don't squench the Spirit." The words squelch and quench had been used to coin the word. This is not too bad a rendition!

How can we "squench" the Holy Spirit? We can do this when we fail to reveal Jesus in our living, both by word and deed. Or when we discourage others by criticism of their spiritual progress. It can be done by faultfinding and withholding our support from ministries developed for His glory—whatever the excuse we give. And if we neglect our worship and inner prayer life with projects not "about our Father's business," these "quench" the Spirit.

Thus the Holy Spirit can be grieved—grieved by a frivolous attitude, a rebellious frame of mind, or spiritual inertia and complacency for the Word, the Work, and the Will of God.

Let our prayer be: *Holy Spirit, keep the fire burning! Remove the dross—until all can see the beauty of Jesus revealed in me!*

He sat by a fire of sevenfold heat
  As He watched by the precious ore,
And closer He bent with a searching gaze
  As He heated it more and more.

He knew He had ore that could stand the test,
  And He wanted the finest gold,
To mold as a crown for the King to wear,
  Set with gems with a price untold.

So he laid our gold in the burning fire,
  Though we fain would have said Him "Nay;"
And He watched the dross that we had not seen
  And it melted and passed away.

And the gold grew brighter and yet more bright;
  But our eyes were so dim with tears,
We saw but the fire—not the master's hand—
  And questioned with anxious fears.

Yet our gold shone out with a richer glow,
  As it mirrored a Form above
That bent o'er the fire, though unseen by us,
  With a look of ineffable love.

Can we think that it pleased His loving heart
  To cause us a moment's pain?
Oh, no! but He saw through the present cross
  The bliss of eternal gain.

So He waited there with a watchful eye,
  With a love that is strong and sure,
And His gold did not suffer a bit more heat
  Than was needed to make it pure.

—AUTHOR UNKNOWN

May 28

This is a faithful saying, and worthy of all acceptation, that Christ Jesus came into the world to save sinners; of whom I am chief (1 Tim. 1:15).

In his letters to Timothy and Titus, fellow soldiers of the cross, Paul used the expression four times: "This is a faithful saying." "This is a faithful saying and worthy of all acceptation . . . godliness is profitable unto all things (1 Tim. 4:9, 8). "This is a faithful saying . . . he abideth faithful" (2 Tim. 2:11, 13). "Not by works of righteousness which we have done, but according to his mercy he saved us . . . being justified by his grace . . . made heirs according to the hope of eternal life. This is a faithful saying" (Titus 3:5-8).

But Paul added the words, "of whom I am chief" (1 Tim. 1: 15). Perhaps he was thinking of the day he consented to Stephen's death and held the coats of those who threw the stones. Perhaps he was thinking of his religious zeal in haling into prison, men and women of the Christian faith in the days of the Early Church. Perhaps he was thinking of the sins of his youthful days which had long since fled into "the womb of time." "The chief of sinners."

John Newton was once a slave trader and stained with the vilest of sins, but after his conversion, wrote the beautiful hymn "Amazing Grace." Near the close of his life, a young minister spoke to Newton of the sorrow of his coming death and the void in losing such a valiant preacher. But Newton told him, "When you reach heaven, you can look for me near the feet of Jesus, sitting close to the penitent thief." Newton also claimed that he was the "chief of sinners." Henry Bosch once wrote, "The deeper the understanding of the Word and the wider the experience in His love, the more humble the true believer becomes."

Those of us who have been redeemed, confess our total unworthiness and praise Him who has saved us from our sins. Like Paul, we see ourselves there and sing gladly as did James Gray:

> *Naught have I gotten but what I received;*
> *Grace has bestowed it since I believed.*
> *Boasting excluded; pride I abase.*
> *I'm only a sinner saved by grace!*

May 29

If we live in the Spirit, let us also walk in the Spirit (Gal. 5:25).

> *Utterly abandoned to the will of God!*
> *Seeking for no other path than my Master trod;*
> *Leaving ease and pleasure, making Him my choice,*
> *Waiting for His guidance, listening for His voice.*

Many years ago Dr. James M. Gray came to Kansas City and preached on the Holy Spirit. In his sermon he said, "Romans 12:1 tells us to give our bodies. But to whom? It is not the Lord Jesus Christ who asks for it. He has His glorious body. The Father is on His throne. But another has come to earth without a body and He is the Holy Spirit. God gives to every redeemed person the privilege and indescribable honor of presenting his body to the Holy Spirit for His dwelling and infilling."

Walter L. Wilson went to his home that night and prostrated himself before the Lord. In the quietness of early morning he addressed this prayer to the Holy Spirit:

"My Lord, I have mistreated You all of my Christian life. I have treated You like a servant. When I wanted You, I called for You. When I was about to engage in some work, I beckoned You to come and help. I have kept You in the place of a servant. Just now I give You this body of mine; from my head to my toe I give it to You. I give You all that I am both within and without. I hand it over to You for You to live in it the life You desire. You may send me where You wish. It is Your body from this moment on." The Holy Spirit accepted Dr. Wilson's offer and he became one of the world's greatest personal soul winners. Have we made this commitment? This is true abandonment to the Holy Spirit! This begins the useful life! This is the victorious life! This is the yielded life!

> *Laid on Thine altar, O my Lord divine,*
> *Accept my will this day, for Jesus' sake.*
> *I have no jewels to adorn Thy shrine,*
> *Nor any world-proud sacrifice to make;*
> *But here I bring within my trembling hand*
> *This will of mine—a thing that seemeth small,*
> *And Thou alone, O God, canst understand*
> *How when I yield Thee this—I yield Thee all.*

—Author Unknown

176

May 30

*They that feared the Lord spake often one
to another: and the Lord hearkened, and
heard it, and a book of remembrance was
written before him for them that feared the
Lord, and that thought upon his name. And
they shall be mine, saith the Lord of hosts, in
that day when I make up my jewels; and I will
spare them, as a man spareth his own son that
serveth him* (Mal. 3:16-17).

It is Memorial Day as these lines are written. The graves in
the cemeteries of our city are decorated with flowers in remembrance of loved ones. Wreaths can be seen honoring the men of
the police force and fire brigades who gave their lives in the line
of duty. And small flags mark the final resting places of brave
young men who died in past wars for the preservation of freedom.

And yet how fleeting is earthly honor, reward, and recognition. How few are really remembered! History records some
great statesmen—a few great composers, poets, and writers. Some
physicians are remembered by succeeding generations for their
contributions to mankind. But all too often the passing years hide
even the greatest of accomplishments. But we are not forgotten
by God! True indeed is the oft quoted proverb: "Only one life,
'twill soon be past; only what's done for Christ will last."

Jim Christy once said, "Life at its longest is all too short.
Health at its best is all too temporary. Death is sure, unless Jesus
comes, and all that is earthly will pass away. Sooner or later we
must release our homes, our possessions, our positions, Don't
hang on too tightly."

But let us hang on to our faith and our service for the Lord.
Let us always seek His kingdom first. His rewards do not fade.
The only true and lasting memorial is to be found in His "Book
of Remembrance." God's grand Memorial Day is coming! Oh,
the joy of being His in that day when He makes up His jewels!

> *Not I, but Christ be honored, loved, exalted,*
> *Not I, but Christ be seen, be known, be heard;*
> *Not I, but Christ in every look and action,*
> *Not I, but Christ in every thought and word.*

> —AUTHOR UNKNOWN

"Seek first his kingdom and his righteousness, and all these
things will be given to you as well" (Matt. 6:33, NIV).

May 31

Jacob their father said unto them, Me have ye bereaved of my children: Joseph is not, and Simeon is not, and ye will take Benjamin away: all these things are against me (Gen. 42:36).

Poor Jacob seems to have reached the end of his rope. Hearing upsetting news from his sons who had just returned from Egypt, he cries out in utter dismay, "Everything's against me!" Joseph had been taken from him; famine was plaguing the land of Canaan; Simeon was being held as a hostage; and now Benjamin, the youngest of the family, was being demanded as a ransom to secure his brother's release. That was almost too much for the aging patriarch to bear! Overwhelmed by these circumstances, he felt that everything had turned against him.

In reality, however, God was working out His wise purposes. When the dust of Jacob's turmoil finally began to settle, it became increasingly clear that all these distressing events were actually intended for his ultimate good. They led to his move to Egypt where under the blessing of the Lord his offspring would become a great nation. Even though he had declared that all these things were *against* him, from God's standpoint everything was going *for* him.

Christian, the same is true for you in the midst of adversity. You may not see it at the time, but the day will come when you will perceive God's kind, providential hand even in the seeming "tragedies" of life. So take courage and be faithful to the Lord. Trust Him and remember the experiences of Jacob. When everything seems to go wrong, dwell upon the wonderful truth that "all things work together for good to them that love God, to them who are the called according to His purpose." Instead of complaining when all things are apparently against you, rejoice with confidence and say, "Everything is going for me!"

—RICHARD W. DeHaan

From *Our Daily Bread*, © 1973, Radio Bible Class.
Used by special permission.

I know not, but God knows;
Oh blessed rest from fear!
All my unfolding days
To Him are plain and clear.

Each anxious, puzzled "Why?"
  From doubt or dread that grows,
Finds answer in this thought:
  I know not, but He knows.

I cannot, But God can;
  Oh, balm for all my care!
The burden that I drop
  His hands will lift and bear;
Though eagle pinions tire,
  I walk where once I ran.
This is my strength, to know
  I cannot, but God can.

I see not, but God sees;
  Oh, all-sufficient light!
My dark and hidden way
  To Him is always bright.
My strained and peering eyes
  May close in restful ease,
And I in peace may sleep;
  I see not, but He sees.

—ANNIE JOHNSON FLINT

June 1

Paul, a prisoner of Jesus Christ, and Timothy our brother, unto Philemon our dearly beloved, and fellow labourer (Philem. 1).

The great apostle called himself
  "The prisoner of the Lord";
He was not held by Roman chains
  Nor kept in Caesar's ward;
Constrained by love alone,
  By cords of kindness bound,
The bondslave of the living Christ,
  True liberty he found.

Oh, happy those who see
  In poverty and pain,
In weakness and in toil,
  Their Father's golden chain;

Who feel no prison walls
  Though shut in narrow ways,
And though in darkness fettered fast
  Can still rejoice and praise;
From sin's dread bondage bought,
  They own their Master's ward,
They bear the brand of Christ,
  Blest prisoners of the Lord!

—ANNIE JOHNSON FLINT

"I trust that through your prayers I shall be given unto you" (Philem. 22).

Saul, as a young man, was a persecutor of the Christian Church. In Philemon he portrays himself as the aged prisoner of the Lord. Paul could have written that he was a prisoner of Rome, but he believed that "all things work together for good to them that love God . . . who are the called according to his purpose" (Romans 8:28). Thus Paul lived in Christ, and therefore he was a prisoner of Jesus, not of a Roman emperor.

Paul was in prison, but he longed to be on the missionary road once more. He desired to see the saints again at Colossae and to visit and stay once again in the home of Philemon. But this was not to be. His race was almost finished! The crowning day was at hand! The victory of faith had been won!

Still, the apostle's heart was in the mission field. He longed to go back. Sometimes our gracious Lord grants this request, other times He says no. It was Paul's time to enter into His rest. How wonderful to know that though He furloughed His faithful worker, He still sees that the work is carried on!

Let me go back! I am homesick
  For the land of my love and toil,
Though I thrill at the sight of my native hills,
  The touch of my native soil.
Thank God for the dear home country,
  Unconquered and free and grand!
But the far-off shores of the East, for me,
  Are the shores of the Promised Land.

No longer young—I know it—
  And battered and worn and gray,
I bear in my body the marks that tell
  Of many a toil-filled day.
But 'tis long to the end of a lifetime,
  And the hour for the sun to set;
My heart is eager for years to come;
  Let me work for the Master yet!

My brain is dazed and wearied
  With the New World's stress and strife,
With the race for money and place and power
  And the whirl of the nation's life.
Let me go back! Such pleasures
  And pains are not for me;
But oh! for a share in the Harvest Home
  Of the fields beyond the sea.

For there are my chosen people,
  And that is my place to fill,
To spend the last of my life and strength
  In doing my Master's will.
Let me go back! 'Tis nothing
  To suffer and do and dare;
For the Lord has faithfully kept His Word,
  He is "with me always" there!

—MARY E. ALBRIGHT

June 2

Giving thanks always for all things unto God and the Father in the name of our Lord Jesus Christ (Eph. 5:20).

I thank Thee God, for colors:
For the crimson of holly berries, the flaming scarlet of
  maple leaves, and sumac along the country lanes in
  autumn.
For the azure blue of the sky, bending over to reflect its
  hue in little lakes set like gems among the high
  mountains;
For the blue of the morning mist that wraps the high peaks
  with its filmy veil of mystery and blends to deepest
  violet in the low places;
For the silvery blue of great waters that dash and spray
  against the jutting crags; and the heavenly blue of
  morning glories that twine about my garden gate.
For the green of the restless sea, the placid lake,
  and the quiet river; the green of the sheltering arms of
  trees pale in early springtime and deep in the mid-
  summer foliage;

181

*For the soft green of rolling plains where cattle browse in
    contentment; the emerald of early wheat, rippling to the
    fingers of the wind.*
*For the gold of sunlight splashing its cheery contrast against
    the shadowed places of earth; the gleaming gold of
    stars that stud the curtain of night; the bright gold of
    sand along the shore; the rich gold in fields of ripened
    grain, the yellow gold in the chalice of every wayside
    buttercup.*
*I thank, Thee, too, for the somber shades: gray in clouds
    and rain; the twilight sky, and all shadows;*
*For the dark shades of brown in fresh-turned earth; in
    roots and stones, and the rough bark of friendly trees.*
*These muted tones complete earth's kaleidoscope of color,
    and make its brighter shades seem lovlier still.*
*With lavish hand Thou hast spread beauty across the world,
    and I know love has planned it all.*

—Kathryn Blackburn Peck
in *Joy in the Morning,* © 1969

"Blessed be his glorious name for ever: and let the whole
earth be filled with his glory; Amen, and Amen" (Ps. 72:19).

June 3

**Whatever you do, work at it with all your heart,
as working for the Lord, not for men, since you
know that you will receive an inheritance from
the Lord as a reward. It is the Lord Christ you
are serving** (Col. 3:23, NIV).

He walked down the aisle with his black gown and hat and
the stripes of green upon his sleeves. As he mounted the rostrum
and turned to receive his green doctoral hood I thought I saw a
few tears form in his mother's eyes. I remembered his birth, the
anguish of a serious illness, the joy of his confession of Christ.
And I thought of another graduation many years before, and for
the first time realized a little how my own mother must have felt
on the night she saw her only son receive his green hood.

In this day of artificial separation of the church into laity and
ecclesiastical hierarchy, we often speak with awe of those "in

full-time service." But the New Testament teaches that all Christians are in full-time service. We all are to be witnesses. All are to faithfully serve Christ. Expenses may have to be made by "making tents," but this does not lower the value of the ministry.

No greater work for the Kingdom can be done than the work of a Christian mother. She who is devoted to her husband and children is also serving Him who loved her. No higher honor, no greater reward can come than this. If it had not been for Eunice and Lois, there might not have been a Timothy. The Church and the sinful world desperately need women and mothers like Lydia and Dorcas and Hannah and Priscilla. Their work is not menial. Christ's servants who sweep with a broom, or cook with pots and pans, and train their children in the way of righteousness, are just as great in the Kingdom as the mighty orator Apollo, or the teacher Barnabas, or the great missionary Paul.

So, Daughter, don't cringe when some unkind soul says, "Oh, you're just a housewife." Lift up your head and proudly say: "I am a full-time worker in His vineyard."

You are serving the Lord Jesus Christ in a mighty and marvelous way!

> *Lord of all pots and pans and things,*
>   *Since I've no time to be*
> *A saint by doing lovely things,*
>   *Or watching late with Thee,*
> *Or dreaming in the dawnlight,*
>   *Or storming heaven's gate,*
> *Make me a saint by getting meals*
> *And washing up the plates.*

> —FAY INCHFAWN

"Be ye stedfast, unmoveable, always abounding in the work of the Lord, forasmuch as ye know that your labour is not in vain in the Lord" (1 Cor. 15:58).

June 4

Stand thou still a while, that I may show thee the word of God (1 Sam. 9:27).

Some saints always seem to be in a hurry. Yet we are admonished to "be still and know." The Psalmist said, "Wait on the

Lord: be of good courage, and he shall strengthen thine heart" (Ps. 27:14). We need to learn to wait on the Lord!

E. E. Wordsworth wrote: "Give God time! Stand still and see His mighty salvation. Even though you are hemmed in on every side and 'Pharaoh's hosts' are pressing hard upon you, the 'Red Sea' will yet open before your eyes (Exodus 14:13-25). Give God time! When the brook is dry and you seem forsaken, remember Elijah's God still lives and He will direct you to Zarephath (1 Kings 17:8-16)."

We are so often in a hurry. But God says, "Wait." In His good and proper times the door will open, the way will be made plain, and He will then invite you in clear unmistakable terms to walk therein. But don't push the door open until the Master unlocks. it. Stand still awhile—and wait on the Lord.

> Sit still, my daughter! Just sit calmly still!
> Nor deem these days—these waiting days—as ill!
> The One who loves thee best, who plans thy way,
> Hath not forgotten thy great need today!
> And, if He waits, 'tis sure He waits to prove
> To thee, His tender child, His heart's deep love.
>
> Sit still, my daughter! Just sit calmly still!
> Nor move one step, not even one, until
> His way hath opened. Then, ah then, how sweet!
> How glad thy heart, and then how swift thy feet,
> Thy inner being then, ah then, how strong!
> Waiting days shall not be counted then too long.

—J. Danson Smith

June 5

Our sufficiency is of God (2 Cor. 3:5).

Christ is our sufficiency. He is sufficient for life and all of its living. Come what may, He is a haven from fear and from storm. When we are weary, He is our Rest. When we are parched from life's thirsts, He is our Water of Refreshment. When the storms come, He is our Rock of Refuge.

Christ is also sufficient for death and for dying. Dr. Truett once said, "Be not afraid. Sickness may get you, a car wreck may get you, disease may get you, a heart attack may get you, an airplane accident may get you—but be not afraid. Jesus says, 'I will be there at the depot of death to meet you and to take you, and will convey you safely across to the other side to be with me.' Be not afraid!"

Moreover, Christ is sufficient for the Judgment. I do not have to be afraid. He is my Advocate. His shed blood has cleansed the record. He has made me righteous. I am in Him and I shall be safe!

But not only is Christ sufficient for life and its living, for death and its dying, and for the Judgment, but He is also sufficient for all eternity! I sat once in the great planetarium in the city of Chicago and saw the vast heavens made real before my eyes. Oh, the vastness of space! And I thought that day, How can I ever find heaven way out there, "the city of the great king on the sides of the north"? And then His word came afresh: "I go to prepare a place for you. . . . I will come again, and receive you unto myself; that where I am, there ye may be also" (John 14:3).

I do not know where God's heaven "raises its fronded palms in air." I cannot comprehend eternity. But I know there shall be no sin there—I know there is no suffering or death there—I know that there is no sadness or sorrow there. "God shall wipe all tears from their eyes" (Rev. 7:17). So much I do not know, but I know that Jesus is there! Jesus, the all-sufficient Christ, and He is enough for me.

I do not ask that God will keep all storms away;
But this I pray; when thunders roar and lightnings play,
He'll shelter me.

Weak though I am, I dread not now the tempter's hour.
My Saviour then will be my shield; I know His power;
He'll strengthen me.

When I must cross the river to that other realm,
No fear I'll know if Christ is near and holds the helm.
He'll pilot me.

Then when I stand before the judge at the great throne—
Guilty? Ah, yes, but bought by Christ; He knows His own;
He'll plead for me!

—BERNICE W. LUBKE

June 6

Jesus answering said, A certain man went down from Jerusalem to Jericho, and fell among thieves (Luke 10:30).

The road to Jericho is still
Trodden by feet of many men;
And, in this modern age, as then
The Levis and the Pharisees
Pass by, unheeding of the plea
Of those who've met with grief and wrong,
Unmindful of their agony.

O, Master, help us understand
That on our road to Jericho
Wounded and maimed shall call to us,
Then may our hearts in mercy go
To them in loving sympathy
To aid, to heal, restore and bless;
Sharing our service neighborly
In Christlike love for their distress,
As good Samaritans may we go
Upon our road to Jericho.

—DELLA ADAMS LEITNER

The road to Jericho is a dangerous road and a downhill road. There are many who travel it. Jesus revealed this parable to a crafty lawyer. His friends were there. Priests were there and other religious figures, but they were totally unconcerned. Curious crowds were there and thieves abounded everywhere—all abusing and injuring the poor and the desperate who walked that sorrowful way.

The Good Samaritan came from a race that was despised and rejected by the Jews of Israel. In that sense he is like the Christ who came unto His own and whom His own rejected. If we would follow our Master and Lord, then we too must walk the road to Jericho as His servants and ministers. Sin and suffering must be our concern, but concern must be turned into "good Samaritan" action. Wounds need to be treated, safety and shelter secured for the homeless, the poor and the outcast succored and cared for. Only in Him are the travellers to "Jericho" made safe and secure.

God pity us if we too "pass by on the other side." The Church of Jesus Christ must never lose its message of hope and salvation from sin, nor its message of concern. Christ, the Great Physician, is walking still the roads to Jericho. May we who know Him ever walk them too, for we do His work today!

I'm broken and seriously wounded,
   The Jericho road has been rough;
Give me not any lofty suggestions—
   The priests have all spoken enough.

I'm weary of many a sermon;
   Too much of too little's been said.
All noble and lofty persuasions
   Can't help if your lying half dead.

Don't speak of a bright road that beckons;
   I'm too crippled to walk in the way;
Tell me not of some footsteps to follow—
   I'm mired in the deepest of clay.

If you know of a Man who is able
   To bind up my wounds and forgive,
Then speak to my poor soul about Him—
   I want to be healed and to live!

My need is the Greatest Physician
   To come without further delay;
A darkness, like night, falls upon me—
   My life is fast ebbing away.

Is there a Saviour called Jesus?
   Does He love me and counts not the cost?
If you know Him—please bring Him! Yes, bring Him!
   I'm dying today—and I'm lost!

June 7

The king said unto Cushi, Is the young man Absalom safe? And Cushi answered, The enemies of my lord the king, and all that rise against thee to do thee harm, be as that young man is. And the king was much moved, and went up to the chamber over the gate and wept (2 Sam. 18:32-33).

"I'll never forget," remarked a man in a Maine fishing village, "the night my two sons were nearly lost at sea. They had taken our boat to cross the water to an island not very far off shore. They neglected to start homeward until dusk. Then a storm came up and intense darkness covered everything. I stood on shore helpless to go to their aid because there wasn't another boat near. Then my thoughtful wife thrust a lighted lantern into my hands. 'Hold it high,' she said. 'They'll see it and row in this direction.'

"I realized how easily the two young lads could become confused and row the wrong way out there on the black waters. So I did the only thing I could do without a boat—I prayed and I held the lantern high. The wind was becoming stronger and my anxiety rose with it. Then I was overjoyed to hear a faint 'Hello!'

"I shouted encouragement and waved my lantern, always keeping it as high as I could. 'Hello, Dad,' I heard Joe call out after a time. And before long, the boat grated on the shore. My lads were safe and home!

"'Thanks, Dad, for the light,' Joe said. 'It was so dark out there! We were rowing in circles for a while until we saw your light.'

"I learned that night the value of a single light held high, and especially one for my sons."

—CHESTER SHULER

A little fellow follows me,
Whate'er he sees me do he tries.
I do not care to go astray,
For fear he'll go the selfsame way.

Not once can I escape his eyes;
Whate'er he sees me do he tries.
Like me he says he's going to be,
That little chap who follows me.

I must remember as I go
Through summer sun and winter snow;
I'm building for the years to be
That little chap who follows me.

—AUTHOR UNKNOWN

Poor David! Listen to him as he weeps: "O my son Absalom! my son, my son Absalom! would God I had died for thee, O Absalom, my son, my son!" There was great tragedy here. David loved his son dearly in spite of Absalom's grievous sins. But the sins of David had returned to haunt the king's household. David's lament tells us that the father must walk in exemplary conduct for his sons to see. The children will be more apt to walk with God if their father does. Many a child has paid a dear price because the father could not hold high a light for guidance to the paths of righteousness!

> He swung on the gate and looked down the street,
> Awaiting the sound of familiar feet.
> Then suddenly came to the sweet child's eyes
> The marvelous glory of morning skies,
> For a manly form with a steady stride
> Drew near to the gate that opened wide
> As the boy sprang forward and joyously cried,
>   "Papa's coming!"
> The wasted face of a little child
> Looked out at the window with eyes made wild
> By the ghostly shades in the failing light
> And the glimpse of a drunk man in the night,
> Cursing and reeling from side to side.
> The poor boy, trembling and trying to hide,
> Clung to his mother's skirts and cried,
>   "Papa's coming!"

—W. C. SAYES

June 8

He has given us his very great and precious promises (2 Pet. 1:4, NIV).

How great are His promises! How marvelous His love!
"I will not forget thee."
"Can a woman forget her sucking child, that she should not have compassion on the son of her womb? yea, they may forget, yet will I not forget thee. Behold, I have graven thee upon the palms of my hands" (Isa. 49:15-16).
"I will not fail thee."
"There shall not any man be able to stand before thee all the days of thy life. . . . I will be with thee; I will not fail thee, nor forsake thee" (Josh. 1:5).
"I will strengthen thee."
"Fear thou not; for I am with thee: be not dismayed; for I am thy God: I will strengthen thee; yea, I will help thee; yea I will uphold thee with the right hand of my righteousness" (Isa. 41:10).

"I will comfort you."

"As one whom his mother comforteth, so will I comfort you" (Isa. 66:13).

"I will be with you always."

"Surely, I will be with you always, to the very end of the age" (Matt. 28:20, NIV).

"I will never leave thee."

"He hath said, I will never leave thee, nor forsake thee" (Heb. 13:5).

Yes, leave it with Him; the lilies all do,
And they grow;
They grow in the rain, and they grow in the dew—
Yes, they grow.
They grow in the darkness, all hid in the night,
They grow in the sunshine, revealed by the light—
Still they grow.

They ask not your planting, they need not your care
As they grow.
Dropped down in the valley, the field—anywhere—
Yet, they grow.
They grow in their beauty, arrayed in pure white;
They grow, clothed in glory, by heaven's own light—
Yes, they grow.

The grasses are clothed and the ravens are fed
From His store;
But you who are loved and guarded and led,
How much more
Will He clothe you, and feed you, and give you His care!
Then leave it with Him; He has everywhere
Ample store.

Yes, leave it with Him; 'tis more dear to His heart,
You will know,
Than the lilies that bloom or the flowers that start
'Neath the snow.
Whatever you need, if you ask it in prayer,
You can leave it with Him, for you are His care—
You, you know.

—AUTHOR UNKNOWN

June 9

While the bridegroom tarried, they all slumbered and slept (Matt. 25:5).

When Jesus comes to reward His servants,
Whether it be noon or night,
Faithful to Him will He find us watching,
With our lamps all trimmed and bright?

—FANNIE J. CROSBY

This parable has been positively tortured in attempts to spiritualize every detail. It is much safer and sounder to let the parable enforce its own lesson.

The picture that Jesus drew was a common one—He always used common things to illustrate great truths. In this parable He was driving home the need for preparedness and watchfulness.

All the virgins thought they were prepared, but five had only an appearance of readiness. Peter exhorts us to "make your calling and election sure" (2 Pet. 1:10). Many have the outward form of Christianity, and mingle with the saints, but have mistaken Christian profession for salvation.

The foolish virgins did not "wake up" until it was too late. The coming of the bridegroom discovered their lack, and they were barred from the feast. The coming of the Lord will be a time of discovery. Those who have depended on appearance will be found unprepared.

But if the wise virgins had not slept, they might have warned the foolish ones in time. Many sleep on in their delusion until it is too late, because too many "wise virgins" sleep on in their security. Let the saints awake!

There is a real personal application here. The lamp of profession may burn for a while with the oil of religious enthusiasm, but only the oil of the Holy Spirit can keep the lamp of witnessing shining till Jesus comes. Let us be certain that we know Him now, and He will not say then, "I know you not."

—J. C. MACAULAY

June 10

Behold, he prayeth (Acts 9:11).

Prayers are instantly noticed in heaven. The moment Saul began to pray the Lord heard him. Here is comfort for the distressed but praying soul. Oftentimes a poor brokenhearted one bends his knee, but can only utter his waiting in the language of sighs and tears; yet that groan has made all the harps of heaven thrill with music; that tear has been caught by God and treasured in the lachrymatory of heaven. "Put thou my tears into thy bottle" (Ps. 56:8) implies that they are caught as they flow. The suppliant may only look up with misty eye but "prayer is the falling of a tear."

Tears are the diamonds of heaven; sighs are a part of the music of Jehovah's court and are numbered with the "sublimest strains that reach the majesty on high." He regards not high looks and lofty words; He cares not for the pomp and pageantry of kings; He listens not to the swell of martial music; He regards not the triumph and pride of man; but wherever there is a heart big with sorrow, or a lip quivering with agony, or a deep groan, or a penitential sigh, the heart of Jehovah is open. He marks it down in the registry of His memory. He puts our prayers, like rose leaves, between the pages of His book of remembrance, and when the volume is opened at last, there shall be a precious fragrance springing up therefrom.

—Charles Haddon Spurgeon

I cannot tell why there should come to me
    A thought of someone miles and miles away,
In swift insistence on the memory,
    Unless a need there be that I should pray.

Too hurried oft are we to spare the thought
    For days together, of some friends away;
Perhaps God does it for us, and we ought
    To read His signal as a call to pray.

Perhaps, just then, my friend has fiercer fight,
    And more appalling weakness, and decay
Of courage, darkness, some lost sense of right—
    And so, in case he needs my prayer, I pray.

Friend, do the same for me. If I intrude
    Unasked upon you, on some crowded day,

Give me a moment's prayer as interlude;
Be very sure I need it, therefore pray.

And when thou prayest, friend, I ask of thee
That thou wilt seek of God not mine own way,
Not what I want, but His best thought for me;
Do thou through Jesus Christ implore, I pray.

—Marianne Farningham and James M. Gray

June 11

Then said the Lord, Doest thou well to be angry? (Jonah 4:4).

Angry words! O let them never
From the tongue unbridled slip;
May the heart's best impulse ever
Check them ere they soil the lip.

Love is much too pure and holy,
Friendship is too sacred far,
For a moment's reckless folly
Thus to desolate and mar.

—D. K. P.

Upon every appearance of anger, the Christian is wise who lets these gentle words of God challenge him, "Doest thou well to be angry?" The unvarying common sense reply is so nearly always No that the believer's best procedure is to get control of self before he deals with his irritants. Anger is a foe to sense! Even in a physical way, it results in harm!

But how about "righteous indignation"? We greatly suspect that this upholstered creature of covering with fair silk, has beneath it some very, very common clay. We fear, in the light of personal experience, that "righteous indignation" is a shabby emotion when God's Word looketh upon it. About the only object at which we are justified in shooting "the lunatic's flaming arrows" is *sin*.

—Richard Ellsworth Day

Dear Lord and Father of mankind,
  Forgive our foolish ways!
Reclothe us in our rightful mind;
In purer lives Thy service find;
  In deeper reverence, praise.

Drop thy still dews of quietness
  Till all our stivings cease.
Take from our souls the strain and stress,
And let our ordered lives confess
  The beauty of Thy peace.

Breathe through the heats of our desire
  Thy coolness and Thy balm.
Let sense be dumb, let flesh retire;
Speak through the earthquake, wind, and fire,
  O still, small voice of calm!

—JOHN GREENLEAF WHITTIER

June 12

Suddenly there came a sound from heaven as of a rushing mighty wind, and it filled all the house where they were sitting (Acts 2:2).

Two noises are recorded in the second chapter of Acts. The noise of a mighty rushing wind and in verse 6, "Now when this was noised abroad—when this noise was heard—the multitude came together."

The first noise was from heaven. It must have been terrific. The language indicates it was like a tornadic wind. But it localized itself in the house where the 120 were gathered waiting for the promise from the Father.

When the disciples were filled with the Spirit, there was joy and ecstasy and jubilance. They came down out of the place where they had been assembled and overcome with spiritual elation they began to attract the gathering throngs. They were making a noise. Jerusalem knew they were there!

I heard of a church that had been in an area for 20 years. A guest speaker went looking for it. He knew its general location but not its exact address. They did not know of it at the local drugstore nor at the only filling station in the town. A taxi driver wasn't aware of it. After driving up one street and down another, they finally found it. It had not been making any noise in that little town.

Some Christians are like that also. They live in communities but no one is aware that they are followers of Christ. Could that be a key as to why the Church today progresses so slowly? Are we making any noise?

—Pastor U. S. Grant

June 13

*He saith unto them, Follow me, and I will
make you fishers of men* (Matt. 4:19).

Simon Peter and Andrew were fishermen of the sea but Christ called them to be fishers of men. This is a noble occupation. There is no greater joy in the Christian life than winning others to Christ.

Three times the Lord Jesus spoke to Peter about fishing and thus about soul winning. Here in our text He said, "Follow me." In Luke 5:4 the Savior said, "Launch out into the deep." In John 21:6, after His resurrection, our Lord commanded, "Cast the net on the right side."

The disciples had toiled the long night through but had caught nothing. These reasons are implied. Jesus was not with them—He stood on the shore. He also had not sent them—they acted on their human impulses. No prayer had been offered—they were depending upon their strength and wisdom, and finally, they were fishing in the wrong spot!

God's successful fishermen are those who are sent by the Spirit and led by the Spirit. Without His guidance we will "toil all night" and catch nothing.

> *Have you toiled all night near the shore in vain?*
> *Push away from the shore, launch out;*
> *Where the flood is deep cast your nets again,*
> *Push away from the shore, launch out;*
> *There a blessing waits for your souls to take,*
> *Haste away from the barren strand.*
> *Toil no more in vain where the surges break;*
> *"Launch out" is your Lord's command.*

—J. B. MacKay

"Let me remind each Christian that the Holy Spirit is still the Lord of the Harvest. He arranges times and seasons. He brings peculiar circumstances which work out for the salvation of men. He alone can make us successful fishermen. Let us learn more and more to depend upon Him to lead us to troubled hearts, and to bring together in His own peculiar way the seeking Saviour and the needy sinner" (Walter L. Wilson).

> He stood upon the shore and watched them toil,
>   Then spoke three simple words, "Come, follow Me."
> And hearing Him, they hung their nets to dry
>   And left their little boats on Galilee.
>
> They did not know the rich rewards ahead,
>   Nor of the power that they would hold someday;
> But answering Him, they followed where He led,
>   And found in Christ the Truth and Perfect Way.
>
> —ROBERT D. TROUTMAN

June 14

I will even make a way in the wilderness
(Isa. 43:19).

"Prayer is the most important spiritual exercise that a Christian can engage in. If one would live a happy, yielded, and victorious life, prayer is essential. We must pray and pray daily. The Bible makes it clear that you can pray at any time, for God never sleeps. His ear is always open to your cry. Prayer is the key of the morning and the bolt upon the night" (Billy Graham).

"In relation to His people, God works only in answer to their prayers" (Andrew Murray).

"You can pray. The door has never yet been forged, the dungeon never yet constructed, the adversary never yet so mighty that excludes God from His people. Pray!" (Robert G. Lee).

"When I was a pastor in quaint, historic old Charleston, I numbered among my friends one Adam Brown. He was an aged negro preacher who conducted a little orphanage on Wadmalaw Island. It was his custom to visit me once a week. Before we engaged in any conversation, his first word was, "Let us pray." He usually prefaced his prayer with a verse from some old, old hymn he had stored in his mind and heart until it was a part of himself.

196

And how he could pray! I was starting out on a preaching mission one morning when Adam Brown prayed: "Lord, bless our brother; make a way for him; *make a way out of no way!*" (Vance Havner).

June 15

From within, out of the heart of men, proceed evil thoughts, adulteries, fornications, murders (Mark 7:21).

The heart of man is a factory of evil things. Now one would think that regeneration would end that operation and in its place establish a shop for the production of good thoughts, but old products keep cropping up on the assembly line sufficiently to warrant timely warnings and exhortations. Part of the apostolic answer to this problem is to keep the plant so busy turning out good thoughts that the others will be crowded out. "Finally, brethren, whatsoever things are true, whatsoever things are honest, whatsoever things are just, whatsoever things are pure, whatsoever things are lovely, whatsoever things are of good report; if there be any virtue, and if there be any praise, think on these things" (Philippians 4:8).

F. W. Boreham in his *Crystal Pointers* tells of the happy soul whose home is the Other End of Nowhere. He has two pockets. One has a hole in it and the other is carefully watched that no hole develops in it. Everything that he hears of a hurtful nature, insult, gossip, or unclean suggestion, he writes on a piece of paper and sticks it into his pocket with the hole. At night he turns out all that is in the pocket without the hole, goes over all that he had put into it during the day and enjoys all the good things that have come his way. Then he sticks his hand into the pocket with the hole and finds nothing there, so he laughs and rejoices that there are no evil things to rehearse. Too many of us reverse the order, putting the evil things in the pocket without the hole and mulling over them again and again. The good things are quickly forgotten. Instead of lending our mind to iniquitous thoughts, it is our privilege to hand it over to the control of the Holy Spirit. By His enabling exercise the mind of Christ can be formed in us.

—J. C. MACAULAY

"Let this mind be in you, which was also in Christ Jesus" (Phil. 2:5).

June 16

Whom the Lord loveth he chasteneth, and scourgeth every son whom he receiveth (Heb. 12:6).

O Savior, whose mercy, severe in its kindness,
  Has chastened my wanderings and guided my way,
Adored by the power which illumined my blindness,
  And weaned me from phantoms that smiled to betray.

Enchanted with all that was dazzling and fair,
  I followed the rainbow, I caught at the toy;
And still in displeasures, Thy goodness was there,
  Disappointing the hope, and defeating the joy.

The blossom blushed bright, but a worm was below,
  The moonlight shone fair—there was blight in the beam;
Sweet whispered the breeze, but it whispered of woe;
  And bitterness flowed in the soft-flowing stream.

So, cured of my folly, yet cured but in part,
  I turned to the refuge Thy pity displayed;
And still did this eager and credulous heart
  Weave visions of promise, that bloomed but to fade.

I thought that the course of the pilgrim to Heaven
  Would be bright as the summer, and glad as the morn;
Thou showed me the path—it was dark and uneven,
  All rugged with rock, and all tangled with thorn.

I dreamed of celestial reward and renown;
  I grasped at the triumph which blesses the brave;
I asked for the palm branch, the robe, and the crown;
  I asked—and Thou showed me a cross, and a grave.

Subdued and instructed, at length, to Thy will,
  My hopes and my longings I fain would resign;
O give me the heart that can wait and be still,
  Nor know of a wish nor a pleasure but Thine!

—SIR ROBERT GRANT

"Blessed is the man whom thou chastenest, O Lord, and teachest him out of thy law" (Ps. 94:12).

June 17

Jesus being full of the Holy Ghost returned from the Jordan, and was led by the Spirit into the wilderness, being forty days tempted [tested] of the devil (Luke 4:1-2).

"[He] was in all points tempted like as we are, yet without sin" (Heb. 4:15), declares the writer to the Hebrews. As the Son of Man He knew our need—as the Son of God He met our need. Because He overcame, He is able to sustain us when we are tempted, making for us a sure way of escape. We belong to a Lord who was tried and proven! He is just the same today!

All who are godly will suffer temptation. The more effective the ministry, the greater the hindrance of Satan to the work. D. L. Moody once wrote, "Watch out for the devil, especially when you come down from the mountain."

But thanks be to our God that "the Lord knows how to deliver the godly out of temptation." Wearing spiritual armor, being fervent in prayer, and looking "unto Jesus the author and finisher of our faith," we can stand as victors on the field of battle!

"We are bound to give thanks always to God for you, brethren beloved of the Lord, because God hath from the beginning chosen you to salvation through sanctification of the Spirit and belief of the truth" (2 Thess. 2:13).

Rejoice, O trembling heart! The Holy Spirit has come to indwell thee, and He will not leave His residence. He has chosen thee as His temple and He will not be driven forth. He has given thee glimpses, yearnings, and firstfruits, which are the earnest of an inheritance that He cannot do otherwise than grant. He has begun a good work, and He will carry it on to the day of Jesus Christ. There are no unfinished portraits in His gallery, no unperfected blocks in His studio. The work which His grace began, the arm of His strength will complete.

—F. B. Meyer

June 18

Watch thou in all things, endure afflictions, do the work of an evangelist, make full proof of thy ministry (2 Tim. 4:5).

The return of our Lord Jesus Christ is called by Paul "the blessed hope." It has been the hope of the Church throughout all the ages. Many signs now point to the consummation of this age and of His returning again. The world is torn with strife and hatred. There is no peace. The fig tree has been in bud and Israel has returned to the land. Men's hearts are fearful and failing as they contemplate "those things which are coming on the earth." Sorcery and witchcraft have deceived many. Satanic worship is practiced by some and many are turned away from the Faith.

We are counselled in many Scriptures, however, not to spend our time in counting signs or setting dates. We may wonder as the signs unfold. In a state of readiness we are to watch for the glorious rays of that bright morning. But with wondering and watching goes working. When He comes, let us be found still planning evangelistic campaigns, endeavoring to start new missionary enterprises, and making "full proof of our ministry." Wonder, watch, and work—but the greatest of these is work! Let us be "about our Master's business!"

> I am waiting for you, oh, my saved ones!
>   For you to go forth
> To the East and the West with my message,
>   The South and the North.
> Go ye, that I come the more quickly,
>   I listen to hear
> My good news of joy and salvation
>   Fall sweet on my ear.
> I gave it in trust for your telling;
>   Still Faithful and True,
> I wait with long-suffering patience
>   With you, and for you;
> I have not forgotten my promise,
>   It is you who are late;
> Must I tarry much longer, Beloved?
>   Oh, hasten; I wait!

—ANNIE JOHNSON FLINT

June 19

Caleb . . . said unto him, Thou knowest the thing that the Lord said unto Moses the man of God concerning me and thee in Kadesh-bar-nea. Forty years old was I when Moses . . . sent me . . . to espy out the land; and I brought him word again as it was in mine heart. . . . I wholly followed the Lord my God. . . . Now therefore give me this mountain, whereof the Lord spake in that day; for thou heardest in that day how the Anakims were there, and that the cities were great and fenced: if so be the Lord will be with me, then I shall be able to drive them out, as the Lord said (Josh. 14:6-8, 12).

Caleb was a man of great faith. He believed God. He walked in His tender care and he was not afraid of choosing a mountain for his inheritance. No valley or pleasant plain for Caleb. No, he was the man of the high road!

The giants of Anakim and its fortified cities would fall, for 40 years had not changed Caleb's beliefs. At Kadesh-barnea his report had said, "We are well able to possess the land." So Caleb was not fearful now.

"Come what may, the Lord's on my side," he said, "but best of all, I am on His side. I wholly follow the Lord." Wanted for this hour—men like Caleb with such a faith!

I want the faith
That envies not
The passing of the days;
That sees all times and ways
More endless than the stars;
That looks at life,
Not as a little day
Of heat and strife,
But one eternal revel of delight
With God, the Friend, Adventurer, and Light.

What matter if one chapter nears the end?
What matter if the silver deck the brow?
Chanting I go
Past crimson flaming
From the autumn hills,

Past winter's snow,
To find that glad new chapter
Where God's spring
Shall lift its everlasting voice to sing.
This is the faith I seek;
It shall be mine,
A faith that looks beyond the peaks of time!

—RALPH SPAULDING CUSHMAN

"You search in vain in Caleb's life to find a single instance where he was pessimistic or cheerless. Caleb was a stunning character. The joy of the Lord belonged to him. 'He wholly followed the Lord' [Num. 32:12]. This is what the Scripture says about him. This was the sublime secret of his character. God said of him, 'My servant Caleb has wholly followed me.' He had the overwhelming testimony of the reality of his devotion to God. In that fact resides the sublime secret of Caleb's marvelous power for God" (George W. Truett)

June 20

I am the way, the truth, and the life; no man cometh unto the Father, but by me (John 14:6).

There is complete exclusion here. He is the life—He is the truth—all else is false. Jesus is *the* way—not *a* way. All those who come to God the Father must come through the Son and His cross. D. L. Moody, in his sermon "The Way Home," said, "Some men try to travel Ecclesiastical Boulevard or Morality Lane or Self-Righteous Avenue or Reformation Alley, but none of these roads lead Home." Since "all have sinned and come short of the glory of God" and "there is none righteous, no not one," atonement and redemption from sin is God's remedy. All must either bow at the Cross or bow later at the judgment. The Cross is God's humbling instrument for a haughty world. Only the Cross leads home. Christ is the way!

I must needs go home by the way of the Cross,
There's no other way but this;
I shall ne'er get sight of the Gates of Light
If the way of the Cross I miss.

—JESSIE BROWN POUNDS

"God, who at sundry times and in diverse manners spake in times past unto the fathers by the prophets, hath in these last days spoken unto us by his Son, whom he hath appointed heir of all things, by whom also he made the worlds; who being the brightness of his glory, and the express image of his person, and upholding all things by the word of his power, when he had by himself purged our sins, sat down on the right hand of the Majesty on high" (Hebrews 1:1-3).

Creation was upheld by the "word of His power." He spoke and miracles were accomplished. But when it came to redemption, there was no word He could speak. He had to go to Calvary himself to accomplish that work.

—AUTHOR UNKNOWN

June 21

Who knoweth whether thou art come to the kingdom for such a time as this? (Esther 4: 14).

This verse speaks of a God-given time, a God-given place, and a God-given person. There was a need that Esther alone could meet but she had been prepared for that hour. God always has someone ready to do His work.

Like the lame man at Bethesda's pool who sadly responded to Jesus' question, "Wilt thou be made whole?" by saying: "I have no man . . . to put me in the pool" (John 5:1-9), so the church's need is not for better programs but better preachers; not for better methods, but for better men! God is always seeking for men to walk His way, work His work, and witness to His Word. He needs men for "such a time as this." What kind of men? Spirit-filled men who then can say, "Thy will—nothing less, nothing more, nothing else."

"The world has yet to see what God can do with and for and through and in a man who is fully and wholly consecrated to Him" (Henry Varley).

"God hath chosen the weak things of the world to confound the mighty—that no flesh should glory in His presence. Let us take our place in the dust and give God the glory! When God delivered Israel in Egypt He didn't send an army. God sent a man, who had been in the desert for forty years and had an impediment in his speech. It is weakness that God wants! Nothing is small

203

when God handles it. Pray, 'O God, give me Thy Holy Spirit!'"
(D. L. Moody).

> Breathe on me, Breath of God,
>   Fill me with life anew,
> That I may love what Thou dost love,
>   And do what Thou wouldst do.
>
> Breathe on me, Breath of God,
>   Until my heart is pure,
> Until with Thee I will one will,
>   To do and to endure.
>
> Breathe on me, Breath of God,
>   Till I am wholly Thine,
> Until this earthly part of me
>   Glows with Thy fire divine.
>
> —EDWIN HATCH

June 22

Ye are the light of the world. . . . Let your light so shine before men that they may see your good works (Matt. 5:14-16).

Read and reread yet again these great words. And any follower of Christ who fails to make it the quest of his life to bring forth his human best could well be held in suspicion. It's a holy motive, transplanted from the Garden of God into our hearts; a godly purpose that makes us perennially determined to possess a fine body, a trained mind, and a radiant spirit. My human best for the Master!

The greatest pleasure is bringing forth our human best to lay it all at the feet of Jesus! Let hands that have a micrometer touch be held out for the King to shackle as He will! Let the mind that soars in familiar visits to poetry's loftiest summits, stand before Him and say, "Dear Son of God, any messages You want delivered?" Let the soul that has been whitened by prayer, and cleansed by fire, cry out unto Him, "Fairest Lord Jesus, give me a place in the heavenly train that waiteth Thy pleasure!"

The highest motivation for individual excellence is that in the present age the man of God is the only visible manifestation of God. The world can never know Jesus save through us! "Ye are the light of the world." Therefore, arise, shine, for thy Light is come. Exhibit before men thy human best, in and for Christ! But also know this. This means dangerous living. High visibility for His sake exposes us to the enemy.

—RICHARD E. DAY

June 23

We love because he first loved us (1 John 4:19, NIV).

"If I speak in the tongues of men and of angels, but have not love, I am only a resounding gong or a clanging cymbal. If I have the gift of prophecy and can fathom all mysteries and all knowledge, and if I have a faith that can move mountains, but have not love, I am nothing. If I give all I possess to the poor and surrender my body to the flames, but have not love, I gain nothing.

"Love is patient, love is kind. It does not envy, it does not boast, it is not proud. It is not rude, it is not self-seeking, it is not easily angered, it keeps no record of wrongs. Love does not delight in evil but rejoices with the truth. It always protects, always trusts, always hopes, always perseveres.

"Love never fails. But where there are prophecies, they will cease; where there are tongues, they will be stilled; where there is knowledge, it will pass away. For we know in part and we prophecy in part, but when perfection comes, the imperfect disappears. When I was a child, I talked like a child, I thought like a child, I reasoned like a child. When I became a man, I put childish ways behind me. Now we see but a poor reflection; then we shall see face to face. Now I know in part; then I shall know fully, even as I am fully known.

"And now these three remain: faith, hope, and love. But the greatest of these is love."

—1 CORINTHIANS 13, NIV

"If you turn to the Revised Version of the First Epistle of John you will find these words: 'We love, because He first loved us.' 'We love,' not 'We love Him.' This is the way the old version has it. 'Because He first loved us,' the effect follows that we love, we love Him, we love all men. We cannot help it. Because He loved us, we love, we love everybody. Our heart is slowly changed. Contemplate the love of Christ, and you will love. Stand before that mirror, reflect Christ's character, and you will be changed into the same image from tenderness to tenderness. There is no other way. We cannot love to order. You can only look at the lovely object, and fall in love with it, and grow into likeness to it. And so look at this Perfect Character, this Perfect Life. Look at the great sacrifice as He laid down Himself, all through life, and upon the Cross, and you must love Him. And loving Him, you must become like Him. Love begets love" (Henry Drummond).

June 24

In my Father's house are many mansions; if it were not so, I would have told you (John 14:2).

Dr. Charles E. Fuller announced one week that he would preach the next Sunday on the subject of "Heaven." Dr. Harry Rimmer, who lay upon his deathbed sent these words to Dr. Fuller: "You say, my brother, that next Sunday you are going to preach about Heaven. I am interested in that land as I have a piece of property there. I didn't buy it, for the Savior purchased it for me with His own blood. For 55 years I have been sending up material, out of which the great Architect, Jesus Christ, is preparing a place for me that will never have to be remodeled or repaired. The foundation rests on Jesus, the Rock of Ages; therefore nothing can destroy it. My ticket to Heaven has no date marked for the journey, no return coupon, and no baggage permit. I may not be here next week when you're talking about that wonderful place, but I will see you there!"

How beautiful the Father's home must be! It is a prepared place for a prepared people, redeemed by His blood out of every kindred and tongue and tribe and people and nation.

Along the Golden Streets, a stranger walks tonight
With wonder in her heart, faith blossomed into sight.
She walks and stops and stares, and walks and stops again,
Vistas of loveliness, beyond the dreams of men,
She who was feeble, weak, and shackled to her bed,
Now climbs eternal hills with light and easy tread—
She has escaped at last, the cruel clutch of pain;
Her lips shall never taste its bitter cup again.
Oh! Never call her dead, this buoyant one, and free,
Whose daily portion is delight and ecstasy!

She bows in speechless joy, before the feet of Him
Whom, seeing not, she loved, while yet her faith was dim.
Along the Golden Streets, no stranger walks today,
But one who, long homesick, is Home at last to stay!

—AUTHOR UNKNOWN

June 25

Be ye transformed . . . that ye may prove
what is that good, and acceptable, and perfect,
will of God (Rom. 12:2).

The will of God is good. No taint of evil or impurity can live in its pure atmosphere. It is like the air of the high mountains, in which microbes of corruption and disease cannot exist.

The will of God is acceptable. The impression produced on those who are unprejudiced, when they come in contact with a life lived only for the will of God, is that it is beautiful; it attracts them; it is acceptable. Our service is acceptable, and His will as we begin to live in it and practice it, makes us men and women of His good pleasure.

The will of God is perfect. There is nothing beyond it. If we travel back to the time before the world was, we can only imagine that perfect peace, perfect joy, and perfect love reigned supreme forever. And why? Because the will of God was done. Whence have come the sorrow, the pain, and the anguish that mar human life today? Why, from rebellion against the will of God. And the Father can only wipe tears from off all faces by winning us back to love and to do His will. "He that doeth the will of God abideth forever."

—F. B. MEYER

"Paul beseeched the Christians at Rome to live in the will of God. He did not command them. Living truly in the will of God only comes with love for God. Paul urged them to present their bodies a living sacrifice. This is a gift. We give ourselves only once" (L. D. Boatman).

"You will never know the will of God unless you are willing to do it" (W. L. Pettingill).

"I find the doing of the will of God leaves me no time for disputing about His plans" (George MacDonald).

My stubborn will at last hath yielded;
   I would be Thine, and Thine alone;
And this the prayer my lips are bringing,
   "Lord, let in me Thy will be done."

Thy precious will, O conquering Saviour,
   Doth now embrace and compass me;
All discords hushed, my peace a river,
   My soul a prisoned bird set free.

Shut in with Thee, O Lord, forever,
   My wayward feet no more to roam;
What power from Thee my soul can sever?
   The center of God's will my home.

Sweet will of God, still fold me closer,
   Till I am wholly lost in Thee.
Sweet will of God still fold me closer,
   Till I am wholly lost in Thee.

—MRS. C. H. MORRIS

June 26

***Thou therefore endure hardness, as a
good soldier of Jesus Christ*** (2 Tim. 2:3).

We are in the King's army, writes Paul, and we are soldiers.
Now a soldier may be a volunteer or a draftee. But in God's army,
all of His soldiers are volunteers. He drafts no man. A soldier must
endure hardship, follow and obey orders, and be courageous and
thoroughly trained. Christ requires no less. But there are other
marks of a good soldier. He must not run from battle nor sleep on
duty, and he may be called upon to die. Paul, therefore, urged the
Ephesian "soldiers" to "put on the whole armour of God." There
is to be no retreat in the King's army and we are to "stand as victors on the field of battle" (Weymouth).
   The Christian life is a life of battle. The enemy of Pilgrim's
soul is both powerful and vicious. We must have a "borrowed
armour." Paul calls it God's armour. It is available to every believer. Our loins must be bound about with the truth to run with
His strength. Our hearts must be kept secure with the breastplate
of His righteousness. Our feet must be shod with His peace to
walk safely in His ways. His helmet of salvation must be worn to

protect our minds and thoughts. We must carry always with us the shield of His faith, and the sword of His Spirit "which is the Word of God."

Christ is the Word which "became flesh and dwelt among us" (John 1:14). And so Paul is saying to each of us, "Put on Christ. Be found always in Him. He is your whole armor. Secure your armor with prayer. Live and fight as good soldiers. You are not on furlough!"

June 27

This I do for the gospel's sake (1 Cor. 9:23).

Discipleship costs something! As followers of Christ, we must willingly surrender our lives to Him and let go of every earthly treasure that might hinder our testimony and fruitfulness. Anything that drains our vigor in the race we must run is a weight that should be abandoned lest it prevent us from attaining full spiritual victory.

General Charles G. Gordon was an outstanding man of God. When the English government wanted to reward him for his distinguished service in China, he declined all money and titles. Finally, after much urging, he accepted a gold medal inscribed with his name and a record of his accomplishments. Following his death, however, it could not be found among his belongings. It was learned that on a certain date he had sent it to Manchester during a famine with the request that it be melted and used to buy bread for the poor. In his private diary for that day were written these words: "The only thing I had in this world that I valued, I have now given to the Lord Jesus." His love for the Savior had constrained him to relinquish his one treasured possession for the relief of the destitute. He would not cling to earthly honor, but casting its last vestige aside, he sought only to serve the Master "for the gospel's sake."

—HENRY G. BOSCH
From *Our Daily Bread*, © 1973, Radio Bible Class.
Used by special permission.

"Then Jesus beholding him loved him, and said unto him, One thing thou lackest; go thy way, sell whatever thou hast, and give to the poor, and thou shalt have treasure in heaven; and come, take up the cross, and follow me. And he was sad at that saying, and went away grieved; for he had great possessions" (Mark 10:21-22).

We are not told his name—this "rich young ruler"
  Who sought the Lord that day;
We only know that he had great possessions
  And that—he went away.

He went away; he kept his earthly treasure,
  But oh, at what a cost!
Afraid to take the cross and lose his riches—
  And God and Heaven were lost.

So for the tinsel bonds that held and drew him,
  What honor he let slip—
Comrade of John and Paul and friend of Jesus—
  What glorious fellowship!

For they who left their all to follow Jesus
  Have found a deathless fame,
On His immortal scroll of saints and martyrs
  God wrote each shining name.

We should have read his there—the rich young ruler—
  If he had stayed that day;
Nameless—though Jesus loved him—ever nameless
  Because—he went away.

—Author Unknown

"This I do for the gospel's sake, that I might be partaker of it with you." Have we placed our treasures on the altar for "the gospel's sake"?

June 28

It came to pass the day after, that he went into a city called Nain (Luke 7:11).

At the city of Nain there was a funeral procession that never reached the cemetery. Luke wrote in this account that there was a young man, "the only son of his mother, and she was a widow," who was being borne to his grave. But Jesus came near! Christ broke up every funeral He ever attended! There can be no "dark valley" when the Lord of life and eternity is present! •

At Nain, there were sorrow, tears, loneliness and death—stark real death. But our Lord is never late. He always delivers on time! Jesus touched the bier and spoke words of glorious resurrection.

Christ is able to do this today and all who are "dead in trespasses and sins" are made alive with eternal life when they receive Him as their own precious Savior.

But there is a day coming when tears shall end and sorrows leave forever and all funeral processions shall cease. Forever we shall be with Him. "Comfort ye one another with these words" (1 Thess. 4:13-18).

> I'm growing very weary, Lord,
>   The day has been so long,
> The morning hours have sped apace,
>   And now 'tis evensong.
> The shadows lengthen on the hills,
>   The sun sets in the west,
> I'm listening for Thy voice to call,
>   "Come home, my child, and rest."
>
> The flowers that bloomed around my path
>   When summer skies were bright,
> They all have faded long ago,
>   And vanished from my sight.
> The mountains that were hard to climb
>   Lie in the distant past,
> And now my pilgrim feet have reached
>   The sunset trail at last.
>
> The valleys they were deep and lone,
>   And tears were often shed,
> When storm clouds gathered dark and low,
>   And thunders roared o'erhead.
> Yet Thou wert there with all Thy love,
>   My trembling hand to hold;
> Thy goodness and Thy mercy, Lord,
>   Could never half be told.
>
> And so I'll walk along the way
>   And thank Thee for Thy care;
> Soon I may hear that shout to rise,
>   And meet Thee in the air.
> Till then, along this sunset trail
>   I'll watch and wait, and pray;
> The morning without clouds draws near,
>   The bright eternal day!
>
> —Mrs. M. E. Rae

June 29

Then said Jesus unto the twelve, Will ye also go away? Then Simon Peter answered him, Lord, to whom shall we go? thou hast the words of eternal life (John 6:67-68).

O grand and glorious fisherman! What a noble commitment! "Though all others leave, I will follow You, for Lord, no other speaks the words of life eternal." Down the passage of the years, no voice has spoken more clearly.

There is a tragedy abroad in the land today. Men are vainly following other footsteps seeking truth when only He is the Truth. Men are vainly looking for flowing fountains but turn away from Him who gives the abundant life. Men are groping the mystic byways seeking a way when He alone is the Way. How sadly the words must have fallen, "Ye will not come to me, that ye might have life" (John 5:40).

You say I'm clinging to an outworn creed;
That Jesus Christ is out of date—passé;
That I must put another in His place,
A new messiah for this present day!

And when I cannot, you're surprised and hurt,
Annoyed—impatient and provoked with me
Because I fail to see in him the "truth,"
The answer to the world's perplexity.

You smile and say, "It is not given to all
To grasp, at once, its vast complexity,"
that "when the time is ripe" I'll know the "truth"
And wonder at my blind stupidity.

How can I answer best this avalanche,
Impassioned with the certainty of youth?
What was the evil quirk of circumstance
That caught you so off guard in search for truth?

How can I give you back your childhood faith,
Restored in all its sweet simplicity?
How can I show you Christ, the Perfect One,
Who was, and is, and evermore shall be?

He is the Truth, the Life, the Light, the Way!
  All I could need or want, I find in Him;
Friend of the friendless; Courage for the day;
  Constant Companion when the path is dim.

How could I put another in His place,
  Who has been more than friend or life to me?
How meet the coming years without His face,
  Waiting at journey's end to welcome me?

Call me old-fashioned—stubborn—what you will,
  Steadfast, unmovable, I shall remain,
Rooted and grounded in the Word, until
  He shall appear, who maketh all things plain!

—KATHERINE MELVILLE

"Jesus said unto him, I am the way, the truth, and the life; no man cometh unto the Father, but by me" (John 14:6).

June 30

I will deliver thee in that day, saith the Lord; and thou shalt not be given into the hand of the men of whom thou art afraid (Jer. 39:17).

This is a precious verse. It declares that our God is able to deliver us. He doesn't state how it will be brought about—the method must be left to Him—but in the dread hour, He will deliver. This should be enough! Rest on His promise.

It is quite human to be afraid, but take courage. He that is with you is greater than they who would devour you. The believer is safe in Jesus' hands. He will put gladness in our hearts (Ps. 4:7).

Like David of old, we may lie down and sleep in peace for our God makes us to dwell in safety. Let some "trust in chariots, and some in horses," but we will remember and trust in the name of our God! (Ps. 20:7).

He does not lead me year by year
  Nor even day by day,
But step by step my path unfolds;
  My Lord directs my way.

Tomorrow's plans I do not know,
I only know this minute;
But He will say, "This is the way,
By faith now walk ye in it."

And I am glad that it is so,
Today's enough to bear;
And when tomorrow comes, His grace
Shall far exceed its care.
What need to worry then or fret?
The God who gave His Son
Holds all my moments in His hand
And gives them, one by one.

—BARBARA C. RYBERG

July 1

Because thou hast forgotten the God of thy salvation, and hast not been mindful of the rock of thy strength, therefore shalt thou plant pleasant plants, and shalt set it with strange slips: . . . but the harvest shall be a heap in the day of grief and of desperate sorrow (Isa. 17: 10-11).

Although the Bible proclaims the love of God, it also warns of His judgments on those who forget Him. If we look honestly at our homeland, we see the rise of paganism with many, like Israel of old, "doing that which seemeth right in their own eyes." Our country needs repentance with a return to "the old paths." If she does not, God will place her on history's rubbish heap.

God warns that though we "plant pleasant plants, the harvest shall be a day of grief and sorrow." Recently the secular press reported some unexpected difficulties in the awarding of prizes for the first babies born on New Year's Day. The apparent winners in four communities were all unwed mothers. When one constantly reads of prominent personalities living "in a meaningful sexual relationship" apart from marriage, thus producing children without a legal father or a wholesome home, we may be certain that a harvest of grief is coming. Has our country become a land that no longer can blush?

Archbishop Sheen recently stated that a large American hotel chain was forced by a labor union to reinstate a dishonest cashier who had been stealing from the company. The excuse used to coerce the hotel was that it had failed to advise the employee when she was hired that "it was wrong to steal." When labor courts and labor leaders ignore the precepts of righteousness in such a callous manner, we have joined "the lesser breeds without the law."

There was once a city named Nineveh that also was very wicked. Jonah was sent by God to preach repentance there and to warn of coming judgment. And Nineveh repented. "So the people of Nineveh believed God, and proclaimed a fast, and put on sackcloth, from the greatest of them even to the least of them. For the word came unto the king of Nineveh, and he arose from his throne, and he laid his robe from him, and covered him with sackcloth, and sat in ashes. And he caused it to be proclaimed and published through Nineveh by the decree of the king and his nobles, saying, . . . Let man and beast be covered with sackcloth, and cry mightily unto God: yea, let them turn every one from his evil way, and from the violence that is in their hands. Who can tell if God . . . will turn away from his fierce anger, that we perish not?" (Jonah 3:5-9).

Billy Graham once said, "I could cry for my country." The time is now for God's people to shed tears for this country, and to pray for individual and national repentance. We must forsake our sin, turn back to God, or we and our nation shall surely die!

> Four things in any land must dwell,
> If it endures and prospers well;
> One is manhood true and good;
> One is noble womanhood;
> One is child life, clean and bright;
> And one an altar kept alight!
>
> —Author Unknown

July 2

When Pilate saw that he could prevail nothing, but that rather a tumult was made, he took water, and washed his hands before the multitude, saying, I am innocent of the blood of this just person: see ye to it (Matt. 27:24).

On the eve of the day of the Crucifixion, the washbowl disappeared from Pilate's palace. No one knew who took it. Some accused Judas Iscariot of selling it but this is plainly libel, because Judas was honest enough to go and hang himself. At any rate, ever since that time, the washbowl remains abroad in the land, carried by infernal hands to where it is needed, and men are constantly joining the invisible choir which performs its imperceptible ablutions therein.

Such as the preacher who sees Dives exploiting Lazarus and dares not tell him to quit because Dives contributes to his salary. The editor who sees a righteous cause misrepresented and says nothing because it might injure the circulation and the advertising. The school superintendent who sees a devoted teacher injured by prominent people and dares not champion her. The good citizen who will have nothing to do with politics because it might hurt his business. The statesman who suppresses principles because they might endanger the party. All these are using Pilate's washbowl.

Listen! Have you heard the splash of water near you?

—ARR. WALTER RAUCHENBUSCH

"I sought for a man among them, that should make up the hedge, and stand in the gap before me for the land, that I should not destroy it: but I found none" (Ezek. 22:30).

God send us men alert and quick
His lofty precepts to translate,
Until the laws of Christ become
The laws and habits of the state.

God send us men of steadfast will,
Patient, courageous, strong and true;
With vision clear and mind equipped
His will to learn, His work to do.

God send us men with hearts ablaze,
All truth to love, all wrong to hate;
These are the patriots nations need,
These are the bulwarks of the state.

—FREDERICK J. GILLMAN

July 3

If my people, which are called by my name, shall humble themselves, and pray, and seek my face, and turn from their wicked ways; then will I hear from heaven, and will forgive their sin, and will heal their land (2 Chron. 7: 14).

Today, alive and active in our land, are all the haughty evils that made Babylon a vermin-infested, briar possessed, animal prowling jungle where the hanging gardens once bloomed. All the besmirching iniquities that made Nineveh a dirty doormat for irreverent feet thrive in our world today. All the sin diseases that made glorious Tyre a meatless skeleton ghastly with grins exist today. All the sins and sinning that made mighty Rome a branch-less tree, dishonorably fruitless, are defiantly rampant now. All the evils that made. Greece—cultured, poetic, artistic, athletic Greece—a crumb in history's rubbish heap are at work in America today. All the blatant unrighteousness that made Egypt a shabby sexton of splendid tombs, and all the greedy selfishness and craze for gold that made Spain a drowsy beggar watching a broken clock, ply their trade with the effrontery of a thief who comes but to steal and to kill and to destroy. They work as silently as moths in chests of fine clothes, as secretly and destructively as mice in a writer's desk, as boldly as drunken men speaking in the wild nightmares of disordered brains. These are iniquities that would "lead our greatest graces to the grave and leave the world no copy."

—ROBERT G. LEE
in *From Feet to Fathoms*

God of our fathers, known of old,
Lord of our far-flung battle-line,
Beneath whose awful Hand we hold
Dominion over palm and pine—
Lord God of Hosts, be with us yet,
Lest we forget—lest we forget!

The tumult and the shouting dies;
The Captains and the Kings depart:
Still stands Thine ancient sacrifice,
An humble and a contrite heart.
Lord God of Hosts, be with us yet,
Lest we forget—lest we forget!

Far-called, our navies melt away;
On dune and headland sinks the fire—
Lo, all our pomp of yesterday
Is one with Nineveh and Tyre!
Judge of the Nations, spare us yet,
Lest we forget—lest we forget!

If, drunk with sight of power, we loose
Wild tongues that have not Thee in awe,
Such boasting as the Gentiles use
Or lesser breeds without the Law—
Lord God of Hosts, be with us yet,
Lest we forget—lest we forget!

For heathen heart that puts her trust
In reeking tube and iron shard—
All valiant dust that builds on dust,
And guarding, calls not Thee to guard—
For frantic boast and foolish word,
Thy mercy on Thy people, Lord!

—RUDYARD KIPLING

"Righteousness exalteth a nation: but sin is a reproach to any people" (Prov. 14:34).

July 4

He said unto them, Render therefore unto Caesar the things which are Caesar's, and unto God the things which are God's (Luke 20:25).

Nations progress through this sequence. From bondage to spiritual truth to great courage . . . from courage to liberty . . . from liberty to abundance . . . from abundance to selfishness . . . from selfishness to complacency . . . from complacency to apathy . . . from apathy to dependency . . . and from dependency to bondage.

A democracy, therefore, cannot exist as a permanent form of government. It can only exist until the voters discover that they can vote themselves largesses from the public treasury. From that moment on, the majority always votes for candidates promising the most benefits . . . with the result that democracy collapses over loose fiscal policy followed by dictatorship.

—ALEXANDER TYLER (1800)

"Freedom can be had and kept only by so much effort that few persons are willing to take the trouble" (Lord Halifax).

"The penalty paid by good men for refusing to take part in good government, is to live under the government of bad men" (Plato).

"Put them in mind to be subject to principalities and powers, to obey magistrates, to be ready to every good work" (Titus 3:1).

> *Father in heaven, who lovest all,*
> *O help Thy children when they call;*
> *That they may build from age to age,*
> *An undefiled heritage.*
>
> *Teach us to bear the yoke in youth,*
> *With steadfastness and careful truth;*
> *That, in our time, Thy grace may give*
> *The truth whereby the nations live.*
>
> *Teach us to rule ourselves alway,*
> *Controlled and cleanly night and day;*
> *That we may bring, if need arise,*
> *No maimed or worthless sacrifice.*
>
> *Teach us to look, in all our ends,*
> *On Thee for Judge, and not our friends;*
> *That we, with Thee, may walk uncowed*
> *By fear or favor from the crowd.*
>
> *Teach us the strength, that cannot seek,*
> *By deed or thought, to hurt the weak;*
> *That, under Thee, we may possess*
> *Man's strength to succour man's distress.*
>
> *Teach us delight in simple things,*
> *And mirth that has no bitter springs;*
> *Forgiveness free of evil done,*
> *And love to all men 'neath the sun!*
>
> —RUDYARD KIPLING

July 5

He said unto me, My grace is sufficient for thee: for my strength is made perfect in weakness (2 Cor. 12:9).

The other evening I was riding home after a heavy day's work. I felt weary and sore depressed, when swiftly, suddenly, as a lightning flash, came, "My grace is sufficient for thee." I reached home and looked it up in the original, and it came to me in this way: "My grace is sufficient for *thee*," and I said, "I should think it is, Lord," and burst out laughing.

I never fully understood what the holy laughter of Abraham was until then. It seemed to make unbelief so absurd. It was as if some little fish, being very thirsty, was troubled about drinking the river dry, and Father Thames said, "Drink away, little fish; my stream is sufficient for thee"; or it seemed like a little mouse in the granaries of Egypt, after seven years of plenty, fearing it might die of famine. Joseph might say, "Cheer up little mouse; my wheat store is sufficient for thee."

Again I imagined a man away up yonder mountain saying to himself, "I fear I shall exhaust all the oxygen in the atmosphere." But the earth might say, "Breathe away, O man, and fill thy lungs ever; my atmosphere is sufficient for thee."

Brethren, be great believers! Little faith will bring your souls to heaven, but great faith will bring heaven to your souls.

—CHARLES H. SPURGEON

He giveth more grace when the burdens grow greater,
  He sendeth more strength when the labours increase,
To added affliction He addeth His mercy,
  To multiplied trials, His multiplied peace.

When we have exhausted our store of endurance,
  When our strength has failed ere the day is half done,
When we reach the end of our hoarded resources,
  Our Father's full giving is only begun.

His love has no limit, His grace has no measure,
  His power has no boundary known unto men.
For out of His infinite riches in Jesus,
  He giveth and giveth and giveth again.

—ANNIE JOHNSON FLINT

There is only one adequate provision for human need—the boundless grace of God. Therefore, hide in it! Hide in it for forgiveness and pardon for a sinful past. Hide in it for keeping—for a troubled present. Hide in it for security—in an eternal future.

Look whose grace it is—"*my* grace." Look what it is! "My grace *is* sufficient." Look when it is is! "My grace is sufficient *now!*" Look for whom it is. "My grace is sufficient for *thee.*"

—Vance Havner
in *Rest a While*

July 6

When they had gone throughout Phrygia and the region of Galatia, and were forbidden by the Holy Ghost to preach the word in Asia, after they were come to Mysia, they assayed to go into Bithynia: but the Spirit suffered them not. And they passing by Mysia came down to Troas (Acts 16:6-8).

They moved forward, and their hearts were set on Bithynia, where they fain would have preached. They were forbidden by the Holy Spirit. The truth declared is that these men in fellowship with Christ, simply could not go to Bithynia. They were driven on. The Spirit of Jesus drove Paul on. There seemed no value in this long journey, striking west. The north was luring him. Bithynia with its scattered tribes was there. He would fain preach, but he could not. So he was driven west, until he came to Troas. There was given to him the vision of a man of Macedonia, and at Troas Luke joined Paul. Now the whole journey is explained. A new door was opened!

In the actual atmosphere of this account, we see Paul strangely puzzled. Quarrelling with Barnabas, parting with him, he wanted to preach the gospel; and so he passed through Syria and Cilicia, and came to Derbe and Lystra, and there he met Timothy. He fain would go on to proconsular Asia, and he could not do it; he was sick, he was ill, an infirmity of the flesh was upon him. He took another direction and went into Galatia and preached there. Then he turned back again. The reason he could not understand. It is a picture of cross currents, of difficulty, of perplexity, and darkness. He felt the lure of Bithynia, and he would go there. No, he must go west, and on he went perplexed. Then came the vision of the man of Macedonia; and when he talked it over with Luke in later days, and Luke would write the story, he told that which at the moment he did not know. The Spirit forbade him to preach the Word in Asia. The Spirit of Jesus drove him ever and ever onward toward Troas. Thus there is stamped the fact of the guidance of the Holy Spirit. And this guidance of the Spirit and driving of the Spirit are placed at the points of supreme difficulty. Circumstances did not prevent. No, the Holy Spirit prevented, these men say.

The supreme value of this story is its revelation of the fact of the guidance of the Holy Spirit, when there is no revelation of the method of that guidance. The Spirit guided by the vision of the man of Macedonia. Here is the revelation of the fact that the Spirit guides, not by flaming visions always, not by words articulate in human ears; but by circumstances, by commonplace things, by difficult things, by dark things, by disappointing things. The Spirit will guide the man who is in the attitude in which it is possible for the Spirit to guide him. Here Paul's attitude of life is revealed—loyalty to the Lord, faith in the Spirit's guidance, and constant watchfulness. It is when a man is in fellowship with the Lord that he sees that the disappointment and the difficulty are also under the guidance of the Holy Spirit. It is the watcher for the Lord who sees the Lord.

—G. Campbell Morgan

July 7

When he was come down from the mountain, great multitudes followed him (Matt. 8:1).

Give us a watchword for this hour
A thrilling word, a word of power;
A battle-cry, a flaming breath,
That calls to conquest or to death;
A word to rouse the Church from rest,
To heed her Master's high behest.
The call is given: Ye hosts arise,
Our watchword is Evangelize!

—Henry Crocker

How wonderful it would be once more to hear the sound of feet hurrying to hear the gospel. How our cities need to be stirred again. Should we not pray earnestly that the Church age may close with another great spiritual awakening as the one which began it at Pentecost? Is not the power of the Holy Spirit and the arm of the Lord still mighty to save?

Let this be our daily prayer: Send a great revival, Lord, and let it begin in me!

> *O for a passionate passion for souls,*
> *O for a pity that yearns!*
> *O for the love that loves unto death,*
> *O for the fire that burns!*
> *O for the pure prayer-power that prevails,*
> *That pours itself out for the lost!*
> *Victorious prayer in the Conqueror's name,*
> *O for a Pentecost!*

> —AMY CARMICHAEL

July 8

To him that worketh is the reward not reckoned of grace, but of debt. But to him that worketh not, but believeth on him that justifieth the ungodly, his faith is counted for righteousness (Rom. 4:4-5).

Thus Paul proclaims the simple message of the Cross. God's righteousness cannot be earned or worked for. It comes as a free gift by faith! He who works to merit God's salvation only increases the debt. God has granted righteousness through the act of believing. To the church at Ephesus, Paul reemphasized this truth. "For by grace are ye saved through faith; and that not of yourselves; it is the gift of God: Not of works, lest any man should boast" (Eph. 2:8-9).

> *Nothing to pay?—no, not a whit;*
> *Nothing to do?—no, not a bit;*
> *All that was needed to do or to pay,*
> *Jesus has done in His own blessed way.*

Nothing to do?—no, not a stroke;
Gone is the captor, gone is the yoke;
Jesus at Calvary severed the chain,
And none can imprison His freeman again.

Nothing to settle?—all has been paid;
Nothing to anger?—peace has been made;
Jesus alone is the sinner's resource,
Peace He has made by the blood of His cross.

Nothing of guilt?—no, not a stain,
How could the blood let any remain?
My conscious is purged, and my spirit is free—
Precious that blood is to God and to me!

—AUTHOR UNKNOWN

D. L. Moody wrote this in the margin of his Bible: "*Justification*, a change of state with a new standing before God. *Repentance*, a change of mind with a new mind about God. *Regeneration*, a change of nature with a new heart from God. *Conversion*, a change of life with a new life for God. *Adoption*, a change of family with a new relationship with God. *Sanctification*, a change of service with separation unto God."

"For all have sinned, and come short of the glory of God; Being justified freely by his grace through the redemption that is in Christ Jesus" (Rom. 3:23-24).

July 9

If it seem evil unto you to serve the Lord, choose you this day whom ye will serve; whether the gods which your fathers served that were on the other side of the flood, or the gods of the Amorites, in whose land ye dwell; but as for me and my house, we will serve the Lord (Josh. 24:15).

This was the day of decision! Joshua gave Israel three choices. They could follow the beautiful idols of Abraham's cultured kin "on the other side of the river"; or the vile idols of

224

the Canaanites in the land where they were dwelling; or, like Joshua, choose the God of Abraham, Isaac, and Jacob.

He warned them that there were two ways they could go. They could choose either the Lord or as McAuley wrote "choose hell by either cultured unrighteousness or debauchery. Either way God is rejected." Their fate would be sealed by the choice they would make.

Joshua and his family would cleave unto the Lord with their whole heart. How wonderful when the head of the household is so respected by his children that they choose the right path also. We need a multitude of "as for me and my house" Christians today. When the father walks in the "paths of righteousness," the children are more apt to follow!

> 'Twas a sheep, not a lamb, that strayed away,
> In the parable Jesus told;
> A grown-up sheep that had gone astray,
> From the ninety and nine in the fold.
>
> Out on the hillside, out in the cold,
> 'Twas a sheep the good shepherd sought,
> And back to the flock safe into the fold
> 'Twas a sheep the good shepherd brought.
>
> And why for the sheep should we earnestly long,
> And as earnestly hope and pray?
> Because there is danger, if they go wrong,
> They will lead the lambs astray.
>
> For the lambs will follow the sheep, you know,
> Wherever the sheep may stray;
> When the sheep go wrong, it will not be long
> Till the lambs are as wrong as they.
>
> And so with the sheep we earnestly plead,
> For the sake of the lambs today;
> If the lambs are lost; what a terrible cost
> Some sheep will have to pay.

—C. D. MILLER

"Believe on the Lord Jesus Christ, and thou shalt be saved, and thy house" (Acts 16:31).

July 10

He that hath the Son hath life; and he that hath not the Son of God hath not life (1 John 5:12).

God makes this very plain in His Word: there is life in His Son. St. Paul, writing to the Ephesian Christians, presents a reminder of this great truth: "You hath he [made alive], who were dead in trespasses and sins. . . . But God, who is rich in mercy, for his great love wherewith he loved us, even when we were dead in sins, hath [made us alive] together with Christ" (Eph. 2:1, 4-5).

But not only do we have life in Christ—we also daily live in Him. Whatever life's circumstances, He hallows them and "we are more than conquerors through him who loved us" (Rom. 8:37).

"Set your affection on things above, not on things on the earth. For ye are dead, and your life is hid with Christ in God" (Col. 3:2-3).

> *Out of the light that dazzles me,*
> *Bright as the sun from pole to pole,*
> *I thank the God I know to be*
> *For Christ the Conqueror of my soul.*
>
> *Since His the sway of circumstance,*
> *I would not wince or cry aloud.*
> *Under the rule which men call chance,*
> *My head with joy is humbly bowed.*
>
> *Beyond this place of sin and tears—*
> *That life with Him! and His the aid,*
> *Despite the menace of the years,*
> *Keeps, and shall keep me unafraid.*
>
> *I have no fear though strait the gate,*
> *He cleared from punishment the scroll;*
> *Christ is the Master of my fate!*
> *Christ is the Captain of my soul.*

—Dorothea Day

July 11

He that saith, I know him, and keepeth not his commandments, is a liar, and the truth is not in him (1 John 2:4).

John writes of the need for holy performance in our daily living. Those who know the Savior must keep His commandments. If we speak of "sanctifying grace," our lives must show it in every aspect and every act and every motive. It is so easy to talk of total consecration and yet not live for Him. Beware of your actions "speaking so loud that none can hear what you say."

I'd rather see a sermon than hear one, any day;
I'd rather one would walk with me than merely
*   tell the way;*
The eye's a better pupil and more willing
*   than the ear.*
Fine counsel is confusing, but example's always clear.
And the best of all the preachers are the men
*   who live their creeds,*
For to see good put in action is what everybody needs.

I soon can learn to do it if you'll let me see it done;
I can watch your hands in action, but your tongue
*   too fast may run.*
And the lecture you deliver may be very wise and true,
But I'd rather get my lessons by observing
*   what you do.*
For I might misunderstand you and the high advice
*   you give,*
But there's no misunderstanding how you act and
*   how you live.*

—Edgar A. Guest

"Having therefore these promises, dearly beloved, let us cleanse ourselves from all filthiness of the flesh and spirit, perfecting holiness in the fear of God" (2 Cor. 7:1).

God knocked at the door of my heart one day
And I looked for a place to hide;
My soul was cluttered and choked with debris
And things were untidy inside.

I needed some time to put matters right,
  Surprised He would call on me.
My soul needed cleaning from bottom to top,
  There were things He should not see.

There were tasks neglected, long overdue;
  Cobwebs to be brushed from the wall;
Rugs to be shaken and windows cleaned up—
  I had not expected this call.

I stood with my hand on the latch of the door
  And gazed at the mess in the room.
When I opened the door, my soul blushed to see
  God had left on my doorstep—a broom.

—Barbara J. Thompson

July 12

I can do all things through Christ, which strengtheneth me (Phil. 4:13).

"I can!" How bracing an affirmation this is when it rests in such a faith as Paul is confessing! It is depressingly easy to find people who know how to say, "I can't." They are well-practiced in it. You have heard this talk. "I can't control my temper." "I can't cope with these jealous thoughts." "I can't tithe my income." "I can't pray in public." "I can't live the holy life." "I can't be a victorious Christian."

The list is almost endless. The refrain is at times monotonous. "I can't! I can't! I can't!"

Now the way out of this impotence is not to blow on one's hands and try a little harder. That is futile. Adequacy comes only through attaching ourselves to the Adequate One. It comes through practicing the confidence that whatever Jesus Christ once was, in the days of His visible life on earth, conquering the "powers of darkness" whenever He clashed with them, *He still is.* He is as availably alive and as vitally available as when He stilled a Galilean tempest or turned the black bereavement of Mary and Martha into a song of hope to celebrate the defeat of death.

Here is something glorious for re-proclamation. The melancholy note of the Christian's incessant defeat, with no ray of hope save the endlessly repeated forgiveness of God, finds expression in "I can't." We need the trumpet music of Paul, "I can do all things through Christ!"

Of course the sharpness, the cunningness, and the persistency of temptation are at times a veritable torture. It was the Paul who knew all this, tasted all this, battled all this, who nevertheless shouted from the top of the battle-heap, "I can!"

How can anyone miss it? The adequate man, every bit as unworthy the last day of his life as on the first day of his conversion, is nevertheless not agloom with sin's bondage and bitterness but aglow with Christ's mercy and masterfulness. He says, "I can!"

—PAUL S. REES
in *The Adequate Man*

"Thanks be unto God, which always causeth us to triumph in Christ" (2 Cor. 2:14).

July 13

His disciples came, and took up the body, and buried it, and went and told Jesus (Matt. 14:12).

John the Baptist had been beheaded by the wicked Herod, and his disciples were therefore greatly saddened and upset. After they had tenderly buried his body, they came with their distress and sorrow and "told Jesus." We as Christians must constantly be reminded that the best thing to do in times of grief or trouble or perplexity is to bring our burden to our Saviour and simply cast our cares upon Him. A poet has wisely written: "In thy weakness, in thy peril, raise to Him a heartfelt call; strength and calm for every crisis comes in telling Jesus all." If problems are pressing in on you from every side, if you are deeply distressed—tell it to Jesus!

—HENRY G. BOSCH
From *Our Daily Bread*, © 1973, Radio Bible Class.
Used by special permission.

God is prepared to keep us in all our ways. The promise is clear: "He shall give his angels charge over thee, to keep thee in all thy ways"—the business ways, the social ways, the ways of service into which God may lead us forth, the ways of sacrifice or the ways of suffering. Let us simply and humbly ask for the fulfillment of the promises. He will answer your prayer. He will be with you in trouble. He will satisfy you with many years of life, or with living much in a short time, and He will show you the wonders of His salvation.

—F. B. MEYER

". . . casting all your care upon him; for he careth for you" (1 Pet. 5:7).

> Are you weary, are you heavy hearted?
> Tell it to Jesus, tell it to Jesus;
> Are you grieving over joys departed?
> Tell it to Jesus alone.

—J. E. RANKIN

July 14

Beloved, let us love one another: for love is of God; and everyone that loveth is born of God, and knoweth God (1 John 4:7).

There is another John 3:16 besides the beautiful verse which says, "God so loved the world, that he gave his only begotten Son, that whosoever believeth in him should not perish, but have everlasting life." It is 1 John 3:16. It was written by the same John, the beloved disciple so close to Jesus. "This is how we know what love is: Jesus Christ laid down his life for us. And we ought to lay down our lives for our brothers" (NIV).

Pastor U. S. Grant asks, "Do you—do I—love the Christian brotherhood so much that we would lay down our lives for the brethren? If so, then let us guard our attitudes and our actions so as not to destroy 'him for whom Christ died.' Our love must be genuine."

In the next verse John asks a very searching question. "If anyone has material possessions and sees his brother in need but has not pity on him, how can the love of God be in him?" If the love of God dwells in us, then we must care and care enough to give and serve.

Henry Drummond wrote: "In the Book of Matthew, where the judgment of the nations is depicted for us in the imagery of One seated upon a throne and dividing the sheep from the goats, the test of a man was not, 'How have I believed' but 'How have I loved?' The test of true religion is not religiousness but Love. Sins of commission in Christ's awful indictment are not even referred to. By what we have not done, by sins of omission, we are judged. It could not be otherwise. For the withholding of love is the negation of the spirit of Christ, the proof that we never knew Him, that for us He lived and died in vain.

"I have enjoyed almost all the beautiful things God has made. I have enjoyed almost every pleasure He has planned for man. But as I look back upon my life, I see standing out above all of life, the experiences when the love of God reflected itself in some poor act of love, and these small things seem to be that which abides. Everything else in all our lives is transitory. The acts of love—they never fail."

It isn't the things you do, dear,
It's the things you leave undone,
Which give you the bitter heartache
At the setting of the sun;
The tender word unspoken,
The letter you did not write,
The flowers you might have sent, dear,
Are your haunting ghosts at night.

The stone you might have lifted
Out of your brother's way,
The bit of heartsome counsel
You were hurried too much to say;
The loving touch of the hand, dear,
The gentle and winsome tone,
That you had not time or thought for,
With troubles enough of your own.

These little acts of kindness,
So easily out of mind,
These chances to be angels,
Which even mortals find—
They come in night and silence,
Each chill reproachful wraith,
When hope is faint and flagging,
And a blight has dropped on faith.

For life is all too short, dear,
And sorrow is all too great,
To suffer our slow compassion
That tarries until too late.
And it's not the thing you do, dear,
It's the thing you leave undone,
Which gives you the bitter heartache,
At the setting of the sun.

—ADELAIDE PROCTOR

July 15

Ahab went up to eat and to drink. And Elijah went up to the top of Carmel; and he cast himself down upon the earth, and put his face between his knees (1 Kings 18:42).

For three and a half years there had been no rain in Israel. Dire distress was present everywhere. But on this day, at Mount Carmel, the rains would come.

Wicked Ahab was there. His usefulness consisted only in being able "to eat and to drink." Mourners over the drought were there, undoubtedly complaining. The seven thousand who had "not bowed their knees to Baal"—Israel's modern religion— were probably in attendance. Obadiah was there. He had supplied the prophets with secret food but also served Ahab. He tried to look out for the glory of God with one eye and his position in Ahab's court with the other. But he could not produce any rain.

And one must suppose that the "bread and water prophets" were there whom Obadiah had been feeding. They had been living in two caves and just existing. These were men of God hiding with His message, and sorely needed in idolatrous Israel.

But one other man was there—Elijah! He was God's man and he made the difference. He could say, "As the Lord liveth before whom I stand"—and such a man always makes a difference! When his knees bent into the ground, this was the sign God had been seeking. The sign of a man prostrate before the Lord brought the sign "of a man's hand in the sky." The clouds came and the sound of "abundance of rain."

One man on bended knee with "his face between his knees" is the method God uses to bring revival in our time. Is the land cracked and parched around you? Take heart. Pray on! Let God see the sign of a man's knees on the ground. He will answer your prayer—sometime, somewhere! The rains will come!

—A. W. Bailey

Unanswered yet? The prayer your lips have pleaded
In agony of heart these many years?
Does faith begin to fail, is hope departing,
And think you all in vain those falling tears?
Say not the Father hath not heard your prayer;
You shall have your desire, sometime, somewhere.

Unanswered yet? Though when you first presented
This one petition at the Father's throne,

It seemed you could not wait the time of asking,
So urgent was your heart to make it known.
Though years have passed since then, do not despair;
The Lord will answer you, sometime, somewhere.

Unanswered yet? Nay, do not say ungranted;
Perhaps your part is not yet wholly done;
The work begun when first your prayer was uttered,
And God will finish what He has begun.
If you will keep the incense burning there;
His glory you shall see, sometime, somewhere.

Unanswered yet? Faith cannot be unanswered;
Her feet were firmly planted on the Rock;
Amid the wildest storm prayer stands undaunted;
Nor quails before the loudest thunder shock;
She knows Omnipotence has heard her prayer,
And cries, "It shall be done, sometime, somewhere."

—OPHELIA G. ADAMS

July 16

**They took knowledge of them, that they
had been with Jesus** (Acts 4:13).

With boldness Peter stood and preached about the crucified
and risen Son of God. This was the same Peter, who but a few
short days before had been afraid of the taunts of a servant girl
and tragically denied his Lord until the hour that the cock crowed.
For three days and nights he had lived in darkest despair. But no
more! Peter had met the risen Lord and had received a new commitment and a fresh ordination. Let the Sanhedrin rage and the
Sadducees threaten. His voice would ring clear and true—"This is
the stone which was set at naught of you builders, which is become the head of the corner. Neither is there salvation in any
other; for there is no other name under heaven given among men,
whereby we must be saved" (Acts 4:11).

Although many would not believe, some did, and about
5,000 were added on this day to the Church. They were convinced by Peter's message and "they took knowledge of them that
they had been with Jesus" (Acts 4:13).

Here is the secret of the great preacher and witness. He must

233

be "with Jesus." His words, his thoughts, his life must always reflect the purity and holiness of his blessed Lord.

Unlearned and ignorant! Yet God has never been frustrated in His purposes by the superficial limitations of His servants. Life's superlative endowment in a servant of God is an adequate experience of Christ. Peter once denied His Lord but now boldness was the endowment needed for the crisis before him.

He and John prayed for boldness! They were filled with the Spirit, and they received boldness! This was after Pentecost. It sets forth the need for Christians to receive a fresh infilling of the Spirit for each new task. One empowerment is not enough. We need ten thousand for every duty. It is sunrise in Pilgrim's life when he learns to pray without ceasing, "O God, fill me with Thy Holy Spirit."

—RICHARD ELLSWORTH DAY

> With frightened lips I shall not ever say
> "I know Him not," for none will question me.
> I shall not need to speak a word today
> To publish to the world my loyalty.
> And yet a hundred times there comes the voice,
> "Know ye this Man—the Master?"
> And a hundred times I make the fateful choice
> As the apostle once of old.
> And every unkind word or straying thought,
> Every look of anger and disdain,
> Says plainly to the world, "I know Him not,"
> And then the cock crows—bitter morn of pain.
> And would indeed today that they might be
> The times I have denied Him only three.

—AUTHOR UNKNOWN

July 17

Thou art my hope, O Lord God: thou art my trust from my youth. . . . Cast me not off in the time of old age; forsake me not when my strength faileth (Ps. 71:5, 9).

The surest way of knowing Christ when the shadows fall is to find Him when life's sun is rising. If He is our Savior when the morning of life breaks, He will also be our Savior when evening comes.

His promise is sure! "And even to your old age I am he; and even to [gray] hairs will I carry you: I have made, and I will bear; even I will carry, and will deliver you" (Isa. 46:4). Happy is the man who seeks the Lord in his youth and walks the years with Him. The pleasures of sin last for such a short season. They cannot compare to the blessings of the way of holiness. Riches untold are the possession of His people. It is wise to seek Him early before the late years come—years when the soul says, "I have no pleasures left."

> E'en down to old age, all My people shall prove
> My sovereign, eternal, unchangeable love;
> And when hoary hairs shall their temples adorn,
> Like lambs they shall still in my bosom be borne.
>
> —GEORGE KEITH

"The devil owns no happy old people."

"Godliness is profitable unto all things, having promise of the life that now is, and of that which is to come" (1 Tim. 4:8).

July 18

In those days came John the Baptist, preaching in the wilderness of Judaea, and saying, Repent ye: for the kingdom of heaven is at hand (Matt. 3:1-2).

Isaiah wrote of those who had "familiar spirits and of wizards who mutter and peep," but such a preacher was not John the Baptist. He came preaching repentance! He had a clear message! Although his ministry was "in the wilderness," and he labored not in a lofty pulpit or an ornate cathedral, yet his ministry bore "fruits unto repentance."

There are two kinds of ministers—those who preach because they have to say something and those who preach because they have something to say. The latter are God's men—even though they minister "in the wilderness."

John preached but few words, yet his message cut like a two-edged sword. He came preaching repentance, but he also came crying. His words were wet with tears. Harry Ironside once said, "Our eyes are too dry." If we would see even the Pharisees "confess their sins," then we must preach God's Word in utter dependence on the Holy Spirit and "in tears."

> I do not ask for mighty words
> To leave the crowd impressed,
> But grant my life may ring so true
> My neighbor shall be blessed.
>
> I do not ask for influence
> To sway the multitude;
> Give me a "word in season" for
> The soul in solitude.
>
> Though words of wisdom and of power
> Rise easily to some,
> Give me a simple message, Lord,
> That bids the sinner come.
>
> I ask no place of prominence
> Where all the world can see,
> But in some needy corner, Lord,
> There let me work for Thee.
>
> No task too great, no task too small,
> Sufficient is Thy grace;
> The darkened heart, my mission field,
> My light, the Savior's face.
>
> —BARBARA CORNEY RYBERG

"Happy is the preacher whose words are such that his Lord can endorse them" (Charles Haddon Spurgeon).

July 19

Giving all diligence, add to your faith virtue; and to virtue, knowledge; and to knowledge, temperance; and to temperance, patience; and to patience, godliness; and to godliness, brotherly kindness; and to brotherly kindness, love (2 Pet. 1:5-7).

Faith is important, for there is no salvation possible apart from faith in the Savior, the Lord Jesus Christ. But Peter urges the believer to add virtue to his faith. This is the quality that makes one likeable. It is moral excellence with faith radiating out to other people.

We are also urged to add knowledge. This is a specific knowledge—a deep and thorough study of the Word of God. A successful and fruitful servant of God must know the Word. Be certain to add knowledge to your faith.

Self-control (temperance) must also be added. This means that such things as hurt feelings, resentment toward others, and bitterness should have no place in the Christian's life. Unchristlike attitudes and reactions are of the flesh and they must be left at the Cross. One cannot talk of salvation and delight in Holy Communion if there is any bitterness or resentment in the heart.

Patience is then to be added—patience with others and with things. And Peter also called for godliness to join with patience. This is really godlikeness. We are to be like Him. Paul also said this. "Be ye therefore followers of God, as dear children; and walk in love, as Christ also hath loved us" (Eph. 5:1).

Finally, add "brotherly kindness and love." Brotherly kindness is a translation from the Greek word *philadelphia*—"a love of the brethren." The word *phileo*, translated "love," is part of this word. It refers to the love of friends. It is a mutual love. But Peter added to this kind of love, the word *agapao*—the love of God. This love must be added to our faith and we shall then "neither be barren nor unfruitful in the knowledge of our Lord Jesus Christ." The life that "adds" is the life of fruitfulness. This is the true faith "that makes us love everybody."

—Robert H. Belton

More like the Master I would live and grow;
More of His love to others I would show;
More self-denial, like His in Galilee,
More like the Master, I long to ever be.

—Charles H. Gabriel

July 20

When he was yet a great way off, his father saw him, and had compassion, and ran, and fell on his neck, and kissed him (Luke 15:20).

The prodigal son did not have a prodigal father. The boy had a free will and the father allowed him to exercise that will, but he longed for his son to be back in his home. And so when the prodigal chose to come back from the sin and the pigpens of the far country, his father ran to meet him.

How did the father see him when he was "a long way off"? D. L. Moody said, "The father was looking for him through the telescope of his tears." That is love! The love a father has for a prodigal son.

Oh, he didn't love his waywardness, his vileness, his filth, or his sins, but he loved his son. The Lord Jesus gave us this parable to teach us that God is like this. The Father loves His prodigal sons and daughters and He is looking for them. His heart too has been broken. He is waiting to forgive our sins and to cover us with a robe of righteousness. He has a ring of sonship for our fingers. He has shoes to enable us to walk His ways. He has a feast spread and waiting.

Yes, the Father is looking for returning prodigals. But they must take the first step toward Him. When one does this, he will find the Father waiting to receive him.

> In the distant land of famine
>   Faining with the swine to feed,
> Oh! how bitter that awakening to
>   My sin and shame and need!
> Dark and dreary all around me—
>   Now no more by sin beguiled,
> I would go and seek my Father,
>   Be a bondsman, not a child.
>
> Yet a great way off He saw me,
>   Ran to kiss me as I came;
> As I was my Father loved me,
>   Loved me in my sin and shame.
> Then in bitter grief I told Him
>   Of the evil I had done;
> Sinned in scorn of Him, my Father,
>   Was not meet to be His son.
>
> But I know not if He listened,
>   For He spake not of my sin;
> He within His house would have me—
>   Made me meet to enter in;
> From the riches of His glory,
>   Brought His costliest raiment forth,
> Brought the ring that sealed His purpose,
>   Shoes to tread His golden courts.
>
> Put them on me—robes of glory,
>   Spotless as the heavens above;

Not to meet my thoughts of fitness,
  But His wondrous thoughts of love.
Then within His house He led me,
  Brought me where the feast was spread,
Made me eat with Him, my Father,
  I who begged for bondsman's bread.

Not a suppliant at His gateway,
  But a son within His home;
To the love, the joy, the singing,
  To the glory I am come.
Gathered round that wondrous temple,
  Filled with awe, His angels see,
Glory lighting up the Holiest,
  And in that glory Him and me.

—FRANCES BEVAN

July 21

Jesus said unto him, No man, having put
his hand to the plough, and looking back, is
fit for the kingdom of God (Luke 9:62).

Five men, Peter, Andrew, Matthew, John, and Paul sat on a hillside overlooking the Sea of Galilee. It was 20 years after Pentecost and they had met by appointment to talk over a crisis in their lives and the future of their ministry.

The work was going hard with them. Paul had suffered the loss of all things. Peter had left all to follow the Christ and he was finding it difficult to support his family. Matthew had just been offered an attractive business proposition.

Peter opened by saying, "Simon the tanner has inherited the estate of his brother, and an old friend of mine in Bethsaida has offered to give me a complete fishing outfit with boats, nets, and tackle, and an established trade in Capernaum. It looks like a providential leading, especially as my wife's mother has opened a boarding house there and it will cost us almost nothing to live with her while we are getting started again. I can make a good living fishing five days in the week and I will have my Sundays free for evangelistic work in the cities around the lake."

Paul said, "Aquila and Priscilla have prospered in the tent making business in Ephesus and they have offered me a position at a good salary to open a branch in Philippi. I can do this work and still have abundant opportunity for Christian work among the churches and this will enable me to lay a little something aside for my old age."

Matthew said, "My story of the life of Christ is having a large sale and is bringing me in enough to pay my expenses, but my business experience tells me that I ought to have a larger margin. Persecution may come and sales would fall off. I have a chance now to take my old position back with added duties and higher salary. This would give me enough to care for the family and to have some left for the rest of you if you need it. And then, too, I would have more leisure time for my writing."

Andrew said, "Peter, do you remember the day when you thought that you had lost your wife's mother? Do you see that sand beach over there? That is where we beached our boat when we quit the fishing business, and where the Master said, 'Fear not, from henceforth thou shalt catch men.' How long a time is henceforth? Do you see that hillside over there? That is where the Master fed the 5,000, and I can see the very spot where that lad stood when I asked him to give up his lunch for the Lord to multiply it. Do you remember how He prayed that day for laborers to be sent forth into His vineyard? Are the fields still white for the harvest? If we are going to continue to pray that others may rise up and follow Him, leaving their all, can we do less?"

A great silence fell over them, and then Paul began to pray. They sensed the light breeze rustling in the nearby trees, remindful of the mighty wind on the day of Pentecost. They heard His words once again, "Launch out into the deep and let down your nets for a draught," and "fear not, from henceforth thou shalt catch men."

The evening caravan for Tyre was just swinging into sight. "Good-by," said Paul. "I must catch the next boat for Ephesus. Aquila will put up the money for a campaign in that old city that will shake the whole of Asia."

"Good-by," said Peter. "Andrew and I will just say farewell to the family and then we will join the midnight caravan for Babylon and then to the East as far as the land of Sinim.

"Good-by," said Matthew. "There is a group of publicans who were going in with me on this tax venture, but I will get them to join me in financing a five-year campaign in Egypt and up the Nile as far as Ethiopia. I have heard from the Ethiopian Treasurer that practically the whole country is open to us with hearts that are hungry for the gospel. Ethiopia will soon stretch out its hands unto God."

"Good-by," said John, and he sat alone till the stars came out and the waves on the beach, impelled by the rising wind, sounded like the voice of many waters, and he said to Him that stood by, "Lord, bless them. I thank thee for Andrew and his deep life and steady faith. Lord, let us ever see Thee before us, ever hear Thy voice, and ever walk and work with Thee, and we will not fear what men can do unto us."

A sudden storm broke over the lake, and I awoke from my dream. Lord, how grateful we are that the apostles of old never turned back but were true to the Great Commission. May we, too, ever walk and work for Thee!

—C. K. Ober

> Go, labor on; spend and be spent,
>   Thy joy to do the Father's will.
> It is the way the Master went;
>   Should not the servant tread it still?
>
> Go, labor on; 'tis not for naught;
>   Thine earthly loss is heavenly gain.
> Men heed thee, love thee, praise thee not;
>   The Master praises—what are men?

—Horatius Bonar

July 22

He saith unto them, But whom say ye that I am? And Simon Peter answered and said, Thou art the Christ, the Son of the living God (Matt. 16:15-16).

Jesus first asked the disciples, "Whom do men say that I am?" There was a variety of answers—but all of them were wrong! Who is He who opened the blind eyes of Bartimeus? Who is this One that stilled the waves of Galilee? Who is this Man who called Lazarus forth from the grave? Who is He?—for even His enemies stated, "No man ever spake as this man."

"Whom say ye that I am?" This is life's most important question. Don't be mistaken in your belief. Peter answered firmly, "Thou art the Christ, the Son of God." God seals men by the choice they make.

The rock of His deity is the foundation of the Church. And any church that isn't established on this foundation, is not His Church; any minister that does not put his faith on this Rock is not His minister; and any congregation that disbelieves His deity is not God's congregation!

It is important to know who Jesus is. It is important to know that His Christhood is linked inseparately with His death and resurrection; but this also must be known—that fellowship with this Christ, the Son of the living God, means the way of the Cross for us too. There can be no following Christ and saving one's life; we can follow Him only by laying it down. And just as He by way of the Cross entered into glory, so it is by losing our life in the way of the Cross, that we find the true life, the abundant life, eternal life.

—J. C. MACAULAY

Lord, I would follow,—yea,
Follow I will;—but first so much there is
That claims me in life's vast emergencies,—
Wrongs to be righted, great things to be done;
Shall I neglect these vital urgencies?

Who answers Christ's insistent call
Must give himself, his life, his all,
Without one backward look.
Who sets his hand unto the plow,
And glances back with anxious brow,
His calling hath mistook.
Christ claims him wholly for His own;
He must be Christ's, and Christ's alone.

—JOHN OXENHAM

July 23

Commit thy works unto the Lord (Prov. 16:3)

In one of David's psalms we are advised: "Commit thy way unto the Lord; trust also in him; and he shall bring it to pass" (Ps. 37:5). Solomon asks that we commit our *works* also.

This week I visited a dear friend in the hospital and his appearance haunted me as I thought of him from days long past. He was a gifted man but evening cocktails gave way to martinis before lunch and then he added vodka to start the day and to give courage for each new task. Life ended for him with a wasted body, a wasted talent, and a wasted soul. He would not believe that "at the last it biteth like a serpent, and stingeth like an adder" (Prov. 23:32).

How different the outcome if he only had committed his work and his way unto the Lord!

—HOWARD WINFIELD

At the first it sweetly sings;
At the last it bites and stings.
At the first it marches proud
At the front of all the crowd.
At the last it takes away
All the glory of life's day.
At the last it tumbles down
To the gutters of the town.

—AMOS R. WELLS

"There is a way that seemeth right unto a man, but the end thereof are the ways of death" (Prov. 16:25).

"If alcoholism is a disease, it is the only disease that is contracted by an act of will. If it is a disease, it is the only disease that is bottled and sold and requires a license to propagate it. If alcoholism is a disease, it is the only disease that produces a revenue for the government, provokes crime, and is spread by advertising. And if alcoholism is a disease, it is the only disease that bars the patient from heaven unless there is repentance" (E. L. Worthington).

I have striven with might and main,
And every time I have failed,
I have risen to fight again,
Yet the same swift foes prevailed;
Now the Victor's power I claim,
Though they draw a thousand swords,
I trust in the Christ who overcame
And the battle is the Lord's!

—BEATRICE CLELAND

"But thanks be to God, which giveth us the victory through our Lord Jesus Christ" (1 Cor. 15:57).

July 24

*This know also, that in the last days peril-
ous times shall come* (2 Tim. 3:1).

Thoro Harris wrote a hymn many years ago that the Church
should be singing today. One verse reads,

> *While the dread hour of darkness*
> *Is settling o'er the earth,*
> *And the Bridegroom is not far away;*
> *And we wait His returning,*
> *O God of boundless grace,*
> *Give me oil in my vessel today.*

"Perilous times shall come," Paul wrote to Timothy. These
dread days are now coming upon us. Paul characterized them as a
time when men shall love themselves. They shall covet everything. They shall be boastful, overbearing, and blasphemous.
Natural affection will not be in them but there shall be an increase
in homosexuality. They shall despise those things which are good.
They shall be traitors to their own wives and to their country.
They shall love pleasure more than God. Their character will be
vicious and they shall be strangers to the truth. No faith or holiness will be in them. However, they will keep a facade of religion
but, Paul wrote, "they will deny the power thereof."

We see this today. The power of the Christian faith is the
gospel—the Good News—how that Christ died for our sins and
was buried and rose again and was seen (1 Corinthians 15). And
this gospel is the power of God to transform sinners and redeem
them. This is the power that religious men (men who are "ungodly," meaning "without God") will deny. In the last days there
will arise men of the cloth who will not be men of the Cross!

As the workers of iniquity increase, let us not fret nor be
surprised. We have been warned that perilous times will grow
worse around us as we near the end of the age. Do not fear.
Rejoice! Maranatha! The Lord is coming!

> *There are many who slumber, but, oh, that I may keep*
> *Faithful watch till the Lord shall appear;*
> *I would watch every sign that the day-dawn is at hand,*
> *And rejoice that His coming is near.*
>
> *"Lo, He cometh! He cometh!" the heavens shall resound*
> *With the shout of the purified throng;*

Let us go forth to meet Him returning on His way,
   Let us join in the angels' sweet song.

Give me oil in my lamp, oil in my lamp,
   Oil in my lamp, I pray;
Give me oil in my lamp,
Keep me shining in the camp,
Until the break of day.

—THORO HARRIS

July 25

After the death of Moses the servant of the Lord, it came to pass, that the Lord spake unto Joshua the son of Nun, Moses' minister, saying, Moses my servant is dead; now therefore arise (Josh. 1:1-2).

This is the beginning of the story of a young man who very early in life gave his heart to God and His service. With 40 years of training under Moses, the day had come for Joshua to do his important work!

Moses' death seemed a tragedy. He had been a great man and valuable to God. But great men die. There comes a time when the work of the Lord's servant ceases. Dr. Walter Wilson wrote, "God buries His servants but carries on His work." Joshuas must be waiting and ready and well-trained when the time comes for them to "arise."

Four promises were given to Joshua, but they are also promises for us today. (1) "Go over this Jordan . . . unto the land which I do give [thee]." (2) "Every place that the sole of your foot shall tread upon" shall be yours. (3) No man shall "be able to stand before thee all the days of thy life." (4) "As I was with Moses, so I will be with thee."

What glorious promises! Let us not be afraid. He will guide and counsel us. Be strong and courageous. He will meet our every need.

"I must wait for four things: First to know whether a work is God's work. Second, to know whether it is God's work for me. Third, I must know if it is God's time for the work; and finally, I need to know whether it is God's way" (George Mueller).

"If he call thee, . . . say, Speak, Lord; for thy servant heareth" (1 Sam. 3:9).

July 26

Owe no man any thing, but to love one another; for he that loveth another hath fulfilled the law (Rom. 13:8).

As Christians we hear much about the urgent need of living for the Lord. It is the theme of our songs and the prayer upon our hearts. But love must be the goal of all Christian living. Although it is essential to stress living for Jesus, the absolute necessity is "loving for Jesus." All else is vain! We may be very orthodox, but without love we are "as sounding brass or a tinkling cymbal" (1 Corinthians 13).

A small-town newspaper once carried as a regular feature the sermons of a local minister. One Sunday his text was from the King James Version, "Though I speak with the tongues of men and of angels, and have not charity . . ." A typographical error came out "clarity." But this is also a necessity. Without charity (or love) there is no clarity in the message we seek to convey to a needy world.

An instructive story is told about a small boy who came from a very poor home. He was shabbily dressed most of the time. Although he liked all of his teachers, one stood out as his favorite. When asked why, he simply replied, "She's so interested in me, she doesn't seem to see my patches." This is the life of the true believer. Are we really "loving for Jesus" while we claim to be "living for Jesus"?

—RICHARD W. DeHAAN
From *Our Daily Bread,* © 1973, Radio Bible Class.
Used by special permission.

July 27

Surely he shall deliver thee from the snare of the fowler (Ps. 91:3).

God delivers His people from the snare of the fowler in two senses: "From" and "out of." First, He delivers them from the snare—He does not let them enter it; and secondly, if they should be caught therein, He delivers them out of it. The first promise is the most precious to some; the second is the best to others.

"He shall deliver thee from the snare." How? Trouble is often the means whereby God delivers us. God knows that our backsliding will soon end in our destruction, and He in mercy sends the rod. We say, "Lord, why is this?" not knowing that our trouble has been the means of delivering us from far greater evil. Many have thus been saved from ruin by their sorrows and their crosses; these have frightened the birds from the nest.

At other times, God keeps His people from the snare of the fowler by giving them great spiritual strength, so that when they are tempted to do evil they say, "How can I do this great wickedness, and sin against God?" But what a blessed thing it is that if the believer shall, in an evil hour, come into the net, yet God will bring him out of it! O backslider, be cast down, but do not despair. Wanderer though thou hast been, hear what thy Redeemer saith—"Return, O backsliding children; I will have mercy upon you." But you say you cannot return for you are a captive. Then listen to His promise—"Surely He shall deliver thee out of the snare of the fowler." Thou hast fallen, and though thou shall never cease to repent of thy ways, yet He that hath loved thee will not cast thee away; He will receive thee, and give thee joy and gladness. No bird of paradise shall die in the fowler's net.

—CHARLES HADDON SPURGEON

July 28

Let your light so shine (Matt. 5:16).
Ye know that our [witness] is true (3 John 12).

> *The glory of love is brightest*
> *When the glory of self is dim,*
> *And they have most compelled me*
> *Who most have pointed to Him.*
> *They have held me, stirred me, swayed me—*
> *I have hung on their every word*
> *Till I fain would rise and follow,*
> *Not them, not them,—but their Lord!*

—RUBY T. WEYBURN

The believer is to be a burning light and a shining witness. D. L. Moody once said, "A holy life will produce the deepest conviction. Lighthouses blow no horns—they only shine." Although the old hymn of P. P. Bliss reads, "Trim your feeble lamp, my brother," oftentimes the brethren, as well as their lamps, are feeble! May holy living be the emblem of our faith and pure light shine to all who see and know us.

> *Christ has no hands but your hands,*
> *To do His work today;*
> *Christ has no feet but your feet,*
> *To guide men in His way;*
> *Christ has no tongue but your tongue*
> *To tell men how He died;*
> *Christ has no voice but your voice*
> *To call men to His side.*

> *We are the only Bible*
> *The careless world will read,*
> *We are the sinner's gospel,*
> *We are the scoffer's creed.*
> *We are the Lord's last message,*
> *Given in deed and word.*
> *What if the type be crooked?*
> *What if the print be blurred?*

> —Annie Johnson Flint

"Sir, we would see Jesus" (John 12:21).

July 29

Even so faith, if it hath not works, is dead, being alone (Jas. 2:17).

James was not denying the great doctrine of salvation by faith so plainly proclaimed by St. Paul. He was simply saying that if we are saved, our works will show it! A believer becomes a new creation and good works must shine forth so that the beauty of Jesus can be truly seen. Good works need to shine forth!

> *What if I say—*
> *"The Bible is God's Holy Word,*
> *Complete, inspired, without a flaw"—*
> *But let its pages stay*
> *Unread from day to day,*
> *And fail to learn therefrom God's law?*

What if I go not there to seek
The truth of which I glibly speak,
For guidance on this earthly way,—
Does it matter what I say?

What if I say—
*   That Jesus Christ is Lord divine;*
*   Yet fellow-pilgrims can behold*
*   Naught of the Master's love in me,*
*   No grace of kindly sympathy?*
*   If I am of the Shepherd's fold,*
*   Then shall I know the Shepherd's voice*
*   And gladly make His way my choice.*
We are saved by faith, yet faith is one
With life, like daylight and the sun.
Unless they flower in our deeds,
Dead empty husks are all the creeds.
To call Christ, Lord, but strive not to obey,
Belies the homage that with words I pay.

—Maud Frazer Jackson

Ye call me Master, and obey me not; Ye call me Light, and see me not; Ye call me Way, and walk me not; Ye call me Life and desire me not; Ye call me Wise, and follow me not; Ye call me Fair, and love me not; Ye call me Rich, and ask me not; Ye call me Gracious, and trust me not; Ye call me Noble, and serve me not; Ye call me Mighty, and honor me not; Ye call me Just, and fear me not; If I condemn you, blame me not.

—*Inscription in the*
Cathedral of Luebeck

"By works was faith made perfect" (Jas. 2:22).

July 30

Weeping may endure for a night, but joy
cometh in the morning (Ps. 30:5).

This was a verse from David's own heart and soul. He knew the depths of sorrow, but often a clearer vision of faith can be seen best through tears. After the tears comes the promise of the joys of the morning!

Should a Christian weep? The answer is "yes." "They that sow in tears shall reap in joy. He that goeth forth and weepeth, bearing precious seed, shall doubtless come again with rejoicing, bringing his sheaves with him" (Ps. 126:5-6).

This verse suggests that our messages and our witnessing must be "wet with tears." At times, some hearts may only be touched by the knowledge that we are praying and crying for their souls. Wesley wept for England and Knox cried "with many tears" for his native Scotland. Revival may be kindled with the tears of the saints on their knees!

Our Lord wept. He shed tears over a city, over a tomb, and over the cross. Over Jerusalem, He wept at their sinfulness. At Lazarus's tomb, He wept over their helplessness. In the garden, He wept over their hopelessness. Jesus shed tears. There were tears in the presence of sin, tears in the presence of death, and tears in the presence of the cross!

But not only did He shed tears—He also dried them! At the tomb of Lazarus, He dried the tears of Mary and Martha. At His own tomb, He wiped away the tears of Mary Magdalene. Christ is the only Comforter for the time of tears. Joy comes in the morning!

> He spoke her name the old familiar way—
> "Mary!" He said, and all her fears
> Were suddenly gone; He heard her say
> "Rabboni!" joyfully, through tears.
>
> So shall it be when in a coming day
> He speaks your name and mine! We'll hear
> Though in our graves we're laid away—
> And, rising up, shall greet Him without fear.
>
> —PAUL G. JACKSON

"God shall wipe away all tears from their eyes" (Rev. 21:4).

July 31

The glorious Lord will be unto us a place of broad rivers and streams (Isa. 33:21).

One of my favorite hymns is "Like a River Glorious," by Frances R. Havergal. The first stanza reads, *"Like a river glorious is God's perfect peace, over all victorious in its bright increase; perfect, yet it floweth fuller every day; perfect, yet it groweth deeper all the way."*

In our text Isaiah is speaking of a future time of peace when the Lord himself will be unto His people "a place of broad rivers and streams." Though this beautiful simile refers primarily to the relationship of Jehovah to the nation of Israel, it also portrays the sufficiency of Christ in the life of the believer; for it shows how He fulfills the deepest needs of our hearts.

Christ is a river of protection. When Isaiah wrote his prophecy, cities encircled by rapidly flowing streams were safe because the waters served as a barrier between them and the enemy. This reminds us that the Lord Jesus is our defender, for His blood covers all our sins and answers every accusation of Satan against us.

Christ is a river of support. Mighty vessels float easily on large tributaries, the buoyancy of the water holding them up. In like manner, our Lord undergirds our lives with His strength when we trust wholly in Him.

Christ is a river of satisfaction. Just as a weary traveler is refreshed by drinking from a sparkling brook, so the child of God is invigorated and finds perfect contentment in Him who is the Water of Life. We have a wonderful Savior who is truly "like a river glorious."

—PAUL R. VAN GORDER
From *Our Daily Bread*, © 1973, Radio Bible Class.
Used by special permission.

August 1

What doest thou here, Elijah (2 Kings 19:9)

Elijah has been called the Peter of the Old Testament. He was a praying man, a powerful man, and a protected man. Through him God wrought many victories, including the destruction of the prophets of Baal. It was following this great victory that Elijah became depressed and afraid. Ahab and his wife Jezebel threatened his life and the prophet fled for 40 days. Finally falling exhausted and defeated, he lay despondent and discouraged beneath a juniper tree. It was there that God came to him and tenderly asked, "What doest thou here, Elijah?"

We do not know his answer, but we know that it is a question which should come to our hearts on many occasions. "What doest thou here" in defeat and discouragement? "What doest thou here" with thy energies and talents? "What doest thou here" with thy time, when the hour is so late and much needs to be done?

The great question of entertainment and amusements for the christian can be answered with careful thought over this question, "What doest thou here? Is it for the glory of thy Lord?"

"I think a Christian can go anywhere," said a young woman who was defending her conduct. "Certainly one can," rejoined her friend, "but I am reminded of a little incident which happened last summer when I went with a party of friends to explore a coal mine. One of the young women appeared dressed in a dainty white gown. When her friends remonstrated with her, she appealed to the old miner who was to act as a guide to the party. "Can't I wear a white dress down into the mine?" she asked him. "Yes, Ma'am," he replied. "There isn't anything to keep you from wearing a white frock down there, but there will be considerable to keep you from wearing one back."

"What doest thou here, Elijah?"

"All things are lawful unto me, but all things are not expedient" (1 Cor. 6:12).

August 2

Keep me as the apple of the eye; hide me
under the shadow of thy wings (Ps. 17:8).

As the apple of His eye, we are the objects of His love, and under His wings we are preserved and protected! The Psalmist elsewhere wrote of dwelling in the secret place and abiding under the shadow of the Almighty (Ps. 91:1). Isaiah spoke of Him as "the shadow of a great rock" and wrote that He had hidden him in "the shadow of his hand" (Isa. 32:2; 49:2). There is safety in abiding under the shadow of His hands and the shadow of His wings. There is also security! If we hide under His wings we shall have peace and rest, and like the mother hen who cares for her brood, we may hide in Him when the night falls.

O precious resting place! No harm can befall us! "He shall cover thee with his feathers, and under his wings shalt thou trust (Ps. 91:4).

> *Under His wings I am safely abiding;*
> *Though the night deepens and tempests are wild,*
> *Still I can trust Him; I know He will keep me;*
> *He has redeemed me, and I am His child.*

Under His wings, what a refuge in sorrow!
  How the heart yearningly turns to His rest!
Often when earth has no balm for my healing,
  There I find comfort, and there I am blest.

Under His wings, O what precious enjoyment!
  There will I hide till life's trials are o'er;
Sheltered, protected, no evil can harm me;
  Resting in Jesus I'm safe evermore.

—William O. Cushing

August 3

In the morning, rising up a great while before day, he went out, and departed into a solitary place, and there prayed (Mark 1:35).

Christ began each day with prayer. Every Christian also needs to begin each day with a foundation of real prayer.

Dr. Mervin E. Rosell has written: "The answer to 'pressure' is prayer. The answer to fear is faith. The answer to worry is God's Word. The answer to guilt is grace. These are not pretty platitudes but workable and vital principles of living."

God's greatest servants have always been those who arose "early in the morning," found their solitary place, and then really prayed!

There is a place where thou canst touch the eyes
  Of blinded men to instant perfect sight;
There is a place where thou canst say "Arise!"
  To dying captives, bound in chains of night;
There is a place where thou canst reach the store
  Of hoarded gold and free it for the Lord;
There is a place—here or on distant shore—
  Where thou canst send the worker and the Word.
There is a place where Heaven's resistless power
  Responsive moves to thine insistent plea;
There is a place—a silent, trusting hour—
  Where God Himself descends and works for thee.
Where is that blessed place—dost thou ask "Where?"
O Soul, it is the secret place of prayer.

—Author Unknown

August 4

Lo, I am with you alway (Matt. 28:20)

It is well that there is One who is ever the same, and who is ever with us. It is well that there is one stable rock amidst the billows of the sea of life. O my soul, set not thine affections upon rusting, moth-eaten, decaying treasures, but set thine heart upon Him who abides forever faithful to thee. Build not thine house upon the moving quicksands of a deceitful world, but found thy hopes upon this rock, which, amid descending rain and roaring floods, shall stand immovably secure. My soul, I charge thee, lay up thy treasures in the only secure cabinet; store thy jewels where thou canst never lose them. Put thine all in Christ; set all thine affections on His person, all thy hope in His merit, all thy trust in His efficacious blood, all thy joy in His presence, and so thou mayest laugh at loss, and defy destruction. Remember that all the flowers in the world's garden fade by turns, and the day cometh when nothing will be left but the black, cold earth. Oh how sweet to have sunlight when life's candle is gone! Then wed thine heart to Him who will never leave thee; trust thyself with Him who will go with thee through the black and surging current of death's stream, and who will guide thee safely to celestial shores. "I am with you always."

—CHARLES HADDON SPURGEON

August 5

Let no man despise thy youth; but be thou an example of the believers, in word, in conversation, in charity [love], in spirit, in faith, in purity (1 Tim. 4:12).

"We do have some reason to expect that a seasoned veteran who has delved for years in the treasures of the Word, especially if he lectures to us about the Promised Land, should bear the fruits of Caanan with him and in him. We shall desire more readily to possess the land if those who advertise it will show us some sample figs, pomegranates, and grapes of Eschol" (Vance Havner).

Paul would later write to Timothy to "preach the word," to "do the work of an evangelist," to "make full proof of thy ministry." But first Timothy must be an example! One wonders if the church today has ever read these parting words from the great missionary.

Our God is a God of love and mercy, but He is also the God of holiness. To have a great ministry, one must be "an example." Faith, love, and purity must be in the life. We may fool a congregation and even a present-day bishop or two—but never the Spirit of God. Is your ministry barren? Then what about your inner living? If you would make "full proof" of your ministry, you must first be an example to all the believers.

Just as I am, Thine own to be,
Friend of the young, who lovest me.
To consecrate myself to Thee,
   O Jesus Christ, I come.

In the glad morning of my day,
My life to give, my vows to pay,
With no reserve and no delay,
   With all my heart I come.

I would live ever in the light,
I would work ever for the right,
I would serve Thee with all my might;
   Therefore, to Thee, I come.

Just as I am, young, strong and free,
To be the best that I can be
For truth, and righteousness, and Thee,
   Lord of my life, I come.

—MARIANNE HEARN

August 6

I thank my God upon every remembrance of you (Phil. 1:3).

Paul opened his letter to the Philippian church with the joy of remembrance in the fellowship of the gospel. He prayed earnestly for this church and literally said, "I hold you in my heart." He made three prayer requests for them. (1) "I pray that your love may abound more and more"; (2) "that you may approve things that are excellent"; and (3) "that you may be sincere and without offense till the day of Christ."

The grandeur of Paul's courage inspired other believers. He was suffering in a Roman prison but it was for the glory of the Cross! The gospel was being proclaimed and, as he preached it, soldiers in Caesar's prison were saved and even some in Caesar's household.

Paul was a faithful servant. The great apostle had an earnest expectation and hope that "in nothing I shall be ashamed" and "with all boldness Christ shall be magnified in me." May we follow in his train!

Paul wrote of one other desire. He said, "For to me to live is Christ, and to die is gain. . . . I am hard pressed between the two. My desire is to depart and be with Christ . . . but to remain is more necessary on your account" (Phil. 1:21-24, RSV). The beatings and stonings, the shipwrecks and the prisons, the hunger and the cold were past. Soon he would go and be with his Lord and Master. He had no fears. Jesus, to whom he belonged, was his faithful Guide. He would lead him safely home! And we too need not be afraid. Christ Jesus is also our Guide, even unto death.

> There is no path in this desert waste;
>   For the winds have swept the shifting sands,
> The trail is blind where the storms have raced,
>   And a stranger, I, in these fearsome lands.
> But I journey on with a lightsome tread;
>   I do not falter nor turn aside,
> For I see His figure just ahead—
>   He knows the way—my Guide.
>
> There is no path in this trackless sea;
>   No map is lined on the restless waves;
> The ocean snares are strange to me
>   Where the unseen wind in its fury raves;
> But it matters naught; my sails are set,
>   And my swift prow tosses the seas aside,
> For the changeless stars are steadfast yet,
>   And I sail by His star-blazed trail—my Guide.
>
> There is no way in this starless night;
>   There is naught but cloud in the inky skies;
> The black night smothers me, left and right,
>   I stare with a blind man's straining eyes.
> But my steps are firm, for I cannot stray;
>   The path to my feet seems light and wide;
> For I hear His voice—"I am the Way!"
>   And I sing and I follow Him on—my Guide.

—Robert J. Burdette

August 7

*He knoweth the way that I take: when he
hath tried me, I shall come forth as gold*
(Job 23:10).

A blacksmith, about eight years after he had given his heart
to God, was approached by an intelligent unbeliever with the
question: "Why is it you have so much trouble? I have been
watching you. Since you joined the church and began to 'walk
square,' and seem to love everybody, you have twice as many
trials and accidents as you had before. I thought that when a man
gave himself to God his troubles were over. Isn't that what the
parson tells us?"

With a thoughtful but glowing face, the blacksmith replied:
"Do you see this piece of steel? It is for the springs of a carriage.
But it needs to be 'tempered.' In order to do this, I heat it red-hot,
and then cool it with water. If I find it will take a 'temper,' I heat
it again; then I hammer it, and bend it, and shape it, so it will be
suitable for the carriage. Often I find the steel too brittle, and it
cannot be used. If so, I throw it on the scrap pile. Those scraps are
worth less than one cent a pound; but this carriage spring is
valuable."

He paused and his listener nodded. The blacksmith continued: "God saves us for something more than to have a good time.
That's the way I see it. We have the good time all right, for the
smile of God means heaven. But he wants us for service, just as I
want this piece of steel. And he puts the 'temper' of Christ in us
by testings and trials.

"Ever since I saw this I have been saying to Him, Test me
in any way you choose, Lord, only don't throw me on the scrap
pile."

—AUTHOR UNKNOWN

"Beloved, think it not strange concerning the fiery trial
which is to try you, as though some strange thing happened unto
you: but rejoice, inasmuch as ye are partakers of Christ's sufferings; that, when his glory shall be revealed, ye may be glad also
with exceeding joy" (1 Pet. 4:12-13).

August 8

After six days Jesus taketh Peter, James, and John, his brother, and bringeth them up into an high mountain (Matt. 17:1).

He took them, and went aside privately into a desert place (Luke 9:10).

There is a time for worship as well as a time for work. There is a "rest that remaineth" for the people of God. Valley work is needed but do not neglect the mountaintop experience where our Lord is glorified, or fail to enter into the desert with Him. A worker must also be a worshipper! If we would see the beauty of Christ transformed in us, we must be with Christ. Slow down, O Christian! "Tarry ye and rest awhile."

> I'm stealing away with Jesus,
> Away from the fretful town—
> I'll walk with Peter and Andrew,
> I'll talk with James and John.
>
> Away from the crowd and the noises,
> At Jesus' feet I'll see
> His face by the whispering waters
> Of the Lake of Galilee.
>
> I opened the sacred pages—
> The din of the city stills!
> With Him I consider the lilies,
> The sparrow, the brooks, and the hills.
>
> And if, like Paul, through shipwreck
> His wondrous power be shown,
> His blood will cleanse my sinning
> And His hand will give the crown.
>
> And so, be it dusk or midnight,
> I go to my rest serene;
> For He walks in the fields of the Scripture,
> By the quiet water's sheen.
>
> —Florence Nye Whitwell

"Ease the pounding of my heart by the quieting of my mind. Steady my hurried pace with a vision of the eternal reach of time. Give me, amidst the confusion of my day, the calmness of the everlasting hills. Break the tensions of my nerves with the soothing music of the singing streams that live in my memory. Help me to know the magical restoring power of sleep. Teach me the art of taking minute vacations of slowing down: To look at a flower; to chat with an old friend or make a new one; to pat a stray dog; to watch a spider build a web; to smile at a child or to read from a good book. Remind me each day that the race is not always to the swift; that there is more to life than increasing its speed. Let me look upward into the towering oak and know that it grew great and strong because it grew slowly and well" (Author Unknown).

August 9

When he ceased [praying], one of his his disciples said unto him, Lord, teach us to pray (Luke 11:1).

The Lord's prayer was given by Christ to His disciples as a model prayer. It is not to be rattled off and treated as a memory piece. An unknown author wrote,

I cannot say "our" if I live only for myself. I cannot say "Father" if I do not endeavor each day to act like His child. I cannot say "who art in heaven" if I am laying up no treasure there. I cannot say "hallowed be thy name" if I am not striving for holiness. I cannot say "thy will be done" if I am disobedient to His Word. I cannot say "in earth as it is in heaven" if I will not serve Him here now. I cannot say "give us our daily bread" if I am dishonest. I cannot say "forgive us our debts" if I harbor a grudge against someone. I cannot pray "lead us not into temptation" if I deliberately place myself in that path. I cannot say "deliver us from evil" if I do not put on the whole armor of God. I cannot pray "for thine is the kingdom" if I am not subject to the King and loyal to Him. I cannot ascribe to Him glory if I am seeking my own honor. I cannot use the word "forever" if the horizon of my life is bounded in the things of this earth.

> *You cannot say the Lord's Prayer,*
> *and even once say "i,"*
> *You cannot pray the Lord's Prayer,*
> *and even once say "My,"*
> *Nor can you pray the Lord's Prayer*
> *and not pray for another,*
> *For when you pray for daily bread,*
> *you must include your brother!*
> *For others are included*
> *in each and every plea,*
> *From the beginning to the end of it,*
> *it does not once say "me."*

—Author Unknown

August 10

Christ was once offered to bear the sins of many; and unto them that look for him shall he appear the second time without sin unto salvation (Heb. 9:28).

When the Savior came, He came to a world that He had made and "the world knew him not." His creation not only failed to recognize Him, it was antagonistic to Him. He was relegated to a stable at His birth. He encountered wild beasts in the wilderness at His temptation. Winds and waves joined forces against His life on Galilee. His own people condemned Him in crucifixion. The sun shone down without any mercy on His parched brow. The earth received the blood that flowed from His wounds.

Yes, the Word was made flesh and He lived among men. He manifest himself as the Giver of Life, but men would not come unto Him that they might have life. He declared himself to be the Bread of Life, but men hungered not for Him. He proclaimed himself the Light of the World, but men chose darkness. He said He was the Resurrection and the Life, but men chose death. He revealed himself as the Shepherd of the sheep, but men would not hear His voice and be gathered.

But this is not the end of the story. He was crucified but He arose! And this same Jesus is coming again!

He is coming again, not to a manger, but to a throne. He will not wear a crown of thorns but the diadems of glory. He will not enter lowly and riding upon a colt, but upon a white charger, having His vestures dipped in blood.

When He comes again, the moon and the stars will fall. The heavens will roll back as a scroll. The mountains will tremble and fall. The earth will rock and reel. When the Plenipotentiary of the skies strides forth on clouds of glory—every eye shall see Him and they that pierced Him and the nations will wail because of Him.

But this is not the full story either. Between His first and second advent, the Holy Spirit is here to bring men and women to Christ. The issue is very simple: "He that hath the Son hath life; and he that hath not the Son of God hath not life" (1 John 5:12). Will you come to Him and receive eternal life?

—U. S. GRANT

"God sent not his Son into the world to condemn the world; but that the world through him might be saved. He that believeth on him is not condemned; but he that believeth not is condemned already, because he hath not believed in the name of the only begotten Son of God" (John 3:17-18).

August 11

They all wept sore, and fell on Paul's neck, and kissed him, sorrowing most of all for the words which he spake, that they should see his face no more. And they accompanied him unto the ship (Acts 20:37-38).

This was a time of sorrow. The elders of the church at Ephesus were deeply moved over Paul's farewell message. They loved him dearly and he loved them. To these saints at Ephesus, he had written his greatest spiritual epistle, and he longed to see Christ formed in them. Now they would see his face no more on this earth.

Sad indeed are the separations of life. Tears fall, but thanks be to our God that one day He shall wipe away all tears from our eyes, and "there shall be no more death, neither sorrow, nor crying."

When life's partings come, let us rejoice in the blessed hope of our being with Christ forever on that glad day when "the dead in Christ shall rise first, and we who are alive and remain shall be caught up with them in the air, forever to be with the Lord" (from 1 Thess. 4:16-17).

He is not here.
We laid him there to rest upon a hillside
Shining with the splendor of an autumn afternoon,
While sun and sky and landscape joined
As if to match the glory of his welcome over there.

He is not here.
He heard a Voice which called his weary spirit,
And went to join the company of those he loved
Who waited for him in the home of God,
Beyond the sunset, over in the everlasting hills.

He is not here.
And yet the mind is filled with memories which the
Passing of the years can never dim. His kindliness,
His gentle, loving ways, his strength;
In which so many placed their trust and trusting, felt secure.

261

He is not here.
We cannot wish him back. For him the trumpets
Loud have blown. His race is over and the crown of life
Eternal rests upon his brow.
For him whose life is hid with Christ in God,
      there is no death.

—EDWARD S. MANN

"Weeping inconsolably beside a grave can never give back love's banished treasure, nor can any blessing come out of such sadness. Sitting down to brood over our sorrows, the darkness deepens about us and creeps into our heart, and our strength changes to weakness. But, if we turn away from our gloom, and take up our tasks and duties to which God calls us, the light will come again, and we shall grow stronger" (J. R. Miller).

The things you loved I have not laid away
    To molder in the darkness, year by year;
The songs you sang, the books you read each day
    Are all about me, intimate and dear.

I do not keep your chair a thing apart,
    Lonely and empty—desolate to view—
But if one comes a-weary, sick at heart—
    I seat him there and comfort him—for you.

I do not go apart in grief and weep,
    For I have known your tenderness and care;
Such memories are joys that we may keep,
    And so I pray for those whose lives are bare.

I may not daily go and scatter flowers
    Where you are sleeping 'neath the sun and dew—
But if one lies in pain through weary hours,
    I send the flowers there, dear heart—for you.

Life claims our best; you would not have me waste
    A single day with selfish, idle woe;
I fancy that I hear you bid me haste,
    Lest I should sadly falter as I go.

Perchance so much that now seems incomplete,
    Was left for me in my poor way to do;
And I shall love to tell you when we meet
    That I have done your errands, dear, for you.

—AUTHOR UNKNOWN

August 12

Let not your heart be troubled . . . in my Father's house are many mansions (John 14: 1-2).

The Father's house is a cure for the troubled heart. A literal translation can read, "In my Father's home are many rooms." I've never lived in a mansion. I might not know how to properly act in one. But oh, the joy of having a room reserved in the Father's home. It is this knowledge that is the cure for the troubled heart. The Father's house is home!

> *In childhood's day our thoughts of heaven*
> *Are pearly gates and streets of gold,*
> *And all so very far away;*
> *A place whose portals may unfold to us—*
> *Some far off distant day.*
>
> *But in the gathering of the years;*
> *With eyes perchance bedimmed by tears,*
> *And hearts oft overwhelmed with grief,*
> *We look beyond the pearly gates*
> *And see a place where loved ones wait.*
>
> *Where all is blessedness and light,*
> *And overall we see the face*
> *Of Him who'll bring us to our own—*
> *Not to a far off distant place—*
> *But rather to our Home!*
>
> —SUE McLANE

"In my Father's house are many mansions; if it were not so, I would have told you. I go to prepare a place for you"

"These words have cooled the hot faces of dying martyrs. They have been a pillow on which the saints of all ages have rested their weary heads. These words take the heat out of life's fierce fever, the pain out of parting, the sting out of death, the gloom out of the grave!" (Robert G. Lee).

Goin' Home!

August 13

The vessel that he made of clay was marred in the hand of the potter: so he made it again another vessel, as seemed good to the potter to make it (Jer. 18:4).

Jeremiah wrote that he had visited the potter's house and had watched him at work. A vessel of clay lay marred. The Word does not say how badly it had been marred. It simply tells us that the vessel had been damaged and rendered unfit for service.

But there was hope! There was a beginning again! The potter took it and made the vessel anew. The future of the vessel lay only in the potter's hands. He made it again!

Just so with the life that is marred. If we will but place ourselves completely in the care of the nail-scarred hands, our God can make us again in the image He desires. Take courage! A vessel of beauty can emerge from His workmanship. We are the clay. Put your trust in Him and ask to be made a vessel meet for the Master's use. He is waiting only for your commitment. In His hands there is beauty again!

> *Have Thine own way, Lord! Have Thine own way!*
> *Thou art the Potter; I am the clay.*
> *Mold me and make me after Thy will,*
> *While I am waiting, yielded and still.*
>
> *Have Thine own way, Lord! Have Thine own way!*
> *Hold o'er my being absolute sway!*
> *Fill with Thy Spirit till all shall see*
> *Christ only, always, living in me!*

—ADELAIDE A. POLLARD

"Christ is building His kingdom with earth's broken things. Men want only the strong, the successful, the victorious, the unbroken, in building their kingdoms. But God is the God of the unsuccessful, of those who have failed! There is no bruised reed that Christ cannot take and restore to glorious blessedness and beauty. He can take the life crushed by pain or sorrow and make it into a harp whose music shall be all praises" (J. R. Miller).

August 14

Paul, an apostle of Jesus Christ by the will
of God, and Timothy, our brother (2 Cor. 1:1).

Paul opened his second letter to the church at Corinth by calling himself an apostle. An apostle is a messenger—a man sent with a message. Some pulpits in our land today are occupied by men like Ahimaaz of old. He was the first minister—the first apostle without a portfolio! He loved to run with tidings except he had no message to give when he came to where he was going! Every present day apostle should ask himself the same question Joab once asked Ahimaaz. "Why wilt thou run my son, seeing that thou hast no tidings ready?" Paul came to Corinth as an apostle with a message: "I am determined to know nothing among you, save Jesus Christ, and him crucified."

The apostle Paul was also an ambassador. "Now then we are ambassadors for Christ, as though God did beseech you by us; we pray you in Christ's stead, be ye reconciled to God" (2 Cor. 5:20).

An apostle and an ambassador! Both go together. An ambassador receives his appointment from the king and he presents his message. He is the king's representative in a foreign land. He serves, not the land wherein he lives, but the sovereign to whom he belongs. Thus Paul could say, "Our citizenship is in heaven." There is a need today for faithful apostles and ambassadors. Men who will say, "I represent the King. This is His message. Be ye reconciled to God."

I am a stranger here, within a foreign land;
My home is far away, upon a golden strand;
Ambassador to be of realms beyond the sea,
I'm here on business for my King.

My home is brighter far than Sharon's rosy plain,
Eternal life and joy throughout its vast domain;
My Sovereign bids me tell how mortals there may dwell,
And that's my business for my King.

This is the message that I bring.
A message angels fain would sing:
"O be ye reconciled,"
Thus saith my Lord and King,
"O be ye reconciled to God."

—E. T. Cassel

August 15

Take my yoke upon you, and learn of me;
for I am meek and lowly in heart: and ye shall
find rest unto your souls. For my yoke is easy,
and my burden is light (Matt. 11:29-30).

On that memorable day when Christ issued this invitation, one might have seen two oxen hitched together, pulling a plow. Joined in a common cause, they divided the work between them. Our Lord, knowing that the leverage of a yoke could be adjusted to give the weaker animal a lighter load while the stronger one bore the greater part, made a spiritual application. He pleaded with men to identify themselves with Him and find life's heavy problems lightened and toil made enjoyable.

J. H. Jowett says, "The fatal mistake for the believer is to seek to bear life's load in a single collar. God does not intend for a man to carry his burden alone. Christ therefore deals in yokes. A yoke is a neck harness for two, and the Lord himself pleads to be One of the two. He wants to share the labor of any galling task. The secret of peace and victory in the Christian life is found in putting off the taxing collar of self and accepting the Master's relaxing yoke."

The Savior offers the "rest" of salvation as a gift. "Come to Me and receive," He says. But in the next verse He speaks of going on into the deeper union of discipleship and letting Him be fully involved in all of life. Wesley pled for this sanctifying grace when he wrote, "let us find that *second* rest!" The full joy of spiritual victory comes not while wearing the chafing collar of an unyielded life. It comes only when we wear His yoke with Him!

—HENRY G. BOSCH
From *Our Daily Bread*, © 1973, Radio Bible Class.
Used by special permission.

August 16

Looking unto Jesus the author and finisher
of our faith (Heb. 12:2).

It is ever the Holy Spirit's work to turn our eyes away from self and to Jesus, but Satan's work is just the opposite of this, for he is constantly trying to make us regard ourselves instead of Christ. He insinuates, "Your sins are too great for pardon; you have no faith; you do not repent enough; you will never be able to continue to the end; you have not the joy of His children; you have such a wavering hold of Jesus." All these are thoughts about self, and we shall never find comfort or assurance by looking within. But the Holy Spirit turns our eyes entirely away from self: He tells us that we are nothing, but that "Christ is all in all." Remember, therefore, it is not thy hold of Christ that saves thee— it is Christ. It is not thy joy in Christ that saves thee—it is Christ. It is not even faith in Christ, although that be the instrument—it is Christ's blood and merits; therefore, look not so much to thy hand with which thou art grasping Christ, as to Christ; look not to thy hope, but to Jesus, the source of thy hope; look not to thy faith, but to Jesus, the author and finisher of thy faith. We shall never find happiness by looking at our prayers, our doings, or our feelings. It is what Jesus is, not what we are, that gives rest to the soul. Keep thine eye simply on Him! Let His death, His sufferings, His merits, His glories, His intercession be fresh upon thy mind. When you awake in the morning or when you lie down at night, follow hard after Him. Look unto Jesus! He will never fail thee.

—Charles Haddon Spurgeon

We would see Jesus—for the shadows lengthen
  Across the little landscape of our life:
We would see Jesus—our weak faith to strengthen,
  For the last weariness, the final strife.

We would see Jesus—other lights are paling,
  Which for long years we have rejoiced to see;
The blessings of our pilgrimage are failing,
  We would not mourn them, for we come to Thee.

We would see Jesus—the great Rock-foundation
  Whereon our feet are set by sovereign grace;
Nor life, nor death, with all their agitation,
  Can thence remove us, if we see His face.

We would see Jesus—that is all we're needing,
  Strength, joy, and willingness come with the sight;
We would see Jesus—dying, risen, pleading—
  Then welcome day, and farewell mortal night!

—Anna B. Warner

August 17

*Wherewithal shall a young man cleanse
his way? By taking heed thereto according to
thy word* (Ps. 119:9).

One can be the finest architect and yet not know the One who is the Rock of Ages and the Chief Cornerstone. It is possible to be a great doctor and never know the Great Physician. A teacher of Philosophy may be totally ignorant of Him who is the Truth. A banker may collect great wealth and never find the Pearl of Greatest Price. And one may attain the highest professorship and not know nor understand, Jesus, the Wisdom of God! How ignorant even the educated who know not the Word!

In Psalm 119 the law of the Lord is described as perfect—it alone converts the soul. The testimony of the Lord is sure—it alone makes wise even the simple. The statutes of the Lord are right—and they rejoice the heart that finds them. The commandments of the Lord are pure—they enlighten the eyes and make pure a vile heart. "The fear of the Lord is clean enduring forever" (Psalm 119:9). The judgments of the Lord are true and righteous—they are more to be desired than the greatest of degrees or the finest of gold. Great rewards are in keeping them and this Word is the only true light for our pathway and the only safe lamp for our feet. Wonderful words of life!

August 18

*As many as are led by the Spirit of God,
they are the sons of God* (Romans 8:14).

From His very birth the Lord Jesus had the Spirit dwelling in Him. . . . He returned from the Jordan full of the Holy Spirit. In the wilderness He wrestled and conquered, not in His own Divine Power, but as one led by the Holy Spirit. The Word says that He was "in all things . . . made like unto his brethren" (Heb. 2:17).

The other side of the truth also holds good: the brethren are in all things made like unto Him. They are called to live like Him. This is not demanded from them without their having the same power. This power is the Holy Spirit dwelling in us, whom we have of God. Even as the Lord Jesus was filled with the Spirit, and then led by the Spirit, so must we be also filled and led by the Holy Spirit.

Let us take courage in this thought. Jesus himself could live thus only through the Spirit. It was after He was filled with the Spirit that He was led forth by that Spirit to the place of conflict and of victory. And this blessing is ours as surely as it was His. We may be filled with the Spirit and we may be led by the Spirit. "Be ye filled with the Spirit" is a command to every Christian. The fulness of the Spirit is absolutely necessary to live a Christ-like life.

—ANDREW MURRAY
in *Like Christ*

Oh, to be like Thee! blessed Redeemer,
This is my constant longing and prayer.
Gladly I'll forfeit all of earth's treasures,
Jesus, Thy perfect likeness to wear.

Oh, to be like Thee! full of compassion,
Loving, forgiving, tender and kind,
Helping the helpless, cheering the fainting,
Seeking the wandering sinner to find.

Oh, to be like Thee! lowly in spirit,
Holy and harmless, patient and brave;
Meekly enduring cruel reproaches,
Willing to suffer others to save.

Oh, to be like Thee! while I am pleading,
Pour out Thy Spirit, fill with Thy love;
Make me a temple meet for Thy dwelling,
Fit me for life and heaven above.

—T. O. CHISHOLM

August 19

Christ also hath once suffered for sins, the just for the unjust, that he might bring us to God, being put to death in the flesh but quickened by the Spirit (1 Pet. 3:18).

He was forsaken by God, that we might be favored of God. He entered into the prison house, that He might set the prisoners free. He went down to the bottom of the pit, that He might lift us up to the bosom of the Father. He endured the sinner's pain, that we might enjoy the Savior's presence. He lost the sunshine of the divine smile, that we might bask in the sunshine of divine love. For a moment He was separated from God, that for an eternity we might be united with God. He suffered for sin, that He might succor the sinner. He bore the burden to bring us the blessing. His hands were nailed to the tree, that in His arms He might bear us to the Throne. God entered into humanity for death, that we might enter into life. Where sin brought man, love brought our Lord, that where He is now, we also may be.

—Robert L. Moyer

O Christ, what burdens bowed Thy head!
  Our load was laid on Thee;
Thou stoodest in the sinner's stead,
  Did'st bear all ill for me.
A Victim led, Thy blood was shed;
  Now there's no load for me.

Death and the curse were in our cup:
  O Christ, 'twas full for Thee!
But Thou hast drained the last dark drop,
  'Tis empty now for me.
That bitter cup, love drank it up,
  Now blessing's draught for me.

Jehovah lifted up His rod:
  O Christ, it fell on Thee!
Thou wast sore stricken of Thy God;
  There's not one stroke for me.
Thy tears, Thy blood, beneath it flowed;
  Thy bruising healeth me.

The tempest's awful voice was heard;
  O Christ, it broke on Thee!
Thy open bosom was my ward,
  It braved the storm for me.
Thy form was scarred, Thy visage marred;
  Now cloudless peace for me.

Jehovah bade His sword awake—
  O Christ, It woke 'gainst Thee!
Thy blood the flaming blade must slake;
  Thy heart its sheath must be.
All for my sake, my peace to make,
  Now sleeps that sword for me.

—Mrs. A. R. Cousin

August 20

Whosoever is born of God overcometh
the world: and this is the victory that overcom-
eth the world, even our faith (1 John 5:4).

Remember there are battles to fight, a war to win and a victory to secure! There is also a world to overcome.

The writer to the Hebrews, in the great faith chapter, closes by describing people of faith as those "of whom the world was not worthy" (Heb. 11:38). Victory requires "going forth unto him outside the camp" (Heb. 13:13). It costs to follow Christ. But the price is just and the return is glorious!

The Taylor family had two sons. The elder chose the bright lights of popularity, politics, and the parliament of England "to make a name for himself." The younger chose "the riches of Christ" and sailed to China where the Holy Spirit used him to establish the great China Inland Mission. When the years passed by, a biographical dictionary listed the name of the eldest son and just these words, "He was the brother of J. Hudson Taylor."

August 21

I charge thee therefore before God, and
the Lord Jesus Christ, . . . preach the word; be
instant in season, out of season; reprove, re-
buke, exhort with all longsuffering and doc-
trine. For the time will come when they will
not endure sound doctrine . . . But watch thou
in all things, endure afflictions, do the work of
an evangelist, make full proof of thy ministry
(2 Tim. 4:1-5).

Did ever a young minister have as great an ordination charge? How these words are needed today! Would you see the "desert to bloom as the rose"? Preach the Word! Would you see the restoration of the "years which the locust hath eaten"? Then preach the Word! Would you see hearts of stone melt into repentence? Then preach the Word! My Word, He says, shall never

271

return to Me void. My Word is sharp and quicker than any two-edged sword, My Word, as the gospel is proclaimed, is the "dynamite" of God unto salvation. Shall we waste our time and the souls of men with words that merely peep?

"When they shall say unto you, Seek unto them that have familiar spirits, and unto wizards that peep, and that mutter; should not a people seek unto their God? . . . To the law and to the testimony: if they speak not according to this word, it is because there is no light in them" (Isa. 8:19-20).

How dear to my heart is the church of my childhood,
Where I took my first step in the straight, narrow way.
The little white church near the thick-tangled wildwood
Where I went with my mother on every Lord's day.
There was no large organ—no high-paid soprano.
The singing was scarcely the best ever heard;
But the man in the pulpit, divinely commissioned,
Poured out his whole soul in proclaiming the Word.
An old-fashioned preacher, a real Bible preacher,
A spirit-filled preacher who honored God's Word.

How thrilling it was just to see him in action,
This soldier of Christ, with his keen, trusty "sword,"
Who wielded his weapon with zeal and devotion
And backed up each thrust with a "Thus says the Lord."
No uncertain sound ever came from his trumpet,
His hearers were moved—yes, convicted and stirred;
And, bowing the knees in wet-eyed confession,
Accepted the truth as revealed in the Word,
By this old-fashioned preacher, this full gospel preacher,
This spirit-taught preacher who honored the Word.

Sometimes, when I listen to ramifications
Of science, that twist my poor brain out of shape,
Or hear the consensus of scholarship's findings,
Regarding our old friend, the anthropoid ape;
As my mind reels confused with drives, plans, and programs,
And world federations toward which we are stirred—
Sociology, politics, newer Freudism—
I sigh for the sermons my infancy heard,
From this old-fashioned preacher, this soul-stirring preacher,
This heartwarming preacher who honored God's Word.

—AUTHOR UNKNOWN

August 22

This one thing I do, forgetting those things which are behind, and reaching forth unto those things which are before, I press toward the mark for the prize of the high calling of God in Christ Jesus (Phil. 3:13-14).

"Robust Christians, that's what the Heavenly Father desires us to be. Robust Christians: the word *robust* comes from an old English term, *robustus*, which meant 'oaken, hard, strong, made of a very hard kind of oak.' That is precisely the virtue our God is desirous of conferring upon us. But He has no way of making us robust save through tribulations. Tribulations for the present seem not joyous; but later—later—when through them God hath conferred on us the peaceable fruits of righteousness—we shall rejoice in yesterday's pommelings more than in yesterday's pleasure" (Richard Ellsworth Day in *The Borrowed Glow*).

"We should never know the music of the harp if the strings were left untouched; nor enjoy the juice of the grape if it were not trodden in the winepress; nor discover the sweet perfume of cinnamon if it were not beaten; nor feel the warmth of fire if the coals were not consumed. The wisdom and power of the great Workman are discovered by the trials through which His vessels of mercy are permitted to pass" (Charles Haddon Spurgeon).

I've dreamed many dreams that never came true;
I've seen them all vanish at dawn.
But enough of my dreams have come true, praise God,
To make me want to dream on!

I've prayed many prayers and no answers came—
Though I prayed and waited long;
But answers have come to enough of my prayers
To make me want to pray on!

I've sown many seeds that fell by the way—
That the birds of the air fed upon;
But I've held enough sheaves in my hands, praise God,
To make me want to sow on!

I've drunk of the cup of sorrow and pain,
I've lived through a night without song;
But I've sipped enough nectar from life's sweetest flowers,
To make me want to press on!

—Author Unknown

August 23

Blessed is the man that walketh not in the counsel of the ungodly, nor standeth in the way of sinners, nor sitteth in the seat of the scornful. But his delight is in the law of the Lord (Ps. 1:1-2).

There is something wonderful about being blest—to have friends and family and health and security. The Psalmist writes about a blessedness the world knows not of. This is the portrait of a man who is blest because he knows and walks with God. There are so many who do not!

The man of the first psalm is blessed because his counsel is of the Lord; his companionship is of the Lord; his conduct is of the Lord; and his considerations, therefore, are of the Lord.

This is the goal of the dedicated and consecrated life. With God's counsel and companionship, we are to be men who walk in holiness and fellowship. We are not to be scornful or haughty. We are not to love sin, but we are to love sinners. As such we exemplify our Lord who first loved us when we were yet ungodly.

To be blest one must learn to walk by His Word, stand with His saints, sit with His sympathy, and delight in His doings. If such is our life, His promise is sure—we shall be like a tree planted by the rivers, with deep-reaching roots. No drought of the soul or of life can harm us because we have an everlasting supply of waters the world knows not of!

"How excellent is thy lovingkindness, O God! . . . Thou shalt make them drink of the river of thy pleasures. For with thee is the fountain of life" (Psalm 36:7-9).

I am drinking at the fountain,
Where I ever would abide,
For I've tasted life's pure river,
And my soul is satisfied:

There's no thirsting for life's pleasures,
Nor adorning rich and gay,
For I've found a richer treasure,
One that fadeth not away.

Is not this the land of Beulah,
Blessed, blessed land of light,
Where the flowers bloom forever,
And the sun is always bright!

—Anonymous

August 24

The path of the just is as the shining light,
that shineth more and more unto the perfect
day (Prov. 4:18).

E. Stanley Jones, the noted missionary-evangelist, gave directions for making the sunset years of life a blessed period of continued fruitfulness. These were some of his suggestions:

Learn something new every day and don't retire—just change your occupation, if necessary, for the Lord.

Do not grow negative in your thinking, but maintain a positive, helpful attitude and strive to be lovable and gracious in all things.

Look around you and then count your blessings. Be thankful each day.

Although your bodily activities are slowing down, your spiritual fervor and strength should increase. Keep active in His service!

> *They say that I am growing old;*
> *I've heard them tell it times untold,*
> *In language plain and bold—*
> *But I'm not growing old.*
>
> *This frail old shell in which I dwell*
> *Is growing old, I know full well—*
> *But I am not the shell.*
>
> *What if my hair is turning grey?*
> *Grey hair is honorable, they say.*
> *What if my eyes are growing dim?*
> *I still can see to follow Him*
> *Who sacrificed His life for me*
> *Upon the Cross of Calvary.*
>
> *What should I care if Time's old plow*
> *Has left its furrow on my brow?*
> *Another house, not made with hands,*
> *Awaits me in the glory land.*
> *What if I falter in my walk?*
> *What though my tongue refuse to talk?*
> *I still can tread the narrow way;*
> *I still can watch and praise and pray. . . .*
>
> *E're long my soul shall fly away*
> *And leave this tenement of clay.*

275

This robe of flesh I'll drop, and rise
To seize the everlasting prize,
And meet you on the streets of gold,
And prove that I'm not growing old.

—JOHN E. ROBERTS

August 25

**Blessed be his glorious name for ever; and
let the whole earth be filled with his glory.
Amen, and Amen** (Ps. 72:19).

This is a large petition. To intercede for a whole city needs a stretch of faith, and there are times when a prayer for one man is enough to stagger us. But how far-reaching was the Psalmist's intercession! How comprehensive! How sublime! "Let the whole earth be filled with his glory." It doth not exempt a single country however crushed by the foot of superstition; it doth not exclude a single nation however barbarous. For the cannibal as well as for the civilized, for all climes and races this prayer is uttered: it encompasses the whole circle of the earth and omits no son of Adam.

We must be up and doing for our Master, or we cannot utter this prayer. The petition is not asked with a sincere heart unless we endeavor, as God shall help us, to extend the kingdom of our Lord and Master.

Is it your prayer? Turn your eyes to Calvary. Behold the Lord of Life nailed to a cross, with thorn-crowned brow and bleeding hands and feet. What! Can you look upon this miracle of miracles, the death of the Son of God, without feeling a marvelous adoration that language never can express? And when you feel the blood applied to your conscience, and know that He has blotted out your sins, you are not a man unless you, from your knees, cry, "Let the whole earth be filled with his glory; Amen, and Amen."

Can you bow before the Crucified in loving homage and not desire to see Him crowned Lord of Lords and King of Kings? Your piety is worthless unless it leads you to plead for the same mercy for the whole world that had been extended to you. Lord, it is harvest-time, put in Thy sickle and reap.

—CHARLES HADDON SPURGEON

August 26

Who hath believed our report? And to whom is the arm of the Lord revealed? He is despised and rejected of men; a man of sorrows, and acquainted with grief; and we hid as it were our faces from him; he was despised, and we esteemed him not (Isa. 53:1-3).

In the great 53rd chapter of Isaiah, the prophet portrays the Son of God as the Man of Sorrows. Concerning the Man of Sorrows he writes that the world believed Him not, desired Him not, and esteemed Him not. John later was to say, "He came unto his own, and his own received him not" (John 1:11).

But the sweetest story ever told by mortal men or angels is the coming of the Man of Sorrows. Although He was to be rejected, yet He came to earth with that foreknowledge. What matchless love was this!

The rejected Man of Sorrows! At his birth He had a borrowed stable. During his ministry, a borrowed home at Bethany. On His triumphal entry, a borrowed beast. On the way to the Cross, a borrowed cross-bearer. In His death, a borrowed tomb. But the Cross was His own. The blood shed was His own. The agony was His own. However, the sin that He bore was borrowed—it was ours! Hallelujah! What a Savior!

"Man of sorrows," what a name
For the Son of God who came
Ruined sinners to reclaim!
Hallelujah! What a Saviour!

Bearing shame and scoffing rude,
In my place condemned He stood;
Sealed my pardon with His blood;
Hallelujah! What a Saviour!

Guilty, vile, and helpless we;
Spotless Lamb of God was He;
"Full atonement!" Can it be?
Hallelujah! What a Saviour!

Lifted up was He to die,
"It is finished," was His cry;
Now in heaven exalted high,
Hallelujah! What a Saviour!

—P. P. BLISS

August 27

Seeing ye put it from you, and judge your-
selves unworthy of everlasting life, lo, we turn
to the Gentiles (Acts 13:46).

Someone once said, "No man has a right to hear the gospel twice, until every man has heard it once!" In this passage of scripture, the apostle Paul turns the missionary movement to the Gentiles. Later in Acts, the Holy Spirit directs Paul to Troas. There he meets faithful Luke and hears the Macedonian cry, "Come over . . . and help us (Acts 16:19). This call drove the great missionary westward, and this cry has driven the missionary Church ever since.

Faithful hands have carried the ministry of healing and salvation to the far corners of the world. When General Douglas McArthur brought the American troops back victoriously across the islands of the Pacific, he was following the steps of faithful missionaries who had answered the Macedonian cry. May we still respond to that call 'til Jesus comes. This is our task! There can be no greater ministry. But strange indeed are its blessings, both to those who give and to those who receive.

An unknown author wrote these verses about how the South Sea islanders (they called them Fuzzy Wuzzies) helped the American soldiers in World War II.

Many a mother in America, when the busy day is done,
Sends a prayer to the Almighty for the keeping of her son,
Asking that an angel guide and bring him safely back.
Now these prayers are being answered on the Owen-Stanley
*   track.*

Though they haven't any halos, only holes slashed in their ears;
Their faces marked with tattoes and scratch pins in their hair;
Bringing back the badly wounded, just as steady as a horse,
Using leaves to keep the rain off, and as gentle as a nurse.

Slow and careful in bad places, on that awful mountain track;
The look upon their faces, makes you think that Christ was
*   black.*
Not a move to hurt the wounded, as they treat him like a saint,
It's a picture worth recording that an artist's yet to paint.

Many a lad will see his mother, and husbands see their wives,
Just because the Fuzzy-Wuzzies carried them to save their lives;

From mortar or machine-gun fire, or a chance surprise attack
To safety and the care of doctors at the bottom of the track.

May the mothers of America, when offering up their prayers,
Mention these impromptu angels with the fuzzy-wuzzy hairs.

—Author Unknown

August 28

Wist ye not that I must be about my Father's business (Luke 2:49).

One of the most dangerous powers of the enemy of our souls is his ability to confuse our thinking on the subject of time. He tempts us to fill our days with golden resolutions and great plans for tomorrow while present opportunities slip like sand through our fingers. He persuades us that spending our time simply abstaining from evil is as profitable as positively doing good.

We may look back but we can never turn back. Our todays may thrill with the memories of lessons learned in yestertimes but tears for time lost do not bring time back. Dreams of a future will also not hurry it to us. We must guard against tears and dreams from making us unfit for God-sent opportunities today! Remember that "with God all things are possible." Not were possible or will be possible, but are possible! Let us not fail to do His work today.

—Edward Lawlor

"Teach us, Good Lord, to serve Thee as Thou deservest. Help us to give and not to count the cost; to fight and not to heed the wounds; to toil and not to seek for rest; to labor and not ask for any reward; save that of knowing that we are doing Thy will. Amen" (Ignatius Loyola).

"Is your place a small place? Tend it with care for He set you there. Is your place a large place? Guard it with care for He set you there. Whate'er your place, it is not yours alone but His who set you there" (John Oxenham).

August 29

When thou passest through the waters, I
will be with thee; and through the rivers, they
shall not overflow thee: when thou walkest
through the fire, thou shalt not be burned,
neither shall the flame kindle upon thee (Isa.
43:2).

Take courage, faint heart. God always leads His people
through. We are never left in the midst of the waters. Does your
heart fear the river? He has promised that the waters will not overflow the soul. And no fire shall burn you, either. He who made
your path will lead you safely, for this God gave His Son for your
redemption and He will never forsake you. No, never!

Elsewhere He has said, "Fear thou not; for I am with thee:
be not dismayed; for I am thy God. I will strengthen thee; yea, I
will help thee; yea, I will uphold thee with the right hand of my
righteousness" (Isa. 41:10). His divine presence is with us. His
divine promise is given and He will strengthen and uphold. His
divine power is manifest in that He will uphold by His right hand.
We need not fear. He is our God . . . our Heavenly Father.

In shady green pastures, so rich and so sweet,
God leads His dear children along;
Where the water's cool flow bathes the weary one's feet,
God leads His dear children along.

Some through the waters, some through the flood,
Some through the fire, but all through the blood;
Some through great sorrow, but God gives a song,
In the night season and all the day long.

—G. A. Young

August 30

Paul, an apostle of Jesus Christ by the will
of God, to the saints which are at Ephesus, and
to the faithful in Christ Jesus (Eph. 1:1).

The Ephesian Christians were addressed as "saints" by Paul in the opening verse of his Epistle. How often we hear the expression, "Well, I'm no saint, you know." If a man thus speaks, he is admitting that he is not a believer or born again. God in His Word has declared that the redeemed are saints. They are *in* Christ, just as the Ephesian Christians were *in* Christ.

The little word "in" is the key word of Ephesians. It occurs 93 times. This is its theme. He has blessed us in Christ—chosen us in Christ—predestinated us in Christ—accepted us in Christ!

And where did these Ephesian Christians live? Paul answers this. They lived at Ephesus—not *in* Ephesus. They lived *in* Christ! Where do you live, O child of God? Not in Kansas City—nor in New York—nor in London. No! You live in Christ!

From the glory and the gladness from His secret place;
From the rapture of His Presence, from the radiance of His
* face—*
Christ, the Son of God, hath sent me through the midnight
* lands;*
Mine the mighty ordination of the pierced hands.
Mine the message grand and glorious strange unsealed surprise—
That the goal is God's Beloved, Christ in Paradise.

Hear me, weary men and women, sinners dead in sin;
I am come from heaven to tell you of the love within:
Not alone of God's great pathway leading up to heaven;
Not alone how you may enter stainless and forgiven—
Not alone of rest and gladness, tears and sighing fled—
Not alone of life eternal breathed into the dead—

But I tell you I have seen Him, God's beloved Son,
From His lips have learnt the mystery; He and His are one.
There, as knit into the body, every joint and limb,
We, His ransomed, His beloved, we are one with Him.
All in marvelous completeness added to the Lord,
There to be His crown of glory, His supreme reward.

Wondrous prize of our high calling! Speed we on to this,
Past the cities of the angels farther into bliss;
On into the depths eternal of the love and song,
Where in God the Father's glory Christ has waited long;
There to find that none beside Him God's delight can be—
Not beside Him, nay, but in Him, O beloved are we!

—C. P. C.
Hymns of Ter Steegen
Translated by Frances Bevan

August 31

*The very God of peace sanctify you whol-
ly; and I pray God your whole spirit and soul
and body be preserved blameless unto the
coming of our Lord Jesus Christ* (1 Thess. 5:23).

*Unto the church of God which is at Cor-
inth, to them that are sanctified in Christ Jesus,
called to be saints, with all that in every place
call upon the name of Jesus Christ our Lord,
both theirs and ours* (1 Cor. 1:2).

*That I should be the minister of Jesus
Christ to the Gentiles, ministering the gospel
of God, that the offering up of the Gentiles
might be acceptable, being sanctified by the
Holy Ghost* (Rom. 15:16).

Fasten thy attention, O believer, upon the care with which
the Scriptures are fashioned to show forth the interest of every
Person of the Trinity in every aspect of salvation. We know the
love of our Lord Jesus; but we are also called upon to remember
the love of God that gave, and the love of the Spirit which is His
glory. Father, Son, and Holy Spirit are in a perfect union of love
and labor for every work which salvation requires—including
sanctification.

Paul writes of God the Father sanctifying us wholly; calls
us sanctified in Christ Jesus; and reminds the Roman Christians
of their being sanctified by the Holy Spirit. The Triune God is
working in our behalf! Sanctification, therefore, is that operation
of God the Father, God the Son, and God the Holy Spirit, through
which the new man, is made perfect in Christ; and shall be, in the
world to come, made perfect like Christ.

—Richard Ellsworth Day

September 1

*Our old man is crucified with him, that the
body of sin might be destroyed, that henceforth we should not serve sin. For he that is
dead is freed from sin* (Rom. 6:6-7).

In the fifth chapter of Romans, Paul emphasizes that our salvation is by faith; that despite the worst sins we have committed, we may have "peace with God through our Lord Jesus Christ." But Paul was afraid that some readers would make this doctrine of salvation by faith the excuse for a "sinning religion." In the sixth chapter he therefore says a dozen times that followers of Christ are to be *dead to sin.*

What does the Bible mean by such expressions? What does it mean to be dead to sin? This much is clear, dead men are no longer troubled by the problems of the living. No stronger term of separation can be used. The apostle asks, "How shall we that are dead to sin, live any longer therein?" (Romans 6:2). The question carries its own obvious answer. He that is dead to sin no longer lives in sin.

Can we read the sixth chapter of Romans thoughtfully and conclude that sinning is consistent with a profession of Christian faith? Surely God means to say to us that salvation through Christ somehow takes a man out of the sin business. God's full work of grace in our lives is designed to do away with sin—all sin in the soul. This is the clear truth that God's Word teaches. But we can be truly dead to sin only when the inner source of sin has been removed ("crucified"), when the old carnal self is dead indeed.

—A. F. Harper

> *Now I will glory in the cross*
> *For this I count the world but dross.*
> *There I with Christ was crucified,*
> *His death is mine; with Him I died;*
> *And while I live my song shall be,*
> *No longer I, but Christ in me.*

—H. A. Ironside

September 2

Then Peter said, Silver and gold have I none; but such as I have give I thee: In the name of Jesus Christ of Nazareth, rise up and walk (Acts 3:6).

The Church's gift is here revealed; "Silver and gold have I none; but what I have, that I give to thee." What hast thou then, O Peter, to give to humanity, lame at the Beautiful Gate, excluded and begging? Said Peter to this man, "I have nothing to give you that will help you to maintain your life while you are a cripple; But I have something to cure the crippled condition; and make you able to earn your own living." This is Christianity!

Christianity has not come into the presence of the World's wounds and woes and agony to give out doles in order to help it bear its limitations. Christianity comes to give men life, and to put them on their feet! Christianity takes hold of a man whose ankles are out of joint, and makes them articulate. Christianity comes to give him life and to make him walk!

If this is the Church's gift, then what is the Church's method? She must speak and work in the name of Jesus Christ of Nazareth, the risen Christ. If we go to lame humanity at the Beautiful Gate in our own name, or in any other name, we may even give them some alms that will help them to bear their disability, but we shall never set them on their feet. It is in His name that the Church must go.

Peter and John went in cooperation. "Look on us," said they. Peter took him by the hand and lifted him. "He took him by the right hand, and raised him up." That is the final thing in the Church's method. We must come to the man that lies at the Beautiful Gate begging alms and take him by the hand. There must be a personal, immediate, and direct contact. The Church standing afar off, and singing a song which she hopes will reach the dweller in the valley does but mock the need. The Church that comes down to the side of the wounded, weary, woebegone world, and holds out her right hand, and lifts, is the Church through which the Christ is doing His own work, through which the Christ will win His ultimate victory.

—G. Campbell Morgan

September 3

Remember the sabbath day, to keep it holy (Exod. 20:8).
Thus saith the Lord God, the Holy one of Israel; In returning and rest shall ye be saved; in quietness and in confidence shall be your strength (Isa. 30:15).

We are living in an age characterized by a lack of quietness, confidence, peace, and rest. Nervousness is the prevailing complaint from many lips. As the consummation of the age approaches, pills have replaced peace—the peace of God. They are a poor substitute! We need rest and quietness for strength—and it comes only by waiting upon the Lord!

> Gone are those Sabbaths, when the very air
>   Seemed hushed to quiet and repose,
> When all the roads that outward led went to
>   The house where prayer and praise uprose.
>
> Within the walls of home there was a calm
>   As in a holy presence; thoughts of gain
> And care were put aside to ponder well
>   How much men labor for is vain.
>
> For little children there was time to learn
>   What childish minds may know of things
> Eternal, and the family chorus sang
>   The songs of age-old worshipings.
>
> Now Sunday comes, a day of rush and speed,
>   Of Careless mirth, far wandering,
> Of gay, yes, of debasing revelry,
>   Of turmoil and of squandering.
>
> And Monday comes, a bitter, weary day,
>   With no new strength for youth or age,
> And headlines in the Monday papers scream
>   Their lurid news across the page.
>
> —CLARA AIKEN SPEER

"They that wait upon the Lord shall renew their strength; they shall mount up with wings as eagles; they shall run, and not be weary; and they shall walk, and not faint" (Isa. 40:31).

September 4

The vessel that he made of clay was marred in the hand of the potter: so he made it again another vessel, as seemed good to the potter to make it (Jer. 18:4).

When the road is long, the days are dark, and storms threaten to overcome our souls, we are prone to cry, "Lord, why? Why this sickness? Why this suffering? Why this sorrow?"

How often we pray that the beauty of the Master be formed in us and yet we forget that God often maketh it from ashes. We pray for the fruit of the Spirit but we cry out against the Husbandman's pruning. Our hearts desire a steadfast faith that will shine as gold, but we dread the purging of the dross! We long to be made in the Potter's image yet we resist when He would mold us and make us after His will. We do not desire to be broken or pressed against the Potter's wheel.

But sickness and sorrow and suffering are the instruments the Potter frequently uses, and He makes His most beautiful vessels with these tools. The most precious gold is that which passes through the refiner's fire. The fruits of the Spirit form abundantly when the Husbandman prunes with His knives.

Take courage. Your part in these trials is to draw close to Christ and trust Him. Joy comes in the morning. The trial of faith does not always last. Though the waters are deep, yet the rivers of sorrow shall not overflow. Strive not against His expressed will. Hinder not the Holy Spirit. He will yet fill your life with the beauty of Jesus and make you fit for the Master's use.

September 5

Many were gathered together praying
(Acts 12:12).

Through the streets of the darkened city, a faithful band of believers silently walked to the home of Mary, mother of John Mark. Their hearts were burdened, for Herod had stretched forth his hand against the Church. James, brother of John and son of Zebedee, had been martyred. Because "it pleased the Jews," Herod had proceeded to make Simon Peter a captive also. And Peter was to die in the morning!

How glorious to read, though, that Peter "was sleeping between two soldiers, bound with two chains, and the keepers before the door kept the prison." Peter was sleeping! And on a night like this! But Peter believed his Lord who in His resurrection majesty had said, "When thou shalt be old . . . another shall gird thee, and carry thee." And Peter was not yet old!

Sleep on, Peter! Christ thy Lord is Master of ocean and earth and sky. Prisons are subject to His power also. He will make a way for you where there is no way!

Peter's faith was greater than the saints who met to pray for him. "Lord, save Peter!" was the heart cry that night. And the Lord worked a miracle. Peter was freed. He came to the door of Mary's home and knocked for entrance. A little maid named Rhoda answered the door. Hearing Peter's voice, excited Rhoda failed to unlatch the door but ran to the prayer room and cried, "Peter is at the door."

"You are mad, child. Be quiet," someone replied. "Lord, deliver Peter," prayed a saint.

"But Peter is at the door," Rhoda insisted.

"Thou art mad, girl. Peter is in prison." And again the prayer, "Lord, deliver Peter."

But the knocking persisted and became louder. Finally they opened the door and there was Peter. We stand amused as the Holy Spirit has Luke pen these lines. "They were astonished!"

At this place in the account are we not prone to quote the words of our Lord, "O ye of little faith." But before we speak thus, let us beware lest our own actions betray us. Do we too believe that God is able, but appear to doubt that He will? Let us exercise our faith. We belong to a mighty God whose Word can never be broken. Hear Him again! "These things have I written unto you that believe on the name of the Son of God; that ye may know that ye have eternal life, and that ye may believe on the name of the Son of God. And this is the confidence that we have in him, that, if we ask anything according to his will, he heareth us: and if we know that he hear us, whatsoever we ask, we know that we have the petitions that we desired of him" (1 John 5: 13-15).

September 6

[Jesus] being assembled together with them, commanded them that they should not depart from Jerusalem, but wait for the promise of the Father, which, saith he, ye have heard of me (Acts 1:4).

Christmas Evans tells us in his diary that one Sunday afternoon he was traveling a very lonely road to attend an appointment, and he was convicted of a cold heart. He wrote, "I tethered my horse and went to a sequestered spot, and walking to and fro in an agony I reviewed my life. I waited for three hours before God, broken with sorrow, until there came over me a sweet sense of His forgiving love, and a new filling of the Holy Spirit. As the sun was setting, I went back to the road, mounted my horse and went on to my preaching appointment. On the following day I preached with such new power to a throng of people gathered on the hillside, that a revival broke out that day and spread through all Wales."

—LETTIE B. COWMAN

Utterly abandoned to the Holy Ghost!
Oh! the sinking, sinking, until self is lost!
Until the emptied vessel lies broken at His feet;
Waiting till His filling shall make the work complete.

Utterly abandoned! no will of my own;
For time and for eternity, His, and His alone;
All my plans and purposes lost in His sweet will,
Having nothing, yet in Him possessing all things still.

Lo! He comes and fills me, Holy Spirit sweet!
I, in Him, am satisfied! I, in Him, complete!
And the light within my soul shall nevermore grow dim
While I keep my covenant—abandoned unto Him!

—AUTHOR UNKNOWN

Today the Holy Spirit is as truly available and as mighty in power as He was on the Day of Pentecost. But has the whole Church, ever since the days of Pentecost, put aside every other work and waited for Him for 10 days that the power might be manifested? Has there not been a source of failure here? We have given too much attention to methods and to machinery and to resources, and too little to the Source of power—the filling with the Holy Spirit. If we were to give ourselves to obey the command of our Lord to the full, we should have such an outpouring of the Spirit, such a Pentecost, as the world has not seen since He was outpoured at Jerusalem. God gives His Spirit, not to those who long for Him, not to those who pray for Him, not to those who desire to be filled always, but He does give His Holy Spirit to them that obey Him.

—HUDSON TAYLOR

September 7

God forbid that I should glory, save in the cross of our Lord Jesus Christ, by whom the world is crucified unto me, and I unto the world (Gal. 6:14).

"Jesus hath now many lovers of His heavenly kingdom, but few bearers of His cross. He hath many who desire His consolation but few His tribulation; many who are willing to share His table but few His fasting. All are willing to rejoice with Him, but few will endure anything for Him. Many follow Jesus into the breaking of the bread, but few to drink of the cup whereof He drank. Many glory in His miracles, but few in the shame of the cross" (Thomas á Kempis).

Precious Savior! How shall I thank Thee for the work that Thou hast done as my Surety? Standing in the place of me a guilty sinner, Thou hast borne my sins in Thy body on the Cross. That Cross was my due. Thou didst take it, and was made like unto me, that the Cross might be changed into a place of blessing and life.

And now Thou callest me to the place of crucifixion . . . where I may be made like Thee, and may find in Thee power to suffer and to cease from sin. Precious Savior! I confess that I have too little understood this. I rejoiced much that Thou hadst borne the Cross for me, but too little that I like Thee and with Thee might also bear the cross. The Atonement of the Cross was more precious to me than the fellowship of the Cross; the hope in Thy redemption more precious than the personal fellowship with thyself.

Forgive me this, dear Lord, and teach me to find my happiness in union with Thee. Show me the hidden glory of the fellowship of Thy cross. Lord, give me to know its full power. I could not break the power of sin. But now I see, this comes only when Thy disciple yields himself entirely to be led by Thy Holy Spirit into the fellowship of Thy cross. The Cross has broken forever the power of sin and made me free. Oh, my Lord, teach me to understand this better. In this faith I say, "I have been crucified with Christ." Take me, Thou Crucified One, and hold me fast, and teach me from moment to moment to look upon all that is self as condemned, and only worthy to be crucified. Take me, hold me, teach me that in Thee I have all I need for a life of holiness and blessing.

—ANDREW MURRAY
in *Like Christ*

O Love that wilt not let me go,
    I rest my weary soul in Thee;
I give Thee back the life I owe,
That in Thine ocean depths its flow
    May richer, fuller be.

O Cross that liftest up my head,
    I dare not ask to hide from Thee;
I lay in dust life's glory dead,
And from the ground there blossoms red
    Life that shall endless be.

—GEORGE MATHESON

September 8

The Spirit itself beareth witness with our spirit, that we are the children of God (Rom. 8:16).

We enter human families either by birth, adoption, or marriage. The Holy Spirit brings us into God's family also by birth—the new birth. When we take the guilty sinner's place and receive the guilty sinner's Savior, we are born again into His family. "As many as received him, to them gave he power to become the sons of God, even to them that believe on his name" (John 1:12).

While Paul tells us that we are also married into God's family through the Son, and John wrote of the bride of the Lamb who had made herself ready (2 Cor. 11:2; Rev. 19:7, 8), the scripture also reveals that we have been adopted into God's family. Adopted children are always wanted!

We once heard William L. Pettingill tell of visiting a dear old saint. On every occasion, when preaching in her city, he would ask concerning her welfare. She always declared, "My Papa is taking care of me.

This is divine truth for "ye have received the Spirit of adoption, whereby we cry, Abba, Father" (Rom. 8:15). The word could be translated, "Papa, O Papa." This is the witness of the Spirit—we are members of His family through His Son. We are children of His love!

September 9

They come to Jesus, and see him that was possessed with the devil . . . sitting, and clothed, and in his right mind . . . and they that saw it told them . . . concerning the swine . . . and they began to pray him to depart out of their coasts (Mark 5:15-17).

There were two outcasts at Gadara that day—the man who had dwelt in the tombs and the Son of God! It mattered not to the Gadarenes that the wild demented man had been healed. It was of no concern to them that he who could not be tamed nor clothed was seen sitting at Jesus feet, healed and restored. No! For their swine were dead! They said, "If this Man stops in our city, the stockyards will suffer." So they asked Christ to depart. The price of pork chops and bacon came first!

Oh, how much Gadara missed! It's lepers remained outside the city gates. It's blind beggars continued to go with tapping canes. And men with withered hands were not made strong again. It is ever thus when the "pork industry" is chosen instead of Christ.

> "Rabbi begone! Thy powers
> Bring loss to us and ours.
> Our ways are not as Thine,
> Thou lovest men, we—swine.
>
> "Oh, get Thee hence, Omnipotence!
>   And take this fool of Thine!
> His soul? What care we for his soul?
> What good to us that Thou hast made him whole,
>   Since we have lost our swine?"
>
> And Christ went sadly,
> He had wrought for them a sign
> Of love and hope and tenderness divine—
> But they—they wanted swine.
>
> Christ stands without your door and gently knocks,
> But if your gold, or swine, the entrance blocks,
> He forces no man's hold. He will depart
> And leave you to the treasures of your heart.
>
> —John Oxenham

September 10

Paul, an apostle of Jesus Christ by the will of God (Eph. 1:1).

One Lord's day, a visiting preacher dressed in a long frock-tailed coat ascended the worn steps of a weather-beaten country church. The door was opened by a faithful usher and the minister said to him, "I am the Reverend John Bryant, Bishop of the Methodist Church by the will of God." The old man shook his hand and replied, "And I am Jacob Schmidt, a shoe cobbler by the will of God. We are glad to greet you, sir."

There is a sublime truth here. We are to live our lives in the expressed will of God. Paul beseeched the Christians at Rome to do this. But today many of us are willing to sing "I'll go where you want me to go, dear Lord, I'll be what you want me to be," and then place reservations as to where we would go and what we will do. Thus we live in His permissive will and miss the mark of great Christian living. We choose God's second best!

How may I ascertain the expressed will of God for myself? George Mueller said this: "I seek at the beginning to get my heart into such a state that it has no will of its own in regard to a given matter. Nine-tenths of the trouble with people is just here. Nine-tenths of the difficulties are overcome when our hearts are ready to do the Lord's will, whatever it may be. When one is truly in this state, it is usually but a little way to the knowledge of what His will is.

"Having done this, I do not leave the result to feeling or simple impression. If I do so, I make myself liable to great delusions. I seek the will of the Spirit of God through, or in connection with, the Word of God. The Spirit and the Word must be combined. If the Holy Spirit guides us, He will do it according to the Scriptures and never contrary to them.

"Next I take into account providential circumstances. These often plainly indicate God's will in connection with His Word and Spirit. I ask God in prayer to reveal His will to me aright. Thus, through prayer to God, the study of the Word, and reflection, I come to a deliberate judgment according to the best of my ability and knowledge, and if my mind is thus at peace, and continues so after two or three more petitions, I proceed accordingly. In trivial matters, and in transactions involving most important issues, I have found this method always effective."

September 11

Wherefore he is able also to save them to the uttermost that come unto God by him, seeing he ever liveth to make intercession for them (Heb. 7:25).

Paul overlooking Mars' Hill preached Christ to the Greeks and spoke of the Resurrection as assuring unto all men that God "hath appointed a day, in which He will judge the world in righteousness" (Acts 17:31). In his letter to the Christians at Rome, Paul wrote that the Resurrection assures the believer of his justification in Christ (Rom. 4:25). In the Epistle to the Hebrews, the resurrection of our Savior assures us of an eternal salvation because He ever lives to make intercession for us. Paul wrote to Philemon saying of the slave Onesimus, "If he hath wronged thee, or oweth thee aught, put that on mine account" (Philem. 18), so we too belong to the risen Intercessor, who at the Father's right hand, intercedes daily in our behalf saying, "Father, put that on mine account. I have paid it."

> *O blessed feet of Jesus! weary with seeking me,*
> *Stand at God's bar of judgment and intercede for me.*
>
> *O knees which bent in anguish in dark Gethsemane,*
> *Kneel at the throne of glory and intercede for me.*
>
> *O hands that were extended upon the awful tree,*
> *Hold up those precious nail prints and intercede for me.*
>
> *O body scarred and wounded my sacrifice to be,*
> *Present thy perfect offering and intercede for me.*
>
> *O loving, risen Savior from death and sorrow free,*
> *Though throned in endless glory, still intercede for me.*

—Author Unknown

"Seeing then that we have a great high priest, that is passed into the heavens, Jesus the Son of God, let us hold fast our profession. For we have not an high priest which cannot be touched with the feelings of our infirmities; but was in all points tempted like as we are, yet without sin. Let us therefore come boldly unto the throne of grace, that we may obtain mercy, and find grace to help in time of need" (Heb. 4:14-16).

September 12

My thoughts are not your thoughts, nei-
ther are your ways my ways, saith the Lord (Isa.
55:8).

A paradox is an apparent contradiction which in reality may conceal a profound and great truth. The Bible contains baffling concepts which would not exist if this Book had been composed by men. Our Lord's thoughts are higher than ours!

Here are some precepts gleaned from the Gospels which upon first reading seem to defy human logic. In them, however, the Lord has designed a wondrous pattern and wise design for the believer. Notice these. We see unseen things (2 Cor. 4:18). We conquer by yielding (Rom. 6:18). We find a rest under a yoke (Matt. 11:28). We are made great by becoming little (Luke 9:48). We are exalted by being humble (Matt. 23:12). We become wise by being made fools for Christ's sake (1 Cor. 1:20). We are made free by becoming His bond servant (Rom. 6:17-29; 8:2). We possess all things by having nothing (2 Cor. 6:10). We wax strong by being weak (2 Cor. 12:10). We triumph by defeat. We find victory by glorying in our infirmities (2 Cor. 12:1-9). We live by dying (John 12:24-25; 2 Cor. 4:10-11).

These divine mysteries embodied in the Christian distinguish him from the unbeliever who finds such thoughts and ways impossible to understand. Only one who has the Holy Spirit to enlighten him can live by the joyous truths hidden in these scriptural paradoxes.

—HENRY G. BOSCH

September 13

Whom having not seen, ye love; in whom, though now you see him not, yet believing, you rejoice with joy unspeakable and full of glory (1 Pet. 1:8).

The author of the Letter to the Hebrews defined faith as "the substance of things hoped for, the evidence of things not seen" (Heb. 11:1). The Lord Jesus gave a special blessing to the saints of faith who have believed in Him. "Jesus saith unto him, Thomas, because thou hast seen me, thou hast believed; blessed are they that have not seen, and yet have believed" (John 20:29).

Helen Keller, blind and deaf from birth, testified to her faith in these beautiful words. "Dark as my path may seem to others, I carry a magic light in my heart. Faith, the spiritual strong searchlight, illumines the way. Although doubts lurk in the shadow, I walk unafraid toward the Enchanted Wood where the foliage is always green; where joy abides; where nightingales nest and sing, and where life and death are one in the presence of the Lord."

And a little blind boy spoke of his faith in words like these:

> *I know what mother's face is like—*
> *although I cannot see,*
> *It's like the way the roses smell,*
> *It's like the secrets fairies tell,*
> *It's like the pure tones of a bell,*
> *All this is mother's face to me—*
> *Although I cannot see.*

> *I know what father's face is like—*
> *although I cannot see,*
> *It's like his whistle in the air,*
> *It's like his step upon the stair,*
> *It's like his arms that take such care,*
> *All this is father's face to me—*
> *Although I cannot see.*

> *I know what Jesus' face is like—*
> *Although I cannot see.*
> *He's everything my mother means,*
> *He's everything my father seems,*
> *He's dearer than my sweetest dreams,*
> *And more than all of these is He—*
> *Although I cannot see.*

September 14

I am persuaded, that neither death, nor life, nor angels, nor principalities, nor powers, nor things present, nor things to come, nor height, nor depth, nor any creature, shall be able to separate us from the love of God, which is in Christ Jesus our Lord (Rom. 8:38-39).

In five passages of scripture, Paul uses the expression, "I am persuaded." This speaks of certainty. There were no doubts in his mind or heart. Perhaps the best known verse is 2 Tim. 1:12: "I know whom I have believed, and am persuaded that he is able to keep that which I have committed unto him against that day."

In our text, Paul is persuaded about love—a love first manifest at the Cross. He wrote, "But God commended his love toward us, in that, while we were yet sinners, Christ died for us" (Rom. 5:8).

Because of Calvary, His marvelous love is mine. Because of Calvary, neither living nor dying, neither powers nor perils, neither things presently seen nor those still to come, neither dangers of sea or sky or hell can ever separate us from the love of God. We are safe under the precious blood!

I hear the words of love, I gaze upon the blood,
I see the mighty sacrifice, and I have peace with God.
The clouds may go and come, and storms may sweep my sky;
This blood-sealed friendship changes not, the Cross is
*   ever nigh.*

—Horatius Bonar

September 15

A certain man named Ananias, with Sapphira his wife, sold a possession, and kept back part of the price, his wife also being privy to it, and brought a certain part, and laid it at the apostles' feet (Acts 5:1-2).

The story of the death of Ananias and Sapphira is very solemn. It is the sad tale of lying to the Holy Spirit. It is a warning to all, for it reveals that, as Ananias, we may give our means—wish to die well as Balaam (Num. 23:10)—bring an offering as Cain (Gen. 4:3)—make a profession as Demas (2 Tim. 4:10)—tremble at the Word as Felix (Acts 24:25)—have a house of gods as Micah (Judg. 17:5)—ask for prayers as Pharaoh (Exod. 8:8)—and yet perish! Ananias and his wife professed, but did not possess. What a difference this makes! Peter said to him, "Satan has filled thine heart."

"Thou hast kept back part." There is a grave lesson here for believers. Ananias stated that he had brought all! Herein lies the sin! Guard thy heart and lips from saying "My all is on the altar" and knowingly hold back part. It is far better to say, "O Christ, here is most of me—make me willing to give my all."

The radiant Christian life is the victorious life found through an unconditional surrender. He who has bought us with himself, deserves His full purchase!

> Go work in My vineyard, I claim thee as Mine;
> With My blood did I buy thee and all that is thine.
> Thy time and thy talents, thy loftiest powers;
> Thy warmest affections, thy sunniest hours.
>
> I willingly yielded My kingdom for thee.
> The songs of Archangels to hang on the tree.
> In pain and temptation, in anguish and shame,
> I paid thy full ransom—My purchase I claim.
>
> —SELECTED

September 16

Caleb . . . said, . . . Forty years old was I when Moses . . . sent me from Kadesh-barnea to espy out the land; and I brought him word again as it was in mine heart. Nevertheless my brethren that went up with me made the heart of the people melt; but I wholly followed the Lord my God . . . now, lo, I am this day fourscore and five years old. As yet I am as strong this day as I was in the day that Moses sent me . . . Now therefore, give me this mountain (Josh. 14:6-8, 10-12).

Caleb was just as strong at eighty-five as he had been at forty. Oh, his beard may have been grayer and there were more lines on his face, but his body and heart were stout! What a wonderful testimony God recorded of him—"He wholly followed the Lord."

Caleb did not change. His spirit and faith and courage grew with the passing years. He was not afraid of the Anakim giants when he was young nor as he grew older. They struck terror to many Israelite hearts but not Caleb's. Why? Because he believed God and claimed His promises—"the land . . . I will give it to you."

Caleb could have chosen a comfortable portion of the land—rich and fertile, but he chose the mountains instead! This meant battles to be fought, rocks to be born away, and trees to be hewed down. No easy life for Caleb—and no compromise. He chose God's best for him. Great victories are not won "picnicking" in green pastures!

When God wants a great servant, He always chooses a busy man. Moses was busy caring for his flocks at Horeb. Gideon was busy threshing wheat by the press. David was watching over his father's sheep. Elisha was ploughing. Nehemiah was serving the king. Peter and Andrew were busy casting fishing nets into the sea and James and John were mending theirs. When God has a great and hard work to do He chooses a hard worker!

—AUTHOR UNKNOWN

September 17

The Lord is my shepherd; I shall not want (Ps. 23:1).

The literal translation from the Hebrew reads, "Jehovah-Saviour" is my shepherd. Yes, David had a Shepherd: Someone to comfort him when he was in sorrow, a Shepherd to seek him when straying, to protect him when in danger, and to lead him safely home when the night drew near. Such a Shepherd is Jehovah-Jesus!

F. B. Meyer said, "As Jehovah, He is sovereign Lord of all. As Jesus, He is all sympathy. As Jehovah, He has all power. As Jesus, He still treads the pathways of this world by our side, whispering sweetly and softly in our ears, 'Fear not, O little flock.'"

Fear not, O little flock
Upon the storm-swept hill;
The Shepherd knows thy path,
He guides thy footsteps still.
His nail-pierced hand will keep
And hold thee safe and fast;
Fear not, O little flock,
He'll bring thee home at last.

—ADELAIDE POLLARD

"He shall feed his flock like a shepherd: he shall gather the lambs with his arm, and carry them in his bosom, and shall gently lead those that are with young" (Isa. 40:11).

September 18

Men ought always to pray, and not to faint (Luke 18:1).

These are our Lord's own words. Every Christian should heed them. His own life was a beautiful example of communion with the Father. If our Savior sought out His Father in the early morning hours, how important it is for us to pray. There is empowerment for service in prayer. If we pray, we faint not—if we pray, He performs!

"But thou, when thou prayest, enter into thy closet, and when thou hast shut thy door, pray" (Matt. 6:6). Privacy for prayer is essential! The outside door must be closed if we are to have the sweetest communion. It is only in the secret place that He whispers to us His dearest words. We must guard against being so busy with our Lord's work that we forget to worship. The Lord Jesus would rather have us at His feet like Mary, than always to be in the "kitchen." Workers can be hired, but never loving disciples.

The weary ones had rest,
The sad had joy that day;
A plowman, singing at his work had prayed,
Lord, help them now!

Away in foreign land they wondered how
Their feeble words had power;
At home the Christians, two or three,
Had met to pray an hour.

Yes, we are always wondering,
Wondering how? Because we do not see
Someone, unknown, perhaps, and far away
On bended knee.

—SELECTED

We seem to stand once more with His disciples at the foot of the Mount of Transfiguration. Our Lord has had His transforming, empowering, communion with the Father, but we have not. We are confronted with a father, presenting the boy, enslaved, the victim of evil, a sad epitome of the world's great need. The Master has commissioned us to relieve such in His name. We rise to the task, little realizing our impotence. We are earnest, sincere, but nothing happens. We are forced to confess defeat. Then the Master comes, fresh from fellowship with His Father. At once the seemingly impossible takes place. The need is met— the child is cured. Amazed and abashed, we ask Him privately, "Why could not we cast him out?" Listen anew to His answer, "This kind can come out by nothing save by prayer."

—NORMAN B. HARRISON

September 19

Peter seeing him saith to Jesus, Lord, and what shall this man do? (John 21:21).

Christians are sometimes troubled by what others are doing— or not doing. Such anxiety may be caused by coveting another's work and position, or by a complaining, murmuring spirit. But it is wrong, for God has said, "In nothing be anxious"; and it is a great destroyer of peace and power in Christian service. The Lord Jesus spoke a word to Peter that may help dispel this form of worry. When Peter asked him what John would do in the future, he answered: "If I will that He tarry till I come, what is that to thee? Follow thou me." The important thing for Peter was not God's will for John, but God's will for Peter.

And so it is with each of us. We may be tempted to bemoan the fact that others travel while we have to stay home; or that we have to travel while others live in ease at home. Other devoted Christians may live in comparative luxury and comfort, while we may suffer privation and trial. But as we heed His word to us, "What is that to thee? Follow thou me," we shall look up instead of around us; we shall walk in His footsteps instead of men's; and as we "consider Him," instead of being dissatisfied with others and with our own place and work, we shall be abundantly satisfied with Him and with His "good, and acceptable, and perfect will" for us.

—THE Sunday School Times

September 20

While they looked stedfastly toward heaven as he went up, behold, two men stood by them in white apparel; which also said, Ye men of Galilee, why stand ye gazing up into heaven? this same Jesus, which is taken up from you into heaven, shall so come in like manner as ye have seen him go into heaven (Acts 1:10-11).

Angels hovered near His crib and sang of His glory. They were near Him at the cross. He said that He could call 12 legions of angels for His defense, but since Jesus came to suffer for the sins of the world, angels did not minister to Him at Calvary.

At the empty tomb again they rejoiced and cried to a sin-sick and saddened world, "The Lord is risen. He is not here. Behold the place where He lay."

In the first chapter of Acts the angels speak again: "This same Jesus, who is taken up from you into heaven, shall so come in like manner as ye have seen him go into heaven." At the sound of the angelic trumpet, the crib and the cross forever past, this same Jesus shall return with the crown of glory resting upon His thorn-scarred brow.

"This same Jesus." He who cleansed the lepers; He who opened the eyes of the blind; He who healed the halt and the lame; He who forgave the sins of publicans and harlots; He who raised the dead—"this same Jesus" shall return!" This is the blessed hope! May we be about our Master's business till the day breaks, the shadows forever flee away, and our faith becomes glorious sight.

"Looking for that blessed hope, and the glorious appearing of the great God and our Saviour, Jesus Christ" (Titus 2:13).

Lo, He cometh! Lo, He cometh!
  Not as once He came to earth—
Meek and gentle, poor and lowly,
  Through the gates of human birth;
Not to walk with feet a-wearied
  Through a world of sin and pain,
By His own despised, rejected—
  Lamb of God, for sinners slain.
Now in majesty He cometh,
  Cloudy splendors wrap Him round;
Wake, ye dead, and list, ye living—
  Hark! the trumpet's awful sound;
Now His face is like the lightning,
  And His eyes are like a flame;
Lion of the Tribe of Judah,
  Heaven and earth adore His name.

Lo, He cometh! Lo, He cometh!
  Bride and Spirit echo, "Come;
Come to heal Thy hurt creation,
  Come to take Thy people home;
Mount the throne, O Son of David,
  Take the sceptre, Prince of Peace;
Come—and hush the drum's loud beating;
  Come—and bid all conflicts cease.
Come—and furl the flags of warfare;
  Come—and sheath the nations' swords;
Come—and reign in truth and justice,
  King of Kings, and Lord of Lords.
Come in power, come in glory,
  Come to take Thy kingdom—come!"
Even so, O King and Bridegroom;
  Even so, Lord Jesus, come!

—Annie Johnson Flint

September 21

. . . for ye serve the Lord Christ (Col. 3:
24).

In the *Screwtape Letters*, C. S. Lewis has Wormwood placed in charge of a new convert. He is instructed how to proceed with his evil purpose in turning a young Christian away from his new-found faith.

One of the points of advice given is to deflect the Christian from Christ to a Cause. The Cause may be ever so righteous and worthwhile, but it is easily corrupted by self-will and so becomes a snare to the soul.

The devil has little fear if a man is devoted to a Cause. What he fears is a man devoted to Christ. A Cause can be selfishly served. Christ displaces selfishness with His own will.

Our loyalty is never safe when we give it without qualifications to a Cause. The Cause subtly becomes "our Cause"—even "our Church." Our loyalty is safe only when it is given without reservation to Christ. Then His mission and His Church becomes our means of expressing our love and obedience to Him.

—Herald of Holiness

Paul wrote to the Christians at Colosse, "He is the head of the body, the church; who is the beginning, the firstborn from the dead; that in all things he might have the preeminence. For it pleased the Father that in him should all fullness dwell" (Col. 1:18-19). May He be our soul's desire! Christ is all—Christ above all—Christ all in all!

September 22

Let your light so shine before men, that they may see your good works, and glorify your Father, which is in heaven (Matt. 5:16).

One day a businessman stopped for a shoeshine. As the young boy shined his shoes, the man remarked, "That's a very dark and stormy sky building up in the west, isn't it, son?" "I really hadn't noticed, Sir," answered the boy, "because I've been busy shining."

This is the Christian's vocation—to shine. God calls us to be a shining witness for Him; "Ye are even my witnessess" (Isa. 44:8). What kind of a witness are we making? Is the lampshade sooty, or bright and sparkling? A shining witness cannot have a grumpy disposition or a scowling face. A Spirit-filled witness should shine out to others with love and joy and peace and long-suffering.

> God gives some men the strength of fire
> To preach in Jesus' name,
> And some, with Pentecostal power,
> Write words that are aflame.
>
> Still others who have found new birth
> From speaking may retreat,
> Yet preach like quiet Lazarus,
> By walking down the street.

—JACKSON L. WEBSTER

"You've got to shine through me, Lord, so my friends will see the light. Help me to keep the windows clean."

—CINDY RANDOLPH

"Ye shall be witnesses unto me" (Acts 1:8).

September 23

Jesus began . . . to do (Acts 1:1).

There is a wonderful expression in Luke's opening verses of the Acts of the Apostles; "The former treatise have I made, O Theophilus, of all that Jesus began both to do and teach." It is a present-tense truth! Christ is still "doing and teaching."

Earlier John had recorded these prophetic words from the lips of the Lord Jesus: "He that believeth on me, the works that I do shall he do also; and greater works than these shall he do; because I go unto my Father" (John 14:12-13); "It is expedient for you that I go away; for if I go not away, the Comforter will not come unto you" (John 16:7).

This is the divine secret! "Tarry and wait in the Upper Room! The Holy Spirit, O little band of believers, is coming to indwell and fill you" (Cp. Luke 24:49). And like a mighty rushing wind or cloven tongues of fire, He fell upon them on the day of Pentecost. There the missionary work of the Church began, and there, through them, Jesus "began to do and to teach." He is still working today through us as the Holy Spirit fills and empowers us for His work.

September 24

And they took Jesus, and led him away
(John 19:16).

He had been all night in agony. He had spent the early morning at the hall of Caiaphas. From Caiaphas He had been hurried to Pilate, then to Herod, and back to Pilate. He had little strength left. They were eager for His blood, and therefore led Him out to die, loaded with the cross. O dolorous procession! Well may Salem's daughters weep. My soul, do thou weep also!

As our Lord is led forth, do we perceive the truth which was set in shadow by the scapegoat? Did not the high priest bring the scapegoat, and put both his hands upon its head, confessing the sin of the people, that thus those sins might be laid upon the goat, and cease from the people? Then the goat was led away into the wilderness, carrying far away the sins of the people, so that they could not be found.

Now we see Jesus brought before the priests and rulers who pronounce Him guilty. God Himself imputes our sins to Him. "The Lord hath laid on him the iniquity of us all." "He was made sin for us." As the substitute for sin, we see the great Scapegoat led away by the appointed officers of justice, bearing His cross.

Beloved, can you feel assured that He carried your sin? As you look at the cross upon His shoulders, does it represent your sin? There is one way by which you can tell. Have you laid your hand upon His head, confessed your sin, and trusted in Him? Then your sin lies not on you; it has all been transferred by blessed imputation to Christ, and He bears it on His shoulder as a load heavier than the Cross. Let not the picture vanish till you have rejoiced in your own deliverance, and adored the loving Redeemer upon whom your iniquities were laid.

—CHARLES HADDON SPURGEON

And can it be that I should gain
An interest in the Saviour's blood?
Died He for me, who caused His pain?
For me, who Him to death pursued?
Amazing love! How can it be
That Thou, my Lord, shouldest die for me?

Long my imprisoned spirit lay,
Fast bound in sin and nature's night;
Thine eye diffused a quickening ray,
I woke, the dungeon flamed with light;
My chains fell off, my heart was free,
I rose, went forth, and followed Thee.

He left His Father's throne above,
So free, so infinite His grace;
Emptied himself of all but love,
And bled for Adam's helpless race.
'Tis mercy all! Immense and free!
For O my God, it found out me.

No condemnation now I dread,
Jesus, with all in Him, is mine;
Alive in Him, my living head,
And clothed in righteousness divine,
Bold I approach the eternal throne,
Redeemed through Jesus Christ, alone!

—CHARLES WESLEY

September 25

Wherefore, seeing we also are compassed about with so great a cloud of witnesses, let us lay aside every weight, and the sin which doth so easily beset us, and let us run with patience the race that is set before us, looking unto Jesus the author and finisher of our faith (Heb. 12:1-2).

Paul never doubted his salvation. He had believed in Christ and he knew that he was the possessor of eternal life through the grace of God and the merits of His Son.

But Paul was constantly urging everyone to run well the race of the Christian life. To the Corinthians he literally said, "and you know that all who run in a race, only one receives a fading laurel wreath—the victor's crown. . . . Everyone who strives for the race keeps temperate in all things. They practice self-denial and they do it to receive an earthly prize. I run and keep my body under subjection, lest by chance, after acting as the herald of the lists who bids others enter, I might find my own self disqualified from running" (from 1 Corinthians 9:24-27).

Is there something in your life that is not pleasing to your Lord?„Are there weights and sins that need to be thrown away lest they trip or overcome you, as the writer of Hebrews suggests?

The Spirit-filled believer must run the race with patience, with constant training, with all encumbrances laid aside, and burdened only with an earnest desire to win. The crowning day is coming!

September 26

I bear in my body the marks of the Lord Jesus (Gal. 6:17).

He was a marked man. When the Lord told Ananias to go and find Paul in the home of Judas on the street that was called Straight, He directed: "Go thy way; for he is a chosen vessel unto me, to bear my name before the Gentiles and kings, and the children of Israel; for I will show him how great things he must suffer for my name's sake" (Acts 9:15, 16).

And the apostle did suffer. Listen as he writes to the church at Corinth: ". . . in labors more abundant, in stripes above measure, in prison more frequent, in deaths oft. Of the Jews five times received I forty stripes save one. Thrice was I beaten with rods, once was I stoned, thrice I suffered shipwreck, a night and a day I have been in the deep" (2 Cor. 11:23-25). Paul was marked with scars for the sake of his Lord. And every true servant of Christ since then has borne some scars, if he has really served the Master.

> *Hast thou no scar?*
> *No hidden scar on feet, or side, or hand?*
> *I hear thee sung as mighty in the land,*
> *I hear them hail thy bright ascended star,*
> *Hast thou no scar?*
>
> *Hast thou no wound?*
> *Yet I was wounded by the archers, spent,*
> *Leaned against a tree to die, and rent*

By raving beasts that compassed Me,
I swooned: Hast thou no wound?

No wound? no scar?
 Yet, as the Master shall the servant be,
 And pierced are the feet that follow Me;
But thine are whole; can he have followed far
Who has not wound or scar?

—AMY CARMICHAEL

God's people have trials. They were chosen in the furnace of affliction. They were never chosen to worldly peace and earthly joy. When the Lord drew up the charter of privileges, He included chastisements among the things to which they should be heirs. God's men must never expect to escape troubles. All of the apostles were made to pass through the fire of affliction and tribulation. It is ordained of old that the cross of trouble should be engraven on every vessel of mercy, as the royal mark whereby the King's vessels of honor are distinguished.

—CHARLES HADDON SPURGEON

September 27

**There is therefore now no condemnation
to them which are in Christ Jesus, who walk
not after the flesh, but after the Spirit** (Rom.
8:1).

To be able to walk and then to run, the child first must be born and then grow to maturity. We cannot "walk by the Spirit" until first we have been to the Cross. It is at Calvary that sins are washed away and redemption comes to the soul. At the Cross, the new birth begins. Regeneration brings us the new nature, "old things are passed away; behold, all things are become new" (2 Cor. 5:17).

Babies that are so lovely and promising at birth, must grow! To fail to do so is a great tragedy. Similarly, the young babe in Christ must mature and walk in the Holy Spirit. The secret of maturity is complete surrender of all of life to Him. Our bodies must be presented as a living sacrifice, holy and wholly His (Rom. 12:1, 2).

It is only then that we can know "what is that good, and acceptable, and perfect, will of God." The joy of the victorious walk comes only to those who lay themselves completely on the altar.

September 28

Thy word is a lamp unto my feet, and a light unto my path. . . . The entrance of thy words giveth light (Ps. 119:105, 130).

The Bible is the Book that contains the mind of God, the state of man, the way of salvation, the doom of sinners, and the happiness of believers. Its doctrines are holy, its precepts are binding, its histories are true, and its decisions are immutable. Read it to be wise, believe it to be safe, and practice it to be holy.

It contains light to direct you, food to support you, and comfort to cheer you. It is the traveler's map, the pilgrim's staff, the pilot's compass, the soldier's sword, and the Christian's charter.

Here heaven is opened and the gates of hell disclosed. Christ is its grand subject, our good its design, and the glory of God its end. It should fill the memory, rule the heart, and guide the feet.

Read it slowly, frequently, and prayerfully. It is mine of wealth, a paradise of glory, and a river of pleasure. It is given you in life, will be opened at the Judgment, and be remembered forever. It involves the highest responsibility, will reward the greatest labor, and condemn all who trifle with its sacred contents.

—Selected

"For ever, O Lord, thy word is settled in heaven" (Ps. 119:89).

Do you want something old, something settled and sure,
That has stood through the ages and still shall endure;
Reliable record of all that is past,
Indelibly graven, forever to last?
Then come to God's Word and the message it brings,
The Book of Beginnings, first cause and first things,
Creator, creation, a story sublime,
The darkness of chaos, the dawning of time,
The world that once was, and the world that now is;
Man made by God's hand, in His image, all His.

Do you want something modern, and startling and new,
As fresh as the morning, as clear as the dew;
Today's current topics brought quite down to date,
Forecast of tomorrow that's never too late?
Then come to God's Word, for its prophecies hold
The symbols of all that the years shall unfold,

A wonderful outline of history's course
From a truly authentic and trustworthy source.
Naught else is so ancient, naught else is so new,
And nothing so wise is, and nothing so true,
While the vivid events of the past it can tell,
And the future's great drama is pictured as well,
Satisfying and full is the message it brings;
The Book of Completions, the end of all things.

—Annie Johnson Flint

September 29

**And he entered again into the synagogue;
and there was a man there who had a withered
hand** (Mark 3:1).

Mark, the stenographer for the Holy Spirit, wrote in his
Gospel of a man with a withered hand who on every sabbath came
to the synagogue. The name of the man is not given. The city is
not identified. All we know is that he came to the synagogue with
a useless, helpless, deformed hand: a hand that had never carried
a burden, never lifted a load, never painted a picture, never
pointed out a safe pathway for wandering feet. As such, he typifies believers everywhere whose hands are so useless that they
have never participated in the joy of giving, so loveless that they
do not know the act of ministering to a sick and suffering humanity, and so feeble that they have not had the thrill of holding forth
the Word of Life to a dying, lost world.

Withered hands can be healed! Jesus said to the man in the
Mark 3 Scripture, "Stand forth." Useless hands can be healed if
we hold them out to Christ. "And he said, stretch forth thy hand,
and he did, and as he stretched forth his hand, it was restored
whole as the other." If we do this, than it can be also said of us,
"there *was* a man who *had* a withered hand."

These hands I give to Thee, my blessed Saviour,
To do Thy will—whatever love demands;
Redeemed and sanctified and in Thy favor,
I gladly yield to Thee this pair of hands.

Compassionate Redeemer, Thou hast saved me;
Thy matchless grace no mortal understands.
When cruel, blighting sin had so enslaved me,
I lifted to the Cross this pair of hands.

310

O take my hands and make them Thine forever.
I would that they respond to Thy commands.
To heal deep wounds and tell the old, old story—
I consecrate to Thee this pair of hands.

To point the lost of earth to Calvary,
To lift the Cross that dying souls may see,
To bring Thy healing touch to darkened lands,
I give to Thee, my God, this pair of hands.

— FLOYD W. HAWKINS

September 30

Thus saith the Lord, The heaven is my throne, and the earth is my footstool: Where is the house that ye build unto me? and where is the place of my rest? (Isa. 66:1).

This unusual verse asks a question: "Where is my house?" In 1 Cor. 6:19 the Lord gives an answer. "What? know ye not that your body is the temple of the Holy Spirit" Yes, we are His holy temple—His home—His house—His earthly dwelling place.

What kind of a house are you building? Be certain that it has a good foundation, and that the foundation is the Lord Jesus Christ. No other foundation can be safely laid, for all others crumble and decay.

But once the foundation is in, the room structure then can start. Dr. Walter L. Wilson suggested these rooms for His house. "The house you build must have a music room in it to sing His Praises; a library room to study and to meditate upon His Word; a living room to really live a testimony and to be a witness; a washroom for the cleansing of soiled hands and feet from the day's toil and grime; an attic and deep closets for the storage of materials to use for the Master; and a big bin to dump the junk and trash that may come into your life."

And then there must be a furnace room—one to adequately keep the whole house warm. And this reminds us that the Holy Spirit is the One who must fill us and possess us, so that we may give warmth and love to all those about us. Yes, such a house for Christ would surely be "the place of His rest." What kind of house are you building?

October 1

There we saw the giants, the sons of Anak,
which come of the giants; and we were in our
own sight as grasshoppers, and so we were in
their sight (Num. 13:33).

The spies who brought back an evil report from the land of Canaan felt that it could not be conquered because it was inhabited by giants. They reported, "We were in our own sight as grasshoppers, and so we were in their sight."

Now who told those spies of Israel that the giants viewed them as grasshoppers? Surely not the giants. Spies don't chat openly with the enemy. Besides, it is not likely that they spoke the same language and thus could not have engaged in conversation.

No, the spies received this notion of the giants' appraisal of them from their own low concept of themselves. Because the spies believed themselves to be like grasshoppers, they assumed that others saw them as such. It is a common error to assume that others view us as we view ourselves.

It is bad enough to see oneself as a grasshopper! But the disaster is compounded when one assumes that others see him as such. It becomes debilitating. This is what happened to the 10 spies. To assume that the Israelites could overthrow the sons of Anak—that grasshoppers could whip giants—was a bit too much for their imagination. They had already forgotten the mighty God who had delivered them from Pharaoh, parted the waters for a way, and protected them on the journey. They were victims of the "vision of smallness" and failed to remember God's greatness. Such an attitude and such a vision can block the work of God in any age.

—James D. Hamilton

"The church has not been short on programs and plans. It has been short on participating and perseverance. It has not been wanting in creeds and contests. It has been wanting in commitment and consecration. Renewal grows best, not on programs and plans, but in the hearts of God's people when they want more of Him" (C. Neil Strait).

"Where there is no vision, the people perish" (Prov. 29:18).

312

October 2

*Let us draw near with a true heart in full
assurance of faith* (Heb. 10:22).

In scripture we read of an evil heart, a blind heart, a deceitful heart, a hard heart, and a stony heart. In Hebrews is found the exhortation to "draw nigh with a true heart." What is a true heart?

A true heart holds no concealed enmity against another nor any hidden murmuring against God. A true heart in all the circumstances of life cries out, "Though he slay me, yet will I trust in him" (Job 13:15).

In a true heart there is no concealed holding to things that displease the Lord. An old preacher once said, "A true heart does not draw nigh to God and say, 'Use me, Lord, use even me just as Thou wilt and when and where,' and then inwardly say, 'But please don't send me to Africa.'" Two things will hinder God in using us: friendships and finances. Our friends must not be outside His will. One cannot sing "Worldly friendships all forsaking," and then mentally "except my unsaved financée." Do you sing "Take my silver and my gold," and then withhold secretly? If we tithe, we lay aside the first tenth for Him. If we just give, we wait to see what we have left and then give what we can spare.

Dr. Trumbull once wrote, "A true heart knows that salvation is not by merit and that remission of and forgiveness of sin is not obtained by good works. A true heart knows that apart from the shed blood of the Cross there is no remission of sin. A true heart knows that the new and living way into the presence of God is the blood-sprinkled way."

"Therefore, brothers, since we have confidence to enter the Most Holy Place by the blood of Jesus, by a new and living way opened for us . . . let us draw near to God" (Heb. 10:19-21, NIV).

October 3

According as he hath chosen us in him
before the foundation of the world, that we
should be holy and without blame before him
in love: having predestinated us unto the
adoption of children by Jesus Christ to himself,
according to the good pleasure of his will, to
the praise of the glory of his grace, wherein he
hath made us accepted in the beloved (Eph.
1:4-6).

Frances Havergal died in June, 1879, and her book *Kept for the Master's Use* was published that autumn. In it she wrote: "Consecration is not so much a step as a course; not so much an act as a position to which a course of action inseparably belongs. Consecration is not a religiously selfish thing. If it sinks into that, it ceases to be consecration.

"Our true aim, if the love of Christ constraineth us, will not be for me at all, but all for Jesus. We want our lives kept, not for our safety but for His glory; not for our comfort, but for His joy.

"The sanctified and Christ-loving heart cannot be satisfied with only negative keeping. We do not want only to be kept from displeasing Him, but to be kept always pleasing Him. Every 'kept from' should have its corresponding and still more blessed 'kept for.' We do not want our moments to be simply kept from Satan's use, but kept for His use; we want them to be not only kept from sin, but kept for His praise.

"Yes, kept for Him! I want to be kept for His sake; kept for His use; kept for His witness; kept for His joy. Kept for Him that in me He may show forth His light and beauty. Kept for Him, that He may do just what seemeth good with me; kept, so that no other lord shall have any more dominion over me, but that Jesus shall have all there is to have—little enough, indeed, but not divided or diminished by any other claim. Is not this, O you who love the Lord—is not this worth living for, worth asking for, worth trusting for?"

> *Take my life, and let it be*
> *Consecrated, Lord, to Thee.*
>
> *Take my moments and my days*
> *Let them flow in ceaseless praise.*
>
> *Take my hands, and let them move*
> *At the impulse of Thy love.*

Take my feet, and let them be
Swift and beautiful for Thee.

Take my voice, and let me sing
Always, only, for my King.

Take my lips, and let them be
Filled with messages from Thee.

Take my silver and my gold;
Not a mite would I withhold.

Take my intellect, and use
Every power as Thou shalt choose.

Take my will and make it Thine;
It shall be no longer mine.

Take my heart; it is Thine own;
It shall be Thy royal throne.

Take my love; my Lord, I pour
At Thy feet its treasure store.

Take myself, and I will be
Ever, only, all for Thee.

—FRANCES RIDLEY HAVERGAL

October 4

When the burnt offering began, the song
of the Lord began also (2 Chron. 29:27).

Abounding joy is the prime characteristic of true and holy religion—a joy unspeakable and full of glory. Is your face somber and dour? Is there no spring in you? Is there something wrong in your inner life, which is choking the spring of joy?

"When the burnt offering began the song began also." The word "began" indicates that it had ceased. For 16 years the song of the Lord had never broken from Levite throats and had not floated through the Temple courts. These courts, intended by David to resound with the praises of God, were silent and still. Why?

King Ahaz had cut in pieces the vessels of the house of God; he had shut its doors, put out all the lights, dispersed the priests, turned the Levites adrift, and had built altars to false gods.

315

Then came a change. Hezekiah became king and he brought the priests and the Levites back to the Temple and ordered them to sanctify themselves and the house of God, and to "carry forth the filthiness out of the holy place."

"Carry forth the filthiness." This must be done before the song can begin. It is also the call of the apostle Paul. "Let us cleanse ourselves from all filthiness of the flesh and spirit." he wrote. In doing this, we must get back to first principles. We are right with God in the exact proportion that we are right with those around us. Let us test ourselves, not by what we are on the Lord's Day but by what we are to those around us every day and to the man we like the least. Also, no secret sin must be tolerated. We must give ourselves entirely to our Lord. Give Him all the keys of your life and hold back nothing. Sing a hundred times a day: "I am His! I am absolutely His!" Then, and only then, will the song of the Lord begin again in you.

—F. B. MEYER

October 5

I will restore to you the years that the locust hath eaten, the cankerworm, and the caterpillar (Joel 2:25).

He is the God of restoration. He can make the desert land bloom with the rose and the barren valleys bring forth fruit. Paul said, "If any man be in Christ, he is a new creature (2 Cor. 5:17). Many a wasted life has found new beauty in the Master's hands. He waits only for trust and commitment.

> 'Twas battered and scarred, and the auctioneer
>   Thought it scarcely worth his while
> To waste much time on the old violin,
>   But he held it up with a smile,
> "What am I bid, good folks," he cried.
>   "Who'll start the bidding for me?"
> "A dollar, a dollar;" then, "Two! only two?
>   Two dollars, and who'll make it three?
> Three dollars, once; three dollars, twice,
>   Going for three—" but no,
> From the room, far back, a gray-haired man
>   Came forward and picked up the bow.

Then wiping the dust from the old violin,
  And tightening the worn, loose strings,
He played a melody pure and sweet
  As a caroling angel sings.

The music ceased, and the auctioneer
  With a voice that was quiet and low
Said: "What am I bid for the old violin?"
  And he held it up with the bow.
"A thousand dollars, and who'll make it two?
  Two thousand! And who'll make it three?
Three thousand, once; three thousand twice,
  And going, and gone," said he.
The people cheered, but some of them cried,
  "We do not quite understand
What changed its worth." Swift came the reply:
  "The touch of a master's hand."

And many a man with life out of tune,
  And battered and scarred with sin,
Is auctioned cheap to the thoughtless crowd,
  Much like the old violin.
A "mess of pottage," a glass of wine;
  A game—and he travels on.
He is "going" once, and "going" twice,
  He's "going" and almost "gone."
But the Master comes, and the foolish crowd
  Never can quite understand
The worth of a soul and the change that's wrought
  By the touch of the Master's hand.

—MYRA BROOKS WELCH

"A new heart also will I give you, and a new spirit will I put within you" (Ezek. 36:26).

October 6

Loosing from Troas, we came with a straight course to Samothracia, and the next day to Neapolis; and from thence to Philippi (Acts 16:11-12).

Paul often looked upon the Christian life as a race. To young Timothy he wrote, "I have finished my course." Each believer is

317

in a race and we need to run as victors. Two things are required of winners. We must run with all weights removed and we must run "a straight course." We cannot win if we zigzag!

Robert E. Hollis wrote of an article he had seen in an old copy of *Preacher's Magazine*. It was signed simply with the initials C. M. A.

"The old farmer unconsciously taught a great truth when he explained about his dog, which had just returned with the carriage from a little drive and seemed thoroughly exhausted as he lay down on the grass panting for breath. ' 'Tain't the road that tires him,' said the farmer, 'but the zigzagging. There wasn't a gate open on the way but he had to go in and examine the whole premises. There wasn't a cat appeared on the path but he had to chase it. There wasn't a dog barked but he just wore himself out barking back and showing fight, so that while we were keeping on the road, he was running over the whole countryside. It isn't the straight travelling that tired him, but the zigzagging.'"

There was a call to go to Macedonia. Paul and Luke set "a straight course." And so must we!

October 7

We know that, if our earthly house of this tabernacle were dissolved, we have a building of God, an house not made with hands, eternal in the heavens (2 Cor. 5:1).

In our Christian pilgrimage it is well, for the most part, to be looking forward. Forward lies the crown, and onward is the goal. Whether it be for hope, for joy, for consolation, or for the inspiring of our love, the future must be the grand object of the eye of faith. Looking into the future we see sin cast out, the body of sin and death destroyed, the soul made perfect, and fit to be a partaker of the inheritance of the saints in light.

The believer's enlightened eyes, by faith, can see death's river passed, the gloomy stream forded, and the hills of light attained on which standeth the celestial city. There the pilgrim enters seeing Christ, embraced in the arms of Jesus, glorified with Him. The thought of the future glory may well relieve the darkness of the past and the gloom of the present. The joys of heaven will surely compensate for the sorrows of earth.

Hush, my fears! This world is but a narrow span, and thou shalt soon have passed it. Hush, hush, my doubts. Death is but a narrow stream, and thou shalt soon have forded it. Time, how short—eternity how long. Death, how brief—immortality, how endless! Methinks I even now eat of Eshcol's clusters, and sip of the well which is within the gate. The road is so, so short! I shall soon be there.

—CHARLES HADDON SPURGEON

> But you will not mind the roughness
> nor the steepness of the way;
> Nor the chill, unrested morning,
> nor the searness of the day;
> And you will not take a turning
> to the left or to the right,
> But go straight ahead, nor tremble
> at the coming of the night,
> For the road leads Home.

—AUTHOR UNKNOWN

October 8

**We all do fade as a leaf, and our iniquities,
like the wind, have taken us away** (Isa. 64:6).

Outside my study window the colors of fall are everywhere. The elm tree stands with its shriveled brown leaves falling from high branches. The sycamore down the street is covering my neighbor's lawn with large, brittle leaves. But the hard maples and the sweet gums are adorned in their leafy garments of burnt red and deepest gold.

Isaiah said, "We all do fade as a leaf." Some fade to an unbecoming nature as old age approaches—just like the elm tree. But some stand out with vibrant colors and majestic beauty. Old age and a life of sin take many away as the wind blows old leaves with the oncoming breath of approaching winter. But how glorious to have lived in His image and will, and to fade in beauty and loveliness. Our testimony must include growing old with grace and sweetness!

Lord, keep my heart attuned to laughter
  When youth is done;
When all the days are gray days, coming after
  The warmth, the sun.
Lord keep me then from bitterness, from grieving,
  When life seems cold;
Lord keep me always loving and believing
  As I grow old.

—Author Unknown

"They shall still bring forth fruit in old age" (Ps. 92:14).

Time rolls on relentlessly, and the farther we leave youth behind, the faster the years seem to slip away. For many people the high noon of their sojourn on earth has passed and the shadows of approaching old age are lengthening across the autumn landscape of their lives. How blessed it is that although "our outward man perish, yet the inward man is renewed day by day" (2 Cor. 4:16). A dear old saint once said, "I am still at work with my hand to the plow and my face to the future. The shades of evening deepen, but morning is in my heart." St. Paul said, "But none of these things move me . . . that I might finish my course with joy" (Acts 20:24). As we grow old, let us allow the Holy Spirit to fill our thoughts, energize our actions, and rekindle spiritual desires and energies. He is able to make us grow old gracefully.

—Henry G. Bosch

From *Our Daily Bread*, © 1973, Radio Bible Class.
Used by special permission.

October 9

Pure religion and undefiled before God and the Father is this, To visit the fatherless and widows in their affliction, and to keep himself unspotted from the world (Jas. 1:27).

A dear old saint once said, "There are two parts to the gospel —the believing and the behaving." They must not be separated for both are of equal importance. If we believe—we shall behave! The Christian is saved only by faith, not by works. But James is correct. If any man is in Christ Jesus, he is surely a new person and good words (the behaving) will follow.

Thus James opens his letter to Jewish Christians of the first century with very sound and sage advice. He literally said this: "You will have trials, but endure them with joy as you walk life's pilgrim way. The testing of your faith is precious and will produce patience. Ask your Father for wisdom for all of life's problems, not just for a few. Don't waver in your faith but endure your trials and temptations by leaning on His arm. Above all, be thankful for all His mercies and gifts."

Then James gives a successful Christian philosophy. Learn to follow his counsel. "Be swift to hear, slow to speak, slow to wrath" (Jas. 1:19). Many a hurt and sorrow could be avoided if we would but yield to the Spirit's guidance here.

And finally, James said, we need to be doers, not just hearers of His Word. Put your faith into action! Tell the world about Jesus—both by your words and by your works!

> *When the voice of the Master is calling*
> *And the gates into heaven unfold,*
> *And the saints of all ages are gathering*
> *And are thronging the city of gold;*
> *How my heart shall o'erflow with the rapture*
> *If a brother shall greet me and say,*
> *"You pointed my footsteps to heaven,*
> *You told me of Jesus the Way."*

—AUTHOR UNKNOWN

October 10

It is finished (John 19:30).

These three very ordinary words burst forth with an eternal brightness when one considers the occasion on which they were spoken and the lips from which they fell. Our Lord had endured six hours of indescribable agony, and death was upon Him. But Christ's three words speak volumes, even yet. In part they are saying to us that:

All prophecy pointing to this hour is finished. And how abundant was that prophecy in the sacred writ of the Old Testament! Hardly a page can be found without some reference to this climactic moment in history.

All sacrifices for sin are now finished. And how many of them dot the horizon of history! From the earliest dawn to this supreme moment the sacrifice of animals—without blemish—was made for sins. But no more!

The destruction of the partition between man and his Maker was now finished. The veil of the Temple was torn from top to bottom a few moments after these words were spoken. God became accessible to all through His Son.

The perfect obedience of Christ to the Father was now finished. He had been obedient all the way, even unto the death of the Cross. He once asked, "Why?" (Matt. 27:46), but not once did He say, "No."

His suffering was now finished. And how He suffered! His miracles were misunderstood—His friends deserted Him—His enemies mocked Him and beat Him. Even His Father hid His face from Him. But now suffering was ending in death.

His atonement was finished. His blood had now been shed. Sin had been cancelled; the ransom had been paid. Mercy and truth had met together and righteousness and peace had now kissed each other (Ps. 85:10).

"It is finished," He cried! And it was the grandest finale of all!

—FLETCHER SPRUCE

October 11

Peter, an apostle of Jesus Christ, To the strangers scattered throughout Pontus, Galatia, Cappadocia, Asia, and Bithynia (1 Pet. 1:1).

Peter opened his first letter by proclaiming some deep spiritual truths. "We are sojourners," he said. We must not live as though this old earth was our only and permanent abode. The Christian looks forward to a better country and his own kindred. There is a city that we seek whose "builder and maker is God." We are truly strangers and pilgrims.

"We are the elect." According to the foreknowledge of God and the work of the Holy Spirit, Peter tells us that we have been chosen in Christ (1 Pet. 2:9). Paul adds that this was known "before the foundation of the world" (Eph. 1:4). This is a divine mystery, but we hold a lofty position in the Beloved.

"According to his abundant mercy [he] hath begotten us again unto a lively hope" (1 Pet. 1:3). This was written by the same disciple who wandered the dark streets of Jerusalem in deep despair until that glorious morning when he received the angel's resurrection message, "Go tell his disciples, and Peter" (Mark 16:7). Our Lord's resurrection has turned death into a living hope.

"We are kept." Sometimes we forget that we belong to a keeping God who is a great and loving Father. Let us rejoice that He is "able to keep [us] from falling, and to present [us] faultless before the presence of His glory with exceeding joy" (Jude 24).

And finally, Peter says "We have an inheritance" (1 Pet. 1:4). Only a true member of the family can receive an inheritance. Others may receive a bequest. But from our risen Savior, as members of God's family, we have an inheritance. It is "incorruptible." Some inheritances undergo decay with the passage of time. But not this one! Some inheritances come from great wealth accumulated by deceit and thievery. But not this one! Some earthly inheritances are lost and disappear. But not this one! "It is reserved in heaven for you."

Let us give thanks and rejoice, as Peter did, that we are saved, redeemed and kept by this wonderful Lord, for we were "not redeemed with corruptible things, as silver and gold, from [our] vain conversation received by tradition from [our] fathers; but with the precious blood of Christ, as of a lamb without blemish and without spot" (1 Pet. 1:18-19).

October 12

He went a little farther, and fell on his face, and prayed, saying, O my Father, if it be possible, let this cup pass from me: nevertheless, not as I will, but as thou wilt (Matt. 26:39).

Gethsemane and Calvary remind us of the proper motives for holy living. Facing death on a cross, our Lord showed us the nature of real consecration: "O my Father, if it be possible, let this cup pass from me: nevertheless not as I will, but as thou wilt."

Absalom, the son of David, was exiled from home for three years. Homesick and ambitious for political power, he vowed, "If the Lord shall bring me again indeed to Jerusalem, then will I serve the Lord" (2 Sam. 15:8). Absalom was not the first nor the last to preface his loyalty to God with an *if*. This is conditioned loyalty. *If* the Lord blesses me, I will serve Him. *If* things go well, I will be a Christian. But conditioned loyalty is no loyalty, and conditioned consecration is not consecration.

True loyalty is seen in our Lord's utter commitment to God's will. It is seen in the action of three devoted young men who, when facing the issue of life or death, declared: "If it be so, our God, whom we serve, is able to deliver us from the burning fiery furnace, and he will deliver us out of thine hand, O king. *But if not*, be it known unto thee, O king, that we will not serve thy gods, nor worship the golden image which thou hast set up" (Dan. 3:17-18).

Is my loyalty to God prefaced by the *if* of Absalom or by the *but if not* of three courageous young men? In my Gethsemanes, can I follow my Lord and say, "Nevertheless not as I will, but as thou wilt"?

—A. F. Harper

October 13

Behold, what manner of love the Father hath bestowed upon us (1 John 3:1).

At one time during his early married life, Thomas Moore left his beautiful bride to spend some six months in foreign service. During his absence, his wife contracted smallpox and became gravely ill. Her lovely features became scarred and disfigured. For weeks she was tortured with the fear that Thomas Moore might leave her when he returned and saw her appearance.

But a friend wrote to him and related the story. When Moore received that letter, he sat at his desk and wrote a long love letter to his wife in England. In it he included this original poem:

Believe me, if all those endearing young charms,
*   Which I gaze on so fondly today,*
Were to change by tomorrow and fleet in my arms,
*   Like fairy gifts, fading away.*
Thou would still be adored, as this moment thou art,
*   Let thy loveliness fade as it will;*
And around the dear ruin, each wish of my heart
*   Would entwine itself verdantly still!*

It is not while beauty and youth are thine own,
*   And thy cheek unprofaned by a tear,*
That the fervor and faith of a soul can be known,
*   To which time will but make thee more dear!*

No, the heart that has truly loved never forgets,
But as truly loves on to the close;
As the sunflower turns on the sun when it sets
The same look which she turned when it rose.

What a wonderful expression of love! But God's love is still deeper and Paul described it so plainly: "God commendeth his love toward us, in that, while we were yet sinners, Christ died for us" (Rom. 5:8). Behold, what manner of love He has given us! There is no greater love! Have you given Him thanks for it?

October 14

Demetrius is well spoken of by everyone
—and even by the truth itself. We also speak
well of him, and you know that our testimony
is true (3 John 12 NIV).

In the New Testament family album three men whose names begin with the same letter stand out as typical of three kinds of Christians today.

There was Demas, who forsook Paul, having loved this present world (2 Tim. 4:10). Doubtless he had started out in dead earnest, maybe with plenty of fire, but the pull of the old life and the charm of the world were too much for him. The Christian's citizenship is in heaven, and whatever does not savor of that is of the world. Any interest that moves ahead of the will of God, be it business or pleasure or ambition, is of Demas.

Then there was Diotrephes, who loved the preeminence (3 John 9). He lived in the days of the Early Church, before the false distinction between clergy and laity had become established. He lorded it over the brethren, opposed dear, saintly John, and refused the visiting ministers, assuming an authority not taught in the Word. His sort is still with us in the minister who bosses instead of shepherding his flock; in ecclesiastical overlords who reject all visiting brethren who do not measure up to their private yardstick; and in any and all who want to rule instead of serve. We are in no danger of running short today in the supply of Diotrephes. And forget not that loving the preeminence is as bad as loving this preset world.

How refreshing it is to move from these two troublesome souls to Demetrius, who loved the truth (3 John 12). Whether or not he was the Ephesian silversmith recorded in Acts 19, now converted, he certainly had a good report from all and also of the truth. His sort is altogether too rare today. He was no celebrity, but we could profitably exchange some of our striking personalities for more of his kind. What would the church do today without his quiet, faithful steady testimony? God help us in such a time to choose the Demetrius way of good report and not the Diotrephes way of loud report!

—Vance Havner
in *Rest Awhile*

October 15

I sought for a man among them, that should make up the hedge, and stand in the gap before me for the land, that I should not destroy it: but I found none (Ezek. 22:30).

The Lord was seeking, not for better methods, but for a better man. He was looking for an individual whom He could use and who would be wholly His. It was hard to find such a one in Ezekiel's time and it is still difficult today.

There was a need for this man. He was needed to "stand in the gap." There was a great void and the Lord desired to fill it. Any man would do *if* he would be completely His! No degrees were necessary. A common fisherman, just like Simon Peter, could do His work!

The Lord sought for a man who would confess Him before the people and faithfully present His Word. Such a one would stand before kings because he would also "stand before Me"— God's man of holiness and dedication. The promise of Ezekiel's day and St. Paul's day is still the same in this day. The call still goes out. Wanted: a man to stand before the Lord and to "fill the gap." The Holy Spirit is looking for such a man. Will you be that one?

October 16

Behold, I stand at the door, and knock; if any man hear my voice, and open the door, I will come in to him, and will sup with him, and he with me (Rev. 3:20).

There is sorrow here! There is tragedy! There is a warning! The church at Laodicea, to whom these words were addressed, had become the church of the closed door. Christ was on the outside knocking!

A church must take three fateful steps if it lapses into spiritual darkness. Its members must lose their penitence; the church corporate must lose its purpose; and the ministers must lose their power. Laodicea "knew not" the loss it had sustained. It had lost its first love!

At Laodicea, the Holy Spirit had called the people into the ministry of Christ and the fellowship of His sufferings. This became unfashionable. Programs replaced prayer, and membership replaced regeneration. The church lost its purpose. It lost interest in evangelism. Gone was a burden for the lost of the city. Gone was the Christ-centered love for the poor. The gospel became polluted. The Holy Spirit removed the candlestick. And Christ was on the outside of the fast-closed door seeking to re-enter.

The Savior called the Laodicean church to repentance! This is the only way the door can be opened. If the church is to become rich, it must repent. If the church is to regain its sight, it must repent. If the church is not to remain empty, it must repent. The alternative is to be spued out of the mouth of Christ.

These are distasteful and harsh words, but thus the Lord spoke so long ago. He stood outside the church's ornate, fast-closed door and knocked. Did they hear?

Is the church of Laodicea with us today? Can it repent? Can the tears fall? Can it hear the sound of knocking at the door? We do not know. But we do know this, that if the earthly, corporate church cannot hear, then also to each man the invitation comes! To him who hears the knock, and in true repentance and faith opens his heart door, the Savior will come in.

Be still, O church! Be still, O my soul! Hush the noisy voices. There is the sound of knocking by a nail-pierced hand at the door!

—HUGHES DAY
in *Layman in the Pulpit*

There's a Stranger at the door,
*   Let Him in;*
He has been there oft before,
*   Let Him in;*
Let Him in, ere He is gone,
Let Him in, the Holy One,
Jesus Christ, the Father's Son,
*   Let Him in.*

—J. B. ATCHISON

October 17

A man shall be as an hiding place from the
wind, and a covert from the tempest; as rivers
of water in a dry place, as the shadow of a great
rock in a weary land (Isa. 32:2).

I live in a portion of the country where in the springtime, low pressure centers often develop over the panhandles of Oklahoma and Texas. As cool polar air sweeps down over the Rockies into the Great Plains it clashes with warm moist air driven northward from the Gulf. As in mortal combat, great storms form and nature's fiercest at times develops—the tornado. One learns early in life, on the plains, the value of a safe and secure storm cellar.

Jesus Christ is such a hiding place from the "tornadoes" of life! He is the all-sufficient Savior for life, for death, and for all eternity. When the biopsy report comes back positive—when a loved one suddenly is taken—when all that we have and hold most dear is swept away—we have a secure hiding place. He is "a covert from the tempest."

Dr. George Truett, pastor for so many wonderful years at the First Baptist Church in Dallas, wrote: "I used to be, when a lad, frightened well nigh unto death at the thought of dying and the Great Judgment. But no more of that now. I have a sufficient Savior.

"When the time comes for me to pass from the earthly scene to the heavenly, He has promised to be there waiting for me. He has promised to convey me to Heaven himself. I needn't be afraid when or where or how I go. The automobile accident may claim me; the airplane disaster may take me; disease may lay its ugly hand upon me—but never fear. When the time comes, Jesus says, 'I'll be there at the depot of death for you and I myself will take you home and there will be no trouble.'

"And then He says, 'I'll be there at the Judgment in your place.' I have put my faith in Christ and He is my Attorney. It is all in my Attorney's hands—He is my Advocate. 'If any man sin, we have an advocate [an attorney] with the Father, Jesus Christ the righteous.' I put my faith in His hands. My life is in His hands. My death is in His hands. My all is in His hands.

"Take my life and manage it. I can't manage it. Take care of me, I can't take care of myself. Save me, I can't save myself. Keep me, I can't keep myself. And He answers back, 'I'll forgive, and I'll save, and I'll guide, and I'll keep you. I'll be with you living and I'll be with you dying, and I'll be with you at the Judgment. And we will live together forever in my Father's home above.'"

Oh, this wonderful, wonderful Christ! Sufficient for all of life! Sufficient for all of death! Sufficient for all eternity!

> When the long night has ended
>   And the storms come no more,
> Let me stand in Thy presence
>   On that bright, peaceful shore.
> In that land where the tempest
>   Never comes, Lord, may I
> Dwell with Thee when the storm passes by.
>
> 'Til the storm passes over,
> 'Til the thunder sounds no more,
>   'Til the clouds roll forever from the sky,
> Hold me fast, let me stand
> In the hollow of Thy hand,
>   Keep me safe 'til the storm passes by.

—MOSIE LISTER
© 1958 by Lillenas Publishing Co.
All rights reserved. Used by Permission

October 18

They that wait upon the Lord shall renew their strength; they shall mount up with wings as eagles; they shall run, and not be weary; and they shall walk and not faint (Isa. 40:31).

Few Christians are willing to engage in the quiet communion with God which enables one to "mount up with wings as eagles." They prefer a constant round of activity or the excitement of being with the crowd. But eagles do not ascend in flocks, and likewise the believer who wants to rise to spiritual heights must be willing to go alone! If he fails to wait upon the Lord, he will soon find that his strength is sapped and his zeal diminished. Only by frequent coming away from the clamor of the world to be with Christ can he gain renewed spiritual vitality and power.

The eagle's flight may indeed be lonely yet it is truly rewarding! The air of the heavenlies is exhilarating, the sunshine of His love shines everywhere, and the view is unhindered by earthly distractions. This is the place of joy where the Christian runs and is not weary. If you would rise to higher ground, then learn the secret of "waiting upon the Lord." By fellowshipping with Him through prayer and the Word, you will be lifted to new heights of victory in Jesus!

—HENRY G. BOSCH
From *Our Daily Bread*, © 1973, Radio Bible Class.
Used by special permission.

I met God in the morning,
When my day was at its best,
And His presence came like sunrise
With a glory in my breast.

All day long the Presence lingered,
All day long He stayed with me;
And we sailed in perfect calmness
O'er a very troubled sea.

Other ships were blown and battered,
Other ships were sore distressed,
But the winds that seemed to drive them
Brought to us both peace and rest.

Then I thought of other mornings,
With a deep remorse of mind,
When I too had loosed the moorings,
With the Presence left behind.

So I think I know the secret,
Learned from many a troubled way—
You must seek Him in the morning,
If you want Him through the day!

—RALPH SPAULDING CUSHMAN

October 19

Teach me thy way, O Lord; I will walk in thy truth: unite my heart to fear thy name (Ps. 86:11).

This prayer should be the heart cry of every child of God—"Teach me thy way." The Lord may guide you by circumstances or doors that both open and close. He may lead you by a pillar of fire by night or by a cloud by day. But he can only teach you from His Word!

Would you grow in grace and stature and in knowledge? Then you must live in His Word. Make His Word the joy of your soul. Whether it be questions of social conduct or social concern, you will find the truth only as the Holy Spirit speaks to you from the Word. What you are to do will be shown you from His Word. Your lifelong commitment in marriage must be in accordance with His Word. "Be not unequally yoked together with unbelievers" (2 Cor. 6:14). Rules of conduct and holiness are made plain as He teaches from His Word.

> *Teach me Thy way, O Lord; Teach me Thy way!*
> *Thy guiding grace afford; Teach me Thy way!*
> *Help me to walk aright, more by faith less by sight,*
> *Lead me with heavn'ly light; Teach me Thy way!*
>
> *When I am sad at heart, Teach me Thy way!*
> *When earthly joys depart, Teach me Thy way!*
> *In hours of loneliness, in times of dire distress,*
> *In failure or success, Teach me Thy way!*
>
> *When doubts and fears arise; Teach me Thy way!*
> *When storms o'erspread the skies; Teach me Thy way!*
> *Shine through the cloud and rain, Through sorrow,*
>   *toil, and pain,*
> *Make Thou my pathway plain; Teach me Thy way!*
>
> *Long as my life shall last; Teach my Thy way!*
> *Where'er my lot be cast; Teach me Thy way!*
> *Until the race is run, until the journey's done,*
> *Until the crown is won; Teach me Thy way!*

—B. Mansell Ramsey

"Wherewithal shall a young man cleanse his way? by taking heed thereto according to thy word. . . . Thy word have I hid in mine heart, that I might not sin against thee" (Ps. 119:9, 11).

"I have more understanding than all my teachers; for thy testimonies are my meditation" (Ps. 119:99).

October 20

They say unto him, We have here but five
loaves, and two fishes. He said, Bring them
here to me (Matt. 14:17-18).

D. L. Moody once said, "When the Lord is your partner, make your plans big." Five loaves and two fishes in the light of human ability is not much. But little is much when Christ has the little. Let not the word "but" hinder you in feeding the multitudes. Do not let your disability cancel out His ability! Look not at human "shortcoming" but at His "long coming." Heed the Master's call—"bring them to me."

Five small loaves and two fishes would hardly satisfy a small boy's hunger—but when he gave them all to the Lord Jesus, he received back more than he and at least 5,000 others could eat. Twelve baskets of bread and fish were left over and all had been satisfied! God multiplies all that we give to Him and it is impossible to outgive God!

"There is a lad here, which hath five barley loaves, and two small fishes: but what are they among so many?" (John 6:9).

> *"My little lad, come now and see,*
> *I've packed your basket carefully.*
> *Five small cakes, they seem so few;*
> *The fishes, all I have, but two.*
> *Your journey may be hard and long,*
> *Among the weary, teeming throng.*
> *If one should hunger, feed him, lad;*
> *For this would make your mother glad.*
> *Seek out the Master, on the way.*
> *Follow close, heed all He has to say.*
> *Here, lad, your basket take and go."*
> *Five thousand? How was she to know,*
> *This hungry multitude was fed*
> *With these five fishes and the barley bread?*

—ADA SHOCKLEY

"There are five things that God can use. 'The weak things, the foolish things, the base things, the despised things, and the things which are not.' When we are ready to lay down our strength and our weaknesses before the Lord, then and only then can He use us" (D. L. Moody).

"God's bakery is still open—there are no union hours there.

He is in the Bread business, and He works miracles with little things and little folks" (Walter L. Wilson).

> *"I have not much to give," he said.*
> *"My talents are so few,*
> *But all I have and hope to be*
> *I gladly give to You!"*
>
> *Not much?—nor had a little boy*
> *Who in a great crowd stood.*
> *But with the simple lunch he gave*
> *They fed a multitude.*
>
> *Not much to give? Perhaps it's true*
> *When viewed in man's false light.*
> *But given with a heart of love—*
> *'Tis great within God's sight.*

—GERALDINE NICHOLAS

October 21

Being justified by faith, we have peace with God through our Lord Jesus Christ. . . . For when we were yet without strength, in due time Christ died for the ungodly (Rom. 5:1, 6).

So that we might clearly grasp what God is doing when He saves us, He has used terms from various phases of life to help us understand. So rich is His salvation that no one idea can plumb its depths.

From the law court, God takes the word *justification.* Cleared in court, acquitted as innocent by the judge, is its basic idea. It views our sin as guilt before the law and stresses Christ's role in bearing our judgment. He died for the ungodly.

From the slave market comes the term *redemption.* It means to be bought out of slavery by the payment of a ransom—our slavery to sin, or legalism; and Christ's own blood is the payment.

From the caste system of the ancient world, God takes the idea of *adoption.* Just as a wealthy man could adopt a slave and give him the full rights of a son, so God welcomes us into His family, and names us as heirs.

From the area of family life, God picks up the term *recon-*

ciliation. It reminds us of our estrangement and separation from Him. We, like the prodigal, are received home through the grace of our Lord Jesus Christ.

—David Allan Hubbard

"But God commendeth his love toward us, in that, while we were yet sinners, Christ died for us. Much more then, being now justified by his blood, we shall be saved from wrath through him" (Rom. 5:8-9).

Jesus, Thy blood and righteousness
My beauty are, my glorious dress;
'Midst flaming worlds, in these arrayed,
With joy shall I lift up my head.

Bold shall I stand in Thy great day,
For who aught to my charge shall lay?
Fully absolved through these I am,
From sin and fear, from guilt and shame.

Lord, I believe Thy precious blood,
Which, at the mercy seat of God,
Forever doth for sinners plead,
For me, e'en for my soul, was shed.

Lord, I believe were sinners more
Than sands upon the ocean shore,
Thou hast for all a ransom paid,
For all a full atonement made.

—Nicolaus Zinzendorf
Tr. by John Wesley

October 22

Behold, what manner of love the Father hath bestowed upon us, that we should be called the children of God (1 John 3:1).

When John dwelt upon the love of God he could find no adequate adjectives to gloriously describe it. One can add nothing to the word that he chose: "God *so* loved the world." Throughout this dispensation of grace many sermons are preached, many songs are written, many paintings depicting God's love are created, but still, they cannot exhaust the full message of that little word "so."

The greatest Lover of all gave the greatest Gift of all, His only begotten Son, that we might receive the greatest blessing of all: for "whosoever believeth in him shall not perish."

There is a miracle here, for He loved us before we first loved Him. Calvary was planned in the loving heart of God and through the willingness of His Son before the very foundations of the world. From the prophesied seed of the woman who was to bruise the serpent's head, to the prophesy of Abraham telling his son Isaac: "God will provide himself a lamb for a burnt offering," to the blood upon the door of the Israelites in Egypt before the avenging angel passed over, to the thunderings of Sinai, to the lambs slain upon many altars, God's love led to a Cross on a hill!

A father one day to his own little son
  A letter of love had penned;
He scarcely could read, so young he was,
  So just at the very end,
"To show him my love," the father said,
"I will close it with a kiss.
This simple sign he will surely know—"
  And he made a sign like this—X X X.
Yes, right at the end where he signed his name
  He added a simple cross,
And the letter was sent, and he knew what was meant,
  The kiss that was told in a cross!

And God wrote a letter, a wonderful book;
  He wrote it o'er earth and sky.
A book that the humble in heart could read
  When lifting their heads on high.
And looking at stars so far away,
  And looking at flowers so near,
They noted the care-free birds' sweet song,
  In them God's care did hear.
Yes, over it all He signed His name,
  On sea, on earth, and on sky.
And the letter was sent, and they knew what it meant,
  Who lifted their eyes on high.

And then when the course of time had run,
  A letter of love was sent.
It was writ so plain that all might read
  And know what the Sender meant.
For there at the end, where all might see,
  A sign that they could not miss;
He placed in the language of childhood's day
  The sign of a child's pure kiss—X.

But why if it told us of God's great love,
    Oh, why was there only one?
My eyes fill with tears, I sob as I see—
    'Twas the cross of His only Son.

And the letter was sent, do you know what it meant—
God's love in the cross of His Son?

—F. HOWARD OAKLEY

October 23

**The disciples took him by night, and let
him down by the wall in a basket** (Acts 9:25).

Little things can be so important. Saul of Tarsus was in that
escape basket but the holders of the ropes only knew that it was
a young convert who, because he had given fearless testimony
concerning Christ, was in severe danger. Perhaps they knew of
his past—but certainly they knew nothing of his future. And yet
their faithfulness saved the life of a young man who gave to the
world most of the New Testament and who would carry to the
Gentiles the gospel of God's redeeming grace. What if they had
failed?

Fletcher Spruce asks, "Who were the disciples who held the
ropes that let Saul down in a basket to save his life? Their names
are not recorded. Often those who do hard work in obscure places
in God's kingdom are unheralded and unsung. They may have
to work at night and frequently they do not see the final results
of their labors. But God sees and He rewards rope-holders whose
arms may ache and whose hands may be burnt. His rope-holders
may be unknown, unpaid, and even unappreicated, but God
rewards and His reward should be sufficient."

Does the place you're called to labor
    Seem so small and little known?
It is great if God is in it,
    And He'll not forget His own.

Little is much when God is in it;
    Labor not for wealth or fame.
There's a crown, and you can win it
    If you'll go in Jesus' name.

—MRS. F. S. SUFFIELD

"A book of remembrance was written before him for them who feared the Lord, and that thought upon his name. And they shall be mine, saith the Lord of hosts, in that day when I make up my jewels" (Mal. 3:16-17).

October 24

I beseech you therefore, brethren, by the mercies of God, that ye present your bodies a living sacrifice, holy, acceptable unto God, which is your reasonable service. And be not conformed to this world; but be ye transformed by the renewing of your mind, that ye may prove what is that good, and acceptable, and perfect, will of God (Rom. 12:1-2).

Paul called this act of entire consecration a "reasonable service." He knew that God required it; he entreated his fellow Christians to do it; but he insisted that it was what every thoughtful Christian should freely choose to do.-

Self-surrender is a reasonable requirement because it is a requirement that every man can meet. If God required talent, some of us would be shut out; if He asked for money, some could not pay. But when God asks for the surrender of myself, He asks for that which is wholly within my power. Jesus did not ask the rich young ruler to sell property belonging to his father, his brother, or his business partner. The requirement concerned only that which was his own: "Go and sell *that thou hast.*" Consecration is reasonable because it is the one condition clearly within my power to meet.

He asks only that you give yourself.

—A. F. HARPER

> Oh, the bitter shame and sorrow
>   That a time could ever be
> When I let the Saviour's pity
> Plead in vain, and proudly answered,
>   "All of self and none of Thee."
>
> Yet he found me; I beheld Him
>   Bleeding on the accursed tree;
> Heard Him pray, "Forgive them, Father;"
> And my wistful heart said faintly,
>   "Some of self and some of Thee."

Day by day, His tender mercy
  Healing, helping, full and free,
Sweet and strong, and oh, so patient,
Brought me lower, while I whispered,
  "Less of self and more of Thee."

Higher than the highest heavens,
  Deeper than the deepest sea,
Lord, Thy love at last has conquered;
Grant me now my soul's desire,
  "None of self and all of Thee."

—THEODORE MONOD

October 25

**One thing I know, that, whereas I was
blind, now I see** (John 9:25).

One day in London's Hyde Park, where anyone can stand on
a box and speak to his heart's content, an atheist was making
sport of an unlettered man who claimed he had found Christ and
that his life had been changed.

The atheist asked, "Do you know anything about Jesus
Christ?"

"Yes, by the grace of God, I do," was the answer.

"When was He born?" was the next question.

The young and ignorant saint gave a wrong answer.

"How old was He when He died?"

Again the answer was wrong.

The atheist with a sneer asked another question and then
said, "See, you do not know much about Jesus."

"I know all too little," was the modest answer, "but I do
know this. Three years ago I was one of the worst drunkards in
the East side of London. Three years ago my wife was a brokenhearted woman, and my children were afraid of me as if I had been
a wild beast. Today I have one of the happiest homes in the city
and my children look eagerly for me when at the close of day I
come home. Jesus Christ has done this for me. This I know."

Such a changed life stands as a shining testimony that cannot
be refuted by all the powers of darkness and unbelief for when the
Master comes, the lame walk, the blind see, withered hands are
made whole, and the dead live again. What a difference Jesus
makes!

Like a blind man who walks in the darkness,
I had longed, I had searched for the light.
Then I met the Master;
Now I walk no more in the night.

For all things were changed when He found me;
A new day broke through all around me;
For I met the Master,
Now I belong to Him.

—MOSIE LISTER
© 1958 by Lillenas Publishing Co.
All rights reserved. Used by Permission.

"I write these things to you who believe in the name of the Son of God so that you may know that you have eternal life" (1 John 5:13, NIV).

October 26

God, who commanded the light to shine out of darkness, hath shined in our hearts, to give the light of the knowledge of the glory of God in the face of Jesus Christ. But we have this treasure in earthen vessels, that the excellency of the power may be of God, and not of us (2 Cor. 4:6-7).

I am Thy bread. Break me up and pass me around to the poor and the otherwise needy of this world. Feed them through me.

I am Thy towel. Take me and dampen me with tears, and with me wash the feet of men who are weary with walking and with working.

I am Thy light. Take me out where the darkness is thick, where it is blacker than black, where no light can be seen on the other side of it, there to shine and let Christ shine even if it seems that no one is taking note.

I am Thy pen, Take me up in Thy hand and, with me, write whatever word Thou wilt, and placard the word where the least and the lost of this world will see it and read it and believe.

I am Thy salt. Sprinkle me on all the things which Thou dost want for men, so that Thy purposes will taste better to them. If people around me do not savor their lot in life, sprinkle me upon them, so that my faith and my love and my hope will flavor their experiences. Spread me out over the people whose faith is about to spoil, even if there is then no part of me remaining to be used for myself.

I am Thy water. Pour me into people who thirst for Thee but do not even know that it is Thee for whom they thirst. Pour into them from me the promise that summer drought will pass and refreshing rivers of water will gush over them if they will but drink of Thee.

I am Thine, dear Lord, Do with me what Thou wilt, when Thou wilt, for whom Thou wilt.

—J. Kenneth Grider

October 27

Without shedding of blood is no remission (Heb. 9:22).

Go quietly, with thy shoes from off thy feet, into Gethsemane. See Jesus there! Drops of blood are streaming down His face. Every pore, like a wee gate that will not stay shut, is open and blood oozes out. What a strange sweat! Not the sweat of men who earn their bread by "the sweat of their brow!" Not the sweat of men who exhaust their strength in athletic struggle. It is the sweat of One whose "soul is exceeding sorrowful unto death." The sweat of One who was "made sin in our behalf," Himself knowing no sin! The Gethsemane blood is the blood without which there is no remission.

Follow Him to Pilate's court. With the cold-heartedness with which men drag oxen forth the slaughter pen, they have dragged Him with sacrilegious hands from the place of His prayer, from the place of His agony, from the place where the shuddering necessity of a world's sin rolled in upon His soul, and they have taken Him to Pilate's judgment hall. In merciless mockery, they put upon Him a purple robe. In unmatched cruelty, they put a crown of thorns upon His brow and press it down, regarding not the nerves it tears and the arteries it punctures. Crimson drops are staining the cheeks that never blushed for shame. This is the shedding of blood without which there is no remission of your sin, of my sins, of all sins!

But if the sight be not too much for you, look again! Hark! Do you hear something hissing like adders in flame? It is the sound of merciless steel lashes of Pilate's scourge biting into His flesh. Do you hear a sound as threads breaking in a tangled loom? It is the scourge tearing His flesh as eagles tear with sharp talons and trenchant beaks the tender flesh of captive lambs. Do you hear a sound as of water dripping from low eaves? It is His blood dripping from His body to the marble floor. And this is the blood without which there is no remission.

But, come and sit down and watch Him there, out yonder on the cross. Look! With earth and hell and heaven as witnesses, in agony unknown He bleeds His life away; in terrible throes He exhausts His soul as His soul is made an "offering for sin!" And while the sun in the heavens refuses to look on that dread scene, the Son of God bleeds from His palms, from His feet, where the nails went, from the brow where the thorns are, from the side where the savage spear went. This is the shedding of blood, the awful shedding of blood, the terrible pouring out of blood, without which, for you, for me, for the whole human race, there is no remission.

—ROBERT G. LEE
in *From Feet to Fathoms*

October 28

*When the chief Shepherd shall appear, ye
shall receive a crown of glory that fadeth not
away* (1 Pet. 5:4).

There is an old song written by George Whitcomb that begins with the words "Glad day, glad day! Is it the crowning day?" There is a crowning day foretold in the Scriptures and there are crowns to be won. In his first letter, Peter writes of the "crown of glory." This is a crown that the Chief Shepherd shall give on that day to all of His faithful pastors—the overseers of the Shepherd's earthly flock. These men have served as loving examples, Peter said, faithfully feeding and caring for His sheep and lambs.

The apostle James writes concerning another crown—the crown of life (Ja. 1:12). This has been called the martyr's crown and will be given to those devoted followers of Christ who lay down their lives for Him and for the gospel's sake. St. John called them "those who were faithful unto death" (Rev. 2:10).

A crown of righteousness is described in 2 Tim. 4:8. In this verse Paul speaks of this crown as waiting for him "in that day" but "not to me only, but to all them also that love his appearing." This apparently is a crown Jesus will award to all who faithfully look for Him, keeping bright the torch of His promise, "I will come again" (John 14:3).

Paul wrote also of the "crown of incorruptibility." This is a crown given for faithfully running the race with Christ's approval of "well done." Paul urges us to run patiently the race set before us, for a crown awaits the victor at the end of the way.

Another crown, and one every believer should win, is recorded in 1 Thess. 2:19. "For what is our hope, or joy, or crown of rejoicing?" The crown of rejoicing! This is the soul-winner's crown. The *New International Version* gives us this beautiful translation: "For what is our hope, or joy, or the crown in which we will glory in the presence of our Lord Jesus Christ when he comes? Is it not you? Indeed, you are our glory and joy" (1 Thess. 2:19-20). Yes, the crowning day is coming some sweet day. Will you receive this crown? Will I? How sad to be in heaven and not have one soul there who shall have cause to say, "I'm here because you told me of Jesus."

Then there is still another crown mentioned in the Word. It is the crown of thorns. "And they . . . plaited a crown of thorns, and put it about his head" (Mark 15:17). This was the crown worn by our Savior at Calvary, where He "suffered for sins, the just for the unjust, that he might bring us to God" (1 Pet. 3:18). Because He took our place, we shall never wear a crown of thorns. As a matter of fact, the Word tells us, we shall actually cast our crowns at Jesus' feet, for they really belong to Him—the Son of God who "loved us and gave himself for us."

And we shall sing:

> Crown Him with many crowns
> The Lamb upon His throne.
> Hark! how the heavenly anthem drowns
> All music but its own!
> Awake, my soul, and sing
> Of Him who died for thee,
> And hail Him as thy matchless King
> Through all eternity.

—Matthew Bridges and
Godfrey Thring

October 29

God so loved the world, that he gave his only begotten Son, that whosoever believeth in him should not perish, but have everlasting life (John 3:16).

There are five great pairs of words in this wonderful passage. The first of these are the two persons of the Godhead, "God the Father" and "God the Son." The second pair of words expresses the Father's attitude toward the whole wide world, namely "He loved" and "He gave." The third pair refers to the objects of His divine love, "the world" and "whosoever"—meaning me and meaning you. The fourth shows us the attitudes of men when God's love and God's gift is acknowledged. They "believe" and they "have." Finally, the last pair of words points to the end of human destiny—if Christ is rejected, we "perish"; but if Christ is received, we have "life everlasting."

In John 3:16 God reveals that He is there. "For God." He tells us that He is interested in men—He "so loved the world." He shows that His thoughts toward us are thoughts of kindness— "He loved." He reveals also that he is omniscient for "He loved the whole world." He tells us, moreover, that His love went to extremes, for "He gave His only Son." And finally he proclaims for all who read to see that He desires our fellowship forever. He gives to us who believe "eternal life."

> *Into a tent where a gypsy boy lay,*
> *Dying alone at the close of the day,*
> *News of salvation we carried, said he:*
> *"Nobody ever has told it to me!"*
>
> *"Did He so love me, a poor little boy?*
> *Send unto me the good tidings of joy?*
> *Need I not perish? My hand will He hold?*
> *Nobody ever the story has told."*
>
> *Bending we caught the last words of his breath,*
> *Just as he entered the valley of death,*
> *"God sent His Son! 'Whosoever,' said He;*
> *Then I am sure that He sent Him for me!"*
>
> *Smiling, he said, as his last sigh was spent,*
> *"I am so glad that for me He was sent!"*
> *Whispered, while low sank the sun in the west,*
> *"Lord, I believe; tell it now to the rest!"*
>
> —Mrs. M. B. Slade

October 30

I heard the voice of the Lord, saying,
Whom shall I send, and who will go for us?
Then said I, Here am I; send me (Isa. 6:8).

Send me to the hearts without a home, to the lives without a love, to the crowds without a compass.

Send me to the children whom none have blessed, to the famished whom none have fed, to the sick whom none have visited, to the demoniac whom none have claimed, to the fallen whom none have touched, and to the bereaved whom none have comforted.

—GEORGE MATHESON

"Then said Jesus to them again, Peace be unto you: as my Father hath sent me, even so send I you" (John 20:21).

So send I you—to labor unrewarded,
  To serve unpaid, unloved, unsought, unknown,
To bear rebuke, to suffer scorn and scoffing
  So send I you—to toil for Me alone.

So send I you—to bind the bruised and broken,
  O'er wand'ring souls to work, to weep, to wake,
To bear the burdens of a world a-weary
  So send I you—to suffer for My sake.

So send I you—to loneliness and longing,
  With heart a-hung'ring for the loved and known,
Forsaking home and kindred, friend and dear one;
  So send I you—to know My love alone.

So send I you—to leave your life's ambition;
  To die to dear desire, self-will resign,
To labor long and love where men revile you;
  So send I you—to lose your life in Mine.

So send I you—to hearts made hard by hatred,
  To eyes made blind because they will not see,
To spend, though it be blood—to spend and spare not—
  So send I you—to taste of Calvary.

—MARGARET CLARKSON

October 31

*There came thither certain Jews from
Antioch and Iconium, who persuaded the
people, and, having stoned Paul, drew him
out of the city, supposing he had been dead.
Howbeit, as the disciples stood round about
him, he rose up, and came into the city; and
the next day he departed with Barnabas to
Derbe. And when they had preached the gospel to that city, and had taught many, they
returned again to Lystra, and to Iconium and
Antioch, confirming the souls of the disciples,
and exhorting them to continue in the faith,
and that we must through much tribulation
enter into the kingdom of God* (Acts 14:19-
22).

"They returned again to Lystra." The Spirit directed Paul
back to the place of stoning. Did his heart skip a few beats when
this message came? It would have been natural, for it was there
the Jews had martyred him. (Even Paul was not certain concerning his death—2 Cor. 12:2.) But the stoning left no doubt concerning the hate at Lystra—the envy—the beating—the bruises! At
Lystra, however, was a young church with new converts that
needed instruction and growth in the Word and love. So back to
the place of stoning he went.

If you are ever called to go back to your Lystra; back where
sorrows abounded, where false witness was given, where soul
and spirit were bruised, remember this. If the Holy Spirit sends
you back "to the place of stoning," He will give you grace and
strength and comfort for the journey; that there, once again,
Christ may be honored and proclaimed.

The cruel stones unerring fell upon him—
Until they deemed his bleeding form was dead;
His worth and work they knew not, and they cared not;
Enough, they madly hated what he said.

God touched him! And he rose, with new life given;
Nor in his bosom burned resentful pain;
And, bye and bye, when need and call both guided,
He to the stoning-place returned again.

Perhaps thou, too, hast tasted cruel stoning—
And would be glad if you came not again
To scenes where surely there awaits thee
The cruel, cutting stones which make life vain.

Yet, if "back to the stones" the Spirit leadeth,
Then thou shalt know there is no better way;
And there, just there, shall matchless grace await thee,
And Christ himself shall be thy strength and stay.

—J. DANSON SMITH

November 1

The eternal God is thy refuge, and under-
neath are the everlasting arms (Deut. 33:27).

Last evening after church, I carried my sleeping grandson to our car for the journey to his home. He is a growing boy, age 6, and my arms tired from his weight. How wonderful to know that the arms of our Lord do not tire but are always strong beneath us. We need fear no failure. His promise is sure, "Even to your old age I am he; and even to [gray] hairs will I care for you: I have made, and I will bear; even I will carry, and deliver you" (Isa. 46:4).

There is safety and security in His arms. Spurgeon said, "He is our shelter and retreat; our abiding refuge. In His arms we find repose from the fatigue and toils of the day."

His everlasting arms are our defense from danger. He holds us securely and He will not let us "dash our feet upon the rocks." His mighty arms are our surety of deliverance as we trust in Him.

Although the everlasting arms are outstretched to bear us up, they were first outstretched upon a cross to bring us in, for the everlasting arms bear the stigmata of nail prints.

The hands of Christ seem very frail,
For they were broken by a nail,
But only they reach Heaven at last
Whom these frail, broken hands hold fast.

—JOHN RICHARD MORELAND

"Faith is just clinging to the everlasting arms, and nothing more" (Theodore L. Cuyler).

November 2

*I say also unto thee, That thou art Peter,
and upon this rock I will build my church; and
the gates of hell shall not prevail against it*
(Matt. 16:18).

The Church is here to stay! It will never perish. The Church
of Jesus Christ can never be destroyed.

Which church, you ask? There are many, many denominations. But I speak of none of these. Denominations are all temporary—many are dying now. But denominations are not the true Church—the eternal Church—the imperishable Church.

The Church that will never perish is that marching army of the redeemed who belong to Christ. They are scattered throughout the whole wide world—throughout the various denominations. These are the blood-bought, born-again saints of God who compose the heavenly membership of the Church eternal. The membership of this Church is invisible—yet discernible. Denominations will perish but the Church will never perish.

Why is this true? It is because of the nature of the Church and its Founder. The nature of the Church is organic, and not organizational. It is spiritual and not material, eternal and not temporal, divine and not purely human. The Founder is Jesus Christ—Truth eternal—the risen Son of God. He builds His Church daily, adding to it those who are being saved. Denominations will die; time will end; but the Church marches onward into the eternities. Praise God, I am a member.

—FLETCHER SPRUCE

The Church's one Foundation is Jesus Christ, her Lord.
She is His new creation by water and the Word:
From heaven He came and sought her to be His holy bride;
With His own blood He bought her, and for her life He died.

Elect from every nation, yet one o'er all the earth;
Her charter of salvation, One Lord, one faith, one birth;
One holy name she blesses; partakes one holy food;
And to one hope she presses, with every grace endued.

Yet she on earth hath union with God the Three in One,
And mystic, sweet communion with those whose rest is won.
Oh, happy ones and holy! Lord, give us grace that we,
Like them, the meek and lowly, on high may dwell with Thee.

—SAMUEL J. STONE

"He is before all things, and by him all things consist: and he is the head of the body, the church, who is the beginning, the firstborn from the dead; that in all things he might have the pre-eminence. For it pleased the Father that in him should all fullness dwell" (Col. 1:17-18).

November 3

Jesus said unto him, No man, having put his hand to the plough, and looking back, is fit for the kingdom of God (Luke 9:62).

Dr. M. R. DeHaan once declared, "Dedication is for life! There is no turning back—ever!" Paul admonished us to forget those things that are behind and to press on. Beware of the backward look!

Over a godly farmer's gravestone, in a small, out-of-the-way cemetery, appears this epitaph: "He plowed a straight furrow!" How we need to do this! The years are going by, but keep your eyes upon Jesus. Be faithful. Follow after Him without wavering. "There must be no turning back."

—HENRY G. BOSCH
From *Our Daily Bread*, © 1973, Radio Bible Class.
Used by special permission.

Growing old but not retiring,
For the battle still is on;
Going on without relenting
Till the final victory's won.
Ever on, nor think of resting,
For the battle rages still,
And my Saviour walks beside me
As I seek to do His will.

Let me labor in Thy harvest
More than ever in the past,
Reaping in what Thou has planted,
Till I dwell with Thee at last;
That before Thy throne eternal
I may have some fruit to bring,
Not my work—the fruit of Calvary,
All Thine own, my Lord and King.

—AUTHOR UNKNOWN

November 4

Wherefore he is able also to save them to the uttermost that come unto God by him, seeing he ever liveth to make intercession for them (Heb. 7:25).

We are sanctified through the offering of Jesus Christ once for all (Heb. 10:10).

David Bulkley, for many years the director of the City Union Mission, loved to quote this first verse but with a slight variation. He would stand in the pulpit and say to the hopeless men before him, "Jesus is able to save to the guttermost—and He wants to."

The writer to the Hebrews declares that the Lord Jesus Christ is able to save "completely," because He ever lives to make intercession to the Father for His own. By Christ's submissive will to the Father's plan, which led Him to the Cross, "we have been made holy through the sacrifice of the body of Jesus Christ, once for all" (NIV).

The gospel brings us, not just something to keep, but Someone to keep us. It is not a work to do, but a Word to be believed concerning a work done. Throughout the ritual of the law in Exodus we search in vain for the blessed words "draw nigh." The words we find are "draw not nigh." A holy God could not look upon sin, and under the law there was no drawing near to God with a full assurance of heart, for the guilty sins were never fully put away but only covered until the "more perfect sacrifice" could be offered.

"This we will do," cried the people. And until darkness fell over the slain Lamb and the veil in the temple was rent in twain, the law demanded a never ending "doing." The work was never finished; the high priest never rested from his labor; and the sacrifices were continually being offered, until the day when, in the fullness of time, the Savior offered himself as the sufficient Atonement for the sins of the world. How glorious to read that once in the end of the age He appeared to finish the work (Heb. 9: 26). The death and resurrection of the Lord Jesus was sufficient "once for all," and by Him we have been made holy.

Free from the law, O happy condition,
Jesus hath bled, and there is remission;
Cursed by the law and bruised by the Fall,
Grace hath redeemed us once for all.

349

Now are we free—there's no condemnation,
Jesus provides a perfect salvation;
"Come unto me," Oh, hear His sweet call,
Come, and He saves us once for all.

"Children of God," Oh, glorious calling,
Surely His grace will keep us from falling;
Passing from death to life at His call,
Blessed salvation once for all.

—P. P. Bliss

November 5

Now, Lord, behold their threatenings; and
grant unto thy servants, that with all boldness
they may speak thy word. . . . And when they
had prayed, the place was shaken where they
were assembled together; and they were all
filled with the Holy Ghost, and they spake the
word of God with boldness (Acts 4:29, 31).

Boldness was the endowment needed by the Christians for
the crisis immediately before them. They prayed for boldness.
They were filled with the Spirit, and they received boldness!

Please remember this event was not Pentecost. It was months
afterwards. Yet the description sounds like Pentecost. Now it cannot be described as a second Pentecost; one Pentecost was enough
to mark the beginning of the Spirit's dispensation.

But it does set forth the need for Christians to receive a
fresh infilling of the Holy Spirit for each new task. This was the
identical group upon which the Spirit first fell. And now He empowers again!

—Richard Ellsworth Day

Child of the Kingdom, be filled with the Spirit!
Nothing but fullness thy longing can meet;
'Tis the enduement for life and for service.
Thine is the promise, so certain, so sweet.
"I will pour water on him that is thirsty;
I will pour floods upon the dry ground.
Open your heart for the gift I am bringing.
While ye are seeking me, I will be found."

—Lucy J. Rider

November 6

Thou wilt keep him in perfect peace, whose mind is stayed on thee: because he trusteth in thee (Isa. 26:3).

Salvation brings us a wonderful Keeper! This verse proclaims it. Though storms and sorrows come our way, eternal peace belongs to each child of God, for He who never slumbers nor sleeps will keep us safe and secure. "In the world ye shall have tribulation: but be of good cheer; I have overcome the world" (John 16:33).

The peace of salvation becomes ours because of our Savior's accomplished and finished work upon the Cross. The peace of security becomes ours when our minds are stayed on Him. Peace comes only through trust! When you are afraid, trust and rest in the Lord; for He is a sure hiding place for the oppressed and a safe refuge in time of distress. "They that know thy name will put their trust in thee; for thou, Lord, hast not forsaken them that seek thee" (Ps. 9:10). Be still and trust!

Be still, my soul; the Lord is on thy side;
   Bear patiently the cross of grief or pain;
Leave to thy God to order and provide.
   In every change He faithful will remain.
Be still, my soul; thy best, thy heavenly Friend
Through thorny ways leads to a joyful end.

Be still my soul; thy God doth undertake
   To guide the future as He has the past.
Thy hope, thy confidence let nothing shake;
   All now mysterious shall be bright at last.
Be still, my soul; the waves and winds still know
His voice who ruled them while He dwelt below.

Be still my soul; the hour is hastening on
   When we shall be forever with the Lord,
When disappointment, grief, and fear are gone,
   Sorrow forgot, love's purest joys restored.
Be still, my soul; when change and tears are past,
All safe and blessed we shall meet at last.

—Katharina von Schlegel
Trans. Jane L. Borthwick

November 7

Our old man is crucified with him, that the body of sin might be destroyed, that hence-forth we should not serve sin (Rom. 6:6).

Christian, what hast thou to do with sin? Hath it not cost thee enough already? Burnt child, wilt thou play with fire? What! When thou hast already been between the jaws of the lion, wilt thou step a second time into his den? Hast thou not had enough of the old serpent? Did he not poison all thy veins once, and wilt thou play upon the hole of the asp, and put thy hand upon the cockatrice's den a second time? Oh, be not so mad! So foolish! Did sin ever yield thee real pleasure? Didst thou find solid satis-faction in it? If so, go back to thine old drudgery, and wear the chain again, if it delights thee. But inasmuch as sin did never give thee what it promised to bestow, but deluded thee with lies, be not a second time snared by the old fowler—be free, and let the remembrance of thy ancient bondage forbid thee to enter the net again!

Transgression destroys peace of mind, obscures fellowship with Jesus, hinders prayer, brings darkness over the soul. There-fore be not the serf and bondman of sin. Turn thee to Jesus anew; He has not forgotten His love to thee; His grace is still the same. With weeping and repentance, come thou to His footstool, and thou shalt be once more received into His heart; thou shalt be set upon a rock again, and thy goings shall be established.

—Charles Haddon Spurgeon

From prayer that asks that I may be
Sheltered from winds that beat on Thee,
From fearing when I should aspire,
From faltering when I should climb higher,
From silken self, O Captain, free
Thy soldier who would follow Thee.

Give me the love that leads the way,
The faith that nothing can dismay,
The hope no disappointments tire,
The passion that will burn like fire;
Let me not sink to be a clod—
Make me Thy fuel, Flame of God.

—Amy Carmichael

November 8

*As the servants of Christ, doing the will of
God from the heart* (Eph. 6:6).

To be a true servant of Christ, one must seek and submit to
His perfect will. What does He want me to do? What does He
want me to be? These are vitally important questions for victorious Christian living.

The Holy Spirit always asks for complete commitment.
Blessed indeed is the one who lays all things at His feet, although
He may return them fourfold at a later date. By such commitment,
we truly become a real servant of Christ "from the heart." While
there is great joy in the soul when salvation is found, greater
joy awaits in full surrender. When the will is completely surrendered, then, and only then, can we prove the real depths of His
love!

> *I owned a little boat a while ago,*
> *And sailed the morning sea without a fear,*
> *And whither any breeze might fairly blow*
> *I steered my little craft afar or near.*
> > *Mine was the boat,*
> > *And mine the air,*
> > *And mine the sea,*
> > *Nor mine a care.*
>
> *My boat became my place of toil,*
> *I sailed at evening to the fishing ground.*
> *At morn my boat was freighted with the spoil,*
> *Which my all-conquering work had found.*
> > *Mine was the boat*
> > *And mine the net,*
> > *And mine the skill*
> > *And power to get.*
>
> *One day there came along that silent shore,*
> *While I my net was casting in the sea,*
> *A Man who spoke as never man before.*
> *I followed Him; new life began in me.*
> > *Mine was the boat,*
> > *But His the voice,*
> > *And His the call,*
> > *Yet mine the choice.*

Ah! 'twas a fearful night out on the lake,
And all my skill availed not, at the helm,
Till Him asleep I waked, crying, "Take,
Thou the helm—lest water overwhelm!"
And His the boat,
And His the sea,
And His the peace
O'er all and me.

Once from the boat He taught the curious throng
Then bade me cast my net into the sea;
I murmured but obeyed, nor was it long
Before the catch amazed and humbled me.
His was the boat,
And His the skill,
And His the catch,
And His my will.

—GEORGE MACDONALD

November 9

Loosing from Troas, we came with a straight course to Samothracia, and the next day to Neapolis; and from thence to Philippi (Acts 16:11-12).

Philippi, Thessalonica, Berea—cities with strange sounding names on the Macedonian road. But Paul came to them, answering the call of the man of Macedonia, and "determined not to know anything among you, save Jesus Christ, and him crucified" (1 Cor. 2:2).

At Philippi, Lydia and her household opened their hearts to Paul and to the Lord Jesus. They were the first converts of the foreign missionary enterprise as the gospel turned westward. Prison doors were also to open. In the jail at Philippi, stocks and bonds awaited Paul and Silas, but also an opportunity to witness to another group of people.

Although bleeding from many stripes, Paul and Silas prayed and sang. No sounds of whimpering fell from their lips. God answered their prayers with an earthquake that shook the city of Philippi and the jail keeper, and his family found salvation as a result.

The next stop was Thessalonica. When Paul and Silas entered the city, the people cried out, "These that have turned the world upside down are come here also" (Acts 17:6). And at Berea, Paul's Christ-centered messages caused them to search diligently the Scriptures to see if what he presented was true. Paul thus built their faith firmly on the Word of God!

Paul, saint and preacher of the open road! His missionary zeal was to lack no horizons and his pulpit was never to be hamstrung by ecclesiastical or political expediency. With bounding enthusiasm he carried the gospel message. Later he would say to King Agrippa, "I was not disobedient unto the heavenly vision."

Thanks be to God that Paul was so faithful, for far beyond the Macedonian highway lay the barbarians of the Western world —and you, and me.

November 10

Be . . . fervent in spirit; serving the Lord
(Rom. 12:10-11).

A clever preacher once took advantage of a horrible pun to make an important point. "Some folks," he said, "are lost in the woulds." People say, "I *would* stay for church but it *would* make the dinner late." Or, "I *would* tithe, but I can't afford it." Or "I *would* teach the class but I don't have time to prepare." The list could go on indefinitely. They are lost in the "woulds." People really lost in the woods are in grave danger. People lost in the "woulds" do not seem to be concerned.

The "woulds" become a hiding place—a refuge from the pressure of recognized duty. Thomas Carlyle said, "Life is not thought, however noble. It is action." Our challenge is to get out of the "woulds" and into reality. Fine purposes must become better actions so that men can see our good works and glorify our Father who is in heaven.

—Herald of Holiness

> *Father, I scarcely dare to pray,*
> *So clear I see, now it is done,*
> *That I have wasted half my day,*
> *And left my work but just begun.*
>
> *So clear I see that things I thought*
> *Were right or harmless were a sin;*
> *So clear I see that I have sought,*
> *Unconscious, selfish aims to win.*

So clear I see that I have hurt
  The souls I might have helped to save;
  That I have slothful been, inert,
  Deaf to the calls Thy leaders gave.

In outskirts of Thy kingdom vast,
  Father, the humblest spot give me;
  Give me the lowliest task thou hast;
  Let me repentant work for Thee!

—HELEN HUNT JACKSON

November 11

**Believe on the Lord Jesus Christ, and thou
shalt be saved, and thy house** (Acts 16:31).

"The preaching of the gospel requires faith; not faith in believing, nor faith in wishful thinking, but faith in Jesus Christ as Lord and Savior. The saving power of Jesus Christ is the one inexhaustible resource God has given to men, but it requires the instrumentality of faith to make it real" (Billy Graham).

On my last sea voyage, I noticed in the stateroom a life jacket hanging on the wall. Beneath it was a sign stating in clear language the purpose of the jacket and directions for its use. But such knowledge is merely educational knowledge. Such information concerning the life preserver is important, but it would never have saved me if disaster had struck the vessel. No, only faith in the life preserver itself could accomplish this. I must believe on the life preserver. This means committing my body to it—putting it on—receiving and trusting myself to it. Such a faith would keep me afloat.

So it is with God's great plan of salvation. Confirmation or creeds cannot save. This is merely assent in the knowledge of the Preserver. Christ must be a personal Savior. Only as I receive Him by faith and trust my soul to Him for salvation, does such knowledge become heartfelt salvation. Believing on the Lord Jesus Christ makes the difference.

November 12

Be careful [anxious] for nothing; but in every thing by prayer and supplication with thanksgiving let your requests be made known unto God (Phil. 4:6).

No anxiety ought to be found in a believer. Great and varied may be our trials, our afflictions, and our difficulties, yet we are counselled not to be anxious. We have a Father in heaven who is almighty and who loves His children. His very joy is to succor and help them at all times and under every circumstance.

We should attend to His Word. "In every thing" includes all. Even the smallest matter of life should be laid before Him. The very little things, the trifling things—everything—should be brought to Him as we live in holy communion with our Father and our precious Lord Jesus.

"By prayer and supplication." We must wait before God with earnestness and perseverance. At all times, "with thanksgiving," we should rejoice before Him. He has saved us from hell, He has given us His Son and the Holy Spirit, and He will not withhold any good thing from us. We have abundant reason for thanksgiving.

"And the peace of God, which passeth all understanding, shall keep your hearts and minds through Christ Jesus." This is so great a blessing, so real a blessing, so precious a blessing, that it must be known experimentally to be entered into, for it passeth understanding. Oh, let us lay these things to heart, and the result will be, if we walk in this spirit, we shall far more abundantly glorify God, than as yet we have done.

—GEORGE MUELLER

November 13

Rejoice in the Lord alway: and again I say, Rejoice (Phil. 4:4).

"Rejoice always" was Paul's victorious song of the soul. Whether in prison or in bonds, in desert wastelands or on the stormy seas, "rejoice" was his battle cry. Paul had joy. It was a joy not in circumstances but a joy in Christ. Through pain and pleasure, through illness and infirmities, His joy remained with and in Paul.

> *Jesus, mine all in all Thou art;*
> *My rest in toil, my ease in pain;*
> *The medicine of my broken heart;*
> *In war my peace, in loss my gain;*
> *My smile beneath the tyrant's frown;*
> *In my shame my glory and my crown.*

> —CHARLES WESLEY

Joy, abundant joy! Eleven times Paul says to these Philippians, "Rejoice!" Five times he flings out his mirthful monosyllable, "Joy." Joy is the courageous cheerfulness of the Christian soul. If there is abandonment to Christ, and not a reluctant giving of ourselves to Him in pinched little fragments, then two things can be said of the gladness that will be ours. It is incessant in its song. "Rejoice always!" It is independent in its source. "Rejoice in the Lord."

The joy that Paul experienced—and extolled—must be seen as the joy in spite of! In spite of a flogging: It was at Philippi that he and Silas, beaten to within an inch of their lives, "sang praises." In spite of fetters—in spite of friendlessness. But his joy was also because of! Not because of prosperity, or pleasure, but because its deep and dependable spring is "in the Lord."

> —PAUL S. REES
> in *The Adequate Man*

November 14

> **These things have I written unto you that**
> **believe on the name of the Son of God; that**
> **you may know that ye have eternal life, and**
> **that ye may believe on the name of the Son of**
> **God** (1 John 5:13).

John had a faith that was sure and certain. The word "know" occurs 26 times in the letter known as First John: "We do know that we know him. . . . Ye know the truth . . . We know that when he shall appear we shall be like him . . . We know that he was manifest to take away our sins . . . We know that we have passed from death unto life . . . We know that he abideth in us .'. . We know that we dwell in him . . . That you may know that you have eternal life."

There is certainty in these words. The knowledge is deep and abiding. These are not fanciful feelings. Feelings may deceive us. Feelings change with our surroundings and our health. We may not always "feel" saved. But if we believe on the Lord Jesus Christ as our own personal Savior, we are saved! We know Whom we have believed. We know that we have eternal life.

Vance Havner, writing in his book *Rest Awhile*, said this: "Don't worry over whether you have repented enough or believed enough or wept enough or prayed enough. Nothing you could ever do would be enough. Saving faith is the faith that believes—that commits. If you have committed to Christ as best you know how, don't loose any sleep for fear heaven will go bankrupt and God go insolvent. Paul didn't say, 'I know how I feel,' but 'I know whom I have believed.'"

This makes all the difference. Let us rest our souls, not on "feeling saved," but on the fact that God says we are saved. This is faith!

> *Three men were walking on a wall;*
> *Feeling, Faith, and Fact.*
> *Feeling got an awful fall*
> *And Faith was taken back.*
> *Faith was so close to Feeling,*
> *He fell too;*
> *But Fact remained and pulled Faith up*
> *And that brought Feeling too!*
>
> —Author Unknown

"What does it say? 'The word is near you; it is in your mouth and in your heart'; that is, the word of faith we are proclaiming: That if you confess with your mouth, 'Jesus is Lord,' and believe in your heart that God raised him from the dead, you will be saved. For it is with your heart that you believe and are justified, and it is with your mouth that you confess and are saved" (Rom. 10:8-10, NIV).

November 15

*Sanctify the Lord God in your hearts; and
be ready always to give an answer to every man
that asketh you a reason of the hope that is in
you, with meekness and fear* (1 Pet. 3:15).

In this portion of his letter, Peter writes concerning God's rules for successful soul winning. First, he urges that we "acknowledge Christ as the holy Lord." This is the rendition of today's text in the New International Version, and it teaches that if we are to be used in winning others, Christ must be crowned as the supreme Lord of our lives. Peter adds, "Be prepared to give an answer." This implies a question being asked. To answer correctly requires study of the Word of God. Young Timothy, early in his career, was thus admonished by St. Paul: "Study to shew thyself approved unto God, a workman that needeth not to be ashamed, rightly dividing the word of truth" (2 Tim. 2:15). The Lord's servant must know the Scriptures in both interpretation and application. This requires a deep and daily study, enhanced with prayer and quietness, revealed and taught by the Holy Spirit.

Not only are we to be "ready to give an answer," but the sentence concludes with "to every man who asks you concerning the hope you have." Fishers of men and women must be Spirit-led people. He must lead and guide to those hearts that are seeking. It is the seeking heart that can be won, and the Holy Spirit speaks only through human lips. If we fail to allow Him to guide and lead, many failures will occur, even though we be eager and zealous.

Finally, Peter wrote these closing words, "Do this with gentleness and respect, keeping a clear conscience." The Lord's servant has a price to pay—the price is a pure and holy life. He must be blameless and without rebuke, "keeping a clear conscience, so that those who speak maliciously against your good behavior in Christ may be ashamed of their slander" (1 Pet. 3:6, NIV).

November 16

*I am the true vine, and my Father is the
husbandman* (John 15:1).

These beautiful words of our Savior were given to the disciples on the night before the Cross. They are found in His message on the "fruitful life."

"My Father is the husbandman . . . he purgeth it." What comfort this should bring. Our hearts are prone to doubt and fear. If only He would not cut so close, we tearfully say. But no, He sees deadness which our eyes have never glimpsed, and because He cares and seeks more fruit for His glory, He must cut deeper. Our part must be to trust. Our Father-Husbandman is doing the pruning, and He who brings the pain will also bring the healing.

"My Father is the husbandman." What care is ours! He will place you, He will plant you, and He will protect you. No harm can come to us, for He has promised that no storm shall break our branches, no scorching sun wither our leaves, and no drought withhold our fruit. "And he shall be like a tree planted by the rivers of water, that bringeth forth its fruit in its season; his leaf also shall not wither; and whatsoever he doeth shall prosper" (Ps. 1:3).

"Herein is My Father glorified, that ye bear much fruit" (John 15:8). What a commission is ours, for He has chosen us and ordained us that we should go and bring forth fruit to His glory! The Lord grant that we shall not disappoint Him.

> Our Master is seeking a harvest,
>   In lives He's redeemed by His blood;
> He seeks for the fruit of the Spirit,
>   And works that will glorify God.
>
> He looks for His likeness reflected
>   In lives that are yielded and true.
> He's looking for zeal in the winning
>   Of souls He's entrusted to you.
>
> He's yearning for someone to carry
>   The life-giving word far and near:
> He's waiting for hearts that are willing,
>   For ears that are open to hear.
>
> Yet nothing but leaves do we offer?
>   Oh, how His loving heart grieves,
> When instead of the fruit He is seeking,
>   We offer Him nothing but leaves!

—Author Unknown

361

November 17

The tongue is a little member, and boast-
eth great things. Behold, how great a matter a
little fire kindleth! (Jas. 3:5).

In one of Billy Graham's sermons entitled "The Sins of the Tongue" he writes, "All too often Christians give excuses for acts of indignation, irritation, impatience, vexation, bitterness, resentment, wrath, pouting, and grudge carrying" We need to face the truth of this statement and James's declaration, too. These are the "sins of the tongue." They must be confessed and forsaken.

The sins of the tongue are many—from designed deception to profanity, gossip, and unkind repetition of someone's past guilt. And how prevalent is criticism and judging of others. Sadly, even some Christians seem to delight in attacking one of Christ's servants, not heeding the dire warning, "Touch not my anointed and do my prophets no harm." He has warned us! Watch your tongue! It can be dangerous! Do not judge, but pray for each other in love!

> *I'm not your judge, Nay!*
> *God forbids me judge the record of your deeds;*
> *But tells me wait, with ready hand,*
> *To love and help and understand.*
>
> *I'm not your judge, Nay!*
> *I'm unfit, God plainly tells in Holy Writ;*
> *He bids me raise and lift you up,*
> *Then pass to you the loving cup.*
>
> *I'm not your judge, Nay!*
> *One upon His throne will judge, in love, His own;*
> *So, over all your faults I cast*
> *Love's sacred mantle to the last.*
>
> —SARAH SPENCER-RUFF

"No man can tame the tongue" (Jas. 3:8). The Psalmist asked, "What shall be done with thee, thou false tongue?" (Ps. 120:3). Is there therefore any hope? Yes, there is hope! A thousand times yes! The Holy Spirit is our hope and in the heart of the believer He can surely tame the tongue. Paul urged us to present our bodies wholly yielded to Him. The Spirit can cure us of criticism, of harsh words, and of unkind language. As we yield to

Him, "the fountain will send forth pure and sweet water." Remembering that the tongue is part of the body, yield it completely to His control and He will "set a watch upon your tongue." He will bring forth the sweet fruits of gentleness, kindness, long-suffering, and love. Give Him your tongue.

November 18

Commit thy way unto the Lord; trust also
in him; and he shall bring it to pass (Ps. 37:5).

If Christ's keeping depends upon our trusting, and our continuing to trust depends upon ourselves, we are in no better position than before, and shall only be landed in a fresh series of disappointments. We can no more trust and keep on trusting than we can do anything else of ourselves. Even in this it must be Jesus only; we are not to look to Him only to be the Author and the Finisher of our faith, but we are to look to Him for all the intermediate fulfillment of the work of faith. We must ask Him to go on fulfilling it in us, committing even this to His power. Without Him we can do nothing. He must work all our works in us! With unbroken and unwavering trust, cease your effort and drop the burden, and now intrust your trust to Him.

"For Thee." This is the beginning and the end of the whole matter of consecration. This makes the difference between forced or formal and therefore unreasonable service, and the reasonable service, which is the beginning of the perfect service where they see His face. This makes the difference between slave work and free work. For Thee, my Redeemer; for Thee, who has spoken to my heart; for Thee, who hast done so much for me. For Thee, my Savior Jesus, my Lord and my God!

—FRANCES RIDLEY HAVERGAL

November 19

Rejoice in the Lord alway; and again I say,
Rejoice. Let your moderation be known unto
all men. The Lord is at hand. Be careful
[anxious] for nothing; but in every thing by
prayer and supplication with thanksgiving let
your requests be made known unto God (Phil.
4:4-6).

A second grader came home from his school's "track and field day" proudly displaying a beautiful blue ribbon. When asked what race he won, he replied, "I didn't win a race. I got the ribbon for stopping at the right place." Of all the boys in the race he was the only one who followed directions and ran by the rules. A blue ribbon for knowing where to stop!

Knowing where to stop in the Christian life is very, very important!

Stop before talk becomes gossip. Talk is harmless, but it so often leads to gossip before one is hardly aware of it. Several men were talking together about a mutual acquaintance when one asked a pointed question about him. His friend replied, "He needs our prayers." His reply was calculated to end a discussion which could have been damaging and to enlist support in place of judgment. He knew where to stop!

Stop before concern becomes worry. Sometimes we assume we "are carrying a burden" when in fact we are worrying. Concern and worry may feel much the same, but they are quite different. Paul admonished, "Be anxious in nothing."

Stop before disappointment becomes bitterness. Life has its disappointments. We have no promise to be carried to glory on beds of ease. We cannot choose our path but, by God's grace, we can choose our attitudes towards what happens to us. Blue ribbons should be given to those who know where to stop. Have you won any lately?

—JAMES D. HAMILTON

"The steps of a good man are ordered by the Lord, and his stops also" (George Mueller).

Ere you left your room this morning,
    Did you think to pray?
In the name of Christ, our Saviour,
Did you sue for loving favor,
    As a shield today?

When your heart was filled with anger,
  Did you think to pray?
Did you plead for grace, my brother,
That you might forgive another
  Who had crossed your way?

When sore trials came upon you,
  Did you think to pray?
When your soul was full of sorrow,
Balm of Gilead did you borrow
  At the gates of day?

                              —MARY A. KIDDER

November 20

Laying aside all malice, and all guile, and hypocrisies, and envies, and all evil speakings, as newborn babes, desire the sincere milk of the word, that ye may grow thereby (1 Pet. 2: 1-2).

And beside this, giving all diligence, add to your faith virtue; and to virtue knowledge; and to knowledge temperance; and to temperance patience; and to patience godliness; and to godliness brotherly kindness; and to brotherly kindness charity [love] (2 Pet. 1:5-7).

God's arithmetic is the old, old math. Addition must be learned before subtraction. Before we "take away" we must first master the science of "adding to." Many of the griefs and disappointments in the Christian life come because we try subtraction before we really have "put on"—have added—the fullness of Christ in our lives.

It is very discouraging business to try to subtract wrong things, for when we begin subtracting, nothing much is left. Taking away from nothing will leave nothing. But if the Holy Spirit is made Lord of the life, He adds and adds and adds. As you yield to Him in surrender, the beauty of Jesus will be formed in you and He will give the fruits of joy, peace, goodness, gentleness, temperance, meekness, and love.

In "Alice in Wonderland," there is an interesting conversation about school. The Mock Turtle says, "I only took the regular course."

"What was that?" Alice asked.

"Reeling and Writhing, of course, to begin with and then the different branches of arithmetic—Ambition, Distraction, Uglification, and Derision."

These are the universal problems of mankind. If we try to subtract them we will surely fail. The secret for their removal is to add! Add Christ in His beauty to your life and all else will disappear. Give diligence to this, Peter said, and although he places love last, if we truly add love, all other fruits will be there in abundance, for "the greatest of these is love."

November 21

I would not have you to be ignorant, brethren, concerning them which are asleep (1 Thess. 4:13).

Paul writes in this scripture to the Thessalonians a wonderful *reassurance*. Literally he said, "I don't want you to be ignorant concerning your loved ones who have died. They are safe in Jesus' keeping. But here is a *revelation* for you. Those who believed in Jesus and are asleep, God will bring with Him when He comes again."

O blessed doctrine of His second coming. The *return* of Christ is the glorious hope of the Church. Not only does this Thessalonian scripture speak of reassurance, of revelation, and of His returning, it also tells us of the *Rapture!* We shall be caught up with our loved ones who have died in the Lord and together we shall meet Him in the air. The consummation of the age of grace is the rapture of His Church.

And so beyond the reassurance, beyond the revelation, beyond the return and the Rapture, lies the *reunion*. What a wonderful word of promise! "Then we who are alive and remain shall be caught up together with them in the clouds, to meet the Lord in the air; and so shall we ever be with the Lord." Redemption shall then be complete—not only from sin's penalty and its power, but saved from its very presence. "And so shall we ever be with the Lord."

But there is one more R in this portion of His Word. It is *readiness*. We are to be ready! Listen as Paul speaks further; "Ye, brethren, are not in darkness, that that day should overtake you as a thief. Ye are children of light, and children of the day. . . . Therefore let us not sleep . . . but let us watch and be sober . . . for

366

God hath not appointed us to wrath, but to obtain salvation by our Lord Jesus Christ" (1 Thess. 5:4-9).

Paul called the Christians at Thessalonica to be ready and to watch, but he also called them to be working. If we are to be ready for His return, we are to be at work for Him. Do not sit on a housetop watching the sky. The Master would have you "warn them that are unruly . . . support the weak, be patient toward all men" (1 Thess. 5:14). As the end approaches, rejoice and pray, "in every thing give thanks . . . quench not the Spirit. . . . prove all things; hold fast that which is good. Abstain from all appearance of evil" (1 Thess. 5:18-22).

Wait! Watch! Work! This is being ready.

November 22

Go your way, tell his disciples and Peter (Mark 16:7).

"And Peter." There is something about this child-hearted, impulsive, wayward man that wins our hearts. Most of us know ourselves better when we know Peter better. J. Wilbur Chapman wrote, "We study him in his failures and we grow discouraged, for if Peter who was so near Jesus in the home of Jairus, on the transfiguration mountain, and in Gethsemane, if he could deny Him, then it is not strange that we should fail in the midst of this sinful generation. How careful we ought to walk! And yet in his successes we rejoice, for if this unlettered, uncultured fisherman could become the great preacher of the Pentecost, and the writer of the Epistles, then there is hope for every one of us."

If Peter was right, he was enthusiastically right. The opposite was also true of him. He was enthusiastically wrong when he said, "Though all men shall be offended because of thee, yet will I never be" (Matt. 26:33). A study of the account of Peter's denial clearly shows that when we are strong in ourselves, then we are weak. Peter failed because of this. It was Peter alone instead of Christ and Peter.

In Mark 14 we read that "Peter followed him afar off." He forgot his vow. He lost all of his joy and power and peace. It all happened because he entered into bad company and warmed himself by the enemies' fire. When Peter had his eyes on the Lord, he was brave enough to walk on the stormy sea. But with his eyes off Christ, he was afraid of a little maid. An unbroken communion is secured by keeping our eyes upon Jesus and setting our affections on things above.

November 23

How long wilt thou forget me, O Lord?
(Ps. 13:1).

How comforting to know that our Father cannot forget His own. His promise is sure. "Can a woman forget her [nursing] child, that she should not have compassion on the son of her womb? yea, they may forget, yet will I not forget thee. Behold, I have graven thee upon the palms of my hands" (Isa. 49:15-16).

Though the banks assign us a number, and to the world we are but a statistic, let us rejoice that our God knows us by our names. Can he forget us or forsake us? No! We are His sheep and the good Shepherd knows His own flock. "He that entereth in by the door is the shepherd of the sheep. To him the porter openeth; and the sheep hear his voice: and he calleth his own sheep by name. . . . I am the good shepherd, and know my sheep, and am known of mine" (John 10:2-3, 14).

Although the Social Security system fails, a computer loses our number, and the world completely forgets us, let us rejoice in His great security. His care is complete; His love changes not, His grace is sufficient; and He has graven our names on the palms of His nail-scarred hands. Since love wrote them there, He will never forget us!

> *This thought is dearer far to me*
> *Than worldly wealth or fame;*
> *However humble I may be*
> *He knows me by my name!*
> *Oh, this Friend divine is*
> *Truly mine,*
> *And He knows me by My name.*

> —W. M. Lightall

November 24

In that night was Belshazzar the king of the Chaldeans slain. And Darius the Median took the kingdom (Dan. 5:30-31).

There is a boundary set in the affairs of nations that drift past the last milestone of God's grace and mercy. This happened to the mighty nation of Babylon. Jehovah had used this heathen nation and their king, Nebuchadnezzar, as His instrument of judgment upon idolatrous Israel. King Nebuchadnezzar came to recognize the God of Israel as "the Most High God [who] ruled in the kingdom of men" (Dan. 5:21). But his son Belshazzar rejected these ancient precepts, desecrated the holy vessels, engaged in debauchery, and led his people into idolatry. Judgment fell on Belshazzar. Judgment also fell on the nation, fulfilling Isaiah's prophecy: "Babylon, the glory of the kingdoms, the beauty of the Chaldees . . . shall never be inhabited, neither shall it be dwelt in from generation to generation" (Isa. 13:19-20).

Through the centuries, nation after nation has been cast on history's rubbish pile. In reading Gibbon's *Decline and Fall of the Roman Empire* certain truths become self-evident. There was a rapid increase in divorce, and the sanctity of the home and marriage were undermined. Higher and higher taxes were levied by the Roman Senate under the guise of social welfare, with free bread and circuses for the people. A mad desire for more brutal sports developed, with pleasure becoming the guiding force in Roman life. Great armies were maintained, but the gravest danger was the moral depravity of both people and leaders. Finally religion decayed, having no longer any real meaning to the people. This is how it happened in Rome. Is this how it will happen today?

Let us replace feasting with fasting—pleasures with prayer—merriment with mourning—and hilarity with repentance. Only in "returning and rest shall [we] be saved" (Isa. 30:15). The Psalmist said, "Blessed is the nation whose God is the Lord; and the people whom he hath chosen for his own inheritance" (Ps. 33:12). We, as individuals and as a nation, need to confess our sins, turning from them to God, and placing our trust "not in chariots nor in horses" but in the Lord of Hosts. History's garbage heap is waiting for those who do not!

"Know ye that the Lord he is God; it is he that hath made us, and not we ourselves; we are his people, and the sheep of his pasture. Enter into his gates with thanksgiving, and into his courts with praise; be thankful unto him, and bless his name" (Ps. 100:3-4).

November 25

Let us come before his presence with thanksgiving (Ps. 95:2).

Thanks to God for my Redeemer,
Thanks for all Thou dost provide!
Thanks for times now but a memory,
Thanks for Jesus by my side!
Thanks for pleasant, balmy springtime,
Thanks for dark and dreary fall!
Thanks for tears by now forgotten,
Thanks for peace within my soul!

Thanks for prayers that Thou hast answered,
Thanks for what Thou dost deny!
Thanks for storms that I have weathered,
Thanks for all Thou dost supply!
Thanks for pain and thanks for pleasure,
Thanks for comfort in despair!
Thanks for grace that none can measure,
Thanks for love beyond compare!

Thanks for roses by the wayside,
Thanks for thorns their stems contain!
Thanks for home and thanks for fireside,
Thanks for hope, that sweet refrain!
Thanks for joy and thanks for sorrows,
Thanks for heavenly peace with Thee!
Thanks for hope in the tomorrow,
Thanks for all eternity!

—August Ludvig Storm

Among the grandest words in the English language are the words "Thank you." How wonderful to be able to say from the heart, "I love You, dear Lord, and I thank You."

I thank You for the beauty of Your creation—for the majesty of the mountains and for the rolling plains. I thank You for the seasons—both for the silent winter and for the windy spring. And for the beauty of the flowers and the blueness of the sky and the melody of the birds.

Yes, we thank You, dear Lord for Your creation. And we thank You, too, for love between man and wife and for homes and children. We thank You for the warmth of the winter hearth—for the quietness of the falling snow, and for the hope of the coming spring!

And most of all we thank You for Your unspeakable Gift—
Your Son Jesus. We acknowledge Your great love in that while we
were yet sinners You had compassion and mercy upon us and
gave Him to us. And we thank You again and again that "whosoever believeth in him should not perish, but have everlasting
life" (John 3:16).

> Thou Life of my life, blessed Jesus,
>   Thou death of the death that was mine.
> For me was Thy cross and Thine anguish,
>   Thy love and Thy sorrow divine.
> Thou suffered the cross and the torment,
>   That I might forever go free.
> A thousand, a thousand thanksgivings,
>   I bring, blessed Savior, to Thee.

—ERNST C. HOMBURG

November 26

**These things I have spoken unto you, that
in me ye might have peace. In the world ye
shall have tribulation: but be of good cheer;
I have overcome the world** (John 16:33).

Three times our Lord used the expression "I have spoken
unto you." "I have spoken unto you that my joy might remain
in you" (John 15:11). "These things I have spoken unto you, that
ye shall not be offended" (John 16:1). Then in our text, that we
"might have peace."

We are living in a world that knows no joy and lacks serene
peace. It is a world of fear and hatred, lust and greed, paganism
and idolatry. The Lord Jesus comes to each of us and says, "Be of
good cheer; I have overcome the world" (John 16:33). His joy and
peace are ours. Bottles of brightly colored tranquilizers should not
be the emblems of our faith.

"There arose a great storm of wind, and the waves beat into
the ship . . . and they awake him, and say . . . Master, carest thou
not that we perish? And he arose, and rebuked the wind, and said
unto the sea, Peace, be still" (Mark 4:37-39). He who calmed the
storm on Galilee is still the same today. Let His Word come into
your troubled heart, bringing you peace and joy.

November 27

Take unto you the whole armour of God,
that ye may be able to withstand in the evil
day, and having done all, to stand (Eph. 6:13).

Someone has said that one mark of an educated man is that he has no bias—no prejudice—no preconception—no intolerance—no discrimination. I halfway believe this.

The half I believe applies to persons. Christians must have no prejudice about people. There can be no pride of race or grace. No pride of creed, of color, or of clime. The root of this is carnal pride. The ground is completely level at the foot of the cross.

However, the half I disbelieve about prejudice applies to principles. Here I have a great bias, an absolute intolerance. We must never compromise against truth.

I told my children that they were absolutely forbidden to run out in front of automobiles—to play with butcher knives—to start fires or strike matches—to drink alcoholic poison. My prejudice came through loud and clear—on principle.

I told my congregation that Jesus Christ is the virgin-born Son of God—that He died for their sins and arose from the tomb —and is coming again. I told them that there could be no compromise in these great truths. Believe on Christ and be saved—reject Him and be lost forever.

I have a strong prejudice in favor of the sinner but against his sins. And I want to teach all men everywhere that truth is truth and love is love—that right is right and God is God—and that tomorrow is good if we don't compromise our principles.

—FLETCHER SPRUCE

I want a principle within
Of watchful, godly fear,
A sensibility of sin,
A pain to feel it near.
Help me the first approach to feel
Of pride or wrong desire;
To catch the wandering of my will,
And quench the kindling fire.

From Thee that I no more may stray,
No more Thy goodness grieve,
Grant me the filial awe, I pray,
Thy tender conscience give;

Quick as the apple of an eye,
  O God, my conscience make!
Awake my soul when sin is nigh,
  And keep it still awake.

Almighty God of truth and love,
  To me Thy power impart;
The burden from my soul remove,
  The hardness from my heart.
O may the least omission pain
  My reawakened soul,
And drive me to that grace again,
Which makes the wounded whole.

—CHARLES WESLEY

November 28

Pray without ceasing (1 Thess. 5:17)

The story is told of a devout christian who acquired a run-down farm. He labored long hours during the summer and his work was rewarded with a fine crop. The banker, from whom a loan had been obtained, came by one day to see the results. He noticed that the old farm buildings had been repaired and painted. The fences were mended, the gardens weeded, and signs of hard work, blessing, and beginning prosperity were apparent. "Sam," the banker said, "the Lord has worked a miracle here." "He sure has," Sam replied, "but you should have seen this place when the Lord had it all to himself."

There is a great spiritual truth here. We are to pray! But we are also to be busy!

Leslie VanInwegen wrote: "Do you feel sometimes, you are getting nowhere in your life? Perhaps you could learn a lesson from a devout ferryman whose daily task was rowing people across a certain stream. On one oar he painted the word *Work* and on the other oar, *Prayer.* When curiosity prompted a passenger to ask what this meant, the ferryman would pull first on one oar and the boat would merely turn around. Then he pulled only on the other oar. The boat turned in the other direction, getting nowhere. He would say, 'To get where I am going I have to use both oars.' The Christian is commanded to pray without ceasing; but at the same time he is commanded to not grow weary in well doing and that we are 'created in Christ Jesus unto good works which God hath before ordained that we should walk in them.' Yes, it takes two oars to row a boat; it takes both prayer and work to reach our goal of satisfying Christian living."

"Be ye stedfast, unmoveable, always abounding in the work of the Lord, forasmuch as ye know that your labour is not in vain in the Lord" (1 Cor. 15:58).

November 29

Be not deceived; God is not mocked: for whatsoever a man soweth, that shall he also reap (Gal. 6:7).

There is a harvest time. We do well to remember its laws. Simply stated, the first one reads—*we reap what we sow!* The sowing of wheat produces wheat—the planting of wild oats yields an abundance of wild oats. We need never be in doubt concerning the harvest!

Men close their eyes to this but not only do we reap what we sow, *we reap far more than we sow.* One grain can produce a hundredfold at harvesttime.

Paul Lawrence Dunbar wrote:

> *This is the debt I pay*
> *Just for one riotous day,—*
> *Years of regret and grief,*
> *Sorrow without relief.*
>
> *Pay it I will to the end—*
> *Until the grave, my friend,*
> *Gives me a true release,*
> *Gives me the clasp of peace.*
>
> *Slight was the thing I bought,*
> *Small was the debt, I thought,*
> *Poor was the loan at best—*
> *God! but the interest!*

And then the final law of the harvest is also true. Often, *we reap long after we sow.*

An irreligious farmer in one of our western states, who gloried in his rejection of Christ, wrote a letter to a local newspaper in these words: "Sir, I have been trying an experiment with

this field of mine. I plowed it on Sunday, I reaped it on Sunday,
I carted the crop to the barns on Sunday. And now, Mr. Editor,
what is the result? It is now October and I have more bushels to
the acre from this field than any of my religious neighbors."

The farmer expected applause from the editor, who was not
a particularly religious man himself, but he opened the paper next
week, there sure enough was his letter just as he had sent it in.
But underneath was this short but significant editorial comment:
"God does not always settle His accounts in October."

> When the seeds that I have scattered
> In the furrows of the years
> Shall be ripened for the harvest,
>   All their stores of hopes or fears;
> When the Master bids me number
>   All the moments that are flown,
> Will it be a joyful harvest
> When I reap what I have sown?
>
> —T. M. BILLS

November 30

**I am debtor both to the Greeks, and to
the Barbarians; both to the wise, and to the
unwise** (Rom. 1:14).

Paul looked upon foreign missionary service as the highest
expression of the Christian life. We listen eagerly to the words
Paul speaks, and we hear him say, "I am debtor to the Greeks!"

"Yes, Paul; we understand how greatly indebted you are to
the Greeks."

And then, as though not noting our interruption, the mighty
missionary continues, "I am debtor to the Barbarians!"

"Why, Paul!" we exclaim; "you in debt to the barbarian!
What did a barbarian ever do for you?"

"You do not understand," our great missionary replies; "I
am in debt to the barbarian, not because of anything the barbarian
ever has done for me, but I am in debt to the barbarian because of
what I can do for him."

O Paul, I am so glad that you realized that you were in debt to
the barbarian! I am so glad that you paid in full that debt of yours
to the barbarian! I am so glad for all that you did for the barbar-

ian, for in those days, my ancestors were all among the barbarians!

—William A. Brown

"Ye shall receive power, after that the Holy Spirit is come upon you: and ye shall be witnesses unto me both in Jerusalem, and in all Judaea, and in Samaria, and unto the uttermost part of the earth" (Acts 1:8).

> Forget them not, O Christ, who stand
> Thy vanguard in the distant land!
> In flood, in flame, in dark, in dread,
> Sustain, we pray, each lifted head!
>
> Be Thou in every faithful breast,
> Be peace and happiness and rest!
> Exalt them over every fear;
> In peril, come thyself more near!
>
> Let heaven above their pathway pour
> A radiance from its open door!
> Turn Thou the hostile weapons, Lord,
> Rebuke each wrathful alien horde!
>
> Thine are the loved for whom we crave
> That Thou wouldst keep them strong and brave.
> Be with Thine own, Thy loved, who stand
> Christ's vanguard in the storm-swept land!

—Margaret E. Sangster

December 1

We know that in all things God works for the good of those who love him, and who have been called according to his purpose (Rom. 8:28, NIV).

> Undaunted be Decembers,
> The sap is faithful yet.
> The giving earth remembers,
> And only men forget.

It is early December as these lines are written. The days are cold and dreary. Winter is now upon us. I am akin to D. L.

Moody in his dislike of winter. He always longed for spring. Once he exclaimed to his family, "Well, the backbone of winter is now broken." "But father," one of the children replied, "winter has just started." "Yes, that is true," Moody answered, "but the days will be getting longer. Yes, the backbone of winter has been broken."

Burris Jenkins must also have felt like this. Years ago he preached a famous sermon with the title "Undaunted by December." This should be the attitude of the child of God. December may be full of pain and problems—the roads may be icy—the temperature frigid—but fear not. December is also full of promise too. The songs of Bethlehem will soon ring out. The stars will shine bright in the crisp nights, and although God's world is silent and still, yet "if winter comes, can spring be far behind?"

Let us not forget St. Paul's wonderful words, even in December, "All things work together for good." Lift up your voice to the north wind and sing, "I am His and He is mine." Do not be daunted by December!

> *Loved with everlasting love,*
>   *Led by grace that love to know;*
> *Spirit, breathing from above,*
>   *Thou hast taught me it is so!*
> *Oh, this full and perfect peace!*
>   *Oh, this transport all divine!*
> *In a love which cannot cease*
> *I am His, and He is mine.*
>
> *Things that once were wild alarms*
>   *Cannot now distrub my rest;*
> *Closed in everlasting arms,*
>   *Pillowed on the loving breast,*
> *Oh, to lie forever here,*
>   *Doubt, and care, and self resign,*
> *While He whispers in my ear—*
> *I am His and He is mine.*
>
> *His forever, only His;*
>   *Who the Lord and me shall part?*
> *Ah, with what a rest of bliss,*
>   *Christ can fill the loving heart!*
> *Heaven and earth may fade and flee,*
>   *Firstborn light in gloom decline;*
> *But while God and I shall be,*
>   *I am His and He is mine.*
>
> —WADE ROBINSON

December 2

Who hath saved us, and called us with an holy calling, not according to our works, but according to his own purpose and grace, which was given us in Christ Jesus before the world began (2 Tim. 1:9).

The apostle uses the perfect tense and says, "who hath saved us." Believers in Christ Jesus are saved. They are not looked upon as persons who are in a hopeful state, and may ultimately be saved, but they are already saved. Salvation is not a blessing to be enjoyed upon the dying bed, and to be sung of in a future state above, but a matter to be obtained, received, promised, and enjoyed now. The Christian is perfectly saved in God's purpose; God has ordained him unto salvation, and that purpose is complete. He is saved also as to the price which has been paid for him: "It is finished," was the cry of the Savior when He died. The believer is also perfectly saved in His covenant head, for as he fell in Adam, so he lives in Christ.

But this complete salvation is accompanied by a holy calling. Those whom the Savior saved upon the Cross are in due time effectually called by the power of God the Holy Spirit unto holiness: they leave their sins; they endeavour to be like Christ; they choose holiness, not out of any compulsion, but from the stress of a new nature, which leads them to rejoice in holiness just as naturally as aforetime they delighted in sin. God neither chose them nor called them because they were holy, but He called them that they might be holy, and holiness is the beauty produced by His workmanship in them. Salvation must be of grace, because the Lord is the author of it: and what motive but grace could move Him to save the guilty? Salvation must be of grace, because the Lord works in such a manner that our righteousness is forever excluded. Such is the believer's privilege—a present salvation; such is the evidence that he is called to it—a life of holiness.

—Charles Haddon Spurgeon

I am not strong, till Thou hast clasped my hand.
I am not fit, till by Thy side I stand.
I am not brave, till Thou hast come to me;
Till Thou hast bound me fast, I am not free.

—Author Unknown

December 3

Blessed be God, even the Father of our Lord Jesus Christ, the Father of mercies, and the God of all comfort; who comforteth us in all our tribulations, that we may be able to comfort them who are in any trouble, by the comfort wherewith we ourselves are comforted of God (2 Cor. 1:3-4).

I remember, very early in my Christian life, having every tender and loyal impulse within me stirred to the depths by an appeal I met with in a volume of old sermons. "All who loved the Lord Jesus should show to others how worthy He was of being trusted by the steadfastness of their own faith in Him." As I read the inspiring words, there came to me a sudden glimpse of the privilege and the glory of being called to walk in paths so dark that only an utter recklessness of trust would be possible.

—HANNAH WHITALL SMITH
in *The Christian's Secret of a Happy Life*

Some day, when our pilgrimage journey is over,
When lessons are past and the schooling is done,
When we share in the glory the Father has given
Through ages unnumbered, to Jesus His Son;

When we shall look back on the way He hath led us
And think of the fears and the dangers thereof;
When we shall remember how oft He delivered,
How many His mercies, how faithful His love;

Ah, then we shall marvel that ever we doubted,
That ever our faith was so weak and so small,
That ever our eyes were so blind to His glory,
Our hearts so unready to answer His call.

And through all eternity how we shall wonder
That we were so slow to believe all His Word;
That we were so slothful in claiming His promise,
So careless of sharing the joy of our Lord.

—ANNIE JOHNSON FLINT

December 4

Always labouring fervently for you in prayers, that ye may stand perfect and complete in all the will of God (Col. 4:12).

John Wesley, preacher of righteousness, stirred all England with the gospel. And then into America came Methodism with its circuit-riding preachers. Wesley once said, "I must have four things in my life. I must have a whole Cross for my salvation, a whole Bible for my staff, a whole church for my fellowship, and a whole world for my parish."

His theology was Christ-centered and Cross-centered. He believed that Jesus died for our sins and that He was able to save. Such a message from the Bible, which he believed to be the Word of the living God, transformed old England. John Wesley also believed in the fellowship of all believers and he wanted the whole wide world for his ministry. Great was his impetus to foreign missions. And out of his ministry came high and holy living, so important to Christian purity and testimony. The Church shall forever be grateful to John and Charles Wesley for the songs they gave us, the holiness they proclaimed, and the old gospel they loved and lived for.

"The Lord make you to increase and abound in love one toward another, and toward all men, even as we do toward you: to the end he may stablish your hearts unblameable in holiness before God, even our Father, at the coming of our Lord Jesus Christ with all his saints" (1 Thess. 3:12-13).

December 5

The angel of the Lord appeared unto him in a flame of fire out of the midst of the bush. . . . And Moses said, I will now turn aside, and see this great sight (Exod. 3:2-3).

So often our sense of values is distorted. We strain toward the spectacular. We strive for the extraordinary. We reach for the sensational. But a life chiefly made up of such extreme situations is abnormal. Much of our earthly pilgrimage is monotonous and humdrum. The tedious round of duties, the constantly recurring petting annoyances—these constitute the long, dismal stretches of our journey.

There must be some reason and purpose in the commonplace circumstances in life. Perhaps we should fail to appreciate the plateau levels and the mountain elevations were it not for the dusty, dreary plains.

But who assumes the prerogative of designating a day or an incident or the routine of life, commonplace? Can it be that our point of view is to blame? If we say with Paul, "For to me to live is Christ," is anything in such living ordinary? If whether we eat or drink, we do all to the glory of God, can any day or any duty be dull?

Oh, for a glorifying vision, a hallowing concept that shall transform the drab into the radiant, the commonplace into the exceptional! Then shall every bush be aglow with God, every day shall be one that the Lord has made, and what hitherto were disturbing irritations now will be stepping-stones to Christlikeness!

—M. A. LUNN

"Every morning lean thine arms awhile upon the windowsill of heaven and gaze upon the Lord. Then with this vision in thy heart, turn strong to meet the day."

> Turn your eyes upon Jesus,
>   Look full in His wonderful face,
>   And the things of earth will grow strangely dim,
>   In the light of His glory and grace.

—HELEN HOWARTH LEMMEL

December 6

Let us now go even unto Bethlehem (Luke 2:15).

I saw the *rush* of Christmas in the throngs of people crowding the city streets—happy but shoving and pushing, walking from store to store looking for last-minute gifts.

I saw the *hope* of Christmas in the wrinkled face of an old man as he sat and gazed at the star at the top of the tree. He had not placed the star there this time. One of the nursing home workers had done this, but he was remembering the star he once had placed on Christmas trees in days long past.

I saw the *kindness* of Christmas when the weary policeman on the corner walked with a lone and gray-haired mother across the busy street.

I saw the *tenderness* of Christmas in the gentle touch of a mother who sang to her baby as she rocked him. She was singing of that other Babe who had come to earth to give so much to us.

I saw the *work* of Christmas as the postman carried his burden of greetings and presents to cheer others, while he carefully walked the icy and dangerous streets.

I saw the *joy* of Christmas in the faces of the youths who carolled for the old and the sick and the infirmed.

I saw the *majesty* of Christmas—and heard it, too—in a church with stained-glass windows while a choir sang the Good News that Jesus had come.

I saw the *humility* of Christmas when I worshipped in a tiny chapel. There was no choir, no great organ, no stained-glass windows, no cushioned pews, no carpeted floors. But the Christ who was born in a manger let His presence be felt there that night.

I saw the *beauty* of Christmas when lights in the homes made a golden pathway across the snow and the stars in the crisp, cold air seemed to shine more brightly for the Lord of heaven and earth.

I saw the *meaning* of Christmas when I saw the empty tomb and heard the angels say again, "He is not here. He is risen."

I saw the *love* of Christmas when I looked again to Calvary!

—RUBY FRANKLIN

December 7

Loosing from Troas, we came with a straight course to Samothracia, and the next day to Neapolis; and from there to Philippi (Acts 16:11-12).

Though the winds may have been contrary, the sails were set and Paul with his companions hastened to Philippi. The Lord's call had been received and He directed their voyage.

There is a lesson here for the young believer. Wait on the Holy Spirit to call you to your place of service. After the message is received, set your course straight. It is true that contrary winds of discouragement and disappointment may blow. But do not despair. The winds are His winds and it is the set of the sail that determines the final destination of the voyage.

Let Christ "trim and set your sails." Enter the ship as Paul did so long ago, commit yourself, and trust Him to guide you to the desired haven where you are to minister. Though the winds be calm or tempest-driven, you will reach your "Philippi" where you are to labor for the Lord. It all depends on the set of the sail! Fear not the wind!

> I stood on the shore beside the sea;
> The wind from the west blew fresh and free,
> While past the rocks at the harbor's mouth
> The ships went north and the ships went south,
> And some sailed out on an unknown quest,
> And some sailed into the harbor's rest;
> Yet ever the wind blew out of the west.
>
> I said to one who had sailed the sea
> That this was a marvel unto me;
> For how can the ships go safely forth,
> Some to the south and some to the north,
> Far out to sea on their golden quest,
> Or into the harbor's calm and rest,
> And ever the wind blow out of the west?
>
> The sailor smiled as he answered me,
> "Go where you will when you're on the sea,
> Though headwinds baffle and flaws delay,
> You can keep the course by night and day,
> Drive with the breeze or against the gale;
> It will not matter what winds prevail,
> For all depends on the set of the sail."
>
> Oh, set your sail to the heavenly gale
> And then, no matter what winds prevail,
> No reef can wreck you, no calm delay,
> No mists shall hinder, no storms shall stay.
> Though far you wander and long you roam
> Through salt sea spray and o'er white sea foam,
> No wind can blow but shall speed you home.

—ANNIE JOHNSON FLINT

December 8

He maketh me to lie down in green pas-
tures: he leadeth me beside the still waters
(Ps. 23:2).

A book well marked with notes and underlined passages
speaks of intense reading. The Bibles used by God's saints indicate such study. Here are a few notes from Psalm 23 found in
Dwight L. Moody's preaching Bible.

> Nearly everyone can repeat this psalm from memory, but not
> everyone from the heart. . . .
> With me is the Lord. Beneath me are the green pastures. Be-
> side me are still waters. Before me a table is spread.
> Around me are my enemies but after me come goodness
> and mercy. Ahead of me is the house of the Lord. . . .
> We have a happy life, the assurance of a happy death, and a
> happy eternity. . . .
> You may talk about Jesus, but as soon as you enter the valley
> you will talk to Him. . . .
> The Lord makes your cup to run over so that others may taste
> too. . . .
> The Shepherd leads and goodness and mercy bring up the
> rear. . . .
> All of God's children have two footmen, goodness and
> mercy coming on behind them.

December 9

When thou prayest, enter into thy closet,
and when thou hast shut thy door, pray to thy
Father, which is in secret; and thy Father,
which seeth in secret shall reward thee openly
(Matt. 6:6).

The Lord Jesus had spent the night in prayer, when one of the
disciples came to Him and asked for instructions in how to pray.
He felt a need to learn and so should we. Here are some of our
Lord's teachings on *the privilege of prayer* based upon Matt. 6:
5-15.

"Enter into thy closet." This speaks of *the place of prayer.*
It should be a quiet spot, undisturbed and secret. Jesus cautions
against those who pray only to be seen of men.

Then He says, "Shut thy door." Here is *the privacy of prayer.* God's greatest prayer warriors have been those who prayed alone. Moody's great campaign in England came as an answer to an invalid's earnest praying for a revival.

Then our Lord adds the word, "Pray." When you are in the secret place—and the door has been closed—pray! All to often, most of us are hurried. We no sooner get the door closed than we are through. "Prevailing prayer" entails earnestness. An old hymn asks, "Have you prayed it through?" This speaks of the place, the privacy, and *the perseverance of prayer.*

The petitions of prayer—what should they be? They should begin with words of praise and thanksgiving; confession and intercession should follow: Then, and only then, should come personal requests. The most gracious words in language are the words, "I thank you." And always, always ask in Jesus name. This is the name that is above all other names, and the only name the Father loves and honors. He is the Way to the throne of grace!

December 10

Rise ye up, take your journey, and pass over the river Arnon: behold, I have given into thine hand Sihon the Amorite, king of Heshbon, and his land: begin to possess it, and contend with him in battle (Deut. 2:24).

"There comes a time when we must 'rise up and begin the journey.' We must not tarry too long on this side of the river. There is a land to conquer and enemies to fight. He calls you 'to begin to possess,' and no victory can come without a battle and without obeying 'marching orders'" (L. D. Boatman).

"Our Father, when we long for life without trials and work without difficulties, remind us that an oak grows strong in contrary wind and diamonds are made under pressure. With courageous hearts may we see in every calamity an opportunity and not give way to the pessimism that sees in every opportunity a calamity" (Peter Marshall).

"Moses my servant is dead; now therefore arise, go over this Jordan, thou, and all this people, unto the land which I do give to them, even to the children of Israel. Every place that the sole of your foot shall tread upon, that have I given unto you, as I said unto Moses" (Josh. 1:2-3).

"Theologically and judicially I know that every believer has everything as soon as he is converted; but experimentally nothing is his until by faith he claims it. God 'hath blessed us with all spiritual blessings in heavenly places in Christ,' but until we set the foot of faith upon them, they do not practically become ours. 'According to our faith,' is always the limit and the rule" (Hannah Whitall Smith).

December 11

Then said Mary unto the angel, How shall this be, seeing I know not a man? And the angel answered, and said unto her, The Holy Ghost shall come upon thee, and the power of the Highest shall overshadow thee: therefore also that holy thing which shall be born of thee shall be called the Son of God (Luke 1:34-35).

"Born of a virgin." Whosoever is lax upon this doctrine, let him face Orr's sentence, through whose closely woven meshes, unworthy thinking cannot escape:

"Anyone who sneers at the crib, cannot help sneering at the cross."

We firmly hold that any man who averts his gaze from the supernatural birth of the Lord Jesus, saying "it doesn't matter" or who rejects the virgin birth as a "fairy tale," impoverishes his devotional life, and endangers his grasp on the Lord's deity.

To evade the virgin birth, one must either reject the Word of God or be disrespectful to it.

Mary said, "How? . . . I know not a man." And Gabriel said, "The Holy Spirit shall come upon thee . . . therefore . . . he shall be called the Son of God." This provided the kind of a Savior faith must have! One whose necessary humanity is assured, derived from His mother; and whose deity is confirmed, derived from His Father.

—RICHARD ELLSWORTH DAY

"When Mary went down into that mysterious vale of motherhood, she came back holding in her arms the Babe whose every nerve carried Divine impulses, whose every bone was of Divine sculpture, and whose every muscle was a pulley Divinely hung" (Robert G. Lee).

A little maid in years,
Shaken by vague dim fears,
Half hoping in her heart
This strangeness would depart.
Bewildered by the light
She'd glimpsed that wondrous night;
Her own familiar world
Through star-lit spaces hurled;
Praying, soul hushed and awed,
At the very knees of God.

The Babe in her arms at last;
The valley of shadow past,
And deep in her woman's eyes
An infinite knowledge lies—
The secret of pain and loss,
The crown of thorns and the cross,
The vision that God had dreamed
Of a sinful world redeemed,
And afar on the shores of time
The light of a love sublime.
She holds to a waiting earth
The Son she has brought to birth!

—MARTHA SNELL NICHOLSON

December 12

Casting all your care upon him; for he
careth for you (1 Pet. 5:7).

Do we really believe this? If we do, why are we so often fretted by the cares of daily life? God our Father has promised that all shall work for good for those who love Him, and we have the assurance that He feels for us in all our trials. He bids us bring everything to Him in prayer, and He has promised to undertake according to each day's need. He is all sufficient and "He careth" for us.

He has also promised to supply all of our needs "according to His riches in glory by Christ Jesus." His credit is infinite. There are assets in abundance, riches of grace, riches of love, riches of mercy, and riches of glory. Whatever the circumstances, there is sufficient supply for every need, either temporal or spiritual. We are prone to doubt and worry. We should trust and enjoy the goodness of our Father's mercies. A motto we have often seen reads, "If you worry you do not trust. If you trust you do not worry." Commit all to Him. Claim His promise. Cast all your cares upon Him. He will meet your every need! He cares for you!

—Harry A. Ironside

December 13

I will instruct thee and teach thee in the way which thou shalt go: I will guide thee with mine eye (Ps. 32:8).

Pilgrim needed a true Guide on his journey to the Celestial City. Hazardous was the path and many pitfalls ensnared the way. How comforting to know that the Lord will be our Guide. What safety! What security is ours!

Asaph wrote, "Thou shalt guide me with thy counsel" (Ps. 73:24). And in Psalm 78 he stated, "So he fed them according to the integrity of his heart; and guided them by the skillfulness of his hands" (Ps. 78:72).

The Lord shall guide us—with His counsel, with His nail-pierced hands, and with His eye. He will deliver us in distress and in the "slough of despondency." He sees in the distance for dangers—both near and far. We need not fear the Way! We may trust His Word! We are safe when He is at work! "For this God is our God for ever and ever: he will be our guide even unto death" (Ps. 48:14).

> *Precious promise God hath given*
> *To the weary passerby*
> *On the way from earth to heaven,*
> *"I will guide thee with mine eye."*
>
> *When temptations almost win thee,*
> *And thy trusted watchers fly,*
> *Let this promise ring within thee,*
> *"I will guide thee with mine eye."*
>
> *When thy secret hopes have perished*
> *In the grave of years gone by,*
> *Let this promise still be cherished,*
> *"I will guide thee with mine eye."*

When the shades of life are falling,
And the hour has come to die,
Hear the trusty Pilot calling,
"I will guide thee with mine eye."

—Nathaniel Niles

"Commit thy way unto the Lord; trust also in him; and he shall bring it to pass" (Ps. 37:5).

"Does the burden seem more than you can bear? The trial so peculiar that the darkness can never be dispelled? The grief too agonizing every to be soothed? The wound too deep ever to heal? Then remember this: only through perfect submissiveness and trust in His guidance and love can God have His perfect way in our lives. Then no affliction is too grievous, no furnace too hot, no price too costly in comparison with entire submission and unconditional trust in Him. He will guide you through! Commit thy way and trust in Him" (James H. McConkey).

December 14

The angel said to them: "Don't be afraid! For I am here with good news for you, which will bring great joy to all the people" (Luke 2: 10, TEV).

A few years ago a striking Christmas booklet was published with the title "If Christ Had Not Come." It was founded upon our Savior's words, "If I had not come." The card represented a clergyman falling into a short sleep in his study on Christmas morning and dreaming of a world into which Jesus had never come.

In his dream he found himself looking through his home, but there were no little stockings in the chimney corner, no Christmas bells or wreaths of holly, and no Christ to comfort, gladden, and save. He walked out on the public street, but there was no church with its spire pointing to heaven. He came back and sat down in his library, but every book about the Savior had disappeared.

A ring at the doorbell, and a messenger asked him to visit a poor dying mother. He hastened with the weeping child and as he reached the home he sat down and said, "I have something here that will comfort you." He opened his Bible to look for a familiar promise, but it ended at Malachi, and there was no gospel and no promise of hope and salvation, and he could only bow his head and weep with her in bitter despair.

Two days afterward he stood beside her coffin and conducted the funeral service, but there was no message of consolation, no word of a glorious resurrection, no open heaven, but only "dust to dust, ashes to ashes," and one long eternal farewell. He realized at length that "He had not come," and burst into tears and bitter weeping in his sorrowful dream.

Suddenly he woke with a start, and a great shout of joy and praise burst from his lips as he heard his choir singing in his church close by:

> O come, all ye faithful, joyful and triumphant,
> O come ye, O come ye to Bethlehem;
> Come and behold Him, born the King of Angels,
> O come let us adore Him, Christ, the Lord.

Let us be glad and rejoice this Christmas season because "He has come." And let us remember the annunciation of the angel, "Behold I bring you good tidings of great joy, which shall be to all people, for unto you is born this day in the city of David a Saviour, which is Christ the Lord" (Luke 2:10-11).

—LETTIE B. COWMAN

December 15

Much more than . . . (Rom. 5:9).

The fifth chapter of Romans has been called the "much more" chapter of the Bible. Over and over again Paul uses this precious expression.

> "Much more then, being now justified by his blood, we shall be saved from wrath through him" (v. 9).

> "For if, when we were enemies, we were reconciled to God by the death of his Son, much more . . . we shall be saved by his life" (v. 10).

> "If through the offense of one many be dead, much more the grace of God . . . by . . . Jesus Christ, hath abounded unto many" (v. 15).

> "For if by one man's offense death reigned . . . much more they which receive abundance of grace and of

the gift of righteousness shall reign in life by one, Jesus Christ" (v. 17).

And finally: "Where sin abounded, grace did *much more* abound" (v. 20).

The "much mores" are full of hope and encouragement for the believer. He who loves us and gave His Son for us will never let us drift beyond His wondrous care. It is the resurrection ministry of the Lord Jesus that has given us so "much more." By Christ's death we have been reconciled to God but "much more" by His intercessory ministry we have been assured of eternal salvation and justification. We are the possessors of His abounding grace. And "much more" of His goodness and love awaits us!

December 16

The Lord opened the eyes of the young man; and he saw; and, behold, the mountain was full of horses and chariots of fire round about Elisha (2 Kings 6:17).

It has been well said that "earthly cares are a heavenly discipline." But they are even something better than discipline—they are God's chariots sent to take the soul to its high place of triumph. Troubles frequently do not look like chariots. They look instead like enemies—cars of misery and wretchedness, which are only waiting to roll over and crush us. But could we see them as they really are—these sufferings, trials, defeats, disappointments, unkindnesses—we would recognize them as chariots of triumph for which our souls have been longing and praying.

When the King of Syria came up against the man of God with horses and chariots, they could be seen by every eye. But God had chariots that could be seen only with the eye of faith. The servant of the prophet cried out, "Alas, my master! How shall we do?" The prophet Elisha sat calmly in his house and only asked, "Lord, open his eyes that he may see."

This is the prayer we need to pray. All around us are God's chariots waiting to carry us to places of glorious victory. Look, then, upon chastening and trials, no matter how grievous they be, as God's chariots to carry you to the high places of spiritual achievement and growth. We must learn how to mount into God's chariots. When they come, climb into His will as a little child climbs into his mother's arms. Let there be no footdragging as you enter. There must be no "ifs." You must learn to accept God's will fully and completely. Shut out every thought save that of complete submission. Learn to say over and over again, "Thy will be done." Trust in His love. Mount thus into His will for you and you will enter a "chariot" and "ride" into the heavens in a way you have never dreamed of. Sorrows, disappointments, losses, and defeats can all be His chariots. Mount into them with a thankful heart. In His shining love, He will carry you up safely in His arms to glorious triumph!

—Hannah Whitall Smith
in *The Christian's Secret of a Happy Life*

December 17

Behold, a virgin shall be with child, and shall bring forth a son, and they shall call his name Immanuel, which being interpreted is, God with us (Matt. 1:23).

There is something about the Christmas season that brings and yet dispels loneliness. The heart turns home and many a song has gained popularity with this theme. A generation ago, crowds thronged the train depots hurrying "home for Christmas," but now it is the great air terminals that bustle with people at Christmastime. But it is still the hope of being "home for Christmas."

Yes, Christ came into the world that we might not be alone. His name, the angel said, would be "Emmanuel." It means "God with us." The Father desired to abolish the loneliness of the sinful heart and gave at Bethlehem His only begotten Son. There is no loneliness in Christ!

In beautiful St. Paul's Cathedral in London hangs the immortal painting of Holman Hunt showing Christ standing at a weedblocked door holding a light. At closer examination, one sees there is no latch on the outside. The door must be opened from within! Are you lonely this Christmastime? Then open your heart's door to Jesus and welcome Him in. Accepting His invitation will bring to you a truly joyous Christmas and He will be with you through all the rest of life's journey.

The holly boughs have all been hung,
The Christmas carols now are sung

To celebrate a Baby's birth;
New joy now gladdens all the earth.
But pause—for pathways, steep and rough,
A baby's hand is not enough;
Men need to know, in Bethlehem
That God himself came down to them.
One further carol lift and tell
Earth's sweetest word—Immanuel:
   God with us!

God with us in the manger bed,
God with us through all years ahead;
For ways too dark and treacherous
God has come down to be with us.
Oh, hear, beyond that Infant cry,
The blessed promise: "I, if I
Be lifted up will draw to me
All men." Beloved, this is He—
Not just a child on earth to dwell,
But Saviour, Lord, Immanuel:
   God with us!

—Helen Frazee-Bower

December 18

**Prayer was made without ceasing of the
church unto God for him** (Acts 12:5).

Is the church suffering from shortness of spiritual breath?
Indeed, is she dying from lack of breath?

Many years ago, Norman B. Harrison wrote, "the Church as
the body of Christ is a living organism, possessed of His life. The
Church's life, corporate as well as individual, in its beginning and
in its continuing, is the very breath of the risen, glorified Son of
God.

"One of the body's activities, both essential to living and also
involuntary, is the act of breathing. The application to the Church
is obvious. She has come upon a day of hectic commotion. Her
activities are varied and many. She is endeavoring to do many
strenuous things. This must call for increased breathing as an
organism. Yet most churches instead of more deeply inhaling at
the fountain of spiritual resources to meet the stress of her pro-

grams, have unquestionably a diminished sense of need. To sustain her own life she must have more prayer."

Is the Church developing spiritual emphysema? The atmosphere she breathes must be heavenly. All too often she has been contaminated with worldly odors and in some quarters noxious and fatal gases have escaped to congregations. This brings spiritual death.

If she is to survive, there must come a return to prayer and a deep conviction of its indispensable value and also our desperate need. Without prayer, churches can do nothing but struggle and gasp and eventually die.

"Without me ye can do nothing" (John 15:5).

December 19

I follow after, if that I may apprehend that for which also I am apprehended of Christ Jesus (Phil. 3:12).

There are three classes of men in the Christian life; the men of the wing, the men of the couch, and the men of the road. The first are those who fly before; they are the pioneers of progress; they are in advance of their fellows. The second are those who lie still; they do not work; they are the invalids who came not to minister but to be ministered unto.

The third class are those who follow the Lamb. They are the ambulance corps. These are the sacrificial souls that come on behind. They do not wish to lead, choosing rather to be in the rear; they come forward only when others are driven backward. They want no glory from the battle, no wreath for the victory, no honorable mention among the heroes. They seek the wounded, the dying, the dead; they anoint for life's burial; they give the cup of cold water; they wash the soiled feet. They are the ones who take in Saul of Tarsus after he becomes blind.

Let others lead, O Lord! I am content to follow. Help me to serve Thee in the background! I cannot fight Thy battles but I can nurse Thy wounded. I cannot repel Thy foes, but I can repair Thy fortresses. I cannot conduct Thy marches, but I can succor those who have fainted by the way.

Write my name amongst those who follow Thee!

O Captain of my Salvation, put me with the ambulance corps!

—GEORGE MATHESON

Count me with the children of the heavenly King;
Count me with the servants who would service bring;
Count me with the ransomed who His praises sing;
Count me, count me.

—W. C. POOLE

December 20

In the beginning was the Word, and the
Word was with God, and the Word was God
(John 1:1).

Jesus asked His disciples on one occasion, "Whom do men say that I the Son of man am?" (Matt. 16:13). Everybody was discussing Him, and the disciples had ready answers: John the Baptist, Elijah, Jeremiah, or one of the other prophets.

The Sanhedrin was discussing Him, too. Imagine this scene. The High Priest speaks, "The name of this man, Jesus, is on everybody's lips. What are you hearing about Him?"

A scholar rises to speak, "I have plumbed the depths of learning, both at home and abroad. I have listened to great teachers, but I chanced to hear Him in the courtyard and never have I heard such wisdom." A doctor of medicine speaks, "I heard of His miraculous cures and decided to see for myself. I was there when He ministered to the blind man, the one who had been blind from birth. Never have I seen such a cure."

With one accord they all decide who Jesus is, and they send one of their members, Nicodemus, to judiciously tell Christ who He is. Listen: "Rabbi [Teacher], we know that thou art a teacher come from God; for no man can do these miracles that thou doest, except God be with Him" (John 3:2).

Nicodemus missed it. So many have missed it since. The Sanhedrin wanted to humanize Jesus. They were willing to accept Him as a wise man, a teacher, one with strange psychic power. But He is more than that!

You say you can accept Him as One who came to show us a better way? He is more than that! He said, "I AM THE WAY." You can accept Him as One who teaches great truths like Buddha? He is more than that. He said, "I am truth." You say you can accept Him as one who shares the philosophies of life? He is more than that. He said, *"I am life."*

This is the Christmas season. Open your heart to this Christ and He will become for you the Truth—the Way—the Life.

—U. S. GRANT

"There was the song in the air, the star in the sky, and whisperings in the hills of a Savior born. The wise men who had been to Bethlehem went home thinking long thoughts about this. Deep in their hearts, as their camel caravan tinkled its roundabout way through the hills, was a freshened assurance of God's eternal nearness. He had not forgotten His world. This is what we celebrate in Christmas—not just a birth but an Incarnation. The Word was made flesh, the living, infinite God was clothed in our human likeness to walk our roads and to dwell with us" (E. Russell Lynn).

"I am come that [you] might have life" (John 10:10).

December 21

Joseph also went up from Galilee, out of
the city of Nazareth, into Judaea, unto the city
of David, which is called Bethlehem (Luke 2:4).

Christmas is surely the season of joy and happiness and its celebration for most of us means home—being home with those we love and with those who love us. But did you ever stop to think about that first Christmas? If Christmas is a time for being at home for us, that first Christmas was a drama of the homeless. No member of the cast of Christmas was home.

Take the shepherds. The only thing we know about them is that they were abiding in the fields, keeping watch over their flocks by night—and that they were not home.

And then the wise men. For them, also, the first Christmas involved a journey that took them away from home. Then there were the angels, the hosts that sang, "Glory to God in the highest, and on earth peace, good will toward men." We certainly cannot detail their daily ministrations, but on that night when Jesus was born, they had a special mission—unlike any before or since, as they heralded the birth of the Savior. That night they were away from their celestial dwelling.

And what of Joseph and Mary? They were away from home. They had come from Nazareth to Bethlehem to be numbered in the census of the empire. The trip was not an easy one, especially for an expectant mother. It really seems intriguing—almost as if there were a divine scheme to it. The event that now means to all of us home and shelter and family and security, meant none of those things on the night when Christ was born.

But what about the Babe of Bethlehem? Why, He was away from home too! David had foretold this when he wrote, "All thy garments smell of myrrh, and aloes, and cassia, out of the ivory palaces, whereby they have made thee glad" (Ps. 45:8). The baby Jesus had not found His home in Bethlehem; He had left it to come to Bethlehem. Isaiah had said His name would be Emmanuel, "God with us." When the eternal Son of God entered into the experience of men, when it pleased Him to be fashioned as a man, it meant forsaking the chambers of eternal glory. When the Word was made flesh and dwelt among us, then He too was away from home (John 1:14).

And then think one last time, who else was away from home that first Christmas? We were. That is why there was a Bethlehem manger and an angel chorus and an infant Savior—because mankind was away from home—you and I and every son of Adam. With sin came spiritual darkness and estrangement. God kept seeking and man kept evading, farther and farther from "home." And so God sent His Son, to show us the way back to God himself, and by the redeeming power of the Cross and the Resurrection. All to bring us back to Him and home! Every manger scene you see is saying that you are away from home, and God is looking for you, to bring you home again. In His love He sent His Son, to take your hand and bring you back into His family, and to dwell forever in His heavenly home.

Home for Christmas! They weren't, because we weren't.

Home for Christmas? By the grace of God it may be so. At home with Him—now, and for all eternity!

—HAL BONNER

December 22

This shall be a sign unto you; Ye shall find the babe, wrapped in swaddling clothes, lying in a manger (Luke 2:12).

What God gives us at Bethlehem is the highest and noblest of all gifts. Yet we can miss the gift if our hearts are drawn to something other than the Holy Child. What made Christmas authentic is its relation to the Savior. And yet the sign of this relationship is not a revelation of power and glory but the sign of the ordinary. The angelic announcement was simple and honest: "The babe wrapped in swaddling clothes." There is no need to make a mistake. The Baby is a baby. The Child is a child. The sign is given in utter simplicity. But it is given so that the shepherds might not make the mistake of the wise men who hunted for the Savior in the palace. The shepherds need not worry or wonder where the Christ might be or what He might be like. The sign is: "[He is] wrapped in swaddling clothes and lying in a manger."

The sign that the angels announced is quite distressing. The ordinariness and the homeliness of Bethlehem is anything but attractive. The uncomfortable stench of the steamy manger scene is not so pleasant as Christmas cards portray. But this is how God came to us—in swaddling clothes and lying in a manger.

Wrapped in swaddling clothes was the Holy Child in whom dwelt all the righteousness and holiness of God. We can come into His presence today with the same kind of joyous faith as did the shepherds. We can come across all of the hurdles of our doubts that stand between us and God. We can cross all the uncertainties that would stand as stumbling blocks between God and us. We can come to receive Him with open hearts. In the Holy Child God gives us the blessing of salvation. The Christ we receive today is the Christ who was once a child but now lives risen from the dead to be our Lord to all eternity. As the Risen Lord He gives us the blessings of heaven.

When the Christ Child came to Bethlehem He came to restore the blessings of heaven to earth. He came to the ordinary to give the extraordinary. In no way did He remain the simple and unadorned child of the swaddling clothes. He stormed the gates of death that He might bring back to us the victory over death. He came to death that He might make us the children of life.

This is the Child of the swaddling clothes. . . .

Let us take Him to ourselves that He may take us unto himself!

—E. RUSSELL LYNN

> That Christmas Day, if you were God,
> And that was your Son on that stable sod,
> Wrapped for death with its sin-cursed sting,
> Would you have made the angels sing?
> Would you have sent a lovely star
> To guide the wise men from afar
> While weaklings did what haters bid?
> Our loving Heavenly Father did.
>
> On the Calvary road, if you were God
> And that was your Son neath the scourging rod

Bearing painful wounds and bitter loss,
Would you have nailed Him to the Cross?
Would you have let Him suffer so
That sinners might redemption know
While this He did their sins to rid?
Our loving Heavenly Father did.

—Author Unknown

December 23

There was no room for them in the inn
(Luke 2:7).

Why was there no room in the inn? Perhaps it was because the inn was truly filled—filled with very important people. Perhaps the innkeeper never knew of the lowly man and woman seeking a place to stay—some subordinate may have turned them away. Perhaps the innkeeper was so busy with important details— the securing of food, the making of beds, the preparation of meals —that he paid no attention to the plight of the young mother. Perhaps he turned them away because he was afraid—afraid that they might embarrass the distinguished people already registered as guests. Perhaps he just didn't care, recognizing that greater wealth could be his by holding the room for more affluent seekers.

Why was there no room in the inn? We really do not know. We only know that "she brought forth her firstborn son and . . . laid him in a manger." The inn missed the Savior of the world. Are you missing Him too?

What could be done? The inn was full of folks:
His Honor, Marcus Lucius, and his scribes
Who made the census; honorable men
From farthest Galilee, come hitherward
To be enrolled; high ladies and their lords;
The rich, the rabbis, such a noble throng
As Bethlehem had never seen before
And may not see again. And there they were,
Close-herded with their servants, till the inn
Was like a hive at swarming-time, and I
Was fairly crazed among them.

Could I know
That they were so important? Just the two,

No servants, just a workman sort of man,
Leading a donkey, and his wife thereon,
Drooping and pale—and I saw them not myself,
My servants must have driven them away.
But had I seen them, how was I to know?
Were inns to welcome stragglers, up and down
In all our towns from Beersheba to Dan,
Till He should come? And how were men to know?
There was a sign, they say, a heavenly light
Resplendent; but I had no time for stars.
And there were songs of angels in the air
Out on the hills; but how was I to hear
Amid the thousand clamors of an inn?

Of course, if I had known them, who they were,
And who was He that should be born that night,
For now I learn that they will make Him King,
A second David, who will ransom us
From these Philistine Romans—who but He
That feeds an army with a loaf of bread,
And if a soldier falls, He touches him
And up he leaps, uninjured? Had I known,
I would have turned the whole inn upside down,
His Honor, Marcus Lucius, and the rest,
And sent them all to stables.

So you have seen Him, stranger, and perhaps
Again may see Him? Prithee say for me
I did not know; and if He comes again,
As He surely will come, with retinue,
And banners, and an army—tell Him, my Lord,
That all my inn is His to make amends.
Alas, alas! To miss a chance like that!
This inn that might be chief among them all—
The birthplace of the Messiah—had I but known!

—Amos R. Wells

December 24

It came to pass, as the angels were gone away from them into heaven, the shepherds said one to another, Let us now go even unto Bethlehem, and see this thing which is come to pass, which the Lord hath made known unto us (Luke 2:15).

The shepherds walked the road to Bethlehem. They were "far from the maddening throng" when the angels brought to them the message. On the quietness of the Judean hills they heard the first Christmas sermon: "In Bethlehem, in the land of Judea, a Savior has been born. Go and see!"

Born a Savior! Not a great teacher or prophet, but the mighty God Incarnate, and He has been born to die!

And so the shepherds believed. "Let us now go even unto Bethlehem, and see this thing which is come to pass" (Luke 2:15). No room for doubt here. Faith manifests itself in the walk to Bethlehem believing that they will both see and find. How blessed to walk this road and find Jesus!

This was God's message to earth's weary nations
  On that first Christmas morn:
"Fear not, for unto you I give a Savior;
  This day the Christ is born."

And still the words are ringing down the ages
  Above the world's despair:
"Fear not, for unto you is born a Saviour,
  And here is rest from care;

"And here is free and plenteous redemption
  For all the sons of men;
Beauty of flame among their dead, gray ashes,
  From death, new life again.

"And here is light for those who sit in darkness,
  And joy for those who mourn;
And here is peace amid the world's disquiet;
  Fear not, the Christ is born."

—ANNIE JOHNSON FLINT

Christmas Eve

That night when in the Judean skies,
  The mystic star dispensed its light,
A man, born blind, moved in his sleep—
  And dreamed that he had sight!

That night when shepherds heard the song
  Of hosts angelic choiring near,
A deaf man stirred in slumber's spell—
  And dreamed that he could hear!

That night when o'er the newborn babe
  The tender Mary rose to lean,
A loathsome leper smiled in sleep—
  And dreamed that he was clean!

That night when to the mother's breast
  The little King was held secure,
A harlot slept a happy sleep—
  And dreamed that she was pure!

That night when in the manger lay
  The Son of God who came to save,
A man moved in the sleep of death—
  And dreamed there was no grave!

—AUTHOR UNKNOWN

December 25

*Being warned of God in a dream that they
should not return to Herod, they departed into
their own country another way* (Matt. 2:12).

The wise men went home by a different road. These words
hold more truth than just what they are saying on the surface.
Christmas should mean that we go home a different way!

We know almost nothing about these wise men—who they
were—how many—where they came from. They were most likely
Persian wise men, counsellors of kings, whose religion was a
crude astronomy. They had caught a bit of Israel's promise, they
had heard some stray notes of their songs of hope, and in their
camel caravan they set out across the desert to Jerusalem, following the star and a brighter light within their own souls. They were
looking for a newborn king, and quite naturally they turned first
to a place where kings were born. They found a king, but one not
to their liking. He was debauched and diabolical, and too deeply
interested in their misssion to be trusted.

So they went on to Bethlehem and bowed themselves down
before a child and in Oriental fashion laid their gifts at His feet.
Their coming was quite providential, for Joseph may well have
used their gifts of gold on his flight into Egypt to save the young
Child's life.

Their mission accomplished, the wise men held consultation
and bypassed Jerusalem on the way home. Let Herod be his own
investigating committee on subversion. They took an obscure
road, and thus provided a symbol of what Christmas should
mean to everyone. Having seen the Christ, they went home a
different way!

The wise men stand as the happy symbols on the first Christmas of what Christmas should mean to everyone. They had an
experience at Bethlehem. They had seen His face. And their first
acts thereafter was to inconvenience themselves. For His sake,
they went out of their way. For His sake, they traveled an obscure
road. They were the first in that long procession since, who
having seen the Christ, go a different way!

Have you been to Bethlehem? Have you looked into His
face? Have you bowed yourself down before the Lord? Will you
join in this great procession?

Wise men have learned to empty their pockets for Him. Wise
men shorten their lives for Him. Wise men inconvenience themselves for Him. Wise men go a different way. Will you?

—E. Russell Lynn

December 26

O foolish Galatians, who hath bewitched
you, that ye should not obey the truth, before
whose eyes Jesus Christ hath been evidently
set forth, crucified among you (Gal. 3:1).

The Galatian Christians were called "foolish" by St. Paul. There were many reasons, but among them was their failure to comprehend the sufficiency of the Cross. Paul wanted them to know that their salvation was Christ and Christ alone. Nothing else could or should be added to His sacrifice. But there is also a simplicity to God's plan of salvation. The Holy Spirit reveals this in the simple words of the gospel invitation—*receive, come, trust, take, believe.*

A young man came to America equipped with a book of prayers and a religious garb but no peace in his heart. It was only after he went back to England that the simplicity of the Cross flooded his soul. "In the evening, I went very unwillingly, to a society in Aldersgate Street, where one was reading Luther's Preface to the Epistle to the Romans. About a quarter before nine, while he was describing the change which God works in the heart by faith in Christ, I felt my heart strangely warmed. I felt I did trust in Christ, Christ alone, for salvation; and an assurance was given me, that He had taken away my sins, even mine, and saved me from the law of sin and death." Thus John Wesley described his conversion.

Spurgeon was saved during the preaching of an untrained yet earnest layman. Spurgeon wrote: "He spun his text for about 10 minutes and then he came up short on the end of his tether." Fixing his eyes upon young Spurgeon, he pointed a long bony finger at him and shouted, "Young man, look to Jesus Christ and you will be saved. Look! Look!" And Spurgeon did look, a simple act of faith, "whereby God sets his seal on the soul." This is the simplicity of the Cross!

> *It is not thy tears of repentance or prayers,*
> *But the blood, that atones for the soul;*
> *On Him, then, who shed it thou mayest at once*
> *All thy weight of iniquities roll.*

> *Look! Look and live!*
> *There is life in a look at the Crucified One,*
> *There is life at this moment for thee.*

—MISS A. M. HULL

December 27

"Leave her alone," said Jesus. "Why are you bothering her? She has done a beautiful thing to me" (Mark 14:6, NIV).

Many people criticize the church for spending money on beautiful windows, an altar, or an organ. Often we hear the words, "It would have been better to give the money to the poor." Sometimes, however, those who criticize the loudest are not well known for their philanthropy.

But many people are touched by a beautiful sanctuary and lovely music. Not many are reached by only free meal tickets. The Lord Jesus laid His stamp of approval upon the "impractical." He said of this woman, "she has done a beautiful thing to me." Others thought she had been guilty of sinful waste when the precious perfume was poured upon Jesus. "Not so," said the Savior.

The Christ spoke often about beautiful things, He did rejoice, of course, in the healing of the sick and the restoring of the lame and the blind, and the Church has a great ministry here. But our sanctuaries also should speak of Him by beautiful windows, Spirit-filled preaching, and lovely flowers. Yes, our Lord is not indifferent to the beautiful things nor to the little lady who arranges the bouquets on the pulpit.

Greeting the stranger with a smile and Christian love is a little thing, but it may well reach someone the minister cannot touch. We need "the little things" and those who bring them and perform them are not unnoticed by the Master. O beloved, learn to do "beautiful things for the Lord Jesus."

—L. D. Boatman

December 28

We should live soberly, righteously, and godly, in this present world (Titus 2:12).

These perilous days call for serious, disciplined living. With diligence we should cultivate habits of devotion to fan the spark of fervor until it becomes a devouring flame consuming every vestige of complacency and indifference.

We are to "walk as children of light" (Eph. 5:8), "that ye may be blameless and harmless, the sons of God, without rebuke, in the midst of a crooked and perverse nation, among whom ye shine as lights in the world" (Phil. 2:15). In our relationships with the world without, our lives should be exemplary. We provide a wide margin of safety if we heed the apostle Paul's admonition: "Abstain from all appearance of evil" (1 Thess. 5:22).

We must have proper ties, not only inwardly and outwardly, but also upwardly. "Set your affection on things above, not on things on the earth" (Col. 3:2). Such close contact with heaven will give to us an aura of "otherworldliness" that will set us apart as "strangers and pilgrims." Those with whom we associate will note that we have been with Jesus.

Only by being Christian in this three-dimensional way—inwardly, outwardly, and upwardly—can we convince the world of the reality, the dynamic quality, the transforming power of the living God ruling in a yielded life.

—M. A. LUNN

December 29

Looking for that blessed hope, and the glorious appearing of the great God and our Saviour, Jesus Christ (Titus 2:13).

There's this strange exhilaration, a sense of expectancy in the air lately. Still, I don't know. Political chicanery, wars and rumors of war, and wispy peace agreements are not the kind of things to make anyone optimistic. It sounds a little like what some preachers have been saying, things about the Jews and their homeland, about famines and the mark of the beast, about the collapse of morality and responsibility, about the ultimate battle of Armageddon.

Could it be, could it be that some of those things are starting to happen? I always thought prophecy was rather remote, irrelevant, far-fetched. Yet now I've got this feeling He may be there, hovering in the wings, waiting for the Grand Appearance at center stage.

The first time He came so quietly. No noise but a baby's cry, the bleat of some sheep, an angel choir singing over the Judean hills. This next time there will be shouting and the trump of God. Triumph.

I get a little nervous. After all, He's the King. I'm not exactly court material.

Still that verse says, "This Jesus shall so come as ye have seen him go." The same One. The One that held small children and healed blind beggars, the One who wept over Jerusalem, who called Zacchaeus by name and fed hungry fishermen by the sea, the One who died. He loved me then and He's the same yesterday, today, and forever.

I can't be afraid. After all these years of following, sometimes warmly, sometimes in doubt, often with rebellion and yearning for the forbidden, following afar and wishing I were near, weary, discouraged, wavering; after following like that, I shall suddenly see and know, know that He is worth it all. And I'm going to be like Him, for I shall see Him as He is.

The same Jesus.

—Maureen Hay Read

"Surely I come quickly: Amen. Even so, come, Lord Jesus" (Rev. 22:20).

December 30

Verily, verily, I say unto you, He that heareth my word, and believeth on him that sent me, hath everlasting life, and shall not come into condemnation; but is passed from death unto life (John 5:24).

A dear old minister friend once said of John 3:16: "It is simply in three parts: God gave—I believe—I have!" The text for today is also a great salvation verse. It has four parts. First, the *plan* of salvation. How simple God makes it. We must "hear his word and believe on him that sent me." No other conditions are to be met.

Then too, this verse reveals the *possession* of salvation. If we hear and believe, we have! "Hath everlasting life," the Savior said. It is a present possession. God's salvation is a free gift to us by believing. We cannot earn it nor do we deserve it.

Jesus also reveals in this verse the *purpose* of salvation. God's purpose is "that we shall not come into condemnation" or the judgment. He loves us and He wants us for himself.

And finally, the *power* of salvation is manifest miraculously for we have "passed from death unto life." Yes, God gave! I believe! I have! And because I believed, I have passed from death into glorious new and eternal life. A new nature is mine—a new creature I am—and I belong to Him forever. But each must believe and receive for himself!

> It is not enough for our faith
>   That others have seen and known Him;
> But each for himself must see,
>   And each for himself must own Him;
> And each must touch the print of the nails,
>   The proof of His claim receiving,
> And each must cry, "My Lord, my God,"
>   And fall at His feet believing.

> —Annie Johnson Flint

December 31

Thou shalt remember all the way which the Lord thy God led thee (Deut. 8:2).

The old year soon will be but a memory. As the days passed, our Shepherd rested us "in the meadow grass and led beside quiet streams." Strength for the journey did not fail. And so our hearts cry out, "Yea, Lord, we do remember all the way Thou has led us."

We remember when the storm broke, our frail bark did not sink. When passions and temptations walked with us, You made a safe way of escape. You safely guided our feet around the Slough of Despondency. And even at a river parting, You were there with eternal hope and resurrection joy!

We do remember, Lord. And we are thankful! And with You as our Guide and Companion and Savior, we move into a new year with abiding faith and trust.

> The open door of another year
>   I'm entering by grace divine;
> No ills I fear and no foes I dread,
>   For a wonderful Guide is mine.
> Through joy or chastening though He lead,
>   In tears though my race be run,
> Whatever my lot, this my prayer shall be,
>   "Not mine, but Thy will be done."

I walk by faith with my heavenly Guide,
  With fearless, unfaltering tread,
Assured that He, who appoints my days,
  Will daily provide my bread.
He'll send more grace should afflictions come,
  And a staff for the pathway steep,
While over me ever by night and day
  My Father His watch will keep.

With perfect trust in His love and care,
  I'll walk to my journey's end;
And day by day He will strength renew,
  And peace to my heart will send.
O blessed Guide, walking all unseen,
  Yet close to my side alway,
Do Thou, who guidest my steps aright,
  Lead on to eternal day!

—GERTRUDE R. DUGAN

New Year's Eve

Another year is dawning!
  Dear Master, let it be
In working or in waiting,
  Another year with Thee!

Another year of leaning
  Upon Thy loving breast,
Of even deeper trusting,
  Of quiet, happy rest.

Another year of mercies,
  Of faithfulness and grace;
Another year of gladness,
  In the shining of Thy face.

Another year of progress,
  Another year of praise;
Another year of proving
  Thy presence "all the days."

Another year of service,
  Of witness to Thy love;
Another year of training
  For holier work above.

Another year is dawning!
  Dear Master, let it be,
On earth, or else in heaven,
  Another year for Thee!

—FRANCES RIDLEY HAVERGAL

INDEX OF POETRY

TITLES and First Lines

A BROOM 227
A father one day to his own little son 335
A little fellow follows me 188
A little maid in years 387
A rushing wind the Spirit came 65
A sacred trust my Lord to me has given 82
ABANDONED 288
ALL THY DAYS 24
Along the golden streets a stranger walks 206
AND CAN IT BE? 306
And should I be afraid of Death? 154
Angry words! O let them never 193
Another year is dawning 409
As Thou didst walk the roads of Galilee 154
At the first 243

BACK TO LYSTRA 345
Believe me, if all those endearing young charms .. 324
BE STILL, MY SOUL 351
Blessed are they who love Him 74
Breathe on me, Breath of God 204
But you will not mind the roughness 319

Child of the Kingdom, be filled with the Spirit ... 350
Christ has no hands but your hands 248
CHURCH ON THE AVENUE 130
COUNT ME 395

Day by day, and with each passing moment 13
DEAR LORD AND FATHER OF MANKIND 194
Do you want something old, something settled ... 309
Does the place you're called to labor 23

Ere you left your room this morning 364
EVENTIDE 162

Father, I scarcely dare to pray 355
Father in heaven, who lovest all 219
Fear not, O little flock 299
FEELING, FAITH, and FACT 359
Fierce was the wild billow 136
FLAME OF GOD 352
For all Thy blessings given 70
For I learn as the years roll onward 170
Forget them not, O Christ, who stand 376
Four things in any land must dwell 215
Free from the law, O happy condition 349
From prayer that asks that I may be 352
From the glory and the gladness 349

GADARA, A.D. 31 291
Give us a watchword for this hour 222
GO, LABOR ON 241
Go work in My vineyard 297
God bless the church on the avenue 130
God gives some men the strength of fire 304
God hath not promised 94
God knocked at the door of my heart one day ... 227
GOD LEADS US ALONG 280
God of our fathers, known of old 217
God send us men alert and quick 216
Gone are those Sabbaths, when the very air 285
Growing old but not retiring 548
GYPSY BOY SONG 343

Hast thou no scars? 307
HAVE THINE OWN WAY 264
He beat me home a little bit 101
He does not lead me year by year 213
He giveth more grace 220
He is not here, we laid him to rest 261
HE KNOWS 11
He sat by a fire of sevenfold heat 174
He spoke her name 250
He stood upon the shore and watched them toil .. 196
He swung on the gate and looked down the street . 189
He walked with God 158
He was better to me than all my hopes 137
Heaven above is softer blue 124
His love is sufficient 155
How dear to my heart is the church of my
    childhood 272
HOW DID THEY KNOW? 19

I am a stranger here, within a foreign land 265
I am drinking at the fountain 274
I am His and He is mine 124, 377
I am not strong till Thou hast clasped my hand .. 378
I am waiting for you 200
I do not ask that crowds may throng the temple .. 92
I cannot tell why there should come to me 192
I could not do without Thee 32
I do not ask that God will keep all storms away .. 185
I do not ask for mighty words 236
I do not know why sorrows bow the heart 107
I don't know about tomorrow 75
I don't look back 54
I have found no satisfaction in the fleeting
    joys of earth 110
I have not much to give 333
I have striven with might and main 243
I have worshipped in churches and chapels 153
I hear the words of love 296
I know not, but God knows 178
I know not how God works His purpose out ... 48
I know not what awaits me 11
I know that my Redeemer liveth 115
I know not where tomorrow's road 142
I know what mother's face is like 295
I like to ponder that word of Scripture 127
I meant to go back 159
I met God in the morning 330
I met the Master 339
I owned a little boat a while ago 353
I remember the years of His hand's deep shadow . 63
I said, "Let me walk in the fields." 87
I shall know by the gleam and glitter 169
I sought the Lord and afterwards I knew 151
I stood on the shore beside the sea 383
I want a principle within 372
I want the faith that envies not 201
I want you to know you are never forgotten ... 17
I will pour water on him that is thirsty 350
I'd rather see a sermon than hear one any day ... 227
If I should die and leave you here awhile 88
If, on a quiet sea 14
If the world from you withholds 119
I'm broken and seriously wounded 187
I'm going by the upper road 100

I'm growing very weary, Lord 211
I'm nearing the end of my journey 162
I'm not your judge 362
I'm stealing away with Jesus 258
In childhood's day our thought of heaven 363
In pastures green, not always 77
In peace let me resign my breath 138
In shady green pastures, so rich and so sweet . . . 280
In the distant land of famine 238
In the secret of His presence 172
Into a tent where a gypsy boy lay 343
It is not enough for our faith 408
It is not the things you do, dear 231
It must have been a blow to Zebedee 46
I've dreamed many dreams 273

Jerusalem's streets had never seen 108
Jesus, and shall it ever be 103
Jesus is passing by 147
Jesus, mine all in all art Thou 358
Jesus, Thy blood and righteousness 334
Jesus, Thy boundless love to me 122
Just as I am, Thine own to be 255

LAD WITH THE FISHES 332
LAUNCH OUT 195
Laid on Thine altar, O my Lord divine 176
Last eve I passed beside a blacksmith's door 89
Lead softly on, dear Lord 21
LESSONS OF THE YEARS 170
Lest we forget 217
Let me go back 180
Little is much when God is in it 336
Lo, He cometh; Lo, He cometh 302
Lord, I have shut the door 72
Lord, I would follow 242
Lord, keep my heart attuned to laughter 320
Lord of all pots and pans and things 183
LOST—A CROSS 50
Loved with everlasting love 124, 377

MAKE ME THY FUEL 352
Man of sorrows 277
Many a mother in America, when the busy day
    is done 278
Many a rapturous minstrel among the sons
    of light 87
MARY 387
May we Thy bounties thus as stewards true
    receive 129
More holiness give me 30
MORE LIKE THE MASTER 237
MY ALTAR 153, 408
MY GUIDE 162
"My little lad, come now and see" 332
My sins laid open to the rod 117
MY SOUL, BE ON THY GUARD 40
My stubborn will at last hath yielded 208

Near the end of a journey long and steep 52
NEW YEAR'S EVE 409
NO SCAR? 307
Not I, but Christ be honored 177
Now I will glory in the Cross 283
NOT MUCH TO GIVE 333
Nothing to pay? no not a whit 223

O blessed feet of Jesus 293
O blessed Lord, whose hand has led me on 152
O Christ, what burdens bowed Thy head 270
O for a passionate passion for souls 223

O LOVE THAT WILT NOT LET ME GO 290
O Saviour, whose mercy, severe in its kindness . . 198
O the Spirit-filled life, is it thine? 25
OCCUPY TILL I COME 82
Oh, that my tongue might so possess 67
Oh, the bitter shame and sorrow 337
Oh, there are heavenly heights to reach 104
OH, TO BE LIKE THEE 269
OIL IN MY LAMP 244
ON THE DOWNWARD WAY 90
Once there was a Christian 80
One by one He took them from me 27
One day upon the green-clad slopes 50
ONE OF THE NINE 159
Our Master is seeking a harvest 361
Out of the light that dazzles me 226

PAPA'S COMING 189
PRAYER FOR PENTECOST 65
Precious promise God hath given 388

Rabbi, begone 291
Ready to suffer grief or pain 103
RECESSIONAL 217
REPLY TO INVICTUS 226
RICH YOUNG RULER 210

Saviour, visit Thy plantation 148
See, Father, I have brought with me 106
SET OF THE SAIL 383
Sit still, my daughter! 184
SO SEND I YOU 344
Some day, when our pilgrimage journey is over . . 379
SOMETIME, SOMEWHERE 232
SPIRIT OF GOD, DESCEND 95
STEP BY STEP 213

Take my life and let it be 314
Teach me Thy way, O Lord 331
TELL IT AGAIN 343
TELL IT TO JESUS 230
TELL ME THE OLD, OLD STORY 40
Thanks to God for my Redeemer 370
That Christmas Day if you were God 398
That night when in the Judean skies 402
THE ALL-SUFFICIENT CHRIST 185
The bearers are unsteady 38
THE BOAT 353
THE BOOK OF COMPLETIONS 309
THE CHURCH'S ONE FOUNDATION 347
THE CROSS 335
The cruel stones unerring fell 345
THE ETERNAL CHRIST 242
THE FUZZY-WUZZY HAIR 278
The glory of love is brightest 247
The great apostle called himself 179
THE HANDS OF CHRIST 346
The holly boughs have all been hung 372
THE INN THAT MISSED ITS CHANCE 399
THE JERICHO CRY 187
THE LOVE OF GOD 34
THE OLD VIOLIN 316
The open door of another year 408
THE PENITENT THIEF 106
THE PRISONER OF THE LORD 179
THE PRODIGAL SON 238
THE RACE 108
THE REFINER'S FIRE 174
THE ROAD TO JERICHO 187
THE SECRET 330

411

THE SET OF THE SAIL 383
THE SIGN OF THE SON OF MAN 127
THE SUNSET TRAIL 211
The things you loved I have not laid away 262
THE TRUE APOSTOLATE 248
THE UNFINISHED SONG 166
The weary ones had rest 299
THE YEARS OF HIS RIGHT HAND 63
There are many who slumber 244
There is a place where thou canst touch 253
There is life in a look at the crucified One 404
There is no path in this desert waste 256
There's a Stranger at the door 327
There's room at the Cross for you 36
They came to the land of Canaan 93
They did not know Christ as they walked along ... 19
They say that I am growing old 275
This holy Book I'd rather own 60
THIS I KNOW 142
This is the debt I pay 374
This is the season of hope and grace 147
THE SAME JESUS 165
This thought is dearer far to me 368
This was God's message to earth's weary nations . 401
Though the storm clouds dark may lower 156
Thou life of my life, blessed Jesus 371
Three men were walking on a wall 359
THY SPEECH BETRAYETH THEE 67
'TIL THE STORM PASSES BY 329
"TILL HE COME" 145
Today on the road I met Him 165
TOUCH OF THE MASTER'S HAND 316
Turn your eyes upon Jesus 381
'Twas battered and scarred 316

'Twas a sheep, not a lamb, that strayed away 225

Unanswered yet? The prayer your lips have
    pleaded 232
Undaunted by December 376
UNDER HIS WINGS 252
Utterly abandoned to the Holy Ghost 288
Utterly abandoned to the will of God 176

We search the world for truth 60
We would see Jesus 267
What could be done? The inn was full of folks .. 399
What if I say 248
What will it profit when life here is o'er 112
When for a little walk we went 101
When from life's feast the glory has departed 29
When the heavenly hosts shall gather 166
When the long night has ended 329
When the seeds that I have scattered 375
When the voice of the Master is calling 321
When the wheat is carried home 42
Who answers Christ's insistent call 84
Wide is the gate that leads to death 90
With frightened lips I shall not ever say 234

Ye call Me Master, and obey me not 249
Yea, I am with thee 24
Yes, leave it with Him; the lilies all do 190
You ask me how I gave my heart to Christ? 124
You cannot say the Lord's Prayer 259
You say I'm clinging to an outworn creed 212
YOU TOLD ME OF JESUS 321

ZEBEDEE 46

INDEX OF AUTHORS AND POETS

Adams, Ophelia G. 233
Albright, Mary E. 181
Alquist, Clarence H. 51
Anatolius 136
Armerding, Carl 152
Atchison, J. B. 327

Bailey, A. W. 232
Baird, Brig. Catherine 155
Barclay, William 17, 30, 56, 84, 119
Beecher, Henry Ward 153, 154
Belton, Robert 62, 237
Bevan, Frances 239
Bickersteth, Edward H. 145
Bills, T. M. 375
Bliss, P. P. 30, 57, 248, 277, 350
Boatman, L. D. 132, 207, 385, 405
Bonar, Horatius 48, 70, 241, 296
Bonner, Hal 397
Borthwick, Jane L. 351
Bosch, Henry G. 137, 148, 209, 229, 266,
                        294, 320, 330, 348
Bower, Helen Frazee 393
Brainard, Mary G. 12

Bridges, Matthew 342
Brown, Catherine Bernard 65
Brown, William A. 376
Burdette, Robert J. 256
Burgeson, Avis 155
Butler, Colvin G. 69

Carey, William 145
Carmichael, Amy 223, 308, 352
Cassel, Dr. E. T. 265
Chesterton, G. K. 108
Chisholm, T. O. 54, 269
Christy, James 177
Clarkson, E. Margaret 45, 49, 143, 344
Cleland, Beatrice 243
Cook, Joseph 60
Corfield, Virginia 27
Coulter, George 21
Cousin, Mrs. A. R. 270
Cowman, Mrs. Charles E. 288, 390
Crocker, Henry 222
Croly, George 96
Crosby, Fannie J. 191
Culbertson, William 37

412

Cushing, William O. 68, 253
Cushman, Ralph Spaulding 93, 202, 330
Cuyler, Theodore L. 346

Day, Dorothea 226
Day, Hughes W. . . . . Unsigned portions
Day, Richard Ellsworth 14, 45, 57, 116, 138, 193,
205, 234, 273, 282, 350, 386
DeHaan, Dr. M. R. 47, 348
DeHann, Richard 37, 178, 246
Dickason, C. Fred 73
Dodge, Kenneth 41
Drummond, Henry 206, 230
Dugan, Gertrude R. 409
Dunbar, Paul Lawrence 374
Dunn, Bruce 131

Fallon, Arthur 135
Farningham, Marianne 193
Fisher, C. William 95
Flint, Annie Johnson . . . 24, 29, 55, 64, 71, 75, 91, 94,
128, 167, 179, 180, 200, 220, 248, 302, 310,
379, 383, 401, 408
Fox, C. A. 104
Franklin, Ruby 382
French, Florence 19
Fuller, Dr. Charles 206

Gabriel, Charles H. 125, 237
Gerhardt, Paul 123
Gillman, Frederick J. 216
Goreh, Ellen Lakshmi 172
Graham, Billy 18, 196, 215, 362
Grant, Sir Robert 198
Grant, Pastor U. S. . 121, 135, 157, 195, 230, 260, 396
Gray, James M. 61, 117, 176, 193
Grider, J. Kenneth 340
Grigg, Joseph 103
Guest, Edgar 227

Halifax, Lord 219
Hall, Mary Lee 88
Hamilton, James D. 312, 364
Hankey, Kate 40, 97
Hanna, Gordon L. 155
Harper, A. F. 283, 324, 337
Harris, Thoro 244, 245
Harrison, Norman B. 300, 393
Hatch, Edwin 204
Havenhill, Leonard 39
Havergal, Frances . . . 22, 33, 250, 314, 315, 363, 409
Havner, Vance 40, 80, 88, 120, 155, 197, 221,
254, 326
Hawkins, Floyd 311
Hayward, M. C. 83
Hearn, Marianne 255
Heath, George 40
Henry, Matthew 120
"Herald of Holiness" 303, 355
Hicks, Anna M. 163
Hoffman, E. A. 147
Homburg, Ernst C. 371
Howe, William W. 129
Hubbard, David Allan 334
Hull, Miss A. M. 404

Inchfawn, Fay 183
Ironside, Harry A. 56, 283, 388

Jackson, Helen Hunt 356

Jackson, Maud Frazer 249
Jackson, Paul G. 250
Jones, E. Stanley 39, 275
Jones, Sam 37
Jowett, J. H. 266

Keith, George 235
Keller, Helen 295
Kempis, Thomas a 289
Kidder, Mary A. 365
Kipling, Rudyard 218, 219

Lawlor, Edward 279
Lee, Robert G. 61, 72, 89, 109, 196, 217, 263, 341
Lehman, F. M. 34
Leitner, Della Adams 186
Lemmel, Helen Howarth 381
Lightall, W. M. 368
Lindgren, Anna J. 25
Lister, Mosie 329, 339
Lockerbie, D. Bruce 108
Lockyer, Herbert 70, 96, 110
Loyola, Ignatius 279
Lubke, Bernice 185
Lunn, M. A. 99, 150, 380, 406
Lynn, E. Russell 58, 105, 140, 396, 398, 403

Macaulay, J. C. 102, 191, 197, 242
McConkey, James 20, 100, 389
MacDonald, George 87, 207, 354
MacKay, J. B. 195
McLane, Sue 263
Mann, Edward J. 262
Marlow, Carol Ann 97
Matheson, George 290, 344, 394
Marshall, Peter 385
Melville, Katherine 213
Meyer, F. B. . . 130, 140, 164, 199, 207, 230, 298, 316
Miller, C. D. 225
Miller, J. R. 262, 264
Monod, Theodore 338
Moody, Dwight L. 21, 82, 86, 111, 123, 155, 202,
204, 224, 238, 247, 332, 377, 384
Moore, Thomas 324
Moorehouse, Henry 33
Moreland, John Richard 346
Morgan, G. Campbell 92, 122, 222, 284
Morris, Mrs. C. H. 208
Moyer, Robert L. 270
Mueller, George 170, 245, 292, 357, 364
Murray, Andrew 53, 144, 168, 196, 269, 289

Neale, John 136
Newton, John 149, 175
Nicholson, Martha Snell 28, 387
Nicholas, Geraldine 333
Niles, Nathaniel 389

Oakley, F. Howard 336
Ober, C. K. 241
Osler, Sir William 101
Oxenham, John 84, 242, 279, 291

Peck, Kathryn Blackburn 52, 107, 182
Pettingill, W. L. 31, 207, 290
Plato 219
Pollard, Adelaide A. 264, 299
Poole, W. C. 395
Pounds, Jessie Brown 115, 202
Proctor, Adelaide A. 170, 231

413

Quayle, Bishop 119

Rae, Mrs. M. E. 211
Ramsey, B. Mansell 331
Randolph, Cindy 304
Rankin, J. E. 230
Rauchenbusch, Walter 216
Read, Maureen Hay 407
Rees, Paul S. 152, 229, 358
Rider, Lucy J. 350
Rimmer, Harry 206
Roberts, John E. 276
Robinson, Thomas R. 67
Robinson, Wade 124, 377
Rosell, Mervin E. 253
Ruff, Sarah Spencer 362
Runyan, William M. 72, 106
Rutherford, Samuel 42
Ryberg, Barbara C. 214, 236
Ryle, J. C. 51

Sandell-Berg, Caroline V. 13
Sangster, Margaret E. 376
Sayes, W. C. 189
Schlegel, Katharina von 351
Scofield, C. I. 99
Sears, L. Wayne 140
Scroggie, John 77
Sheen, Archbishop 215
Shockley, Ada 332
Shuler, Chester 188
Simpson, A. B. 170
Sizoo, John 23
Slade, Mrs. M. B. C. 343
Smith, Hannah Whitall .. 82, 114, 122, 379, 386, 392
Smith, J. Danson 158, 184, 346
Speer, Clara Aiken 285
Spruce, Fletcher 65, 108, 111, 126, 130, 322, 336, 347
Spurgeon, Charles Haddon ... 15, 118, 141, 161, 192, 220, 236, 247, 254, 267, 273, 276, 305, 308, 319, 352, 372, 378, 404
Stanphill, Ira 36, 75, 76
Stearn, D. M. 91
Stoddard, William S. 137
Stone, Samuel J. 347

Storm, August Ludvig 370
Strait, C. Neil 16
Styles, John H., Jr. 154
Suffield, Mrs. F. W. 23, 336

Taylor, Husdon 288
Thackeray, W. M. 153
Thomas, Mary S. 47
Thompson, Barbara J. 228
Thompson, Robert H. 35
Thring, George 342
Tindley, G. Albert 119
Toplady, Augustus 15
Tozer, A. W. 66
Troutman, Robert D. 196
Troy, Grace E. 113
Truett, George 184, 202, 328
Tupper, Flora B. 156
Tyler, Alexander 219

Valby, Dr. 138
VanGorder, Paul R. 251
VanInwegan, Leslie 373
Varley, Henry 203

Waggoner, C. W. 110
Walker, Ralph 131
Warner, Anna B. 267
Webster, Jackson L. 304
Welch, Myra Brooks 317
Wells, Amos R. 38, 160, 243, 400
Wesley, Charles 306, 358, 373
Wesley, John 18, 380, 404
Weyburn, Ruby T. 247
Whittier, John Greenleaf 60, 93, 194
Whitwell, Florence Nye 258
Wilson, Walter L. 145, 176, 196, 245, 311
Wordsworth, E. E. 184
Worthington, E. L. 243
Winfield, Howard 243

Young, G. A. 280

Zinzendorf, Nicolaus 334

SUBJECT INDEX

Abiding in Christ 141, 143, 167, 171
Adoption 333
Ahab 232
Ahimaaz 57
Ambassadors for Christ 265
Ananias and Sapphira 297
Anger 195
Anxiety 118, 357
Arithmetic, God's 365

Barabbas 98
Barbarians, The 375
Belief 372, 407
Belshazzar 89
Bible, The 59, 88, 309

Blood of Christ, The 296, 333, 340
Boldness of the Disciples 233, 350

Caleb 201, 298
Calvary 105, 115, 116, 269, 334
Care of God 19, 96
Christlikeness 53, 268
Christ, the Savior 91, 115, 150, 305, 342, 404
Christ, the Son of God 172, 212, 241, 395
Christ, the Way 202
Christian Example 254
Christ's Glory 168
Church, The 31, 78, 130, 157, 283, 326, 347
Communion with Christ 144, 147
Conduct, Christian 43, 251

Consecration and Dedication . . . 39, 82, 83, 207, 314,
337, 339
Conversion 18, 84, 123
Commitment 382
Cross Bearing 66, 83
Cross, The 50
Crowns, The Christian's 341
Crucifixion of Self 66

Death 51, 74, 89, 154, 162, 261, 318, 319
Decision 224
Dedication 133
Deliverance 85
Demas 39, 325
Demetrius 325
Discipleship 209

Eagle's Flight 329
Emmanuel 392
Emmaus 18
Enoch 158
Evangelism 222
Everlasting Arms, The 346

Faith 15, 75, 135, 320, 358, 409
Family of God, The 353
Father, God the 111, 168, 290, 334
Finished Work of Christ 124, 349
Fishers of Men 46, 136, 195
Following Christ 43, 99, 348, 394
Forgiveness 175
Fruit of the Spirit 47, 360

Gadara 291
Gifts and Giving 80, 123
Glory 58
God's Care 139, 142, 169, 229, 280, 387
Grace 220, 378
Grammar 82
Grieving the Spirit 173
Growing Old 275
Gospel, Preaching the 39
Guidance 11, 142, 388

Hands 310
Harvest, The 374
Heaven 100, 206, 263
Holiness 122, 337, 378, 405
Holy Spirit 20, 24, 30, 64, 173, 221, 304, 350
Home 100, 263
Home for Christmas 396
Husbandman, The 361

Immortality 318
Inn, The 399

Jericho 186
John 137
Joshua 224, 245
Joy 28, 47, 131, 315, 357
Judging Others 362
Judgment 89, 214, 368, 374
Justification 333

Kadesh-Barnea 104
King's Army, The 208

Lameness 78
Laodicea 336
Lepers, The 146, 159

Life in Christ 113, 226
Light 187, 247, 338
Loaves and Fishes 332
Looking to Christ 54, 266
Lord's Day 284
Lord's Prayer, The 259
Lord's Supper, The 144
Love 33, 53, 58, 205, 230, 246, 324, 334, 342
Love of the Brethren 230
Loyalty to Christ 323
Lying 163, 296

Man of Sorrows 277
Mary, Mother of Christ 386
Memorial Day 177
Missions and Missionaries . . 179, 239, 278, 354, 375
Mother 153
Moulded like Christ 264

Naaman, the leper 120
Nain, Funeral at 210
Nail-scarred Hands 368
Names of Jesus 165
Nation, The 214
New Birth 407

Old Age 234, 319

Paul 132
Peace 32, 151, 357
Penitent Thief, The 105
Peter 367
Phoebe 76
Plumbline, The 138
Potter, The 264
Prayer 37, 70, 71, 192, 232, 253, 276, 286, 299,
373, 384, 393
Prayer of the Savior 49
Preaching the Word 50, 56, 235, 271
Prejudice 372
Priestly Ministry of Christ 73
Prodigal Son, The 111
Prodigal Son's Brother, The 140
Prodigal Son's Father, The 237
Promises of God 94, 189, 234
Purity 197

Reaping and Sowing 374
Reconciliation 333
Redemption 269, 321, 349
Remembrances 17
Rest 266, 284
Restoration 316
Resurrection, The 18, 107, 114, 126, 134, 293
Revival 148
Rich Young Ruler 99, 209
Road to Bethlehem, The 401
Rock of Ages 68
Rope Holders, The 336
Running Life's Race 306

Salvation 35, 109, 124, 213, 223, 305, 342, 356,
358, 404
Sanctification 282, 308, 314
Second Coming of Christ . . . 127, 191, 200, 244, 301,
366, 344, 345
Serving Christ 182, 204, 279, 303, 405
Shepherd, Christ the Good 19, 77
Sickness and Sorrow 285
Soldiers of Christ 208

Soul Winning 46, 86, 102, 145, 195
Speech of the Christian 67
Spirit-filled Life 24, 64, 176, 337, 393
Spiritual Emphysema 393
Stocks and Bonds 354
Stones 345
Storms 135
Strength 94
Sufficiency of Christ 338
Surrendered Life, The 308
Swaddling Clothes 397

Talents 82
Tears 210, 251
Temptation 101
Testimony 325, 405, 258, 329
Thankfulness 70, 181
Thanksgiving Day 370
Thomas 62
Threshing Time 42
Tithing 27, 80, 128
Tongue, The 362
Touch of the Master 146

Trust 51, 155, 178, 213

Unbelief 93

Victorious Living 44, 149

Waiting on the Lord 44, 48, 161, 183
Watchfulness 200
Wesley, John 380
Will of God, The 207, 353, 292
Winter 376
Wise Men, The 403
Witness and Witnessing 47, 186, 227, 247, 248,
303, 360
Withered Hands 310
Word of God 60, 271, 309, 330
Worrying 118
Worship 284
Wounds of Christ 116

Youth 254

Zebedee 46

SCRIPTURE INDEX

Genesis:
5:24 158
33:14 21
42:36 178

Exodus:
3:2-3 380
20:8 284

Numbers:
10:2-12 44
13:27-28 104
13:33 312

Deuteronomy:
2:1 93
2:24 385
8:2 . . . . 63, 408

11:11-12 106
32:31 68
33:25 13
33:27 346

Joshua:
1:1-2 245
1:5 . . . . 81, 189
14:6-12 . . . . 201, 297
24:15 224

Ruth:
3:2 42

1 Samuel:
9:27 183

2 Samuel:
18:19-23 56
18:32-33 187

1 Kings:
18:42 232
20:28 12
22:2-5 161

2 Kings:
5:17-18 120
6:16 125
6:17 391
19:9 251

2 Chronicles:
7:14 217
20:17 48
29:27 315

Esther:
4:14 203

Job:
19:25 114
23:10 257

Psalms:
1:1-2 274
5:8 164
13:1 368
14:1 112
17:8 252
20:6 63
23:1 . . . . 19, 298
23:2 . . . . 77, 384
27:14 161
30:5 249
32:8 388
37:5 363

40:2 41
46:10 48
57:1 96
66:16 109
71:5, 9 234
72:19 . . . . 182, 276
77:6 147
77:10 63
78:19 129
84:11 94
85:6 148
86:11 330
91:1 171
91:3 246

Psalms:
95:2 370
116:15 162
118:24 16
119:9 268
119:89 . . . . 88, 309
119:105 309
119:130 309

Proverbs:
4:18 275
16:3 242

Isaiah:
6:8 344
9:6 165
17:10-11 214
26:3 351
30:15 284
31:5 96
32:2 . . . . 32, 328
33:21 250

40:31 329
41:10 .... 63, 189
42:16 139
43:2 .... 78, 280
43:19 196
49:15-16 189
49:16 64
53:1-3 277
53:5 116
55:6-7 41
55:8 294
55:11 59
64:6 319
66:1 311
66:13 190

Jeremiah:
18:4 .... 264, 285
29:11 142
39:17 213

Ezekiel:
22:30 326

Daniel:
5:4-5 89
5:30-31 368
6:20 85

Joel:
2:25 316

Amos:
7:7 138

Jonah:
4:4 193

Habakkuk:
3:2 148

Malachi:
3:16-17 177

Matthew:
1:23 392
2:12 403
3:1-2 235
4:1 101
4:19 195
5:14, 16 ...... 204, 303
5:16 247
6:1 80
6:6 384
8:1 222
8:2-3 146
9:2 37
11:29-30 266
14:12 229
14:17-18 332
14:33 135
16:15-16 241
16:18 347
17:1 258
18:2-3 97
24:30 127
25:5 191
26:39 323

27:15-21 98
27:24 215
28:1 126
28:20 .... 190, 254

Mark:
1:19-20 46
1:35 253
2:5-12 38
3:1 310
5:15-17 291
7:21 197
8:34 83
10:22 99
12:41 27
14:6 405
16:7 367

Luke:
1:34-35 386
2:4 396
2:7 399
2:10 389
2:11 402
2:12 397
2:15 .... 381, 401
2:48-49 86
2:49 279
4:1-2 199
7:11 210
9:10 258
9:62 .... 239, 348
10:30 186
11:1 259
14:16 35
15:13 111
15:20 237
15:25 140
17:12-17 159
18:1 299
19:2 150
19:13 82
20:25 218
23:42 105
24:33-34 18

John:
1:1 395
1:2-14 60
2:1-2 28
3:3 69
3:16 342
5:24 407
6:67-68 212
9:25 338
13:14 143
14:2 .... 206, 263
14:16 30
15:1 360
16:33 371
17:1 58
17:8, 14 134
17:9 49
19:16 305
19:30 .... 124, 321
20:21 344
20:24 62
21:3 136
21:21 300

Acts:
1:1 304
1:4 287
1:10-11 301
2:2 194
2:4 20
3:1-2 78
3:6 283
4:13 233
4:29, 31 350
4:31 64
5:1-2 296
5:4 163
8:29 145
9:11 192
9:25 336
12:5 393
12:12 286
13:46 278
14:19-22 349
15:3 84
16:6-8 221
16:7 14
16:11-12 ...... 317, 354, 382
16:31 356
17:6 39
19:34 26
20:22 11
20:37-38 261
27:25 155

Romans:
1:14 375
1:15 102
4:4-5 223
5:1, 6 333
5:9 390
6:6 352
6:6-7 282
8:1 308
8:14 268
8:16 290
8:28 376
8:38 .... 39, 23, 296
12:1-2 .... 207, 337
12:10-11 .... 149, 355
13:8 246
15:16 282
15:20, 25 39
16:1-2 76

1 Corinthians:
1:2 282
1:14 132
1:17-18 66
2:1-2 50
6:11 122
9:23 209
10:31 130
11:23-26 144
13 205
13:8 58
15:16-17 107
15:54 100

2 Corinthians:
1:1 265
1:3-4 .... 87, 169, 379
3:5 184

4:6-7 .... *339*
5:1 .... *318*
5:17 .... *123*
7:1 .... *31*
8:5 .... *133*
8:9 .... *129*
9:7 .... *128*
12:9 .... *220*

Galatians:
3:1 .... *404*
5:22 .... *47, 53*
5:25 .... *176*
6:7 .... *374*
6:14 .... *289*
6:17 .... *307*

Ephesians:
1:1 .... *280, 292*
1:4-6 .... *314*
1:14 .... *168*
4:15 .... *67*
4:25 .... *67*
4:29 .... *67*
4:30 .... *141*
5:3-4 .... *67*
5:18 .... *24*
5:20 .... *181*
5:25-27 .... *157*
6:6 .... *353*
6:13 .... *372*
6:18-20 .... *72*

Philippians:
1:3-4 .... *17, 255*
1:21, 23 .... *154*
3:12 .... *394*
3:13-14 .... *273*
4:4 .... *357, 364*
4:6 .... *70, 118, 357*
4:8 .... *151*
4:13 .... *228*

Colossians:
3:1-3 .... *113*
3:12 .... *121*
3:23 .... *182*
3:24 .... *303*
4:6 .... *67*

4:12 .... *34, 380*
5:24

1 Thessalonians:
4:13 .... *366*
5:17 .... *373*
5:19 .... *173*
5:23 .... *282*

2 Thessalonians:
3:1-2 .... *92*

1 Timothy:
1:15 .... *175*
2:8 .... *71*
4:12 .... *43, 254*

2 Timothy:
1:5 .... *153*
1:9 .... *118, 378*
1:12 .... *75*
2:3 .... *208*
3:1 .... *244*
4:9-10 .... *39*
4:1-5 .... *271*
4:5 .... *200*

Titus:
2:8 .... *67*
2:12 .... *405*
2:13 .... *406*

Philemon:
1 .... *179*
22 .... *180*
18-19 .... *55*

Hebrews:
1:1-2 .... *172*
1:3 .... *115*
4:14 .... *73*
4:15 .... *74, 91*
7:25 .... *293, 349*
9:22 .... *340*
9:28 .... *260*
10:10 .... *349*
10:12-13 .... *73*
10:22 .... *313*
10:24-25 .... *157*
11:6 .... *18*

12:1-2 .... *54, 131, 266, 306*
12:6 .... *198*
13:5 .... *190*

James:
1:6 .... *37*
1:26 .... *67*
1:27 .... *320*
2:17 .... *248*
3:5 .... *362*

1 Peter:
1:1 .... *322*
1:7 .... *15*
1:8 .... *295*
2:1-2 .... *365*
3:15 .... *360*
3:18 .... *269*
5:4 .... *341*
5:7 .... *387*

2 Peter:
1:4 .... *189*
1:5-7 .... *236, 365*

1 John:
2:4 .... *227*
2:6 .... *167*
3:1 .... *324, 334*
4:7 .... *230*
4:9-10 .... *33*
4:19-21 .... *137, 205*
5:4 .... *271*
5:12 .... *226*
5:13 .... *358*

3 John:
1 .... *22*
12 .... *247, 325*

Revelation:
1:5 .... *166*
3:14-15 .... *95*
3:20 .... *326*
5:9 .... *167*
21:1 .... *109*
21:4 .... *51, 74*